# Images of Schoolteachers in Twentieth-Century America

Paragons, Polarities, Complexities

# Images of Schoolteachers in Twentieth-Century America

## Paragons, Polarities, Complexities

Pamela Bolotin Joseph
Gail E. Burnaford

*EDITORS*

St. Martin's Press    New York

*To our students—our colleagues*

*Editor:* Naomi Silverman
*Managing editor:* Patricia Mansfield-Phelan
*Project editor:* Diana Puglisi
*Production supervisor:* Elizabeth Mosimann
*Art director:* Sheree Goodman
*Cover design:* Rod Hernandez
*Cover art:* Clockwise from top: Jason Hill; illustration from *Starring First Grade,* by Miriam Cohen, illustrated by Lillian Hoban; Rod Hernandez; Rachel Weidman; photograph by C. Orrico/Superstock, Inc.

Library of Congress Catalog Card Number: 92-62799

For information, write:
St. Martin's Press, Inc.
175 Fifth Avenue
New York, NY 10010

ISBN: 0-312-09073-0

## Acknowledgments

**Figure 10-1.** Copyright © 1988 by Lillian Hoban. By permission of Greenwillow Books, a division of William Morrow & Company, Inc.

**Figures 10-2 and 10-3.** From *Miss Nelson Is Missing* by Harry Allard and James Marshall. Illustrations copyright © 1977 by James Marshall. Reprinted by permission of Houghton Mifflin Company. All rights reserved.

**Figure 10-4.** From *The First Days of School* by Jane Hamilton Merritt. © 1982. Used by permission of the publisher, Julian Messner/A Division of Simon & Schuster, New York.

**Figure 10-5.** Illustration by Amy Schwartz from *Annabelle Swift, Kindergartener* by Amy Schwartz. Copyright © 1988 by Amy Schwartz. Used with permission of the publisher, Orchard Books, New York.

**Figure 10-6.** Illustration by Lillian Hoban from *The New Teacher* by Miriam Cohen. Illustration copyright © 1972 by Lillian Hoban. Reproduced by permission of Macmillan Publishing Company.

**Figure 10-7.** From *We Laughed a Lot My First Days of School* by Sylvia Root Tester. Copyright © 1979 by Children's Press, and used with permission.

**Figure 11-1.** By Frank Cotham. Copyright © 1983 by Frank Cotham. Reprinted with permission of Frank Cotham.

*Acknowledgments and copyrights are continued at the back of the book on page 290, which constitutes an extension of the copyright page.*

*We have pursued teacher images . . .*

*Abuser, Actor, Adversary, Advocate, Animator, Artist*
*Baby-sitter, Bad teacher, Bore, Buffoon*
*Caricature, Child, Colleague, Companion, Controlled,*
    *Controller*
*Dentist, Director of a play, Disciplinarian, Door closer, Door*
    *opener, Drill sergeant, Dynamo*
*Eccentric, Elder, Empowerer, Engine, Exception*
*Father, Female, Fool, Friend*
*Gardener, Good fairy, Good teacher, Guide*
*Healer, Helper, Hero, Heroine, Human being, Humiliator*
*Ideal, Inspiration, Intellectual, Interpreter, Iron butterfly*
*Joker, Juggler*
*Leader, Learner, Liberator, Light breeze*
*Male, Manager, Martyr, Matriarch, Maverick, Mechanic,*
    *Member of mainstream culture, Moral force, Mother*
*Nonconformist, Nonentity, Novice, Nurturer*
*Ogre, Oppressor, Orchestra conductor*
*People-pleaser, Parent, Pawn, Pedant, Plant, Potter,*
    *Presence, Problem-solver, Producer, Professional,*
    *Protector, Puritan, Pushover*
*Robot, Role model*
*Sadist, Saint, Savior, Scholar, Schoolmarm, Scientist,*
    *Smiler, Soldier, Stereotype, Storyteller, Supporting player*
*Therapist, Tyrant*
*Victim, Villain, Visionary, Voyager*
*Witch, Woman, Worker*

# Preface

There appears to be a growing awareness that survey courses in teacher education providing prodigious amounts of data about the profession are not sufficient to prepare students to become teachers or to help practicing teachers empower themselves for continued growth and professionalism in their field. Consequently, professors in schools of education are looking for texts that offer examples of scholarship and research, while interacting with student readers in a relevant and meaningful fashion.

*Images of Schoolteachers in Twentieth-Century America* offers prospective and experienced teachers studying in schools of education (and in informal settings) the opportunity to engage in critical thinking and dialogue about the teaching profession. This book also has value as a resource for the study of American culture. The chapters discuss the imagery surrounding teachers in this society in a variety of contexts and media. Teachers' own voices are represented, as well as the voices of children in classrooms and literary/media artists who imagine and evoke images of teachers in our culture.

This book is designed as a springboard for instructors and students working as colleagues to engage in thought and dialogue about *what it means to be a teacher* in American society. The chapters are meant to create conversation about schoolteacher images, roles, and relationships with students. In addition, the text offers an array of primary source materials, which we hope will stimulate examination of the teaching profession and what it means to have an identity as a schoolteacher. Whether our readers are just entering the profession, are experienced educators, or are students of American culture, the chapters are written to invite participation in a variety of activities that we believe will expand awareness of teaching and teachers in America.

Each chapter presents an interpretive framework in which readers can examine the roles and relationships of teachers in schools. At the end of each section, the *Continuing Dialogue* offers a range of activities for discussion, writing, and research opportunities for students. In this sense, the book embodies the view that a text is not a definitive authority, which includes all the information students need to know about a subject, but rather a source and resource to stimulate thinking and further investigation.

It is our hope that readers will use the activities together with others reading this book as a means of more thoroughly exploring the teaching profession and the various genres that portray it. Activities are designed to be undertaken in small groups or alone, and often require the participation of children and adults in classrooms and communities. Through such activities veteran teachers, as well as teaching candidates and students in teacher education or liberal arts courses, can engage in qualitative research about their profession and American culture. We also view the reference materials provided for each chapter as valuable starting points for further investigation. It is our hope, too, that readers will explore contexts and media that interest them which are not within the realm of this book. We believe that the reading of this book should be a collaborative process; we welcome ongoing and dynamic involvement for readers as fellow responders and researchers.

This process approach to teacher education reflects our belief in the value of enabling teachers to be researchers in their professions. Both those preparing to become teachers and those returning to college for advanced degrees are currently being encouraged to pursue research that is personally relevant and intellectually meaningful. This book presents models of ways to view and to conduct such research. Some chapters approach research as a qualitative endeavor, in which interviewing, observation, and dialogue are crucial components. Other chapters address the topic of teacher imagery through the study of literary texts, thus demonstrating a type of research that resembles literary criticism, within a particular social setting. Students utilizing this text could engage in independent studies, research projects, or masters' theses, following a line of inquiry begun in one or more of these chapters.

The book is organized in four parts: Part I presents a conceptual framework and explains the three research focuses around which the Chapters in Parts II, III, and IV are organized; Part II reveals the classroom in which contemporary teachers and students are called upon to share their metaphors of schoolteachers along with past generations of teachers who have portrayed their lives and teaching through oral history; Part III involves images of teachers created in American culture through the media of television, film, and song lyrics; and Part IV searches for images in children's textbooks, textbooks written for teacher audiences, adult fiction, and children's literature.

We wish to call attention to the subtitle of this book—*Paragons, Polarities, Complexities*. We think these three ways of classifying teacher images provide a valuable framework for us as authors and will be useful for students. We may view the nature of images in some sense as an interweaving of the apparent images and metaphors we associate with teachers in our immediate past and in the euphoric stereotypes we present to young children as they enter school; the diametrically opposed stereotypes of teacher as hero and teacher as villain; and the much more complex portraiture of teachers as they see themselves through their own lenses of self coupled with those of society. Many of the chapters also raise the issues of social class, gender, and race as these concepts intertwine with perceptions of teacher images historically and currently. Through specific activities and questions and through instructors' encouragement of parallel and original research, we believe this book will encourage further scholarship and reflection on these issues, which are imperative to understanding the teaching profession and the role of schoolteachers in American culture.

We view this text as an original piece of scholarship, written by teacher-educators who work daily with teachers in public schools. Since Lortie's study of schoolteachers (1975), continuing research has been conducted on the nature of the profession and the people who work within it. Many of these works propel readers toward an imaginative and emotional involvement with their studies. We continue this dialogue, while expanding the focus to include the analysis of teachers as they appear in American culture—in film, music, television, literature, textbooks, and the words of children and teachers themselves.

Our approach has been eclectic. We have called on a variety of contributors who have established knowledge and research in qualitative methodology, literature, and the media. It is our hope that our study reveals essential imagery that inspires dialogue as well as providing interesting materials that enrich both instructors' and students' visions of their course.

## Acknowledgments

Shortly after daybreak on a cold December morning several years ago, our colleagues joined us for a meeting during a faculty retreat at Lake Geneva, Wisconsin. We asked them to discuss an idea for a book about the images of teachers in American society and culture. Some of our colleagues began the meeting with us, others drifted in and sat down (not knowing we were not just eating breakfast) but then stayed, becoming actively involved in the conversation. Some were intrigued and began to imagine their own contributions, while others were elated because we touched on their fervent interests that they had already developed through their research and teaching. This core of potential authors identified their friends and colleagues who also shared these interests. And a book had begun.

The contributors have engaged in this project with enthusiasm, joy, and satisfaction. This satisfaction stems from the recognition that this book is a gift to all of us because we have long wanted such a resource to have for our work as teacher educators. But despite the intrinsic rewards that always accompany the fulfillment of a long-desired project, we still wish to give the contributors our thanks for their work as researchers and writers. We also thank them for their stimulating, sympathetic, and humorous conversations and company as colleagues and friends.

When early drafts of the introduction and some chapters were sent to the publishers, one editor responded with enthusiasm, respect for our ideas (even when the work was still in somewhat embryonic form), steadfast belief in this project, and friendship. To that editor, Naomi Silverman, we wish to express our appreciation and great affection. We also want to thank our project editor, Diana Puglisi, associate editor Sarah Crowley, and all the other staff members at St. Martin's whose names we do not know, for their important contributions to making this book a reality.

Also, we are grateful to Brian Farrell, Jordana Joseph, Heather Dunn, and Kate Kellogg, who pitched in to help us when we needed it most; we never would have met our deadlines without their hard and careful work.

Finally, the completion of this book was strengthened by the helpful criticisms of reviewers who were asked to respond to the manuscript. We thank Brian Deever (Georgia Southern University), Mari Koerner (Roosevelt University), Gene Provenzo (University of Miami), and Betty Sichel (C. W. Post Campus, Long Island University) for their suggestions and their enthusiasm. To know beforehand that other teacher-educators envision bringing our book into their courses has been extremely gratifying.

Pamela Bolotin Joseph
Gail E. Burnaford
*Editors*

# Contents

Preface     vii

## Part I.   Introduction

1. Contemplating Images of Schoolteachers in American Culture
   *Pamela Bolotin Joseph and Gail E. Burnaford*     3

   Continuing Dialogue     24

## Part II.   Teachers and Children

2. Constructing and Discovering Images of Your Teaching
   *Joseph Fischer and Anne Kiefer*     29

3. Reflections in a Mirror: Teacher-Generated Metaphors from Self and Others
   *Sara Efron and Pamela Bolotin Joseph*     54

4. Across the Generations: Conversations with Retired Teachers
   *David Hobson*     78

5. Good Women and Old Stereotypes: Retired Teachers Talk about Teaching
   *Nancy Green and Mary Phillips Manke*     96

6. A Mosaic: Contemporary Schoolchildren's Images of Teachers
   *W. Nikola-Lisa and Gail E. Burnaford*     116

   Continuing Dialogue     142

# Part III. Screen and Song

7.  A Teacher Ain't Nothin' But a Hero: Teachers and
    Teaching in Film
    *William Ayers*                                                 147

8.  Just Fun—Dreams of Revenge: Images of Teachers in
    the Lyrics of Rock, Pop, and Folk-Protest
    *Fletcher DuBois*                                               157

9.  From Our Miss Brooks to Mr. Moore: Playing Their
    Roles in Television Situation Comedies
    *Ken Kantor*                                                    175

    Continuing Dialogue                                            190

# Part IV. Literature and Textbooks

10. Teacher as Gatekeeper: Schoolteachers in Picture Books
    for Young Children
    *Ann M. Trousdale*                                             195

11. Personal Memories and Social Response: Teacher
    Images in Literature for Older Children
    *Gail E. Burnaford*                                            215

12. Opening and Closing the Door: Urban Teachers in
    American Literature, 1900–1940
    *Rosalind Benjet*                                              231

13. The Sentimental Image of the Rural Schoolteacher
    *Mary Phillips Manke*                                          243

14. "The Ideal Teacher": Images of Paragons in Teacher
    Education Textbooks before 1940
    *Pamela Bolotin Joseph*                                        258

    Continuing Dialogue                                            283

Afterword: The Dialogue Continues                                  285

Contributors                                                       287

Name Index                                                         291

Subject Index                                                      295

# Images of Schoolteachers in Twentieth-Century America

Paragons, Polarities, Complexities

# I

---

## Introduction

# 1

## Contemplating Images of Schoolteachers in American Culture

Pamela Bolotin Joseph
Gail E. Burnaford

I n our lives, we have collectively known thousands of teachers. They have recited multiplication tables with us, attended class picnics with us, and shared Shakespeare with us. They have pleaded with us, coaxed us, and scolded us as we made our way through the labyrinth of learning in schools. If we take a moment, we can conjure up images of teachers in our own experiences who made some sort of impression on us; our private images stem from our responses to the women and men who taught us. We also hold impressions of schoolteachers through the memories and imaginations of others. Throughout American culture, we find images reduced to pedantic and foolish stereotypes or to teacher heroes—who are creative, intelligent individuals, leaders and courageous renegades. Images of teachers in American culture have been created through various media— literature, film, music, television commercials. Furthermore, those of us who are teachers or want to become teachers also have images of ourselves and the kind of teachers we believe we are. We strive to define ourselves, even though we know that images of schoolteachers—real teachers who have come before us, imaginary characters, and imagined roles defined for us by society—affect how others view us and perhaps how we portray ourselves.

This book examines some of the images of teachers as they are portrayed in a variety of media at various points in the twentieth century, viewed through the lenses of image-makers from literature and popular culture. We have pursued teacher images by conceiving this book as a composition of various genres that integrate scholarship and personal response as

3

the chapters are read and juxtaposed with others; individual chapters cast light on others. We also seek images created by teachers themselves and the students they teach. A major purpose of the book is to investigate the patterns and themes that emerge as we look at the images made conscious and distinct in the texts, stories, films, and narratives of teachers and students. These patterns may then contribute to a rich dialogue on the question, "What does it mean to be a teacher?" The contributors have attempted to unveil the assumptions, the contexts, and the layers of meaning that surround teacher imagery in American culture. We provide this book as a forum for getting in touch with such influences on our lives.

We deem the question, "What does it mean to be a teacher?," as vital to this book; it links the chapters together, and it connects the authors to the readers as we imagine our mutual pursuit of answers to this question for what it means to ourselves and for American culture.

We realize that a person's sense of self as a teacher does not spring from a uniquely individual concept of self-definition as a professional. We must take heed that "while we are immersed in our personal history, our practices are not simply the products of our intent and will" (Popkewitz, 1988, p. 379). Moreover, we recognize that "individual and collective identities are constructed on three sites: 1. the biologically given characteristics which we bring to every social interaction; 2. givens that are often covered over by social relations, family, school; 3. and the technological sensorium that we call mass or popular culture" (Aronowitz, 1989, p. 197). Our understandings of what it means to be a teacher stem from our own personalities and development, from what we have learned implicitly and explicitly from our families, communities, and our schooling, and from the messages in the culture that surrounds us.

Teachers develop understandings of their work, relationships with students, and concepts of themselves through various sources. Students' ideas of teachers, their parents' expectations, administrators' attitudes, portrayals of teachers in the media and public opinion, the idealized images given to teachers by those who mediate their entrance into the profession, as well as the advice and experiences handed down from past generations of teachers, contribute to our understanding of what it means to be a teacher. We need to ponder all those who have in some way represented schoolteachers—either by generating images of respect or, conversely, by diminishing the profession's status—and to come to terms with how their responses have influenced us.

We envision our work as contributing to the study of teaching and education that acknowledges teachers as a primary source of knowledge for researchers (Carew & Lightfoot, 1979). Teachers themselves educate us about their work and, as we have found, reveal much about American culture through their reflections about families, children, or society. Our scholarship demonstrates the potency of the experiences of teaching and schooling through stories and narrative (Carter, 1993; Witherall & Noddings,

1991), so that we can learn from the voices of adults and children in schools—from the past and present—and not just from reports and commissions that cannot reveal human feelings, hopes, and concerns. We also believe that the provocative questions and implications of this research continue the traditions of feminist research methods (Nielsen, 1990) because our contributors often substantiate and emphasize the voices and interpretations of women as teachers and as students.

Our readers must integrate knowledge from past and present, from understandings of the teaching profession through the experiences of the women and men who teach, and from impressions and depictions from diverse genres. We urge our readers to actively pursue connections that the editors or contributors did not explicitly make, and to pursue an innovative avenue of research that we characterize as interactive. Finally, we must think about the influence of history, society, and culture on the image-makers and on ourselves, pondering Joel Spring's (1992) comments about images in American life: "What people know, what they believe in, and how they interpret the world have an important effect on their choices and consequently their actions" (p. 2). For our readers who are or plan to be educators, we intend this book to help you think about your choices and actions in your classrooms, schools, and communities.

## The Aims of Image-Seeking

> **image** *n*. 1. A representation or likeness of a real or imaginary person, creature, or object. 2. A mental representation of something not perceived at the moment through the senses; mental picture. 3. The way in which a person or thing is popularly perceived or regarded; a public impression (Funk & Wagnalls, 1989).

When we consulted a popular dictionary to determine just what this word "image" might mean, we discovered three definitions. As we contemplated what each implied for our scholarship, we realized that the three ways of thinking of image responded to our purposes for this book as well as to the three audiences we imagine reading it.

The first definition refers to an image as *a likeness,* perhaps real, perhaps imaginary. Why might we attempt to portray likenesses of teachers? We do so because prospective teachers need to consider what it means to be schoolteachers—in their classrooms and within American society. Critics of teacher education maintain that "most colleges and universities tend to focus on the ideal rather than the real" (Hoy & Rees, 1977, p. 24). Consequently, people enter teaching without participating in critical reflection about the challenges of teaching, the problems they will face, and their own reactions to the experience of being a teacher. A compelling reason why we initiated this work was because we envisioned that conversations with veteran teachers could help entering teachers better reflect on their chosen profession and their lives as teachers. Teachers-to-be should face the reality of how uncertain, controversial, and full of conflict this profession is in the eyes of those who are professionals, students and families, and the public. We also desire to engage prospective teachers in conversations about their impressions and dreams, their hopes and fears. Teacher education should build on or rebuild what teachers and teachers-to-be already believe about their work (Feinman-Nemser & Folden, 1986). Teacher education must provide sufficient opportunities to fully imagine what it is like to be a teacher. We hope that this study of images will provide reflection as "an intellectual experience," which is an important component to teacher education (Clandinin, 1986, p. 176).

We are mindful of research that confirms that new schoolteachers who have been motivated to teach because of their sense of their calling and altruism fall into despair when they suffer disillusionment in their occupational choice. Failure to anticipate the difficulties of teaching indeed hastens the departure of promising candidates from their profession (McLaughlin et al., 1986). We must encourage prospective schoolteachers to explore personal motivations and expectations, and to think about the complexity of their roles and purposes. They need to be continually asked to imagine their profession and how it is beheld because of its special nature of working with children and adolescents. They need to ponder the varied responses to teachers from students, parents, communities, and the popular media or culture, and to explore their own feelings about these reactions. Interacting with stories, evoking the memories of teachers and those who have been taught, and joining in conversation about film or television portraitures of teachers may give new teachers an added awareness of this profession in this society and its personal meaning as well.

So, too, we consider what Margaret Mead (1951/1962) suggests in *The School in American Culture*, that cultural images contribute to the enculturation of teachers into their profession. "The teacher who is adequately trained to represent the order of the past, the dignity and beauty of tradition, must, in the course of her training come to terms with her own past," writes Mead (p. 28). A teacher or one aspiring to be a teacher may acknowledge the verity of teaching as she has been taught, substituting "the demands which her parents and teachers made upon her for a new set of demands, which she will make, in the same tone of voice, upon her pupils" (p. 28). If we examine the recollections that might be the foundations for teacher behaviors, new understanding may develop. The cultural imperatives to represent obedience and order are handed down to the teacher from generation to generation, Mead declares.

Many teachers (during their educational preparation and their subsequent lives in schools) have had no time to reflect on the questions, What is it that I really want to be? What is a teacher? How do the expectations about teaching prescribe or perhaps even enslave teachers in the classroom? How do the images of teaching form and limit the curriculum, affecting not just how we teach but what we teach? And why have teachers received so little status, power, and authority as professionals in their schools and within American society?

Such critical questioning leads us to consider whether the enculturation of teachers has to be understood by using the theory of hegemony by which we conceptualize teachers as a "subordinate group consent[ing] to the existing social order" (Giroux & Simon, 1989a, p. 8). Our contributors inform us that "good" teachers imagine dedication as appropriate lack of pay and lack of militancy; they accept their subordinate—perhaps even underclass—position in society; they don't compete for money or authority. These are distressing thoughts for people entering teaching and imagining themselves as empowered professionals. These issues also are troublesome to our contributors who all have been curious about the nature of such expectations that evolve from our individual pasts, collective present, the dynamics of society, and the pasts and presents of teachers themselves.

A second definition of this word "image" which we found in our dictionary is *a mental representation of something not perceived at the moment through the senses*. We might probe these images not immediately perceived through the senses because schoolteachers often teach in isolation (Apple, 1986; Chapman & Lowther, 1982). They may have never known or contemplated how fellow teachers live in and with their profession.

Schoolteachers may not have reflected about how administrators, parents, community members, or media respond to them, not because of who they are, but because of personal memories or stereotypes and consistent cultural behaviors that go unquestioned or unchallenged. Often, such personal feelings about what it means to be a teacher persist despite contradictory experiences. An expansion of those perceptions to include the scope of teacher imagery—not just in the immediate classroom but in novels, on television, and in the hearts and minds of former and present students—adds depth and breadth to our understanding. The unseen becomes more accessible; we can thus discern the reactions of others as we create our self-definitions as teachers. As schoolteachers connect with the experiences of teachers and students and imaginatively enter into dialogue with the image-makers, we hope that they will gain understanding of the meaning of teaching.

Furthermore, it is necessary to contemplate the relationship of the teacher to schooling. Although we must start with our own experiences as students and as teachers, we must expand our imagination to consider what is outside our immediate experiences.

Teachers' interpretations of their roles contribute to the way students experience schooling. Teachers may perceive their roles as directly responsive to the school system's mandated curriculum, regardless of their students' prior knowledge or preferences in their own learning. In fact, scholars of popular culture point to teachers' lack of empathy with their students' experiences. "Students from subordinate groups, especially marginalized groups, face a curriculum which demands a certain kind of learning," writes Carnoy (1989) about education and culture in American society; "the method of teaching this curriculum assumes a desire to succeed on the school's (and society's) terms, no matter how irrelevant or uninteresting the content" (p. 21). So, too, do others (Aronowitz, 1989; Fine, 1989; Lipsitz, 1990) write about the failure of schools to intellectually or emotionally engage youth from low-income and working-class families.

If we have liked school and have succeeded in mastering what our teachers have set out for us to accomplish, can we imagine the experience of schooling from the point of view of those for whom the classroom has little significance? Can we empathically understand the experiences of those who view schools as harsh places that select and weed out, ignoring those who are not easily taught? In addition, can we imagine the perspectives of those who are not represented in stories of classrooms and the memories of teachers? We must reflect not only about what it means to be a teacher but also what it means to be a student.

There is a third definition of "image" in our dictionary, and it is that which is *popularly perceived or regarded; a public impression.* This interpretation of image turns our attention to schooling as portrayed in American culture, including popular culture.

We understand the power of image in popular culture or media and literature in creating our sense of reality—of what is possible, normal, usual.[1] "This is how anything imaginational grows in our minds, is transformed, socially transformed, from something we merely know to exist or have existed, somewhere or another, to something which is properly ours, a working force in our common consciousness," explains anthropologist Clifford Geertz (1983, p. 41). Thus, an author's, songwriter's, filmmaker's vision of teachers and schooling becomes part of popular sensibilities and understandings, excluding the discernment of other examples. An example of this cultural consciousness, the image of urban schooling as "the blackboard jungle," hurts both the teachers and youth whose behaviors can only be seen as stereotypes of popular culture.

Artistic forms of expression engage our imagination and teach us the commonplaces of our culture. It is through children's literature (Taxel, 1989), music (Grossberg, 1989; Shumway, 1989), and television (Aronowitz, 1989) that identities are formed, good and bad are named, and standards and aspirations are established. In *Time Passages: Collective Memory and American Popular Culture*, Lipsitz (1990) asserts that "hegemony is not just imposed on a society from the top; it is struggled for from below, and no terrain is a more important part of that struggle than popular culture." Lipsitz continues, "Cultural forms create conditions of possibility, they expand the present by informing it with memories of the past and hopes for the future; but they also engender accommodation with prevailing power realities, separating art from life, and internalizing the dominant culture's norms and values as necessary and inevitable" (p. 16).

Popular culture is pervasive, but some adolescents, and adults, too, seem particularly captivated by the sounds, words, and visual sensations of popular culture; they experience incessant imagery. Having been bombarded with the negative imagery of schools and teachers in films and commercials aimed at adolescent and preadolescent audiences, we take to heart Giroux and Simon's (1989b) assertion that "popular culture . . . is not insignificant in shaping how students view themselves and their own relations to various forms of pedagogy and learning" (p. 221).[2]

It is not just popular culture that diminishes the image of schoolteachers and schools. As we examine the social and political values of communities and American society, we observe the political irony that education is a panacea (at least during election campaigns). In actuality, however, education often is not a high national or local priority. We read opinion polls that inform us that teachers are denigrated in American society, that many parents would not want their children to grow up and become teachers. (We have even heard teachers tell us that they don't want their own children to become teachers.)

Moreover, in academic life, American history and culture often are taught with scarcely a mention of schooling, even though schooling will consume young peoples' lives for many years and determine the adulthood they will experience. We must question why teaching and schooling often have so little significance to those who seek to understand American life. Ultimately, it is this third definition that must capture our interest and provoke our analysis; what does it mean to be a teacher, not only in our own eyes, but also in the conceptualizations of others within American culture in the twentieth century?

## Conceptualizing Images: Paragons, Polarities, Complexities

Although there might be various titles that could introduce this book about teacher images that well may illustrate the themes and issues in our writing, as chapters were generated, we continued to gravitate toward the notion of "paragons, polarities, and complexities." The schoolteachers described in various chapters include ideal teachers, horrible teachers, and other characterizations that do not lend themselves to simplistic description. Furthermore, these three concepts attracted us because as we wrote our own chapters and read and discussed the chapters of contributors, we realized that the title represented not only the images found in various media, but also the progression of our thinking about the book and its organization.

At first, we were fascinated by the negative image of teacher as buffoon and witch. (We are still amazed at the recurrence of the witch in fictional accounts as well as in narratives of teachers themselves.) We (who are teachers and work with so many lovely, caring people who teach) had difficulty understanding why obnoxious caricatures permeated American popular culture. Then we became more curious about the teacher as friend and hero, about the manifestation of the teacher ideal. Eventually, the juxtaposition of both kinds of images seemed to be a promising framework for the book.

As contributors began sharing and discussing their manuscripts, however, we realized that this diametric conception of image did not do justice to the book, particularly in explaining the relationships between teachers and students and the self-reflection of teachers as they interpret who teachers are and what they do. At that point, we reassessed our own research, recognizing dimensions that we had not seen before. For example, when we studied image in order to delineate the portrayals of relationships between teachers and students, we realized that teachers may indeed be something other than friend or foe, empowerer or controller. We better understood that teachers must choose their actions and purposes (encompassing their affiliations with students) within complicated contexts. We began to comprehend teachers as human beings who make decisions encumbered by powerful forces in their schools, communities, and American society generally. We even felt the need for some sympathetic response to caricature: why have the teacher-ogres ridiculed in popular culture become so hateful, so angry?

We use the conceptualization of images as paragons, polarities, and complexities in order to give our readers a basis for discussion, a way of considering and probing the images they encounter in the chapters and in other sources. We hope that this title stimulates reflection and conversation but does not confine our readers within too rigid boundaries.

### Paragons

Undoubtedly, some portrayals of schoolteachers produce images of remarkable human beings, people who sacrificed their private lives and even their health in order to devote themselves to their profession. In picture book after picture book, in countless teacher education textbooks, and in a multitude of films, images of schoolteachers—loving and smiling, noble, or heroic—continually appear. In such accounts, teacher paragons wish to do more than just their jobs in a limited academic sense; they are good and helpful people who demonstrate unfailing moral purpose and patience.

When extraordinarily positive images of schoolteachers exist, one commonality seems evident: the teacher as paragon must do for students what others in their lives cannot do. In the representation of the paragon, it is the schoolteacher alone who can introduce learning to the child. It is the schoolteacher who can understand children's anxieties and recognize their talents when others in the students' environment cannot, who stands with students and against the forces that otherwise would harm or stifle them. Little drama is engendered by a story that depicts a teacher working in harmony with parents, communities, schools, and students. Whether realistic or simply a necessary dramatic element, the paragons created by authors or filmmakers seem to be special adults who do not just teach but do battle with the negative influences in the students' environment. Similarly, such good teachers also enter into the memories and portraits of schoolchildren and teachers themselves who idealize the teacher who "saves" students—from corrupt systems, from the scorn of peers, and from negligent families.

Paragons, however, must be understood through the perspectives of their beholders. Ideal traits vary depending on the image-makers' audiences and purposes. For example, the good teacher in books for very young children emerges as a version of the good fairy or the good witch who helps the child enter a strange and scary world. That this paragon in primary literature generally is a woman who never demonstrates the features of commonplace motherhood—impatience, frustration, or possibly interests in the world other than children themselves—demonstrates to children that the teacher is a wonderfully benign creature. Schoolteachers portrayed in fiction for older children, television, and film must be more than good. They must also be courageous, insightful, and humorous, and they must relate to young people in ways that other adults seem unable to do in order to have relationships of equality and trust with the students. In the literature of rural America, schoolteachers must be savvy, keeping ahead of their wild pupils in anticipating their mischievous challenges. Paragons in textbooks must be self-sacrificing, self-controlled, and subservient. Even teachers themselves contrast paragon images of "true teaching professionals" who really "give themselves to the kids" with those who punch time clocks and lack dedication. We have found time and time again that teachers conceive of money as tainted. The paragons' admired attributes differ from genre to genre; nonetheless, we discover certain prescribed patterns suggesting the unique role of teachers.

We have also come to see that paragon images must be poked and probed. For example, the wonderful nurturing image of teacher as parent can be provoking if we allow ourselves to realize that the parent is nurturing and caring, but may also be controlling, dominating, or even abusing. Or, our contributors have discovered that the "best" of teachers may ignore the intelligence of their students, imposing the teachers' versions of proper education without any cognizance of students' unique needs, strengths, or creative powers. Therefore teachers' moral callings reflect their own values but not the values or aspirations of those whom they teach. We realize that some teachers actually see themselves (or are advised to see themselves) as soldiers—combating and overpowering students and their families, not collaborating with them.

## *Polarities*

The images that we envision as polarities are particularly apparent in memories of individuals. Eliot Wigginton, teacher and Foxfire founder from Rabun Gap, Georgia, characterizes how he begins each school year with his ninth-grade English classes (Wigginton, 1985). He asks his students to write about the memorable moments they have had in their school years thus far. Students sometimes relate brief flashes of memory from kindergarten, from third grade, or perhaps from eighth. Teachers in their roles as leaders and authority symbols figure prominently in those memories. "I remember when Miss Smith screamed at me to be quiet in the fourth grade; I remember my face getting red and the tears choking my eyes"; "I remember when my teacher came to my house to see my project on birds; she really treated me like I was special." (So, too, have we discovered polarities when we ask undergraduate and graduate students in teacher education or renewal courses to describe poignant memories of their young lives as students.)

Polarities similarly exist in popular culture. Authors who describe childhood and adolescent experiences in classrooms remember with gratitude or with excruciating pain the teachers who helped them believe in their own talents or who stifled and ridiculed them. Then, loving images of teachers become juxtaposed with fear; in the eyes or memories of students, the schoolteacher as the good mother changes into the wicked witch. We discover cruel and insensitive teachers in literature, film, and narratives about schools; such images are sometimes portrayed in ridiculous fashion, but sometimes the horror experienced by the child predominates. Many accounts about teachers have quite circumscribed formulas; there are good teachers and bad teachers, noble or preposterous ones, sentimentally remembered classrooms and chaotic school environments. Polarities exist in the characterizations of different teachers as healers or wounders, teachers who are sensitive or callous, imaginative or repressive. Such polarized portrayals seldom allow us to contemplate a teaching professional—a human being—who has magnificent moments or forgivably absurd ones. Often schoolteachers are described and remembered as caricature and stereotype, not as human beings.

The preponderance of polarities in twentieth-century images of teachers provokes our curiosity and concern about those schooled in the United States. Why, we must ask, do such dichotomies of image popularly appear in film, on television, in literature, and in the accounts of children?

Do simplistic, dichotomized images reflect a collective present that appears to be "true" to the memories of audiences? Our own memories of teachers may possibly be the starting point for an investigation of images. To what extent are images of teachers—as mothers, as eccentrics, as villains—a function of our personal memories? Have we remembered with grave distortion? Or, is it not possible that the kernels of truth behind docile, pedantic, or harsh images may indeed exist, creating a disheartening or frustrating portrayal of schooling? Shall we believe that some truth lies behind these depictions that demonstrate the small moments of injustice in classrooms and predominant patterns within school systems? Do the images of popular culture "also provide meaningful connection to our own pasts and to the pasts of others?" (Lipsitz, 1990, p. 5).[3]

Imagery, however, like myth, may derive validity not from reality but from people's belief in it. H. J. Gans maintains that "a society's art, information, and entertainment do not develop in a vacuum; they must meet standards of form and substance which grow out of the values of the society and the needs and characteristics of its members" (Gans, 1974, p. 67). How have we been conditioned to perceive teachers in certain roles because of predominant stereotypes in American culture? And what are the needs of members of American society? Or, at the very least, what needs do the publishers of textbooks and literature or the producers of film and television interpret as societal requirements? "Rarely do we ask about the origins and intentions of the messages we encounter through the mass media; sometimes we forget that artists have origins or intentions at all, so pervasive are the stimuli around us" (Lipsitz, 1990, p. 5).

May we blame the image-makers for the often negative perception of schoolteachers in American culture? Do the creators of popular culture who make schools and teachers the butt of their jokes need to relive and fantasize their own adolescent rebellion? It appears that the "experiences of being young involve struggles between youth and adults" and that these struggles have become "increasingly visible since the end of the second world war" (Grossberg, 1989, p. 104). Are such topics simply profitable because of large youthful audiences? Do they serve to reinforce a perspective that ridicules respect for knowledge or tradition? Grossberg (1989) notes that in recent popular culture "never has youth talked so much, nor had so much expertise and knowledge" (p. 105)—obviously, in contrast to adults, parents, and teachers.

Our contributors also question: can negative images function as subversive catalysts, or are they only an outlet for anger, thus dispelling the energy emanating from anger that might challenge and change the status quo? Or must we simply come to terms with the fact that there is nothing sacred about being a teacher and that schoolteachers are "fair game" (along with people of other occupations) for humorous treatment and that humor can be tender, uplifting, and not necessarily cruel?

No matter what the image-makers' motives might be, we have to consider that personal memory may be displaced by the images of popular culture (Lipsitz, 1990). And memory often perpetuates the negative, the horrible image—driving out remembrances of pleasant experiences.

Unfortunately, the cultural memories that produce negative portrayals may affect the teaching profession. Mary Tanzy Crume (1989) contends that teachers are disgruntled in their profession and that young people are discouraged from entering the profession because of an image crisis. She notes that literature and film are the vehicles through which people most often see teachers and schools; thus, these media must share a portion of the blame for this crisis: "Novels and films may add substance and credibility to the impressions that their audiences already hold, harden their attitudes, and convince them they have learned more about the real-life teachers that novelists and filmmakers have supposedly used as models. The potency of these images is increased if books and movies show similarities in their treatment of teachers" (p. 36). Memory and media thus affect the images that students, the public, and teachers have of the profession. Crume warns us that "if these images are largely negative, they may give the public further justification for a lack of support of education" (p. 36). Crume's argument must be given serious consideration, especially by those who wish to become schoolteachers and those of us who define ourselves as teachers. Our contributors also fear the constraints caused by imposed images and call for teachers to liberate themselves from such an imposition.

### Complexities

The research presented in these chapters renders not only simplistically positive or derogatory representations, but also images of teachers as complex and rich. The authors have found fascinating portrayals of schoolteachers. We began to think about teacher images as complexities as we read the accounts of teachers themselves, first as they struggled with stereotypes of themselves that they felt did not do justice to their work or purpose, and then, as they contemplated their own images. The metaphors for self-definition that teachers themselves create certainly are not polarities or paragons. Rather, they describe the intricacy and creativity of the teaching process in which the teacher might have many kinds of relationships with students as well as with parents and administrators. Our research also demonstrates that popular culture may occasionally reveal the complexity of the relationship between teacher and student. Some stories and narratives allow readers or viewers to respond to teachers as individuals, to empathically share laughter and pain with schoolteachers as humans, not as stereotypes.

Perhaps our understanding of teachers and teaching will be informed only by searching for the heterogeneity that images offer. We learn more from the profound descriptions of teaching as struggle and complexity than from caricature and stereotype. The teachers' voices, the visions of authors and filmmakers who probe deeply and imagine the intricate relationships among human beings—among teachers and students—may teach us much more about what it means to be a teacher.

Finally, our contributors remind us that it is not enough for scholars simply to call complex images of teachers and teaching to our attention. The experiences and reflections revealed in narrative and dialogue from teachers and students, and among the authors' insights about various genres, mutually benefit teachers and prospective teachers, and could ultimately inform students and parents as well. What forum have schools and universities provided for informing each other of our hopes, moral purposes, and self-definitions? How can teachers convey to the American public the complexity of their purposes and experiences when the schoolteacher image has been so deeply molded by paragon and polarity? We are hopeful that the readers of this book can utilize it as a catalyst for serious and sensitive dialogue among all participants and critics of schooling in the United States.

## Commonalities of the Schoolteacher Image in American Culture

Although they examine various contexts, time periods, and media, the chapters presented here illustrate common insights about the experiences of teachers and the response to teachers. We wish to call the reader's attention to several themes or threads crucial to our understanding of American culture that appear as we view this book as a whole.

One commonality is strikingly apparent—the frequent theme of the negative image, the terrible teacher. The image of schoolteacher as obnoxious caricature permeates American popular culture (including media not covered in this volume, e.g., television commercials), in the portrayals of schoolchildren, in the concerns of teacher education textbook writers, and in the discourse of schoolteachers as they describe their conceptions of how others view them. These caricatures or stereotypes are numerous and differ from one another, but all are negative and all reduce the teacher to an object of scorn, disrespect, and sometimes fear. Teacher as buffoon and bumbler, as rigid authoritarian, and as terrifying witch—with uncontrolled and irrational flights of anger and punishment—all pervade the material studied by the contributors. That these negative images become present in the self-portraits of teachers through their awareness of how others see them, and in different sources of media, suggests that American society has not provided for a respected role for the teacher. This fact, as driven home by the numerous accounts and descriptions in this book, provides a critical understanding of the teaching profession and one's life as a teacher. It also conveys an essential point about American culture: teachers and what they represent are not valuable to this society.

Hofstadter (1962) suggests that the image of the teacher is significant to our understanding of American culture. In *Anti-Intellectualism in American Life* (1962), he writes: "The figure of the schoolteacher may well be taken as a central symbol in any modern society. The teacher is, or at least can be, the first more or less full-time professional representative of the life of the mind who enters into the experience of most children (p. 309) .... [and] from observing how teachers are esteemed and rewarded they quickly sense how society looks upon the teacher's role." (p. 310). In many other cultures, the teacher is esteemed because of one society's reverence for learning. Responses to the teacher and education undoubtedly reflect on a culture's predilection toward thought, growth, and, if not enlightenment, certainly toward traditional wisdom.

What does the treatment and depiction of teachers say about American society? How do negative caricatures convey the life of the mind in the United States? It is clear from our scholarship that Americans have not schooled their children to believe in an ideal of a respected scholar who cultivates the intellect. We must also realize that even "good" teachers, the nurturing, kindly friend, father or mother, may not represent the life of the mind as much as they reveal their goodness and benevolence. A good teacher may mean much to a student emotionally, but the appreciation for intellectual stimulation does not routinely echo in the construction of teacher images in the areas explored by our contributors.

We certainly do not find images of teachers as transformative intellectuals, as educators who "go beyond concern with forms of empowerment that promote individual achievement and traditional forms of academic success" (Giroux, 1989, p. 138). According to Giroux, "Acting as a transformative intellectual means helping students acquire critical knowledge about basic societal structures, such as the economy, the state, the workplace, and mass culture, so that such institutions can be open to potential transformation" (pp. 138–139). Teachers who critically examine American culture and society and encourage critical inquiry in their students seldom appear in narrative, literature, or other media. The lack of images of teacher as critical thinker helps produce what Spring (1992) calls an ironic situation—"that the supposed protectors of democracy, the public schools, do little to promote a political culture that would help a democratic society survive" (p. 5).

The failure of the transcending image of the teacher as an intellectual or as the adult who leads students toward intellectual pursuits—toward analyzing and challenging existing conditions of community and society— parallels another commonality. The "successful" teacher (or at the very least one who is hired and keeps a job) does not awaken students' intelligence. Such teachers value order; order is what they strive for, what they are paid for. Throughout the century, it appears that "good" teachers have controlled their classrooms, their students, and themselves, and they in turn have suffered the domination of the community. Fine (1989) believes that in American society today, "the typical classroom still values silence, control, and quiet" (p. 160). It may not be tantamount to a caricature, but the stereotype of the teacher representing control presents an unpleasant, stifling image. Furthermore, we find that the drama depicted in several genres centers on the struggle for power and control as students are seen as threats to the teacher's ability to order (to govern) and to create order (structure or organization).

Mead (1951/1962), writing at the midpoint of the twentieth century, proposes that the image of the American schoolteacher is a "distillate" of ideas, a blending of stereotype and actual experience. She imagines a nondescript person (a woman) of "indeterminate age, of the middle class, and committed to the ethics and manners of a middle-class world" (p. 5). This teacher works to control the instincts of her students and finds that her major duty is to prepare students for conformity. What does her student think of her? What, in fact, shall we all think of her?

> In the emotional tone which accompanies the image there will be respect, a little fear, perhaps more than a little affection, an expectation that she will reward his efforts and struggles to learn and conform, and a spate of delighted memories of those occasions when he himself perpetrated feats of undetected mischief. She stands in his mind on the borderline of childhood, urging, beckoning, exhorting, patiently teaching, impatiently rebuking a child in whom the impulse is strong to escape the narrow bounds of the school room into the outdoors where birds are nesting, or the sunlit pavements are waiting for marbles (p. 5).

Mead opens a Pandora's box of questions. Will the sunlight always be outside the classroom? Why can't the classroom be an alive and a spontaneous place? Does this image doom the teacher to never crossing the line—never becoming the child and sharing with a child's delight the pleasures of play and learning? Mead's version of schooling in which the teacher stands on "the borderline of childhood" preparing a child to conform to the world of work brings to mind the view that the discipline of the classroom can be likened to the discipline of the factory assembly line: ". . . school is an activity, from the point of view of all its participants, that systematically denies pleasure; in fact, one of its most valuable features from the view of the dominant anticulture is its regime of discipline and the conversion of play into labor" (Aronowitz, 1989, p. 202). Training in school, then, becomes training for the world of work, as defined by those who direct the workers and control the labor force. Taxel (1989) echoes this perspective, referring to the "chilling evidence of the extent to which classrooms are dominated by the world views and the ideological perspectives of those occupying positions of socioeconomic and political preeminence in society" (p. 205).

Regardless of class considerations, several educational theorists and researchers conclude that curriculum and class discussions represent adult interests—neither the daily lives of adolescents (Fine, 1989; McNeil, 1981) nor the popular culture that "is appropriated by students and is a major source of knowledge for authorizing their voices and experiences" (Giroux & Simon, 1989b, p. 221). And yet, in our work and experience, we know there are teachers who legitimize the voices and interests of their students. Images of such teachers are seldom found in popular culture (except, perhaps, to be ridiculed). Thus we ask, is our memory of teachers woven into our self-definition of our struggle in childhood for identity and independence, of our conflict with freedom and control?

We cannot ignore a particular detail in Mead's stereotype: the teacher is a woman. This schoolteacher image is one of docility and order. Is our concept of the schoolteacher intertwined with issues not only of class but also of gender? Are teachers (regardless of their sex) associated with "traditional" feminine images of obedience and submission? Grumet (1988) writes, "the structure of the school replicates the patriarchal structure of the family" (p. 85). Furthermore, Grumet reminds us, teachers (primarily women) are usually trained and evaluated by men. Several chapters in our text also reveal that the teacher is a white woman, thus suggesting that stereotypical teachers in American culture are depicted as nonblack, nonethnic representatives of the middle-class.[4] Schoolteacher images, however, must be understood within an inclusive social context; seldom are images of leadership found among females, Afro-Americans, and working-class people in popular culture (Aronowitz, 1989, pp. 203–204). The "social order" is also enacted in children's literature (Taxel, 1989, p. 205).

The contributors perceive that gender and race are important concepts for understanding images of schoolteachers, though less important notions than the issue of submission. The submissive image displays the schoolteacher's realm in a classroom of children, dealing with often mundane concerns of discipline and orderliness. This image does not portray teachers as dynamic characters in the school or as vigorous members of the community. The contributors find that the docile teacher is a pervasive stereotype. Moreover, submission enters into interviews with contemporary teachers. We find that the image of docility and submission outrages them, not because they feel it is incorrect portraiture, but because it points out the worst frustration in their work—that of perceived or real powerlessness.

Nonetheless, another theme also emerges in the research of the contributors: the image of empowered teachers, professionals who celebrate their influence and creativity. Throughout diverse genres, as well as teacher narratives, we discover teachers who have a *presence*.

In textbooks, film, television, literature, and most prominently, in the interviews conducted with schoolteachers, images of strength and potency also exist. By their presence, their sense of who they are, they captivate their students, become mentors, and consistently—moment by moment, day by day—lead young people to identify with them as strong forces, as adults who are proud of their chosen work and life choices. Perhaps not in the school or in the community, but certainly in the classroom, there are images of teachers as leaders.

We also have to understand the presence of the teacher as a moral force. Our contributors often find verification for research suggesting that schoolteachers perceive themselves as people who do not teach just to make a living (Joseph & Green, 1986; Lortie, 1975). For some, the attraction is working with young people; others want to help, and some want to mold or make changes. Teachers devise metaphors of themselves as gardeners, as potters, as orchestra conductors, as problem-solvers, as therapists. They see themselves as people who try to make the world better in both small and great ways. And so, we must participate in the joy of the schoolteachers—in real life, memory, and culture—as they celebrate their artistry, their creativity. There are teachers who make things happen, who feel contentment and excitement because of what they do and what changes they can make. Although they may not always imagine themselves the heroes and saints portrayed throughout popular culture and the literature of teacher education, the schoolteachers represented in our book view their presence as vital to their students' destinies.

## A Collaborative Process

We offer this book with the hope that our readers will use it as an incentive for further study and reflection. This book does not attempt to "cover" all possible material about schoolteachers in twentieth-century America. We believe that our students in teacher education and American culture classes must be our colleagues by exploring with us and contributing to our study.

The collaborative process is very important to us and to our contributors. In fact, we have experienced a peculiar tension in writing this book because we (editors and contributors) are uncomfortable with textbooks that "tell" students all that they should know. In our teaching, we attempt to prevent ready acceptance of someone else's analysis that thereby closes minds instead of opening them to numerous possibilities for interpretation before making intelligent judgments. Our teaching depends to a great extent on primary sources that allow students to read and think about issues and ideas without mediating interpretations.

We also know the value of thought-provoking concepts that inspire readers to see paths that they had never considered before. We cannot write without interpreting and analyzing, and yet, it is very important to us as teachers that readers contemplate and challenge our ideas. For that reason, we encourage dialogue about this book not only as readers respond individually but also in conversations among students or among instructors and students. Furthermore, we would be delighted if our investigations encourage students to do their own studies. In fact, we hope that the choice of similar topics by several contributors with their different approaches to inquiry will suggest to our readers that there is not *one* way to pursue scholarship; the chapters represent a diversity of orientations, styles, and the contributors' values about knowledge and research. We have provided "Continuing Dialogues" at the end of each section to encourage further research, but certainly we welcome other avenues for readers' involvement.

We would like this book to serve as an impetus for more exploration of the imagery surrounding teachers in this society; we hope that we can spark interest in teacher images through various genres and time periods. (For example, we have not explored the visual arts, and so we encourage readers to discover the image of teachers in magazine illustrations and cartoons.) There are images of schoolteachers—diverse, uncomplimentary, and idealized—throughout American popular culture, and it would be impossible for our contributors to have studied all aspects of American culture.

We invite our readers to continue our studies by interviewing colleagues, former schoolteachers, students, parents and administrators. Or they may want to write their own autobiographies in order to get in touch with the schoolteacher images that propelled them toward and away from becoming teachers themselves. We believe that this book's strength will be in its ability to encourage conversation about schooling and teaching, to help our readers reawaken and appraise their own memories of schoolteachers. We also encourage readers to become aware of their own emotional responses to the images presented in these chapters. The contributors themselves responded with pride, exhilaration, compassion, sadness, and anger to what they encountered in their studies. What are our readers' responses? And why have they been so provoked?

We also want readers to consider the image-makers in their various contexts in this book. Who were the writers, the film producers, the former and present school people who articulated these images? What were their memories, and what illusions and stereotypes influenced them? We are constantly reminded of the impact of the public voice and eye on the language of imagery. Writers, producers, and book editors all anticipate the reactions of their readers, judge the appeal of their work, and perhaps consciously stimulate interest, humor, or controversy. We must ask then to what extent their work reflects imagination and to what extent it reflects American culture. As Daniel Cottom (1989) reminds us, "the range of meaning in a text is always severely limited by the politics put into play by a particular approach" (p. 21). It is necessary for our readers to question the politics—the motivations—that help to create literature, film, and even memory.

Furthermore, reliance on one or a few interpretations of image is untenable as we approach this material from our various viewpoints and multiple experiences with teachers and as teachers. Cottom (1989) also explains the intricacies of interpretation of text within a cultural perspective: "We cannot be justified in giving any text, even the simplest joke, an interpretation that excludes the possibility of differing and contradictory readings" (p. ix). We hope that the readers will supplement our constructions and interpretations of image. We hope that, together, our scholarship will help us all discover much about ourselves and our sense of what it means to be a teacher.

Ultimately, for our readers who work as schoolteachers or who plan to become teachers, we want this book to be a starting point for reflection about their goals and purposes. The relationship between teacher and student represents the essential dynamic of the teacher's purposes (often within the constraints of the given school system and community). The chapters help us to understand that what it means to be a teacher is far more than teaching skills and subjects. For example, schoolteachers "open doors" by cherishing and encouraging young people's talent and individuality, by mediating between the world of the child and that of the adult, by offering friendship, guidance, and even love. We also see how schoolteachers "close doors" by representing an uncaring adult world, a world that seems irrational, unfair, and unforgiving.

We have written this book with the commitment to provide a text that creates intellectual and emotional experiences as it stimulates our readers to observe and critically contemplate the complexity of images that surround teachers and schools. Our book is intended for anyone who has an interest and curiosity about teaching and teachers in twentieth-century America. We hope that it will be valuable for both entering and experienced teachers, that it will stimulate discussion and reflection about the profession. We also believe our study is a resource for students of American culture who perceive the creation and maintenance of images as essential components of our understanding of cultural behavior, norms, and values. But what the student of culture values as important scholarship, so must we all. We cannot understand the nature of the teaching profession without contemplating its place in the context of American culture. We must probe deeply and ask questions about the diversity of images—both personal and public—and reflect on the ramifications of these images for schoolteachers, their students, and our society.

## NOTES

1. The line separating popular culture and other cultural expressions such as literature, theater, or art is drawn amidst great controversy and compelling conflicting viewpoints (see Gans, 1974). We do not feel capable of drawing this line here, although a potentially useful demarcation may, in fact, be how schooling distinguishes what is worth studying and what is not (see Aronowitz in Giroux & Simon, 1989a).

2. Giroux and Simon (1989b) also suggest the power of popular culture to challenge the influence of prevailing cultural values: "Popular cultures may contain certain aspects of a collective imagination which make it possible for people to surpass received knowledge and tradition. In this sense, popular cultures may inform aspects of a counterdiscourse which help to organize struggles against relations of domination" (p. 227).

3. Neil Sutherland (1992) warns us that "memory is not only fallible, but it is also shaped by the circumstances that prompt it . . . . each life story is told or written from the point of view of the present and is designed to convey a message to the present" (p. 237). However, he sees value in fictionalized accounts of childhood because "their writers may set them down earlier in life than do autobiogra-

phers" and "the professional skill of novelists enables them to describe events of childhood more sharply, more precisely, more completely than the less articulate" (p. 245).

4. We wonder whether teacher education programs concerned with minority recruitment have dealt with such cultural issues; why would teaching be attractive to people of color who from childhood have had impressions of teachers as submissive and white?

## REFERENCES

Apple, M. W. (1986). *Teachers and texts: A political economy of class and gender relations in education.* New York: Routledge & Kegan Paul.

Aronowitz, S. (1989). Working-class identity and celluloid fantasies in the electronic age. In H. A. Giroux & R. I. Simon (Eds.), *Popular culture, schooling, and everyday life* (pp. 197–217). Granby, MA: Bergin & Garvey.

Carew, J. V. & Lightfoot, S. L. (1979). *Beyond bias: Perspectives on classrooms.* Cambridge, MA: Harvard University Press.

Carnoy, M. (1989). Education, state, and culture in American society. In H. A. Giroux & P. L. McLaren (Eds.), *Critical pedagogy, the state and cultural struggle* (pp. 3–23). Albany, NY: SUNY Press.

Carter, K. (1993). The place of story in the study of teaching and teacher education, *Educational Researcher, 22* (1), 5–12, 18.

Chapman, D. W. & Lowther, M.A. (1982). Teachers' satisfaction with teaching. *Journal of Educational Research, 75*(4), 241–247.

Clandinin, D. J. (1986). *Classroom practice: Teacher images in action.* London: Falmer Press.

Cottom, D. (1989). *Text & culture: The politics of interpretation.* Minneapolis: University of Minnesota Press.

Crume, M. T. (1989). Images of teachers in films and literature. *Education Week,* October 4, p. 3.

Feinman-Nemser, S. & Floden, R. E. (1986). The cultures of teaching. In M. C. Wittock (Ed.), *Handbook of research on teaching* (3rd ed.) (pp. 505–526). New York: Macmillan.

Fine, M. (1989). Silencing and nurturing voice in an improbable context: Urban adolescents in public school. In H. A. Giroux & P. L. McLaren (Eds.) *Critical pedagogy, the state and cultural struggle* (pp. 152–173). Albany, NY: SUNY Press.

Funk & Wagnalls New Encyclopedia. (1986). New York: Rand McNally & Company.

Gans, H. J. (1974). *Popular culture and high culture: An analysis and evaluation of taste.* New York: Basic Books.

Geertz, C. (1983). *Local knowledge: Further essays in interpretative anthropology.* New York: Basic Books.

Giroux, H. A. (1989). Schooling as a form of cultural politics: Toward a pedagogy of and for difference. In H. A. Giroux & P. L. McLaren (Eds.), *Critical pedagogy, the state and cultural struggle* (pp. 125–151). Albany, NY: SUNY Press.

Giroux, H. A. & Simon, R. I. (1989a). Popular culture as a pedagogy of pleasure and meaning. In H. A. Giroux & R. I. Simon (Eds.), *Popular culture, schooling, and everyday life* (pp. 1–29). Granby, MA: Bergin & Garvey.

Giroux, H. A. & Simon, R. I. (1989b). Conclusion: Schooling, popular culture, and a pedagogy of possibility. In H. A. Giroux & R. I. Simon (Eds.), *Popular culture, schooling, and everyday life* (pp. 219–235). Granby, MA: Bergin & Garvey.

Grossberg, L. (1989). Pedagogy in the present: Politics, postmodernity, and the popular. In H. A. Giroux & R. I. Simon (Eds.), *Popular culture, schooling, and everyday life* (pp. 91–116). Granby, MA: Bergin & Garvey.

Grumet, M. R. (1988). *Bitter milk: Women and teaching.* Amherst, MA: University of Massachusetts Press.

Hofstadter, R. (1962). *Anti-intellectualism in American life.* New York: Random House.

Hoy, W. K. & Rees, D. E. (1977). The bureaucratic socialization of student teachers. *Journal of Teacher Education, 28*, 23–26.

Joseph, P. B. & Green, N. (1986). Perspectives on reasons for becoming teachers, *Journal of Teacher Education, 37*(6), 28–33.

Lipsitz, G. (1990). *Time passages: Collective memory and American popular culture.* Minneapolis: University of Minnesota Press.

Lortie, D. C. (1975). *Schoolteacher: A sociological study.* Chicago: University of Chicago Press.

McLaughlin, M. W., Pfeiffer, R. S., Swanson-Owens, D. & Yee, S. (1986). Why teachers won't teach. *Phi Delta Kappan, 67*(6), 420–425.

McNeil, L. (1981). Negotiating classroom knowledge: Beyond achievement and socialization. *Curriculum Studies 13*, 313–328.

Mead, M. (1951/1962). *The school in American culture.* Cambridge, MA: Harvard University Press.

Nielsen, J. M. (1990). *Feminist research methods: Exemplary readings in the social sciences.* Boulder, CO: Westview Press.

Popkewitz, T. S. (1988). What's in a research project. *Curriculum Inquiry 18*, 379–400.

Shumway, D. R. (1989). Reading rock 'n' roll in the classroom: A critical pedagogy. In H. A. Giroux & P. L. McLaren (Eds.), *Critical pedagogy, the state and cultural struggle* (pp. 222–235). Albany, NY: SUNY Press.

Spring, J. (1992). *Images of American life: A history of ideological management in schools, movies, radio, and television.* Albany, NY: SUNY Press.

Sutherland, Neil. (1992). When you listen to the winds of childhood, how much can you believe? *Curriculum Inquiry 22* (3), 235–256.

Taxel, J. (1989). Children's literature as an ideological text. In H. A. Giroux & P. L. McLaren (Eds.), *Critical pedagogy, the state and cultural struggle* (pp. 205–221). Albany, NY: SUNY Press.

Wigginton, E. (1985). *Sometimes a shining moment: The Foxfire experience.* Garden City, NY: Anchor Books.

Witherall, C. & Noddings, N. (1991). *Stories lives tell: Narrative and dialogue in education.* New York: Teachers College Press.

# Continuing Dialogue

1. Write a letter that you wish you had written to a schoolteacher whom you have known.

2. What are your memories of schoolteachers from books that you have read or television shows you have seen in your childhood? Do the images portrayed in these media complement your own personal memories?

3. Write about your experiences as a student in classrooms (eventually, discussing your recollections within a small group). What teachers emerge in your mind as unforgettable? What are the positive recollections? What are the negative? Do you consider an individual teacher or several teachers as important to your formative experiences? Can you recall the names of your teachers from early years? Do you remember better the names of male or female teachers? Why do you think you have these impressions?

4. Write a paragraph describing a composite of the schoolteacher in American culture today (refer to Mead's version, published in 1951, on pp. 16–17). Reflect on what influenced the creation of your composite image of the schoolteacher and on the similarities and/or differences between your portrayal and Mead's.

5. Write a paragraph describing what you would imagine as an excellent or ideal teacher.

6. Interview (possibly in collaboration with others) adults who do not work in classrooms or schools and then interview some who do. Try to interview men and women from a variety of age, class, and ethnic groups. (Consider asking questions such as: Do you believe that schoolteaching is a respected profession? Would you want your son or daughter to become a teacher? How do you describe your own classroom experiences as a former student? Or, complete sentences such as: "Teaching is like . . . ," "I remember most vividly a teacher who . . . ," "My favorite teacher. . . . The most important job for a teacher is. . . . Teachers spend most of their time. . . .") Also discuss if the memories and beliefs of those who become teachers and those who choose other occupations reveal some pronounced differences, or if there are differences among the interviewees along the lines of gender, social class, or ethnicity.

7. Interview university faculty (not in teacher education) and ask them their attitudes about schoolteachers. For example, do they see the roles of

schoolteachers as being similar to their roles as university faculty? Why did they choose university teaching rather than public school teaching?

8. If you are a schoolteacher or have decided to enter the teaching profession, what were/are your expectations of your work? How do you think the American public perceives your role and status? What were/are the rewards you perceive about being a teacher? What difficulties do you anticipate?

# II

Teachers and Children

# 2

# Constructing and Discovering Images of Your Teaching

Joseph Fischer
Anne Kiefer

*I believe that the image is the great instrument of instruction. What a child gets out of any subject presented to him is simply the images which he himself forms with regard to it* (Dewey, 1897/ 1959, p. 28).

We sat on small chairs in Margaret's middle-grade reading lab and talked about the revolutionary school reform being implemented in Chicago. She had been at M. School, a predominantly Hispanic, inner-city school, for most of her twenty-seven years of teaching and was eager to share her thoughts: "I think a lot of us feel that we can see the end of our career and we would like great things to happen at the schools. I think we are more in control now. Some people feel very frightened and others just want to grab the ring and run with it. So I think it is a wonderful thing to happen. It is making us all young again." Margaret began to talk about reading, how she got children to share their experiences and how she hoped they would always love books. "You have to help children get excited about reading. When you start talking to kids and getting the kid that does not like to read to tell you some things he knows about whales, then he gets hooked. You do not have to tell him to do this, do that. He is already part of the story because he already told you he knows about whales."

Helping children "be part of the story" is central to Margaret's teaching. For her, the story does not merely originate from books but is a lived experience, a relationship she builds with and encourages among her students.

29

We talked several times during the spring of 1990 and Margaret continued to portray her views about her teaching, her students and her colleagues. These images comprise her autobiography of teaching; they seem to say—"this is what I have done; this is what I have created. This is me." We will see that similar imaging is at work for all the teachers described in this chapter.[1]

The teachers we studied talked about how they viewed their work, how they portrayed their teaching and how they thought others saw them. The interviews, then, served as a mirror for reflection and were, to a large extent, an encounter for mutual explorations of the images that guide teachers in their work.

We discovered that, throughout their teaching careers, teachers not only hold diverse images of themselves but also actively construct these images (a process referred to in this chapter as "imaging"). Teachers told how their views about teaching changed during their careers, and they mused about how the images and the process of imaging served them in their teaching.

Another interesting finding was that teachers had multiple images of their work, indicating the multifaceted nature and the complexity of their profession. Moreover, while some images were clear and vivid, others were tentative and emerging, perhaps indicating that the process of creating and capturing images develops with reflection and a deeper awareness of one's interactions with students.

Our research revealed that, although many images of teaching are given or imposed on teachers, the most profound ones are actively constructed during teaching practice. The images that teachers create of their work appear to result from a conscious process of doing, describing, and naming. We found that it is the reflective teacher who constructs images about professional roles and practices.

Given the time and opportunity for reflection, teachers can describe their lives focusing on the changing images of themselves that they have experienced over their years of teaching. The complexity of their images reflects the tasks they have, the jobs for which they receive a salary, and even more importantly, the roles they play in the lives of their students, of other teachers, and of the administrators in the system in which they work.

This chapter has three major divisions: the first, images of teaching, gives portraits and stories; the second presents background on creating and capturing images; and the third provides interpretations of teacher images. Our conclusion focuses on the uses, implications, and ramifications of both the images themselves and the process of imaging.

## Images of Teaching: Portraits and Stories

The world, I said, has its influence as nature and as society on the child. He is educated by the elements, by air and light and the life of

> plants and animals, and he is educated by relationships. The true educator represents both: but he must be to the child as one of the elements. . . .
>
> In spite of all similarities every living situation has, like a new born child, a new face that has never been before and will never come again. It demands of you a reaction which cannot be prepared beforehand. It demands nothing of what is past. It demands presence, responsibility: it demands you (Buber, 1961, pp. 90, 114).

While we captured a multiplicity of images from a wide range of teachers, the following case studies are presented because they represent important dimensions of images and of the process of creating images. The case studies suggest that images are multiple, change over one's teaching career, and grow in meaning and usefulness in informing and even shaping practice. Furthermore, the teachers who spoke to us are witnesses to Buber's belief that teaching demands our presence—"it demands you." A given, contrived, or conventional image of our work does not usually enlighten us. The unique image as self, as personality and character, is worthy of contemplation and brings joy to our teaching and to student learning.

### Irene

Irene has been teaching at M. School for the past twenty-one years. She was working in her computer writing lab, preparing for the next group of students before our interview began. Toward the end of our conversation she began to describe how her teaching had changed over the years.

> I used to be extremely structured. Everything went by schedule, because that is how I was taught initially. And now, because I feel freer as a teacher I understand more of what I am doing. Now I can let things go and let the children kind of pick up where they would like to work from, whereas before it was only what I felt should be done.
>
> I was very strong on discipline, but now I can let them go off in groups and I feel more at ease with my own style than I did in the beginning. I thought that I needed to have everybody's attention at all times. Now I do not feel that need.

Irene's change in teaching style was slow and painful. After observing her colleagues and reflecting on her teaching, she began to try out new ways of doing things.

> The few times I did let go of the discipline, things did happen anyway. So it made me feel freer in doing it again. But, it was a good ten years before I started asking myself, "what is happening to this class?"
>
> It was a very slow process for me. Other teachers were willing to do all these things, and I used to see them doing that, and I thought, "I cannot stand all that chaos in that room!"

Irene stated that she had learned from her colleagues during her long career, and she acknowledged her debt to them. Whenever she has an opportunity, she lets the teachers know what their children are doing in her writing lab. She hopes that, as a result of recent school reform initiatives in her district, teachers will have more time to interact, to share ideas, and to talk about what is happening in the classroom.

Irene's early images of teaching confined her to the role of taskmaster, giver of information; she found it necessary to constantly seek the children's attention. In her desire to change, she began to look more closely at what was happening among her students and turned to her colleagues for guidance and new ideas. In her struggle she began to find herself, her presence among the children. Of significance was her realization that in order to change her teaching, she needed to observe her students more closely and to design her teaching around their interests.

Irene's experiences exemplify a major finding of our research. Teachers need to feel free in their work in order to be creative, grow professionally, and find satisfaction and fulfillment in what they do. If they merely continue to follow given and constricting roles and functions, their teaching will atrophy. It is useful for teachers to examine the images they hold and to sort out and deal with those that do not enhance their growth. Constructing images of our teaching thus requires weighing possibilities and making choices. In essence, it is a moral act.

### Sarah

Sarah's first job at M. School, twenty-six years ago, was teaching Spanish to gifted non-Hispanic children. They wrote plays in Spanish, gave presentations at schools with large Hispanic populations, and every year went to the State Fair in Springfield to submit projects about Hispanic culture. She also noted with pride, "I used to take my classes to the university to demonstrate to the student teachers. I would talk to the audience and then my students would actually put on a demonstration of how they would speak in Spanish."

Her program no longer exists, but her fluency in her second language serves her well in speaking to her predominantly Hispanic seventh and eighth graders. Sarah reflected on the many changes that have occurred during her teaching career at M. School. What seems constant is her view of teaching as an adventure: "Every year you have new students, new things to explore with them and I think every day is an adventure. I mean, it is in a constant state of flux and I think this is very important. Working with children gives one a sense of being young and active and always being aware of what is going on in the world. Because children are naturally very curious, they keep you going, more or less."

Sarah's longevity in the same school gives her an intergenerational view of her students and their families. She attends class reunions and weddings of former students. Students and faculty at M. School are like a family.

> It is exciting when the kids come back year after year, you watch the generations go. I mean they come back with their children. We have children of students that we taught going to our school and you can see that it is a continuing family.
>
> The children and the faculty, we're all like a family. There is a great feeling of familial emotion and caring and I think that the children feel comfortable. It is their home away from home, and the kids feel that we are their second parents. For the most part I think the children respect us, and they understand that we are telling them things for their own good, just as their mother or father would.

Like a counselor, Sarah gets involved with the emotional problems of her students.

> There has to be more than just reading, writing and arithmetic. There has to be a feeling of emotion, a feeling of the child knowing you care about him as a total human being, not just as a test score on a piece of paper.
>
> These kids are filled with problems, they have many concerns, and they need to talk to somebody. The teacher must be involved with the children. You cannot come in and say, "Open your book to page five," and that is the end of the relationship.

Sarah offered that she feels like a jack-of-all-trades, that she wears many hats. Teaching can be hectic, and Sarah feels pulled in many directions.

> I am living in a much more mechanized society, a much more rapidly developing one. We work in a very fast pace, we are all pressured, and life seems more complicated. We are all in a hurry, we are on schedule. I feel I have to breathe on a schedule. And people become frustrated with that. I describe myself sometimes like a hamster on a wheel. I never get anywhere. We do not know how to relax and be in tune with nature.

Moreover, teachers are not valued or recognized in our society, Sarah feels. In many societies, she noted, teachers are held with more respect and even reverence.

> The most important thing today is recognition, admiration, someone to pat us on the back and say, "You are important, you made a difference, we need you." People have to have positive strokes. In order to function and to blossom you need recognition and praise. Just as the children need positive strokes to make them feel good, so do we.

> A teacher has fears, needs and concerns and anxieties, just like
> anyone else does. And I think that it is very important that they be
> recognized and supported.

Sarah sees herself in multiple roles. Like a parent and a social worker
she gets involved with her students, but she feels there is never enough time
to do what has to be done, and she is always on a schedule. She finds
teaching an adventure; there is something new each day. Like the elder in a
village, Sarah rejoices in seeing generation after generation come to school.
Some even come back and tell her, "You made a difference in my life."

It is not clear to what extent Sarah has integrated her many roles and
whether or not she sees some central image of herself. Her acceptance of
diverse responsibilities may be related to her feeling of being overwhelmed.
It appears, too, that many of her rewards are external, beyond her control.
Her parent-like role is rewarded when her students grow up and away, and
she awaits their return to voice their appreciation. While she attends to her
students' emotional problems, they ultimately have to solve their own. During
many of our conversations together, Sarah's internal satisfactions with
her work seemed elusive.

### Kate

Kate teaches in a tiny makeshift classroom at the end of the hall, cluttered
with books, chairs, her desk, and a computer. The one window at the
back was barely visible as piles of materials were stacked on the window
sill. A group of her seventh grade students sat in a circle as Kate read a
story. This was her thirtieth year of teaching.

> I just gave a short story the other night to this class and if they read
> it and enjoyed reading it, they would have come back to me and told
> me that they really liked the story.
> They need to hear my voice with inflection in it and they need
> to connect with it. I call it bonding. You cannot do it before someone
> takes you there. They won't taste other things unless you lead them
> to it. All my children would be reading these teenage love books if
> they could choose what to read.

Kate was asked how she "took them there." She described how she
carefully selected the stories they read together, tried to imagine what students
would get connected to, and which books would enhance their experiences.
When she was successful in her choice, the students would build a
trusting relationship with each other and with her. In reading the stories
together, they would come to share a common experience and eventually
speak a common language. And, in their memories they would always have
the image of talking about a much-loved book with Kate, in her tiny room at
the end of the hall.

So far this year their favorite book has been *Lottery Rose*, about an abused child, and they still talk about it. You have to understand that most of these children have never read a whole book until I get them. They look forward to other books I am giving them now, because they wonder, is it going to be as good as *Lottery Rose*? The boy in the story turns out to be a winner. He learns to communicate with people, which he could not even do before. That kind of a theme got them stimulated to reading.

And you really have to touch those feelings in them. They are so numbed by television, and it is on such an adult level, either violence or sex. For them to tune into people's real feelings, it does not happen very often. They are thrilled with what is going on in these movies, but they do not feel the feelings. But to touch them, that does not happen often, and it happened with this book. They were touched.

Kate's best preteaching experiences at the university were with "real" teachers during practice teaching. In our conversation, she went back to long ago when she was a student.

In the beginning of the sophomore year we went into the classrooms and worked all the way to our junior year observing teachers. By the time we got into student teaching we were not overwhelmed by the classrooms, or were not terrified. We knew what we were getting into. I do not know how many methods courses you give a student, but it really does not have a value until you actually get into a classroom.

I remember the students. There were thirty in the classroom. The children all seemed to be using what they were doing; they were trying to accomplish something. They were grouped and there was a lot of interplay. And that was something I enjoyed doing. That was an impression! More impressions I do not remember. It must have been pleasant, because I continued on. It was something to look forward to, teaching. I could not wait to teach.

As a college student, Kate's images of teaching were positive and based on close observations of teachers relating to students. She began to construct images of herself as a teacher from her impressions of classroom life among students. Thus, her images were reality-bound, originating from experiences, from the practice itself.

In a previous interview, Kate related how she could not wait to get into teaching. Why had she been so attracted to teaching? Her reply helps explain why she was able to change the way she viewed herself and to focus on her central role as educator. "I always loved drama, and I always think that teachers are kind of mini actors. I just do not mean that a teacher must be an actress and present dramatic presentations. What drama really is, is a little bit of life; it is taking ideas and making things happen with them. I do not know another way of saying it. That is what I believe. In drama of course there is conflict and you get plenty of conflict in teaching."

Over the years, Kate came to a deeper understanding of what it feels like to have developed a bond with students. In reading together she both learns from them and leads them to a larger world. But, as we shall see, to arrive at this realization she needed to make a conscious effort to change some of her ways.

> There was a time in my life when I played the many roles of a teacher. I was the confessor, the mother, the problem-solver, friend, the person they turned to when they have a serious problem. Some teachers still try to do that. I have moved away from that and I have to tell you I did that purposely.
>
> Children will absorb you and it is very hard to pull back and to work back with ideas. It is very hard to be a social worker, a psychologist, and an educator at the same time. I did it and it was draining.
>
> I made the decision that I was trying to get a different point of view: to not go to the person, but to start with the literature and then it became personal. When you start getting personal with a child, it is very hard to get back to being an educator. But if you start with an idea in literature and those things involve their personal problems, a lot of them can be solved by themselves; not with the teacher lifting up, but solving themselves through literature. To me that was more important.

Kate also elaborated on some of the ways she tries to start with an idea in literature to help her students learn to reach beyond themselves. Through literature she hopes they will develop their own strategies to solve their problems and find their own meanings.

> On Monday two children from M. School died in a fire. One was in kindergarten and the other in first grade. I knew them. It was tragic and there were quite a few teachers affected by it. They really had a hard time handling it. That is a tragedy and a problem you cannot hide away or run from. But you cannot constantly involve yourself in the problem, you need to reach out for something else. We need to learn to grow from the problems.
>
> They need somebody to listen to them. Our priority is to educate them and to help them look for solutions. Literature can get them to a different kind of plateau in life. For example, after reading *Lottery Rose*, if a student has a problem of being abused, he knows that a child can survive that kind of problem. Through the story he knows that he can turn to others for help. He can find his way, which the

child did in this story; there are rays of hope out there. Saying it in a book is more real to me.

Kate decided to change when she found her role as a problem-solver too draining and she began to question her role as an educator in these situations. She turned to literature to see how it might help lead students out of their problems, to help them reach out and not get overwhelmed. This thought came to her one day as she was counseling a child and urging her to reach out beyond her problems. "I knew then I was giving this advice to myself," she told me.

Earlier, in her own studies, the groundwork for these insights had been laid. She realized, "You cannot reach out, or lead, unless someone previously has taken you there. . . . One of my small talents is painting. I did art work when I was young, and even though I loved to paint and I loved to do drawings, I never bonded with art until I got the right kind of a teacher who led me in there. I had him in a class and he made me feel that there was something to paint that was worthwhile. He made it alive."

What teaching might become was the topic of our last interview. Kate talked about some of her concerns and her visions for schooling.

> The bad part of teaching is that there is so much junk involved besides the drama. If it would just be drama, it would be a wonderful profession to be in.
>
> Reading for so many years was based on skills, and we did that for a long time. Many of our children turned out to be proficient readers by using merely skills, but if you asked me whether or not that is truly educating a child, I would say no. Children have to be connected to literature. They have to enjoy it, and it must take them beyond themselves.
>
> What is happening to our educational system is that students are not allowed to create anymore. I would love to see students become independent readers, independent learners. I would like to see children getting together to work together. I would love to see children grab books because they are thrilled by a subject.

### Maria

Maria was interviewed on one of the hottest spring days; the temperature in the school was close to 95 degrees. Maria taught in a small room that was created by walling off a section of the hall near the windows. The day was too hot for the computers to be used, so the twenty children from grades 1 and 2 worked in two groups. The very quiet ones slowly looked through magazines for pictures of objects that they could use for their personal dictionaries. Her responsibility as an ESL teacher is to provide ways for the children to acquire English.

Maria believed that there are pressures on these children that go beyond the usual urban pressures.

> I grew up in Chicago but it was different then. I went to a school
> near here. When I started school, I did not know English and came
> to be afraid of the school, the teacher and even of the other children.
> When I came to the school door in the morning, the sounds over-
> whelmed me. I spent the days being as quiet as I could so no one
> would notice me and ask me any questions. Even with that, I was
> terrified. I don't remember events, or teachers or specific children. I
> just remember the fear.

The children in her classroom were not afraid. They were quiet but their
stillness seemed to be the result of the heat, not distress. The children who
searched through magazines had an intensity that emanated from involvement in a task. They talked in low sounds to each other about the pictures
they chose and about the way to say the names of the pictures.

> When I started teaching here we had only a few children who did
> not know English. Now each classroom has ten or fifteen children
> who need help. They need understanding. They need to be taught
> things that the other children already know. I can feel the fear
> again when they start in my group, and I spend as much time on
> getting the children to relax as I do on English. Once they see me as
> a person who knows what and how they feel, we can actually begin
> learning English.

The group of children sat with the teacher around the table. She talked
about the tiny furniture spread out before them. On the table she also placed
what looked like a blueprint or floor plan of an apartment. The squares and
rectangles were labeled for rooms of the apartment. Maria said things like:
"I put the sofa in the living room"; "I put the tub in the bathroom." Despite
the distracting heat, the children watched her closely and listened to her
words. Then the teacher asked the children to perform certain of the activities that she had been doing. They began to respond with confidence to the
directions as the teacher explained them. Maria noticed this, too, and chose
one of the children to be "the teacher."

> I used to spend my time with the alphabet and the sounds of the
> letters. I went to some ESL workshops, and they told us that the
> children need to develop some oral language that they can use to
> analyze for the sounds. There are so many teachers who don't under-
> stand that. They keep asking me to teach reading so the children
> won't "get so far behind." I think I spend a lot of time just talking to
> the other teachers trying to help them understand. I even ask them
> to come down here to see the class so they will have an idea how

little they [the students] can do with English. I think I need to get some more information. . . . I almost said ammunition.

Some of the children began to pack up their things and prepared to leave the group. At about the same time, other youngsters appeared at the door and looked around for empty places. It seemed that this class was a "pull-out" program, and the children were scheduled for brief periods during the day as they came from their mainstream classrooms for ESL. When we talked about this later, Maria explained: "I am trying to get a firmer schedule. That's one reason I want the teachers to come and see us 'at work.' They are concerned that the children will 'fall behind' in their classrooms. I understand their concern but would like them to really see how little English the children understand. My husband keeps telling me just to do my job and not worry so much about the children and the other teachers. But I see my job as not just providing ESL lessons, but also helping the children and the teachers to understand language and language learning."

Maria often spoke of the lives of the children and the needs she recognized in them. It was clear to us that much of her empathy arose from her own experiences and her desire to do whatever she could to help these children.

Margaret, Irene, Sarah, Kate, and Maria shared their present images of themselves as well as how the imaging process had been occurring in their lives. They do not represent types, yet they do serve to illustrate patterns of images and processes of imaging in teachers' lives.

The next section begins an interpretation of images and imaging based on, and illustrated by, these lives.

## Creating and Capturing Images

To understand the nature and implications of teacher imaging, it is useful to consider some of the main sources of the images and the factors related to their construction. We can only begin to speculate on some possible origins, but we believe that the following three areas are worth consideration: (1) constructed images, (2) ideal images, and (3) given images.

### Constructed Images

Teachers construct images about their teaching by reflecting on their experiences with students. The images that teachers create during their careers are related to their work. The process of imaging and the practice of teaching develop together. Images emerge from the practice itself, and inform and even guide it. When the image informs practice and is viewed as useful, the teacher includes it in her repertoire. Similarly, "given" images (from tradition, society, and the media) may undergo modification or elaboration and deeper understanding as teachers examine the consonance between the images of teaching and their teaching practice.

Images are constructed, especially when teachers begin to reflect on and become more aware of the nature of the relationships and interactions taking place in their classrooms. The constructed images originate from "both sides"—from the interchange between students and teacher, and from consciously engaging in conversation. In brief, image building takes place during social interactions; the images emerge from the mutual act of teaching and learning.

Creating and capturing images about teaching can be viewed as essentially an autobiographical narrative. Teachers comprehend their work by telling stories about it, and the images they create are the basis for these stories. Moreover, both teachers and students become storytellers. Shared experiences lead to conversations about them, and hence to a shared describing and naming of what has been lived. Buber suggests that in naming their experiences of creating and telling their story, teachers and students embrace and name the world (Genesis:1). The most profound images of teaching, and hence the most powerful stories, are created in "I–Thou [you]" types of encounters, of "meeting in the middle," of forming a meaningful bond with students (Buber, 1961).

Students are socialized into the roles and images teachers expect of them, but also mutually share in constructing and creating the images of teaching and learning. The importance of student imaging can be illustrated by considering what can happen when teachers need to step out of their classrooms. The "controlling" teacher carries with her the sanctions of behavior and often feels the need to appoint a student monitor. The teacher who has established a bond with her students leaves behind an image of a relationship, a commitment, a sharing of norms. Thus, students do not feel abandoned or free to "go out of control." They have internalized an image of the relationship between them and their teacher which guides their behavior. To us, Dewey's (1897/1959) words seem particularly relevant as we think about how images are constructed through social discourse: "I believe that the only true education comes through the stimulation of the child's powers by the demands of the social situation in which he finds himself. Through these demands he is stimulated to act as a member of a unity, to emerge from his original narrowness of action and feeling, and to conceive of himself from the standpoint of the welfare of the group to which he belongs" (p. 20).

### Ideal Images

Images emerge, too, when teachers examine their own beliefs, values, and ideals about teaching and learning. However, unlike the situation in which they construct images through interactions, teachers look mainly inward to more idealistic or ideal models. "I believe teaching should be like this, no matter what this particular class or school is like," is an example of this kind of imaging. Another may be, "Schools ought to be places for the development of the intellect; unfortunately, these types of children are not capable of that sort of intellectual rigor."

Images about teaching may originate from early and significant models of relationships—parent and child, pupil and teacher (Bowlby, 1988). Socialization into particular images of self-identity and self-esteem takes place during these early relationships. Career models and images of adult roles begin to be formulated during this time and tend to continue into adulthood. These often are idealistic types of images and models, and more realistic ones await entry and socialization into the work setting (Lortie, 1975). Most teachers remember the teachers they had when they were students, and these often serve as role models or ideal images (for better or for worse) for their teaching.

Similar types of images—symbols, icons, and mandala objects that tap a community's consciousness (see Bruner, 1986; Campbell, 1990; Jung, 1972)—could also shed some light on teacher imaging. For example, iconographic imaging (especially that from worship or ceremony settings) may have had an especially profound impact on certain children and, hence, are instructive for understanding particular kinds of teacher-student relationships. A study of the image of teacher as icon would surely help explain why some students overly idealize their teachers and why some teachers place themselves on altars or pedestals.

### Given Images

The expectations that society, tradition, parents, and the school system have of teaching tend to result in teachers accepting (either actively or passively) the culture-bound images of teaching. We call these "given" images. The office of teaching, the institutional role, shapes the images held by the teacher. Babysitter, caretaker, monitor, recordkeeper, parent, disciplinarian, trainer, moral model, expert, authority, subject specialist, tester, grader, and cafeteria supervisor are some examples of roles that teachers assume because of institutional requirements, tradition, and cultural mores. Teachers often accept "given" images as their destiny or as legitimate requirements of their role.

Curiously, the teaching profession provides for little role differentiation. Teachers are responsible for professional, paraprofessional, clerical, and even housekeeping duties. Even when teachers work mainly outside of the classroom, much of their work is clerical and managerial rather than central to instruction. Few teachers are employed in schools as researchers, instructional leaders, or curriculum developers. And even when principals create opportunities for teachers to define a new role, too many teachers return to given roles, and do not maintain an image of themselves as instructional leaders. The question we might ask is, what hold do given images have on teachers' professional identity?

Undoubtedly, the three areas discussed above overlap, and it is probably true that teachers hold images of each kind. As teachers examine the images of their work, a consideration of their origins may illuminate why some images speak to them and inform their practice, while others are mainly a burden and constrict teaching potential. Our belief is that, once teachers begin to actively create their own images of their work, they will discover their unique images, those that reveal something of their individual presence, their person. Perhaps then they will begin to help create more professional opportunities for themselves in their schools.

The following section continues the exploration and interpretation of images of teachers and teaching by revealing the "presence and person" of those who spoke to us. We perceive these revelations as growing, dynamic, and full of life—animating the practice of teaching for teachers and those who would be teachers.

## Interpreting Teacher Images

What meanings and possible interpretations can be discerned from the many images portrayed by our teachers? How might we group teacher images so that we can better understand them?

Based on the case studies presented here and discussions with teachers conducted over the past five years, we have created the following groupings (or types) that illuminate common meanings and interpretations embedded in the specific images. These groupings not only serve to highlight essential aspects of the teaching self, but also illustrate how relationships among teachers and students are created and maintained.

    I. *Those referring to the teaching self*
       Teacher as Interpreter
       Teacher as Presence
       Teacher as Elder
   II. *Those referring to relationships between teacher and students*
       Teacher as Child
       Teacher as Advocate
       Teacher as Therapist
       Teacher as Parent
       Teacher as Animator
       Teacher as Companion
       Teacher as Storyteller

We will now discuss these images and, whenever possible, illustrate them with material from our interviews as well as the writings of others who have influenced our interpretations.

### Teacher as Interpreter

This typology of images portrays teachers as interpreting what happens in the classroom and as constructing meanings about the teaching-learning relationships taking place. What these teachers have in common is their ability to learn from their work, to be open to a new level of understanding of what they do, and, when necessary, to be willing to change. In so doing, they become experienced teachers.

Constructing images of teaching is fundamentally an act of interpretation and, thus, a valuable guide for effective and satisfying teaching. Tracy (1987) believes that good interpretations are "those that enrich our experience, allow for understanding, aid deliberation and judgement, and increase the possibilities of meaningful action," and concludes that "to understand at all is to interpret. To act well is to interpret a situation demanding some action and to interpret a correct strategy for that action . . . to be 'experienced' is to have become a good interpreter" (p. 9).

We are reminded of Irene's struggling to change old images of her work, of trying to give up the confining models of teaching she had been following. She learned from her students and her colleagues and created new images and interpretations of herself: a teacher who is freer, who is not so bothered with demanding the students' attention and who is now able to share decision-making with her students. Her new perspective has given her a deeper understanding of her teaching. It has liberated her.

Kate's learning was equally dramatic. While always a very independent teacher who was familiar with sharing leadership, she came to a new awareness of her relationship with students. From being overwhelmed with students' emotional problems, she has learned to engage her students in literature where they are invited to develop strategies for self-examination and problem-solving. When she looked at herself as problem-solver, confessor, and mother, she felt absorbed and thought that she was avoiding her teacher role. Now, she sees herself as educator, one who leads students to examine their lives through literature and to reach beyond themselves.

### Teacher as Presence

Teachers with a central image, a clear and vivid focus of what they do, seem to have in common a sense of their own personality, point of view, and individuality. They have a style of teaching; that is, they have a presence. The teachers have sifted through the multiple images that could be held and have centered on those that most aptly speak to their uniqueness and the way they relate to students. They have examined their life experiences and realize that their teaching reflects their character. The unforgettable teacher is one whose presence is felt by her students; her countenance is imprinted on their memories.

Playwright and recent president of the Czech Republic, Vaclav Havel, writing to his wife Olga while he was in prison, talked about the absence of her presence. His reflections on the meaning of human existence and on human personality speak eloquently to the image of teacher as presence.

> You mention that almost every day you speak about me and with someone and thus I am, in some small way, present at home . . . and that leads me to a theme I sometimes ponder, the question of what human existence really is, viewed in space and time. . . .
>
> Human personality is a particular view of the world, an image of the world, an aspect of the world's Being. It is as if it were a light constantly reilluminating the world; a crystal in which the world is constantly being reflected. . . .
>
> We therefore imagine the other person not merely as someone we know from the past . . . but we know him and experience him as an integral part of our own present and future and our own potentialities . . . a dimension of our own existence (Havel, 1989, pp. 138–142).

Margaret and Kate most vividly illustrate this grouping of teacher as presence—the teacher as "I." Their colleagues view them as role models and frequently turn to them for advice. Margaret views school reform in her district as an opportunity to place her mark on her school. She intends to "grab the ring and run with it." She feels in control, is happy with her profession, attends conferences, gives in-service sessions for her faculty, and urges her colleagues to try out new ideas. Her views about teaching reading are based on her long years of practice and her familiarity with research. She has experimented with different methods and has sorted out what works and what does not. Margaret sees herself as a reading specialist and a lover of literature, and this interest manifests itself in her teaching and in her relationships with colleagues.

Kate's experience in art and drama helps her define her view of herself and her teaching style. Her reflection about how she relates to students not only led to changes in her teaching, but also gave her insights into her own personal development. She is more aware of her feelings toward students and the limitations of trying to solve their problems. She has come to the realization that problems can lead to growth and that struggles can be liberating. Just as she learned to find deeper meaning and worth in her art studies, she is now helping students find meaning in the books they read. Kate engages her students in the world of ideas, and her presence is felt among them.

### Teacher as Elder

Most teachers noted that a major reason for becoming a teacher was to share their knowledge, to hand down what they had learned. This grouping of images we have named: teacher as scholar, as expert, and as elder. High school teachers, in particular, view their main role as "subject-matter" specialists. (They are teachers of Math, English, Biology, History, etc.)

The larger reality of this grouping of images is that the teacher has "been there." This is teacher as adult and grandparent (and similarly, as mentor, model). She has a sense of continuity in life, is aware of the changes, growth, and development of humans, of the journey they take, and of the cultural values they hold. She has experienced the joys and pains of life, and she shares her insights of the lived life with her students.

Moreover, she has experienced the traditions, the ways of the culture, and is a party to the wisdom of the community (folklore and legends handed down). As elder, the teacher embodies not only the accumulated knowledge of the community, but the moral dimension as well. She not only wants to share these, but also invites the young to contribute to this wisdom.

### Teacher as Child

Nearly all teachers interviewed stated that they entered teaching because they wanted to work with children, with young people. Many told us that they feel young in working with children, that they enjoy the sense of wonder children have, and that they, too, experience a sense of adventure, of the new, and even of awe in their teaching.

Ayers (1990) writes that teachers must have "reverence for each child and humility in the face of each interaction. Teaching is for many teachers a way of being healthy. Creativity in healing as in teaching is, in Winnicott's words, 'the retention throughout life of something that belongs properly to the infant . . . the ability to create the world.' " (p. 21).

Similarly, DuBois (1989) recalls how Rabindranath Tagore, in discussing the characteristics of the true educator, focuses on the need to be open and awake to children, and to become like children:

> . . . clearly education comes out of ("is the gift of") joy resulting from the association with the teacher's mind which is avid for learning. It is not merely that teacher's experience in the field, but rather his openness to life, his wakefulness. In this he is like a child. Tagore believed that true teachers were "born," not made. He says here that "the born teacher is the man in whom the primal child responds readily to the call of children." Due to his childlike quality the teacher can be a friend to children and is considered one "of their own species."

Teachers who view themselves as child-like identify with and affirm their students. The teachers remember what it was like when they were children, and thus are able to enter into communion with their students.

### Teacher as Advocate

I became a teacher because I had such bad teachers. I thought maybe I could help other children.

I remember wishing, even as a youngster, that I could be the teacher and do something better.

I thought maybe I could help some kids learn. I wanted to make up for what was happening to children. It just wasn't fair. Since then I have seen children and parents lost in some bureaucratic processes or even some unfair practices that made me mad.

The above quotations from our interviews help to identify a grouping of images of teachers as advocates for children. The ideas that they express relate to the sense of protectiveness or defense of children. Children need to be protected from "bad teachers," from bureaucratic idiocies, from unrealistic expectations, from abuse, from dangers to their physical and mental well-being.

Maria summed up the ideas related to being an advocate when she described her efforts to help other teachers understand language and language learning among children whose first language is not English. Her own life experiences and her feelings from her childhood seem to have made her empathic toward the children who are being rushed into reading a language they do not understand. Maria expressed her understanding of what the children were "going through" and gave a sense that her work might help and should help them. Her concern for her students pushed her to extra work with the other teachers in the school.

Children need help to learn to resist pressures from insensitive adults or other children. All teachers help children, but those teachers who image themselves as advocates see their role as including special efforts to see that the rights of children are protected, that the feelings of children are respected, and that children are affirmed.

### Teacher as Therapist

Many teachers we interviewed see themselves as providing emotional support for their students. A frequent position, especially among primary school teachers, is that teaching had to be concerned with both the cognitive and emotional development of students. How to help students with their emotional problems, however, posed a dilemma for teachers. Balancing their major role of educating with that of therapist or counselor was a frequent challenge.

After much reflection, Kate decided to move away from the role of "confessor, mother, and problem-solver." She felt absorbed by the many personal problems students brought to her, and she now feels more comfortable in helping students through literature. Sarah, on the other hand, sees one of her essential responsibilities as helping students deal with their emotional problems. Her belief is that once student feelings are dealt with it is possible to work on academics. Sarah admitted, however, that this is tiring, especially with the busy schedule she is expected to follow.

Writing about the emotional component of teaching and learning, Salzberger-Wittenberg, Henry, and Osbourne (1983) note the importance of helping children understand their feelings. They discuss how children elicit emotional responses from teachers: ". . . the effect a student or group of students has on us may be a valuable indication of the kind of feelings they want us to have. These may be ones of being idealized and admired and all sorts of positive aspects of a relationship, but more often what is deposited in us are the feelings the other one cannot bear or cannot bear on his own, such as helplessness, confusion, panic, guilt, despair or depression. He may need another person to help with them" (p. 59).

In trying to come to terms with how they might deal with students' personal problems, teachers need to be aware of the kinds of feelings students elicit from them. We comprehend that such reflections would help teachers better understand their own feelings toward students and assist them in creating positive relationships in their classrooms.

### Teacher as Parent

This grouping of images overlaps with the one above. Teacher as parent is a prevalent image and open to many interpretations. Some teachers readily portray themselves as second parents to their students. Others shy away from such images and even deny any type of resemblance with their style of teaching. The many interpretations of teacher as parent make this grouping a particularly fruitful one for analysis. We can recall some of the multiple images of parents—from nurturing, caring, sharing, giving, and guiding, to controlling, dominating, abandoning, rejecting, and abusing—in order to begin to understand the possible interpretations of this image for teachers.

We must also consider that how children relate to their teachers, to a large extent, is influenced by the kind of relationship they have with their parents. Bowlby's (1988) attachment theory enlightens our understanding of parent-child relationships and has implications for teacher-student relationships.

> Ethological theory regards the propensity to make strong emotional bonds to particular individuals as a basic component of human nature, already present in germinal form in the neonate and continuing through adult life into old age (pp. 162–163).

The pattern of attachment consistent with healthy development is that of secure attachment, in which the individual is confident that his parent (or parent-figure) will be available, responsive,
and helpful should he encounter adverse or frightening situations.
With this assurance, he feels bold in his explorations of the world
and also competent in dealing with it (p. 167).

Salzberger-Wittenberg, Henry, and Osbourne (1983) directly address
the parenting issue faced by teachers: "The task of the teacher may be
thought of as resembling the parental function: that is, to act as a temporary
container for the excessive anxiety of his students at points of stress. It will
mean that he will experience in himself some of the mental pain connected
with learning, and yet set an example of maintaining curiosity in the face of
chaos, love of truth in the face of terror of the unknown, and hope in the face
of despair" (p. 59).

In addition to being "temporary containers" of student feelings, the
above authors see an additional role that teachers might play in helping
students face problems. They believe that teachers are important in helping
students think through and organize their thoughts and feelings and hence
help them come to terms with them: "The pupil's ideas and thoughts are
aided by a teacher who assists him in ordering them, particularly at such
times when the learner becomes overwhelmed by too much undigested
knowledge. The teacher's capacity to be reflective and thoughtful about data
rather than producing ready answers enables the learner to internalize a
thinking person. He in turn will produce new conjunctions of thoughts and
meaning which may set off in the teacher a new combination of thinking
about his subject" (pp. 60–61).

Of the case studies presented in this chapter, Sarah's discussion of her
role as parent provides the most data for such an analysis. She feels happy
that her school is like a family, that she knows her students' brothers and
sisters, and that the students feel comfortable with their teachers. It is not
clear how Sarah interprets her role as second parent, but we have some clue
from her statement that she believes that the children "respect us, and they
understand that we are telling them things for their own good, just as their
mother or father would."

Parent as moral authority appears to be Sarah's idea of what it means to
be a second parent. She is pleased that there is a feeling of trust among
students and faculty. Not so clear, however, is the extent to which she fosters
independence and decision-making among her students. The mutuality of
the relationship seems less evident.

### Teacher as Animator

This grouping encompasses images of teacher as catalyst and as activa-
tor. A basic feature here is intrinsic motivation—that originating internally
from the interests of the student. The teacher's role is one of activating this

interest. Dewey (1897/1959) puts this aptly: "I believe that interests are the signs and symptoms of growing power. I believe that they represent dawning capacities. Accordingly the constant and careful observation of interests is of the utmost importance for the educator" (p. 29).

Margaret, Irene, and Kate have learned to observe and nurture the interests of their students, and over the years they have found ways to cultivate the "dawning capacities" of their children. In bonding with their classes, they activate the potential for growth. Margaret demonstrated how she helps her students become part of the story, and Kate reflected about building trust among her students and helping them relate to the books they read together.

A variant of this grouping is the teacher as actor, as dramatist. Some teachers understand themselves as being engaged in a drama with their students, as mutually participating in a play. Kate explicitly stated this analogy when she noted that she saw teaching as drama, as bringing "a little bit of life" to the classroom, of "taking ideas and making things happen with them." This is possible when one finds utmost value in what one does. In such valuing, a bond is activated and a drama unfolds.

### Teacher as Companion

As we look back over the images, we see that many center around relationships, the special bond that creative teachers forge with their students. We call this grouping teaching as companion. The essence of this type of relationship is one of mutual benefit for teacher and student. When teachers try to see students from the student's perspective, they begin to enter the relationship in a more meaningful and intimate way. A similar viewing must take place among students. Rather than an "I–It" type of relationship, teacher and student enter an "I–Thou" type of relationship (Buber, 1961). The teaching-learning relationship becomes one of a dialogue, an encounter, and not merely one of playing out institutional or traditional roles.

Kate most clearly represents this grouping, though all the teachers studied, to some extent, are companions to their students. Sarah's image of being a "second parent" to students indeed reflects a kind of companionship. And if the parent and child role is symbiotic in nature, the companionship is one of mutual benefit. However, when the parent role is one of controlling or maintaining dependency, it is quite different from the companionship concept discussed here.

For example, Kate explicitly stated that she read to her students in order to create a bond between them and the story. She recalled her own art teacher as an example of the bonding she has in mind. The bond is to an idea, to a craft, a talent, a story, a desire for something worthwhile and meaningful. Her students bond within the context of literature—a literature she selects (that begins with them and takes them to a larger world). She learned that the "bond" implied in becoming involved with students' personal problems may befit a therapist or social worker, but it did not meet her idea of an educator. Kate is a companion to her students in a world of ideas, a world of literature. Together they share their views of the book being discussed. They become companions in exploring literature and the diverse meanings it holds for them.

### Teacher as Storyteller

Teachers do not merely act out a prescribed role, but create roles and opportunities for learning among their students. Working together, students and teachers share experiences and even tell the story of what happens when they are together in the classroom. They create special names for what they have shared, thought, and felt together. They capture a way of life. And when they record what they do, we all benefit from their insights (Coles, 1989; Richardson, 1964; Wigginton, 1985).

In some ways Sarah is an example of a storyteller. She sees generations of students come to her class, and she talks to them about their brothers and sisters. They attend weddings and reunions, and they share memories of what it was like when they were together at M. School. She is open to their stories, their problems, their personal lives. However, it is not clear to what extent the students are co-authors of these stories and what deeper messages and meanings are portrayed in them.

Kate, Margaret, and Irene are more actively engaged in storytelling with their students. Margaret elicits students' interests and experiences so that she can help them become "part of the story." Literature and experiences are linked in Margaret's classroom. Similarly, Irene believes that the best stories come when students feel comfortable in playing with ideas, writing journals, and reading each others' writings. Kate selects stories that speak to the life experiences of her students. She reads aloud to them so they can hear her voice and get into the story. She asks them to try to connect the stories they have read, so that they can find the images they hold; these images serve as a foundation for storytelling.

---

## Conclusions and Further Reflection

Our comments on imaging generated from conversations with teachers, and our interpretations and perceived implications of these images are preludes to learning about teachers and teaching.

When teachers begin to construct images of their work, core meanings of teaching/learning relationships manifest themselves. That is, teachers begin to see their work as one of learning, being, comprehending, and affirming what students do. They begin to be aware of themselves as healing, creating the setting, and bonding with their students. Some, too, tell the story of what they or their students have created.

Throughout this chapter we have mentioned implications of teacher images and imaging. We have spoken of the areas where this focus would prove helpful and places where the information might be applied. We now wish to bring these remarks to an explicit level and to describe how this information might be used.

First, in conversations with teachers we ("we" as researchers, teacher-educators, colleagues, or fellow students) can offer the opportunity for them to reflect on their sense of themselves. This means that we can listen to and nurture the "emerging" images to bring those images to the level of consciousness where they can continue to inform the teachers' practice in the classroom.

Second, we can assist teachers in integrating their images of themselves with possible teaching behaviors. We can focus on choices available and how those choices fit or do not fit with the images of the self that already exist. Thus, consonance will develop between those images and what the teachers do in the classroom. We can also focus on the negotiating process necessary for change of behaviors. The self-image may have to change in order to accommodate changing practices in the classroom.

Third, in preparing for the initiation of teachers into the teaching profession, we can help new teachers to anticipate the differing images of teaching they will meet in their positions as the "new kids." The culture of the schools in which they work will either support or deny the new teachers' images of teacher and teaching, as Bruner (1986) helps us understand: ". . . a culture is as much a *forum* for negotiating and renegotiating meaning and for explicating action as it is a set of rules or specifications for action. . . . It is the forum aspect of a culture that gives its participants a role in constantly making and remaking the culture—an active role as participants rather than as performing spectators who play out their canonical roles according to rules when the appropriate cues occur" (p. 123).

Fourth, in staff development programs, we can make reflecting on teacher images a part of the assessment of the school environment, as a place to nurture the teacher as educator.

And fifth, we can emphasize for teachers that their work with students is enhanced by their increasing sense of themselves. We believe that it will help them to recognize that same need in their students and help their students to create positive and helpful images of themselves as learners—learner as creator, as interpreter, as companion or storyteller.

Furthermore, we also need to reflect on how schools, culture, tradition, and lack of differentiation of role often force teachers into roles other than their principal one as educator. All the teachers interviewed had images of their work that reflected some aspect of the cultural/social context. The message given is that the essential role of the school as a place for education is being corrupted (Goodlad, 1979). Sarah finds that American culture does not revere teachers as other societies do. We recall her voice of warning: "In order to function and to blossom you need recognition and praise." While she finds satisfaction in her work, she wonders how many young people will enter teaching, given the low status afforded the profession. Kate is similarly concerned that the school system does not cultivate creativity and has lost sight of its essential purpose of educating children.

Even the strongest teachers, those who actively construct images of their work, are heavily influenced by the often uncaring and negative environment in which they teach. Positive teacher images compete with cultural images that far too often do not nurture the teacher as educator. When this happens, how can we ask teachers to share the wisdom of the culture with the young? How can teachers create a community of learners when their role is being endangered?

By constructing and reflecting on images of our teaching selves, we can get in touch with our feelings, values, and character. We begin to realize which images of our teaching enhance our feelings of self-worth and expand our roles as teachers, and which ones limit, confine, and even cripple us. We learn to look into the mirror of our inner selves and find ways to know and to love our work, our students, ourselves. Imaging about the significant aspects of teaching helps us find meaning in our work.

The challenge is to find images that liberate us and take us to a deeper awareness of ourselves, of others, and of the world. We believe that conscious focus on images and their influence will help free both the teachers and society from imposed images and the damage these imposed images may cause. Our hope is that someday we can all say as Irene did: "And now, because I feel freer as a teacher I understand more of what I am doing. Now I can let things go and let the children kind of pick up where they would like to work from." Once we feel free of restraining images and roles, we are able to share our presence with our students and create a learning community with them.

## NOTE

1. Data for this study were collected over a period of five years, from 1984 to 1990. Both authors worked in staff development programs with five inner-city Chicago public schools over an extended period of time, and thus were able to become familiar with the culture of the schools as well as to build relationships of trust with teachers. This greatly facilitated the discussions with teachers. Notes taken during and after these discussions were analyzed for the images they contained.

   Structured interviews did not characterize this part of the study. Rather, the discussions were an outgrowth of the working relationships that the authors established with the teachers.

   During the second and later part of the study, a sample of teachers was extensively interviewed on three different occasions. Broad questions relating to the school reforms being implemented in Chicago, the career histories of the teachers, new ideas they wanted to work on in their classrooms, and how they viewed their work and their teaching, guided these interviews. With the teachers' consent, the interviews were recorded and transcribed to facilitate analysis.

M. School is an inner-city, predominantly Hispanic, school in Chicago. Margaret, Irene, Sarah, and Kate are from M. School; all were interviewed by Joe Fischer. Maria is from another inner-city school in Chicago; she was interviewed by Anne Kiefer.

In addition, the authors teach in the field-based master of education program at National-Louis University in which an intact group of teachers work together with a core instructor for two years. This program results in considerable bonding between students and professors, permitting candid and in-depth dialogues and reflection about teaching. These experiences provided an additional rich source of information for the study.

## REFERENCES

Ayers, W. (1990). Teaching and the web of life: Professional options and folk alternatives. *Holistic Education Review, 3,* 19–21.

Bowlby, J. (1988). *A secure base.* New York: Basic Books.

Bruner, J. (1986). *Actual minds, possible worlds.* Cambridge, MA: Harvard University Press.

Buber, M. (1961). *Between man and man.* Boston: Beacon Press.

Campbell, J. (1990). *The hero's journey: Joseph Campbell on his life and work.* San Francisco: Harper & Row.

Coles, R. (1989). *The call of stories: Teaching and the moral imagination.* Boston: Houghton Mifflin Company.

Dewey, J. (1897). *My pedagogic creed 9.* In M. S. Dworkin (Ed), *Dewey on education: Selections* (pp. 19–42). New York: Teachers College Press.

DuBois, F. (1989). *The true teacher: Rabindranath Tagore and Martin Buber.* Frankfurt/M.: Arnold Kopcke-Duttler [Hrsg].

Goodlad, J. (1979). *What schools are for.* Bloomington, IN: Phi Delta Kappa.

Havel, V. (1989). *Letters to Olga.* New York: Holt.

*The Holy Bible, King James Version.* (1966). Philadelphia: National Publishing Company.

Jung, C. G. (1972). *Mandala symbolism.* Princeton, NJ: Princeton University Press.

Lortie, D. (1975). *School teacher: A sociological study.* Chicago: University of Chicago Press.

Richardson, E. (1964). *In the early world: Discovering art through crafts.* New York: Pantheon, Random House.

Salzberger-Wittenberg, I., Henry, X. & Osbourne, X. (1983). *The emotional experience of learning and teaching.* London: Routledge & Kegan.

Tracy, D. (1987). *Plurality and ambiguity: Hermeneutics, religion, hope.* New York: Harper & Row.

Wigginton, E. (1985). *Sometimes a shining moment: The Foxfire experience.* Garden City, NY: Anchor Press.

# 3

# Reflections in a Mirror

## Teacher-Generated Metaphors from Self and Others

Sara Efron
Pamela Bolotin Joseph

*As a teacher I am like a* dentist. *The dentist tells you what you have to do to have good teeth, but essentially you have to do it. Some days it is as hard as pulling teeth. And if they didn't brush their teeth last night, they come back and you can't get near them because they have bad breath. And you have this faint feeling as if they fail you in some way, or you failed because you did not press upon them the importance of doing it. They come with cavities and you have to fix them. They come to you two hours before you have to turn in the grades and they ask, "What can I do?" "Well, you really should have brushed. Let's see if I can fill it. We'll stick some silver in there and see if it holds. But next time remember to brush!"* (F, 44, High School, Small Town)

Teacher as dentist—an unusual description of schoolteaching—and yet, this metaphor informs us, allowing us to understand how one teacher views her work, her purpose, her relationship with students. This metaphor reveals a person who does not see herself as a creative power—a dynamic force in the lives of young people. Rather, it is a metaphor of struggle (of "pulling teeth"), of compassion ("Come . . . What can I do?"), of failure and perseverance. It portrays a teacher who finds her work difficult and often unsupported, but ultimately she persists because she cares about her students.

If we want to capture the "essence" of what teaching is in the eyes of a

teacher, if we want to understand how teachers make sense of their work—
to acquire an empathetic understanding from within—we believe that we
must explore an artistic form of image that can grasp and reveal the not
always definable emotions. Metaphor is "a unique and enduring and irre-
placeable way to embody the truth of our inward lives" (Abbs, 1981, p. 491).

But our opinions of ourselves, social scientists suggest, depend not only
on self-perception but also on the responses of others; thus, self-definition
is both a process of individual experience and a social product (Cooley,
1902/1983; Mead, 1934; Thomas, 1980). Although an individual is an independent actor capable of innovating and initiating actions and reflecting
on them, behavior is influenced by the opinions and attitudes of a "generalized other" (Nias, 1985). Thus, we may ask, are schoolteachers' sense of
who they are—their metaphors of self—cast by their expectations of themselves as professionals? Is their sense of identity and self-worth based on
responses from students, administrators, and parents? We must consider
the idea that teachers' self-images are not molded by a single layer of
perception, but reconstructed through multiple perspectives that individual teachers reflect on in order to make sense of internal and external
images of themselves as professionals.

Also, we wondered, do their perceptions of self reflect a passive acceptance of external forces? Or, as research about teaching suggests (Lieberman
& Miller, 1984; Nias, 1985), is self-definition the result of dynamic interactions in which individuals confront their realization of professional self and
negotiate it with the images of others? Does one teach not only to satisfy
self-expectations, but also to fulfill the felt needs of students, parents, and
administrators?

This chapter explores teachers' images of themselves through metaphor.
We asked these schoolteachers to share their memories, perceptions, and
feelings by asking questions about images they held of teachers—of their
own professional selves, of their former teachers, of themselves when they
first began to teach, and of teachers through the eyes of others, thus attempting to conceptualize how teachers perceive themselves through and with the
awareness of how they are perceived by students, parents, and principals.

These conversations about image and metaphor originate from interviews with twenty-six teachers who work in diverse public school populations—urban, suburban, small-town, and rural schools varying across the
total social-economic continuum and all grade levels from kindergarten
through high school.[1] They possess various years of experience, differing
levels of involvement with the communities in which they teach, and a
multitude of purposes for why they teach. We have provided some of the
demographic information with their narratives so that our readers can appreciate the teachers' diversity as well as their commonalities regardless of
age, gender, or classroom. These teachers describe themselves as "career
professionals"—not "paycheck teachers" who work only from week to week
in order to survive or "get by." The teachers in this study liked their work

and respected their profession. Not one person suggested that teaching was an unfortunate career choice; no one felt that the difficulties of the job make the gratification not worthwhile.

We asked teachers to generate metaphors of their professional selves in order to elicit both an intuitive and an intellectual awareness of their understanding of what it means to be a teacher. We found that the multifarious aspects and the complexities of teaching emerged in the teachers' responses. The images and metaphors reveal these schoolteachers' interpretations of their professional existence—their sense of purpose and their daily practice. The images the teachers brought forth evoke self-doubt, anger, and cynicism, but they also symbolize narratives of celebration in which this group of professionals expressed their fulfillment            career choice and their work.

## Metaphors of Self-Definition

In this chapter metaphors are used in             clarify, contain, and understand the inner values, beliefs, and             that arise out of the teacher's experience in the classroom's lif             teacher's professional life. The need for clarification is apparent             researchers' characterizations of teachers' workplaces. Lorti             intains that teaching tasks provoke feelings of apprehension: "Uncertainty . . . can be transformed into diffuse anxiety and painful self-doubt, which reduce the psychic rewards of classroom teaching" (p. 161). "Metaphor becomes an extraordinary powerful tool through which the teacher can express more fully the meaning of what he or she does in an ambiguous work setting" (Provenzo et al., 1989, p. 551).

Abbs (1979) points out the advantages of symbolism, particularly language symbolism, over rationalism and empiricism when it comes to analyzing a multifaceted situation. The rationalist and the empiricist tend to ignore the thoughts, feelings, and sensations that seem confusing or multidimensional; the result is our reduced, scant understanding of experience of mind and spirit: "We are creative centers constructing a world we can inhabit out of a world which is terrifyingly dense, and seemingly indifferent. Through the powers of symbolism, and particularly through the powers of language, we are able to grasp our own inner being and assert values, beliefs and aspirations. These are meaningful simply because they arise out of our existence in personal and endless attempts to clarify, to contain, to understand" (Abbs, 1979, pp. 42–43).

Metaphor (from the Greek *metapherein*: "to bear change") draws parallels between apparently unrelated phenomena. It allows us to attend to likenesses, to relationships, and to underlying patterns in seeking what Aristotle called similarities in dissimilarities; "through metaphorical thinking, divergent meanings become unified into the underlying patterns that constitute our conceptual understanding of reality" (Pugh et al., 1992, p. 3). Metaphorical thinking contributes to our identification of conceptual categories that may not be obvious or previously acknowledged.

For teachers, "metaphor provides a means by which they can construct and express their understanding of social reality when the definitions and understandings presented to them fail to provide adequate meaning" (Provenzo et al., 1989, p. 569). Similarly, Ricoeur (1977) indicates that the use of metaphor can be a means of taking control of the unknown and unexplained and of assuming responsibility and authority over experiences confronting the teacher.

School setting is a complex existence with myriad layers of interactions and meanings. This intricacy calls on teachers to gain understanding and meaning in this setting. The search for metaphor can be seen as a drive to name, to categorize, and to gain insight and thus clarify the immense and rich complexity of teachers' lives in schools (Bowers, 1980). There is irony in the notion that scientific categorization of teaching into discrete steps can capture the artistry and complexity of teaching. It is also paradoxical, as Eisner (1985) asserts, that in the professional socialization of educational research, the use of metaphor has been regarded as a sign of imprecision, while, in fact, "for making public the ineffable, nothing is more precise than the artistic use of language" (p. 227).

When we attempt to gain insight into teachers' self-images as seen through their individual lenses, the use of metaphor seems natural; metaphorical language enables teachers to reveal what Ball (1972) describes as the "core-self" among the range of meanings of "being a teacher." We find that metaphor allows teachers both intuitively and rationally to engage in a reflective process about their personal notions of their roles in schools. We discover that through metaphors, consciously or unconsciously, the teachers portray their personal philosophies of what teaching is, their own vision of their goals as teachers, and their sense of classroom realities. It is apparent that these teachers' relationships with students seem to shape their self-images and also provide an understanding of their "core meanings" of being teachers.

## Patterns of Teachers' Metaphors of Self

As we attempted to analyze teachers' images of self, we saw that the metaphors may be viewed as several dichotomies, all telling us about teacher-student interaction. Although we will explain the metaphors through these patterns, images overlap as teachers imagine themselves as performing varying and perhaps contradictory roles.

The first dichotomy suggests two patterns, the artistic versus the mechanical teacher. The artistic teacher seeks to create—to allow students to reveal their own talents and artistry, to provide the medium in which students can bloom. The mechanical teacher keeps the educational machine operating. Teachers who describe themselves with this metaphor do not seek creativity in themselves or in their students; they emphasize functioning and managing. The second dichotomy reveals the teacher as parent, as the all-knower who believes that the students must have the guidance of the powerful adult. In the other side of the dichotomy we see playfulness, the excitement of working with young people. This side is the teacher as fellow learner.

Images of the artistic teacher include the light breeze, play director, actor, orchestra conductor, juggler, gardener, and potter:

> Maybe as a *light breeze*, touching the students, maybe bending a little bit this way or that way. Sometimes it is a warm breeze, when it is cool outside, but sometimes it's a cool and refreshing breeze when they are too excited (F, 53, Junior High, Suburban).

> A *director of a play* who takes students with all the talents and skills they have, and in a class situation, makes each one shine as the leading lady or man on stage (M, 44, High School, Small Town).

> I am kind of like an *actor*. Before he goes on stage he peers in his closet to see what outfit needs to be worn at that specific situation. Depending on the students and their needs, I choose the kind of hat I am going to wear. Sometimes I have to change the act while I am on stage. It depends on the kids you are with. Sometimes you have to be one thing to one group and another thing to another group (M, 32, Elementary, Small Town).

> I am like an *orchestra conductor* working with my hands to show them what I am saying. Trying to maintain this side while the other side is doing something else, and this person in the back is talking. And another one has a very private need that I have to attend to just now. So it is very much like conducting an orchestra (F, 26, Junior High, Suburban).

> One sometimes feels like a *juggler* because you are trying to keep everything going, and make sure that it is going successfully. . . . Encourage the children who need encouragement and also recognize children who are doing well; give them a little spin by saying, "You are doing a great job, keep going." And all through this time you have to know what you are doing, have to be attuned and aware to this special balance between these different needs (M, 30, Elementary, Suburban).

> A *gardener*. Whatever they have in the seed can bloom fully. A healthy plant. I take whatever they come with, with whatever they

bring, and let them be what they can be (F, 44, Elementary, Small Town).

The artistic teacher, as the above metaphors illustrate, generates movement, excitement, and sensitivity. As the "light breeze" metaphor implies, the teacher touches the students but does not shape or transform them. The students keep their own presence which the teacher cherishes and allows to come alive.

There are other images of the artistic teacher, however. This pattern of metaphor can also suggest the teacher who more forcefully molds and shapes in order to allow the students' talents to reveal themselves. The artistic teachers do not always describe their work as enjoyable because they feel a tension between themselves and their students; they push and they pull as they try to motivate and stimulate their students. Clearly, some artistic teachers have a stronger sense of their own force or power:

> A *potter*—shaping clay, where you try to get the flaws out, and you try to bring out the best that is within each student. I shape them into an ideal of what I see. I see a certain thing that a student needs in order to succeed. I have a motto that I present to the students in the beginning of the year that says: "All students are gifted. They just open up their packages at different times." I am the one who helps them open that package (F, 50, Junior High, Suburban).

> I don't like the metaphor of molding the mind, because I don't think that I am molding their minds. I don't want to mold their minds; I want to stimulate them. I give them something to respond to that isn't necessarily a positive response all the time . . . but they do respond, and I go for that. I don't care if they hate it—I just love to see the response (F, 42, Elementary, Small Town).

There were few teachers who epitomized the other side of the dichotomy— the mechanical teacher. Only two metaphors were created emphasizing a well-ordered machine:

> An *engine* that is well taken care of. Everything works the way it is supposed to work. Everything goes the way it is supposed to go. There is a set rhythm and reason to why things work in the way they do. I lead by example (M, 29, High School, Small Town).

> A *manager* or a *leader*. Too often we consider ourselves just as teachers, but in fact we forget that we are leading about 150 kids a day. They are coming in and you are leading them in terms of instruction, you are leading them in terms of discipline, in terms of getting along with other people (M, 28, High School, Suburban).

So, too, may we include "the dentist" who, using the human body as the well-cared-for machine, sees her role as keeping the students functioning.

But in this study, the mechanical teachers do not keep their machines working merely in order to conform to a school hierarchy; they strongly feel a
sense of responsibility and devotion to students who need stability and
discipline—so these teachers believed.

As we explored the second dichotomy, we saw few examples of the
"teacher as learner." Only one teacher solely expresses her relationship with
students as fellow student:

> I see myself as a *learner*. I am learning each and every day; I learn
> with my students. My students know that I don't know everything. I
> am proud of it (F, 33, Elementary, Urban).

Another viewed himself fundamentally as a co-student—"I am not the 'all-
knower.' " He also discussed other self-images; as fellow voyager on a journey, he pictured himself as the captain of the ship and then as a gardener
"planting ideas in students' minds" (M, 41, Elementary, Urban). Similarly,
another teacher explained,

> I could consider myself a *guide*. I am showing the students the way,
> guiding them towards and helping them to see their potentials and
> helping them to develop their skills. I am interested in helping
> them see themselves in a positive way. I am kind of a guide in a
> forest preserve; you're going with them and experiencing with them
> (M, 33, Elementary, Suburban).

The fellow learner delights in the growth and stimulation of the teacher
along with the student, even if their roles are not considered equal.

In the metaphors of teacher as parent or surrogate parent, however,
there is little sense of equality in the relationships between teacher and
student. These metaphors portray the strongest presence of the teacher as
well as suggest that, without the teacher's influence, the students would be
without guidance—adrift, without nurturing or basic care-giving.

> I think that sometimes I feel like a *mother*, that I am giving care
> and loving that might not be there. Sometimes I feel like a mother
> or best friend. I am not only giving but also nagging. Nobody ever
> put guilt trips on some of my kids. They never feel guilty about not
> doing anything . . . the Jewish/Italian mother syndrome. I fill that
> void. "You didn't do your homework, but I expected you to. . . ."—a
> mother (F, 36, High School, Urban).

> Actually I tell the kids all the time that I am like their second
> *father*, because I try to be more like a friend to all rather than just a
> teacher. I realize that they have lots of problematic situations at
> home, so I treat them with respect so they feel that they can come to
> me and talk with me about things that they would normally not
> talk with teachers about (M, 37, Elementary, Urban).

A *helper*. You find yourself being a social worker, the teacher, the mother. You have so many roles to play, so many hats to wear in any given day, so you need to be there to assist them in any way possible. You have to be able to do that in order to be a good teacher. There are so many things that influence the kids' lives that you need to be aware of and to be as of much help to them as you possibly can (F, 45, Elementary, Urban).

I am an *iron butterfly*. Strong but with the sensitivity to flit from flower to flower and draw out what is needed in it. But yet very organized and structured and strong (F, 35, Elementary, Urban).

Furthermore, through this dichotomy we can understand that "the potter" is less an artistic metaphor and more a figure of strength and guidance; we have a greater sense of her power and far less understanding of the students—the unformed, somewhat lifeless class. Nonetheless, it is perhaps the image of the "iron butterfly" that epitomizes the teachers who want to make an impact on students' lives. These teachers describe themselves as sensitively attuned to students' needs as individuals, but they represent themselves in the active role of leadership. The "iron butterfly" may flit from student to student, but she is not a "light breeze." She characterized her classroom as a "democratic dictatorship" in which she responds to her students but "has the last word." The mother, the father, the helper, and the iron butterfly care passionately about their students and believe, as teachers, they know what is best for them. The parent metaphor may describe the sensitivity and friendship that these teachers offer students, but ultimately, the teacher is the all-knower, the powerful adult who must save students from themselves.

## Memories

Where, we must ask, do these metaphors come from? We tried to answer this question by asking the teachers to remember their images of their own teachers and of themselves before and at the time they themselves became teachers.

All teachers have themselves been pupils. Throughout their many years of schooling, they have formed images of teachers and teaching. Once the students move to the other side of the desk as teachers, the image they formed as students is one of the most powerful influences on their assumptions about teaching. Teacher candidates establish a "teacher role identity" based on former teachers, childhood events, and former teaching experiences (Crow, 1987). The influence of past perceptions of teachers is twofold: (1) their decision to enter the occupation and (2) the manner in which future teachers assimilate intuitive and taken-for-granted assumptions about teaching (Lortie, 1975). In addition, we suggest that the memories of former experiences may indeed influence to some extent the way schoolteachers teach.

Many of the twenty-six teachers in our study described their former teachers with warmth and respect:

> Most of my teachers I really liked. I saw them as friendly, warm people . . . intelligent, interested in me as a person. There were pleasant relationships (F, 53, Junior High, Suburban).

> I was always fascinated by teachers. I wanted to be a teacher. I thought it was neat, the way they had so many kids looking up to them. They just seemed to know how to handle everything. They always knew the right thing to say and do (F, 24, Elementary, Suburban).

For some, this respect bordered on awe of the all-powerful, all-knowing figure.

> I went to a parochial school. The teachers were nuns. I saw them as bigger than life, invisible, invulnerable, all-seeing, all-knowing, very much in control in every situation (F, 42, Elementary, Urban).

Among our interviewees, only a few teachers held what they considered to be unpleasant recollections about schooling and teachers.

> I was in awe of teachers. I went to a public school in a very small rural community. We were thirteen in my class up to eighth grade. I was intimidated by my teachers. I was very afraid of some of them, because I considered them to be very powerful. I thought my role was to do what they expected all the time, knowing that the consequences would not be pleasant if I did not meet their expectations. They tried, I believe, to mold my mind (F, 44, Elementary, Small Town).

> I didn't like school at all. I felt teachers were cold. I didn't feel that they were people I could ever approach—not in an academic nor in a personal way. I felt put off by many teachers. I was not a bright student at all, and many times I could feel the frustrations of the teacher. That had to do a lot with my feelings toward school. That is why I disliked it so much (F, 27, Elementary, Suburban).

The interviews suggest that, although the former teachers' ability to influence students and to appear competent did seem attractive to many of the interviewed teachers, those with uncompassionate or strict "all-powerful" former teachers entered teaching themselves in order to provide wonderful school experiences for students. Most interviewees, however, found that their memories about teachers were characterized by respect and warmth as well as appreciation of how teachers could influence and control their classes. They told us that their own attraction to the teaching occupation was influenced by these memories.

Self-image also becomes constructed from memories of themselves as beginning teachers—their motivations and hopes. How did these school-teachers remember themselves when they first decided to become teachers? How did they imagine the teaching profession? The interviewees' answers can be divided into two major categories. First, they believed that teaching would be a fun, happy job that would provide stimulation and spontaneity through working with children or adolescents:

> I wanted to do fun things with kids. I wanted learning to be a great experience in which everything is new and unexpected. All my life I knew that I was going to be a teacher, and I looked forward to the day when I would teach my own class (F, 33, Elementary, Urban).

Second, they saw that teaching could make an impact on the lives of the students and thus, ultimately, would allow the teacher to make a contribution to society.

> I wanted to make a difference in my own way. I wanted to let them see that a teacher doesn't necessarily have to be one that stands at the chalk board all the time, one that is human as well. I have seen a little bit of both since I have been teaching. I wanted to let them know how much I care (F, 40, Elementary, Urban).

A few teachers also entered the profession because of their love of subject matter or because they learned that they had teaching or leadership ability. A few mentioned that their career choice was influenced by the summer vacations that teaching provides, although the schedule was not their primary motivation.

Their self-expectations had to be modified because of the challenges of reality once they stepped into their own classrooms. All of the teachers in our study expressed the discrepancy between the image they had of what teaching would be like and what they eventually experienced in the classroom. Only two teachers described the first year as a "dream come true." The rest talked about the "harsh awakening." The awakening included their disillusionment about students' eagerness to study or about their own ability to excite and influence their pupils.

> I saw myself as someone who would make everybody absolutely love reading as much as I do. "Oh," I thought, "They will be so thrilled to read all these wonderful books and poetry." I had a very rude awakening. It was a disaster! The students weren't anything like I thought they would be. Instead of "Oh, it's great to be here!" they went, "Do we have to be here? Why do we have to do this? These are such boring stories." That just devastated me to think that they would not like it.

It was so upsetting to me that they didn't like what I like, so I went to second grade (F, 50, Junior High, Suburban).

I expected every child to be excited by everything that I had to tell them. I expected them to react to me in a positive way. I expected to see their little eyes light up and their little brains increase. I was disappointed, and still am, that children are not as excitable as I thought or felt they should be. I don't see them reacting to a lot of things. I think that they are numbed by just being placid. At times I feel like I am a television set. You wave your hands and say: "React!" I don't care, I don't care if it's bad, I don't care if it is good, I want to see something. That's my biggest frustration (F, 44, Elementary, Small Town).

These teachers did not expect that the demands of the profession would be as great as they turned out to be. Research suggests that many new teachers say that teaching was more difficult than expected; they found their tasks harder and more taxing than anticipated (Lortie, 1975).

I didn't think it was nearly as difficult as it is. I didn't realize the amount of preparation that was needed nor did I realize the amount of emotional stress that is involved in teaching. Never did I realize how involved emotionally you become with the students. In my first year teaching when the students didn't get something that I was hoping they would get, or when I saw them emotionally distressed about something and there was nothing I could do about it. . . . that was so frustrating. That was something I didn't expect when I was going into teaching (F, 24, Elementary, Suburban).

Their formal training, some teachers asserted, was inadequate by itself to meet the actual challenges faced in the classroom. They had to focus on the needs of the children in their own class and find for themselves the meaning of being a teacher. They felt that they had to rely on themselves for survival and success.

After college, where you had all these method courses that told you that you do a little motivation skit for the students and then they'll learn. At first you feel very disappointed and you feel very unprepared. But then common sense takes over and you realize, "I do have skills behind me. I can use those and my common sense to make things work." After a while you do find out the things that get results and those that don't. You use elimination. At first when I came out I was disappointed because it was not as the book said it was going to be. Because the first job I had was on the west side of Chicago and the books didn't prepare me for any of that. Nothing whatsoever. They didn't prepare me for kids putting rocks in your car, none of that. You just thought it is going to be utopia when you came out to teach. It isn't that way (F, 45, Elementary, Urban).

My first year was a disaster, because I was put in one of the worst eighth-grade classes that the school had ever encountered. As a result of that, I ended up with a group of kids who actually challenged me to a duel. I was only 21 and actually looked younger than many of those eighth-graders. They refused to accept this young guy as a teacher (M, 32, Elementary, Urban).

Whether the discrepancy between expectations and reality is as dramatic as many teachers report has not been verified by research. The hardship of the first two years may represent a kind of investment, a dividend to achieve the successful conquest of the challenges presented by classes, pupils, or circumstances (Woods, 1979). Perhaps teachers almost have a need to believe in the "baptism by fire" myth as a means of sustaining their "craft pride." Hardships "are like battle-scars to be shown as evidence of how tough it was and how much professional honor is due to them for finally emerging victorious" (Cole, 1985, p. 98).

The schoolteachers had to make sense of the experiences of the first years by generating new images of teachers and teaching. Certain "critical incidents," the key events within the first eighteen months of teaching, represent one of the crucial phases within one's career as a teacher. These "critical incidents" create a challenge about one's self-image and identity as a "proper teacher." "As a result of the challenges some of these claims are dropped, others are made real. Some that become parts of the identity are confirmed, others are renounced" (Measor, 1985, p. 75).

The memories teachers have of their own school experiences and the expectations they held when entering the profession seem to provide the foundation for the self-metaphors they hold. It appears that metaphor weds the teachers' practical present experience with these memories and expectations they have brought with them to the present day. The metaphors that the teachers used to describe themselves as professionals reflect neither the harsh "awakening" of the early experiences nor their disillusionment. The majority of teacher-generated metaphors reveal teacher as artist or teacher as parent, demonstrating their sense of creative powers and strong presence of self.

## Teachers' Image in the Eyes of the Students

Do the metaphors of self stem from students' reactions to the teachers? On one hand, when asked about the most rewarding part of their profession, all the teachers who participated in this research talked about the feeling of satisfaction they derive from interaction with their students, especially when small recognitions of thanks and appreciation are given. They talked about feeling good when the students learn and improve. Some concentrated on the entire class, whereas others focused on individual students and how they could affect their students' lives. On the other hand, when asked how they imagine their students' perception of themselves as teachers, they expressed little sentimentality; dismal and even ugly images emerged.

Only the kindergarten and primary grade teachers imagine that they enjoyed the unreserved affection of their students:

> At my students' age, they love teachers. They almost see them as mothers. Quite often when they talk to me while they are relaxed they'll call me "Mom" or "mother" and they'll say, "I am sorry." But I'll tell them, "That's OK because you are with me five hours a day. I can understand that." So in the first three levels, they see you as someone to comfort them and to be of help (F, 45, Elementary, Urban).

As children grow older this unquestionable love turns into a more complex attitude toward school in general and teachers in particular. As one of the kindergarten teachers said,

> The little ones love the teachers. They love me. Between 9 and 18 we lose something there. It starts in elementary school, in fourth or fifth grade. They start to get the "school hate" feeling about that time. I don't know how to explain it (F, 44, Elementary, Urban).

Some of the teachers believed that their students have different images of teachers depending on the teachers' personalities and style of teaching.

> It really depends on the personality of the teacher. Some are *The Teacher*. You don't think of them in any other terms. They are serious in their job, demand respect, are very formal. Others are pals. They are good teachers, but still they are friendly. Kids can talk with them freely on every subject in the world, but still they expect learning and behavior in the class. Another kind of teacher is someone who loses all sense of control over students. The kids do whatever they want in the class and "it ain't learning. . . ." So it really depends on the personality of the teacher (F, 26, Junior High, Suburban).

> I am judged many times on the amount of work that my course requires. That's how students quickly sum you up: How much work is required. Another way they do it is by the "cool scale," how cool you are. Are you someone that is in tune with them as teenagers? The third way, how much respect you show them, how do you treat them in the classroom? There is a big difference in class when a student does not bring something and you scream at him and yell in front of the whole class, or whether you ask him to see you after class and you talk it over with him. That is a big difference and they judge you on that (M, 28, High School, Suburban).

Others recognized with regret that students saw the interrelation between students and teachers as "us against them." When asked for their images in the eyes of the students, these various depictions were revealed: disciplinarians, order-givers, uncaring, necessary evil, or, as one teacher described it:

> A person who is consistently telling you, "Work! work!" . . . Paper work constantly and a person who ignores the other parts of your life. Somebody standing there and giving instructions (F, 40, Elementary, Urban).

Teachers explained this perception in several ways. Some saw this negative image as being "owned" only by the failing students and not by the successful ones.

> Many students see the teachers as being on an ego trip for power and control. They think that they are baby sitters. Other students, who do well in school, look at teachers as role models, they appreciate their efforts. They respect their knowledge. And there are a lot of students who have no feelings one way or the other (F, 44, High School, Small Town).

White teachers who work in mostly minority urban schools imagined students' feelings of estrangement.

> I think they see the teachers living outside of their own personal world, kind of separated. My students are black and most of their teachers are white. I feel that we are as foreign to them as they are foreign to us. And there is not that crossover. They think that in our eyes, "we know it all" but yet we couldn't make it on their street (F, 42, Elementary, Urban).

Feelings of estrangement also exist in situations in which teachers shared the racial or social-economic background of the students. Many of the teachers in the study report that students view teachers as enemies. The teachers attribute their deteriorating images and loss of prestige and appreciation in part to the attitude toward authority at large.

> The teachers are authority figures and they [students] resent it. They see you as a surrogate parent, and they don't respect their own parents either. We just take over where the parents leave off—with the mouthiness, and the disrespect (F, 50, Junior High, Suburban).

The issue, explains one teacher, is not just students' response to the teaching profession.

> I don't know if it is just the image of teachers or the image of authority in general. I don't think there is much respect for police officers, or any other job where somebody is in charge. Too much

questioning of authority, too much of a feeling of "free will." On the other hand, it is not so bad. Our country is based on having free will. But we also must have laws. There is too much of the care-free attitude. It hurts education (M, 32, Elementary, Small Town).

But the negative attitudes of students may change over time as hard work and growth become appreciated.

What is the image of the teacher in the eyes of the students? In their eyes I am a witch. They think I am too strict. They are scared of me being their teacher. That is during the school year. But after the end of the year and in the following years, they appreciate what I have given them: discipline and learning habits (F, 33, Elementary, Urban).

These interviews suggest that many of these teachers would rather wait for their eventual reward—the appreciation from the mature student who later comes to have high regard for the teacher's efforts. Rather than caring about immediate popularity, the interviewees seem to respect their own visions about teaching and find satisfaction when their students ultimately understand their aspirations. For example, they experience deep gratification when students come back to school after several or many years and tell them that now their teacher efforts make sense—that the teachers have been a powerful influence.

Recent research states that teaching is a client-centered occupation and that students become a potent influence in shaping and reinforcing teachers' values and actions (Nias, 1985). These studies also report that the greatest satisfaction for a teacher may be the feeling of being rewarded by one's students. "Isolated in their classrooms, teachers receive feedback for their efforts from the words, expressions, behavior, and suggestions of the students" (Lieberman & Miller, 1984, p. 2). However, the discrepancy between teachers' metaphors of self and their imagined perspectives of students makes clear that the greatest reward of teaching may be the teachers' intrinsic satisfaction of knowing that they are working to accomplish their own essential goals.

## Through Parents' Eyes

As in the case of the students, there is little sense of the teachers' artistry and power when they picture images that parents have of them. The teachers interviewed here interpreted their interactions with parents as being different and more complex than the potentially ideal model in which teachers and parents view each other as working cooperatively in a shared understanding and team effort toward achievable goals (Epstein, 1987;

Rosenholtz, 1989). The teachers speculated that differences among the various images held by parents stem from teachers' perceptions of their communities and the previous school experiences of adults.

Most of the schoolteachers who felt that parents support the teachers and are involved in their children's learning work in what they perceive as affluent communities. They commented:

> Parents really support the teachers in this school. It is expressed in their volunteering for every special event (M, 30, Elementary, Suburban).

> What I say to the parent holds weight. In this community they respect education (F, 27, Elementary, Suburban).

At the same time, parents in affluent communities seem to expect too much from their children and put too much pressure on them.

> Parents are very involved with the teaching process here. There are some absurd concerns that a bad first or second year is going to ruin their child's chances for Harvard (M, 24, Elementary, Suburban).

However, some teachers feel somewhat threatened by parents who call the teacher's authority into question because of their higher social status.

> I am teaching in a community that is rather affluent. Most of my parents, both of them, have a degree. Many are former teachers; many have excellent positions in companies. They don't put teachers on a pedestal. They see themselves definitely equal if not better than the teachers in educational background, etc. Instead of accepting what the teacher says, they want to argue about it, and have their input in every decision that you are making (F, 50, Junior High, Suburban).

A few teachers working in less affluent communities thought that the parents' view of teachers was a direct result of the specific quality of each teacher:

> First and foremost how much you help their child. If you are someone who sets high standards and lets the kid just hang there without help. . . . parents are very negative about that. But if you make the effort to help the child and communicate with the parents, they are very receptive (M, 28, High School, Suburban).

Often these teachers pointed to their loss of prestige, authority, and power. They attribute this loss not only to criticism from parents, but also to parents' lack of support for teachers when children misbehave in school.

> Today there is not so much respect, especially not from parents. There is not as much support at home. When I was young and there was a problem at school, my parents would deal with me. Now the

> parents call the teacher. . . . trying to find out what the teacher did
> that was wrong, not what their child did . . . trying to point the
> finger at the teacher (M, 32, Elementary, Small Town).

This lack of respect for teachers' expertise provokes frustration when, despite their years of experience, their educational recommendations are received with suspicion or even outright rejection.

> Today the frustrations that I have are caused by the lack of parental
> interest and support and sometimes lack of respect. I tell the parents "I really feel that the child needs another year to grow, to go to
> developmental first grade." They will say "No, no." They reject the
> proposal. Wouldn't they accept my professional opinion if I was a
> businessman or an accountant? They don't trust us, they don't value
> our advice. That's hard. It does not seem that they trust us that we
> know what we are doing. It is a poor public image. Some feel "they
> are silly to teach, they could make more money doing something
> else. They are not important members of society." Maybe some had
> poor teachers, or cruel teachers in the past that color their perception (F, 44, Elementary, Small Town).

The parent-teacher relationship often seems fraught with tension. Some teachers attribute the strain between parents and teachers to parents' fears that the teacher is a competitor for their child's attention and devotion.

> I think that they see teachers as a threat. They think that teachers
> have far more influence over their children than they want the
> teachers to have. Sometimes they resent them, because they feel
> that they don't see that part of the child (F, 44, Elementary, Small
> Town).

Others explain the tension as a reflection of the parent's personal experiences as a student.

> Depends on their experiences. Many parents live their life through
> their kids' experiences. If they were frustrated with their school
> experiences, they see an opportunity "to right some wrongs" (M, 29,
> High School, Small Town).

Teachers who work in impoverished urban areas regard the parents' rejection of teachers as estrangement because teachers do not live in the community and because the parents have unhappy memories or feelings about schooling.

> Parents think that we don't understand their community and their
> needs. They are afraid of us in many respects and they are intimidated by us because many of them didn't have successful school
> experiences (F, 42, Elementary, Urban).

Others associate this resentment with feelings of fear and inferiority which the parents feel toward the teachers.

> They see us as a threat. They are threatened by a lack of education. They respond in two ways: either they fight with us or they are very offensive. They say, "You don't have a right. Why did you do this or that?" Or they are very passive because they fear they can't compete with what you can say. I don't really think it is respect. It is fear or envy or they end up feeling inferior (F, 36, High School, Urban).

A glimpse of the complexity of the parents' perceived attitude was given by a teacher who was frustrated because of parents' irresponsibility.

> "It is your job, don't bother me." No matter what discipline and scholastic problems I have with their children, they don't want to know. It is my job, in their eyes, to solve all their children's problems. They don't want to be called or bothered by it (F, 42, Elementary, Urban).

And yet, the same teacher felt that she needed to involve parents in their children's education, and so she organized a "homeroom club" for parents.

> I had a very special homeroom club for parents this past year, where parents and children came together to class once a week and worked together. That core group of parents thought it was the best thing that ever happened to them. They imagined me as someone very helpful and generous (F, 42, Elementary, Urban).

When we compared the teachers' memories of their own parents and childhood experiences, we saw clearly the incongruity between memories and current situations. Memories reveal that the parents of the teachers thought of teaching as an esteemed occupation; they respected teachers and insisted that their children do likewise. The interviews, however, demonstrate threat and conflict. Today, these teachers must "win" the respect of the parents; it is not given gladly.

Conversely, the teachers have little respect for the parents. They criticize parents for failing to discipline and to give good moral values, for not valuing education and thus producing unmotivated students, for disrespecting the teaching profession and passing along this disrespect to their children. Indeed, if they defined themselves through the parents' eyes, it is doubtful that these schoolteachers would find much joy or satisfaction from their profession.

## Through Administrators' Eyes

Research indicates that the relationship between teachers and principals, and in particular, the attitude of the principal toward the teacher's role, is of paramount importance in a teacher's work life (Lieberman & Miller, 1984). In many ways, principals shape the organizational conditions under which teachers work. The image of their roles as teachers in the eyes of the principals may explain, in many instances, their realization of reward or frustration from their profession.

In most instances, the teachers we interviewed for this research work for different principals. The teachers carry their own personal experiences of day-to-day interpersonal relationships with individual administrators, and yet, the interviewees basically generated four images that they believed all principals have of teachers.

The first image is that of "pawns in a game," a game "we don't even know that is being played" (F, 36, High School, Urban). Teachers who raised the pawn image felt they were tools used by administrators to advance their own careers.

> Our administrators see us as a group of people who can help them to achieve their goals; I can do my job without them. They have an agenda that often comes from the school board and they turn to the teachers to carry it out. But I don't find in many of them that their motive is to make a better school or a better community. They want to advance, they want to move up. I find it very distasteful. I find many of them want to move out to a different school, to a better position. Many of them are really not interested in helping teachers or students. They are interested in helping themselves (M, 28, High School, Suburban).

As part of this political game, teachers perceive the contradiction between the image of teachers as presented by the administrator to the public and their real attitude toward the teachers.

> Whenever they are in public and are speaking about teachers they are very positive. "We have the best teaching staff in the state." "Our teachers are committed." They always boost your ego at the beginning of the year. Whenever they try to sell a referendum in the paper they praise the teachers. They like the public to think that they are very supportive of their teachers and that they picked the best to be in their school. I've known some teachers who in times of trouble don't get any support from the same administrators. But of course there are individual administrators who behave differently (F, 44, High School, Small Town).

The second image that these teachers believe that administrators have of them is that of "loyal soldiers"; this means "doing the administrator's bidding, putting their plans into action" (M, 44, High School, Rural). This image projects powerless teachers, who are limited in their ability to assert control or influence in the work setting. The interviewees postulate that their inability to influence decisions affects the school environment.

> The administration does not understand these children's needs. I
> think there should be a lot more give-and-take between the adminis-
> tration and teachers. The administration is not in the classroom
> and they don't realize all the things we have to deal with. We get
> such a variety of students, in so many different situations; if they
> could just come in and understand a little bit better what we deal
> with each day, maybe some of the curriculum wouldn't be pushed
> onto us and the state tests wouldn't be given so often. The curricu-
> lum comes as a decree from the administration. They buy curricu-
> lum programs, they jump on bandwagons and we have to follow
> suit. We have to follow their curriculum and plans whether we
> agree or not because we don't get much input into the process. We
> should have a chance to choose too, or see what is in this curricu-
> lum, and to ask questions before it is thrown to the classroom. We
> are handed the curriculum and are told, "Here is what you are going
> to do next year" (F, 50, Elementary, Urban).

This frustration intensifies when teachers perceive that their administrators have no sense of what is happening in their classrooms.

> The farther they are removed from the classroom the poorer their
> perception of teachers. The longer they are administrators, or if
> they have never been in the classroom, the less they know what is
> going on there. Most of them have been teachers at some point, but
> the longer you are out of the classroom, the harder it is to remember
> what it is like there. So I think that their expectations are out of
> focus (F, 42, Elementary, Small Town).

A more positive image rendered in many interviews is that of the "competent professional." In talking about this image, these teachers assumed
that principals who select their own staff trust their teachers and respect
their skills.

> Administrators want the teachers in their school to be the best. And
> they scout for the best. The administrators respect the teachers
> because they hired the teachers. My experience has been with ad-
> ministrators who are open-minded; they say, "this is the guideline;
> go ahead and just follow the outline. You fill in the missing spots"
> (F, 24, Elementary, Suburban).

As "competent professionals," the teachers have a high level of work autonomy and serve as their own judges in what should be done in their classrooms, particularly in making decisions about curriculum. The teachers
appreciate this autonomy.

Still, some teachers believe that the administrators need to provide
more guidance and direction for their work activities.

> In my school we have a say in what we are going to teach and how to
> teach it. We pretty much have a free hand. For example, this year

> with my language class, I changed it to a writing workshop. I had no
> problem with the administration. I feel powerful in my school, in
> some ways too powerful. Our administrator likes to delegate every-
> thing to a point of frustration. Whatever you ask, she would say
> "Fine, you handle everything." When you are a busy teacher you
> don't want the responsibility. You want her to take care of it (F, 50,
> Junior High, Suburban).

The highest level of feeling good and confident about one's own work
was found among those teachers who perceived their image in the eyes of
their administrators to be that of a "colleague."

> We have a collegial relationship. Teachers and administrators have
> common goals; you can't separate their roles. We are here for the
> kids. These kinds of feelings are fostered here (M, 24, Elementary,
> Suburban).

Or, as elaborately described by another teacher from the same school district,

> The principal definitely feels respect for teachers. The teachers see
> the kids, they know the development process. The administrators
> see the potential strength of the teachers. There is a lot of input the
> teachers need to have in order to make those daily, local decisions.
> In fact, that is the process we are doing right now in this school and
> in this district. There is a lot of teacher input in what goes on, from
> curriculum to schedule and everything else that is included in a
> school day. Things are happening here, not because the principal
> says so or wants it that way, but because the teachers and the staff
> met together and came up with what they believe is best for the
> school. Each school in the district has its own school council build-
> ing. The principal is actively involved in the decision-making, but
> there is a very definite trend toward more teacher input and parent
> input. The Board of Education has changed his [the principal's] role.
> But that is his style anyway. His leadership style is to delegate—to
> allow to a lot of teachers input rather than dictating what should be
> done in the school (M, 30, Elementary, Suburban).

The four teacher images that these teachers attribute to administrators
(pawns, loyal soldiers, competent professionals, and colleagues) suggest that
administrators' specific behaviors and attitudes as well as their expectations of teachers contribute to these teachers' sense of professional compe-
tence; the administrators who facilitate the teachers' professional goals are
the ones they respect. Clearly, shared decision-making and collegial relationships make the difference as to whether or not teachers imagine themselves
in their schools as strong and empowered professionals or as puppets in a
cynical kind of "educational" game. But there is little evidence to suggest

that they feel like "puppets" or "pawns" in their classrooms. First and foremost, "We are here for the kids" is a motivation and vision that pervades the interviewees' cognizance of their own teaching.

---

## Conclusions

Through these articulations of beliefs and conceptions we have learned that only by asking teachers to speak for themselves can we know how they make sense of their work and how they construct images through interactions with the school community and through day-to-day experiences in the classroom. The teachers interviewed spoke frankly and thoughtfully. They were reflective, raising and refining questions and expressing misgivings about their public and personal images.

The metaphors and images they revealed described their joys and sorrows, expectations and frustrations, and the rewards and stresses of their professional experiences. Their work does not come easy, despite their hopes and enthusiasm. The metaphors and images this study depicts reveal the struggle that teachers experience as they shape their relationships with students as well as the contradictions they realize as they contemplate how students, parents, and administrators perceive their work. Furthermore, self-image comes as a response to a tension, the balancing act between various competing goals—power and engendering, creativity and control, activity and passivity. It is within this intricacy of images that teachers live and work.

We have searched for the social construction of teacher metaphors and found that this study portrays professionals who rely on their own sense of themselves and their beliefs about teaching for their self-definition. The metaphors teachers use for themselves seem to emerge from their memories of their own love and respect for schooling—for teachers who were powerful and stimulating—and from their own parents who believed in the nobility, or at the very least, the authority of the teaching profession. Ultimately, we understand their metaphors as each teacher's personal investment in caring for children and young people.

The mirror into which the teachers look to generate self-image obstructs discouraging or disillusioning reflections. Their sense of self appears firmly embedded in their own sense of competency and their belief in the possibilities manifest in the profession of teaching.

## NOTE

1. Interviews were conducted during the spring term of 1990 with graduate students studying for a master's in education—curriculum and instruction—in the

Graduate Field-Based Program Master of Education at National-Louis University. The interviews were one component of a study focusing on teachers' perceptions of themselves as moral agents in which cohorts of field-based students (approximately fifteen in each cohort) participated in a discussion about moral values and then answered a questionnaire about their understanding of their roles as moral educators. A total of 180 teachers (graduate students) completed questionnaires.

The interviewees were selected because they were representative of the population (180) who filled out the questionnaire; thus, age, gender, type of community, race, and opinions on the questionnaire were factors in the selection process, as was the questionnaire respondents' willingness to verbalize their ideas in the comment section provided on the questionnaires. Twenty-six teachers were interviewed within several months after they had participated in the class and the questionnaire.

Semistructured interviews were used to collect data. These interviews were 45 to 90 minutes long and were tape-recorded (audio) and transcribed verbatim for analysis. Interview protocols were followed, although some questions were inserted, changed, or omitted in order to preserve the conversational tone of the interviews by trying to accommodate the unique characteristics of the interviewees.

The separate focuses of the interviews were, first, the metaphors given to the teachers (by themselves and others) and, second, their characterizations of themselves as moral educators. We chose these focuses because of our strong research interests in both themes; we kept our thinking and writing about these themes somewhat separate because of the scale and complexity of both. At this point, no formal attempt has been made to correlate the responses in the two categories, but it is our informal understanding that the teachers who saw themselves more directly as moral educators construed metaphors of themselves as teachers in active leadership roles.

We characterize the analysis of the interview data as an example of grounded theory. Bogdan and Biklen (1982) note that grounded theory allows conclusions to emerge from the bottom up, from distinct pieces of collected evidence that are interconnected. Therefore, we read and studied the interviews by reading the words and sentences of the teachers and allowing themes or ideas to emerge rather than looking for validation of hypotheses. The data were examined, and the interviews were compared in a constant search for connections, oppositions, and repetitions and the development of ideas within each interview and among all the interviews. We organized the data according to a three-coded framework: answers to direct questions, themes that emerged in the form of recurring images or descriptions, and actual metaphors used by the teachers. Glaser and Strauss (1967) refer to such data organization as the constant comparative method: categories are generated, common themes emerge, and relationships and similarities become clear.

## REFERENCES

Abbs, P. (1981). Education and the living image: Reflections on imagery, fantasy, and the art of recognition. *Teachers College Record, 82*(3), 474–496.

Abbs, P. (1979). *Reclamations*. London: Heinemann Educational Books.

Ball, D. (1972). Self and identity in the context of deviance: The case of criminal abortion. In R. Scott & J. Douglas (Eds.), *Theoretical perspectives on deviance* (pp. 158–186). New York: Basic Books.

Bogdan, R. C. & Biklen, S. K. (1982). *Qualitative research for education: An introduction to theory and methods*. Boston: Allyn & Bacon.

Bowers, C. A. (1980). Curriculum as cultural reproduction: An examination of metaphor as a carrier of ideology. *Teachers College Record, 82*(2), 267–289.

Cole, M. (1985). "The tender trap?" Commitment and consciousness in entrants to teaching. In S. J. Ball & I. F. Goodson (Eds.), *Teachers' lives and careers* (pp. 89–104). London: Falmer Press.

Cooley, C. H. (1902/1983). *Human nature and the social order*. New Brunswick, NJ: Transaction Books.

Crow, N. M. (1987). Preservice teachers' biography: A case study. Paper presented at the annual meeting of the American Educational Research Association, Washington, DC.

Eisner, E. W. (1985). *The educational imagination*. New York: Macmillan Publishing Company.

Epstein, J. L. (1987). Parent involvement: What research says to administrators. *Education and Urban Society, 19*, 119–136.

Glaser, B. G. & Strauss, A. L. (1967). *The discovery of grounded theory: Strategies for qualitative research*. Chicago: Aldine.

Lieberman, A. & Miller, L. (1984). *Teachers, their world and their work*. Alexandria, VA: ASCD.

Lortie, D. (1975). *Schoolteacher: A sociological study*. Chicago: University of Chicago Press.

Mead, G. (1934). *Mind, self and society*. Chicago: University of Chicago Press.

Measor, L. (1985). Critical incidents in the classroom: Identities, choices and careers. In S. J. Ball & I. F. Goodson (Eds.), *Teachers' lives and careers*. London: Falmer Press, pp. 61–77.

Nias, J. (1985), Reference groups in primary teaching: Talking, listening and identity. In S. J. Ball & I. F. Goodson (Eds.), *Teachers' lives and careers*. London: Falmer Press, pp. 105–119.

Provenzo, E. F., McCloskey, G. N., Kottkamp, R. B. & Cohn, M. M. (1989). Metaphor and meaning in the language of teachers. *Teachers College Record 90* (4), 551–573.

Pugh, S. L., Hicks, J. W., Davis, M. & Venstra, T. 1992. *Bridging: A teacher's guide to metaphorical thinking*. National Council of Teachers of English, Urbana, IL. ERIC Clearinghouse on Reading and Communication Skills No. ED341 985.

Ricoeur, P. (1977). *The rule of metaphor: Multi-disciplinary studies of the creation of meaning in language*. (R. Czerny et al., Trans.). Toronto: University of Toronto Press.

Rosenholtz, S. J. (1989). *Teachers' workplace: The social organization of schools*. New York: Longman.

Thomas, J. (1980). *The self in education*. Slough: NFER/ Nelson.

Woods, P. (1979). *The divided school*. London: Routledge & Kegan Paul.

# 4

# Across the Generations

## Conversations with Retired Teachers

David Hobson

L eaving the university campus behind, I often head out to work with one of several groups of classroom teachers in their school buildings in the so-called field. These teachers are experienced professionals who spend four hours one day after school each week with me, a university professor, and fifteen of their colleagues during our two-year master of education program in curriculum and instruction.

The teachers and I talk together, share practice, and wonder out loud about what to do with many of the real issues facing us in our everyday teaching lives. Rather than the more usual "listening to experts" approach that seems to characterize so much of teacher education, we seem to be most open to the teachings and wonderings of our colleagues. We listen closely to the stories that seem to come from an experience base that we all recognize. We give each other a hearing; we offer each other empathy and help.

Consequently, when the editors of this text told me they were conceiving a book around the question, "What does it mean to be a teacher?"—and that they wanted to produce a book that involved a collaboration between many persons and perspectives—I thought immediately that I would like to collaborate with the thirty-two classroom teachers with whom I work. Since many teachers would be reading this text, it seemed especially meaningful to actively involve teachers in the process of its construction, and to invite them to take part in conceiving, conducting, and consuming research about education.

It was important to me to find a way to be guided as much as possible by the teachers with whom I have been working. I wanted to try to decrease my own influence on exactly how we would proceed, on what specific questions we would ask, on precisely how the interviews would be conducted. Eventually, as I participated in dozens of discussions about all these issues, I tried to abstain from judging the various ideas that surfaced and to affirm the possibility that each person might proceed in the way he or she thought best. Throughout the process, I reiterated the idea that I thought it important that we (as experienced teachers with eyes and ears well tuned by many years of working with children in classroom settings) take seriously our own good judgment about what was significant, proceeding with diminished dependence on me (the university professor) as an expert. Here are some of the decisions we reached:

We would talk with retiring teachers. Who better than persons like ourselves, but even more experienced and presumably wise, to talk with about what it means to be a teacher? How better to gather insights informed by long years of classroom experience?

We decided to leave the specific lines of inquiry in each of the interviewer's own capable hands. Why not make this a collaborative and exploratory investigation? We would see where it would lead.

Interviewers generated a list of the questions they found interesting. Next we formed small groups of six and brainstormed some more. Then we shared what we had generated in groups of sixteen. We were not, of course, unschooled: Between ourselves, we had about five hundred years of teaching experience!

Next, with my guidance, we broke down into triads and conducted some interviews, role playing with one another. For about thirty minutes, one person interviewed; the second person responded; and the third person attempted to record. Then, another round began and we reversed roles. Finally, in a third round, we reversed again. At the end of the session, we talked about the interviewing experience we had just enacted.

Some interviewers had asked just one or two questions and followed the intriguing path that the respondent took. Others asked numerous questions, also to good effect. Some interviewees felt they had enjoyed a very satisfying hearing, while others confessed to having felt manipulated and heard not at all. Nearly all agreed that taking notes was next to impossible; we would use tape recorders all around. Much food for thought was generated that afternoon.

Over the next several months, each of the classroom teachers in my groups conducted an interview with a retired teacher. The interviewers then wrote reactions to the sessions they conducted. We exchanged tapes among ourselves and wrote further responses to interviews conducted by colleagues. Finally, I listened to the tapes and made transcripts of the conversations. I wondered and pondered. I wrote a draft chapter. Some excerpts were shared with an additional group of classroom teachers, and the ensuing discussion was transcribed. Finally, a later draft was put in the hands of the entire group of teacher-researchers with the invitation to respond in writing. Further collaborative analysis, conducted in small groups in the way of

Van Manen (1990), ensued. Using all these materials, I sat down to write again.

Much of the pleasure of this investigation lies in the collaborative aspect I have been sharing with my colleagues. Sharing the process of conceiving this work, sharing drafts as they have come along, and sharing discussions of what all this material might mean with my teacher-researcher colleagues has been a most satisfying aspect of the project.

Without doubt, this writing is primarily mine. For all my efforts to involve classroom teachers in the design and implementation of this interview project and despite all the writings in response which many individuals penned along the way, the two central facts remain that (1) I am the university instructor and as such have had a powerful influence throughout and (2) I did the actual writing. Still, this is an intentional collaboration. For all its limitations, this is a deliberate effort to amplify the wonderings of thirty-two classroom teachers in conversation with a like number of retired teachers. It is my hope that the participation of many teachers in the ways I've described will help this work strike a more responsive chord than had I done it alone.

This chapter centers on the oral histories of thirty-two retired teachers identified from personal and professional networks of acquaintances and interviewed by an equal number of midcareer teachers. All of the participating teachers were white, middle class, and suburban—as were the retired teachers. All but two of the interviewers and interviewees were female. Most of the retired teachers were in their sixties and seventies, a few were in their eighties, and one was 92.

What follows is a rendering of these teacher-to-teacher interviews, with statements from the retired teachers' recollections serving as frameworks for discussion. As we looked more closely at the experiences and perceptions of retired teachers, we contemporary teachers constructed meanings and pondered questions about the images retired teachers have of themselves and their profession, reflecting on the question, "What does it mean to be a teacher?"

## "Teaching One Grade Was a Cinch!"

While listening to the tapes, I often burst out with appreciative laughter over the sense of genuine amazement that filled some teachers' voices as they talked with the old timers. It wasn't that the information they were learning was so surprising, because stories of one-room schoolhouses, of being unable to teach if you were married, and of having to carry in wood for the fire are familiar to teachers who have perused history of education texts. It was more a feeling of incredulity that this very person with whom one was conversing and laughing and meeting in real human terms had actually been there. This was not ancient history! These stories were within the experience of this older woman, a retired teacher who was not so different from the interviewer. It was a heartwarming experience for me when I heard the genuine respect that persons from each group expressed for each other.

Two generations of classroom teachers met in these conversations. For example, one present-day teacher, upon hearing about the one-room school-house, put it this way: *"It seems incredible to me that just one person was responsible for so many children while doing eight different things at the same time. Do you ever look back and wonder how you ever did it?"* (The voices of the contemporary teachers—the interviewers—will be presented in italics throughout this chapter in order to distinguish them from those of the retired teachers.) The retired teacher replied laughingly, "I do. I do. Especially after teaching one grade. Teaching one grade was nothing after you had taught eight! Teaching one grade was a cinch!"

More taped laughter. Then silence. These small silences occurred with some frequency as I listened to the tapes. Having worked with these present-day teachers for four hours once weekly for two years, I could almost imagine their thoughts as they contemplated the subject matter at hand, in this case the thought of teaching eight grades at once.

And there was much about which to feel some astonishment:

> You had to fix the fire in the morning. You had to do your own janitor work. You had to go out and pump water and bring it in. They didn't have indoor toilets then. No flushing. They would clean them out once a year.

> You had to go up on Sunday afternoon and start the fire. You did what they called "banking" it. You put on a lot of coal and shut the draft so it would burn all night. In the morning you kept it going by putting more coal on and you kept it going all week. Every night before going home you had to bank the furnace. That was the worst thing, I think. I probably remember that because I said, "Never again" after I left.

> When I first started it was a rural school with an outhouse and a pump outside for the water and the big furnace in the room. You couldn't have any plants or anything in the room because it all froze overnight. And you had the 8th grade boys take turns bringing in the water in the big cooler. We were all drinking out of the same dipper. They were all farm kids who walked to school, so when they came in they had wet clothes and they put them on the furnace to dry. It smelled like a barn!

> I started teaching in 1930 at the age of 18 for $85 per month. And that included doing the outside chores which meant throwing in wood. We'd form a line to throw the wood into the basement and

then we'd all go in and pile it up. I boarded across the street and the gentleman there started the fire in the morning. And there was sweeping, carrying in the water and cleaning the outdoor toilet.

Upon listening to this last interview, a present-day teacher commented, *"I can't imagine doing that!"* And the retired teacher replied, "I can't either. I don't know how I did it. Except that I went to school there and so I kind of took over. And I was the last teacher they had before it closed down. Most of the country schools were closing then."

I was intrigued by the images of the schoolteacher of the past, seemingly far different from those cast by present-day professionals: teacher as custodian, janitor, day laborer—those were all tasks that teachers used to perform in addition to actual teaching. But, on closer inspection, although some of the specific tasks are different, I realized that teachers today also complain about the plethora of nonteaching tasks that call them away from the work of teaching. As one contemporary teacher mused, *"I stopped to think about all the nonteaching tasks I do. If someone interviewed me in fifty years they might also be shocked at the things I do!"* As I listened to teachers from two generations speak about this issue, I thought it striking how much things have changed in this regard, yet remained the same in that the preponderance of nonteaching tasks present in teaching is as much a cause for complaint now as it was then.

## "Well, in My Day, Girls Usually Went into Teaching."

A favorite question employed by the interviewing teachers was, "Why did you become a teacher?" The responses form a familiar pattern reminiscent of Lortie's (1975) research, of how it happened that certain persons became teachers.

> I think I've always known that I would be a teacher. My father had always said to me that he knew I was going to be a teacher because I used to organize the whole neighborhood, put up horses and give them stools or something to sit on and then . . . play teacher. And I'm the oldest and so I just became the authority figure and the person they looked up to and the babysitter . . . I've been having schools since I was eight years old.

> I decided to be a teacher in the second grade, being the oldest; it came kind of naturally with brothers and sisters. I don't remember wanting to be anything else. We used to play school all the time, imitating the school routine, sitting at desks at home. . . .

I always enjoyed school, and we had so many kids so close together that it was a natural thing to come home and share the things I learned. It was a fun thing to do.

The family context was a formative influence. Apparently, teaching was often an activity that emerged out of the "natural" family responsibility of looking after the younger ones, a responsibility that evolved into many a lifelong career. And for many teachers, it was a loving responsibility. One retired teacher who now substitutes occasionally explained, "I've always wanted to be a teacher from when I was a child. I've always loved school and I still love school. That's why I'm still here." When the interviewer interjected, *"You've really never had any doubts?"* she replied, "No. I've always loved school from the time I was a little bitty. I substitute because I still love teaching, I love the contact with the children, the looks on their faces is a reward that can't be matched in any other way."

It was extremely interesting to me, as I studied the tapes, how self-aware some of these retired teachers appeared as they looked back on their decisions to become teachers. Memory does not simply reveal the past as a set of facts comprising a particular reality that can be excavated by our finding and questioning these supposed eyewitnesses. Embedded in their statements are clues by which several of the teachers themselves call into question the seeming obviousness of some of their statements and go on to offer additional explanation and insight.

I don't think I thought too much about other possibilities at the time. Certainly most of the females were at school for nursing or teaching, and a lot of the girls I knew were there for the MRS. degree, and many of them—that's what they came out with. . . . Well, there weren't that many choices. I wasn't aware of that many things to do. I wouldn't choose that way now. The people that I knew became teachers.

All through my childhood and young adulthood it was taken for granted that I would become a teacher because you became teachers or nurses when I was that age. Perhaps if I had been exposed to other vocations, I might have gotten interested, but. . . .

The ensuing silence was deafening as interviewer and interviewee paused with no more words to say. I sensed confusion, but perhaps the pause created a realization that the availability of jobs limited and shaped choices, and that certain decisions seemed "natural" at the time. But the world had changed during the intervening years, and one might not be inclined to choose that way again.

The teachers contemplating their vocational choices did not specifically identify the gender structure of jobs as an important factor in much of their work decisions. As a result of research by Weiler (1992), among others, we can read these retired teachers' own portrayals of their decisions to become teachers more critically, and we can question how "free" these choices really were considering the restrictions and limitations on women's roles and work at the time. Similarly, if a young woman pictures herself as a teacher, a nurse, or a caretaker and if she is able to perceive few other options, then her fulfillment of the role may perpetuate that which is familiar—the feminine, the nurturing one, the mother.

I am compelled to wonder about the young persons who are entering the teaching profession today. To what extent are their choices to be teachers shaped and limited by forces and conditions operating well outside of their awareness? Will they, fifty years from now, be second-guessing themselves with the considerable benefit of hindsight? The interviews disclose retired teachers saying over and over again words to the effect that, "I didn't think too much about it at the time," and "it seemed the natural thing to do." Teacher-educators may provide aspiring and new teachers with a real opportunity to think carefully about the full context surrounding the decision to become a teacher.

## "It's Nice If You're a Mother Because . . ."

The matter of teaching and mothering also explicitly emerged, but from the perspectives of many retired women teachers, it was mothering first, then teaching. Clearly, they saw the profession as a supplement to one's primary mission—raising a family—and not a legitimate focus entirely in its own right. They defined "normal" life as family life; and teaching was an extension of the familiar in a woman's life.

> I grew up respecting the field of education, realizing what a wonderful thing it is for a married woman to be with her family during vacation time and to have a "normal" life during the summer. Sure you're busy at night but you are also home with your family, you are there at dinner time, so I saw many advantages.

> In my instance teaching has been a wonderful supplement to raising a family. I was able to be with my children when they really needed me. I felt it was a wonderful profession to supplement the income which was necessary if you wanted your children to go to college . . . and for other goodies in life.

> I think there are several occupations that, for females, have the connotation of being a "female job" and one just uses it as a supplemental kind of thing, that it's not really a career. Teaching is like that.

Contemporary teachers, however, raised some questions on the matter of teaching being supplementary to parenting. One young teacher wrote with feeling: *"Oh yeah, says who? Maybe for that "old granny" that was interviewed. Teaching is a legitimate career in and of itself. Sure, it fits in nice with motherhood, but maybe motherhood is a supplement to a strong career!"* After affirming that she, too, had combined parenting with teaching, another present-day teacher offered this rejoinder: *"The interviews perpetuate the idea that teaching is great for a family, a 9–3 job allowing time for the mother's role. And summers off! Only to a degree is this really true. I've spent too many hours, after my children were asleep, grading papers, planning lessons, doing report cards. And what about the summer spent planning new curriculum? We teachers are hurting ourselves and our image if we don't discuss these aspects as well."*

It was apparent to me that serious questions were being raised, and they were being raised primarily by some of the younger teachers who were single or married and without children. The contemporary teachers' responses motivate me to consider how the role of teacher is being redefined by young women entering the profession who do not see it necessarily as supplementary to raising a family. What of the women who do not see the income as merely secondary? What of the self-definitions and professionalism of those who feel more ownership in their careers because teaching was chosen actively and thoughtfully—from a wider array of occupational possibilities than those even imagined by retired teachers or teachers who entered the profession in earlier times?

## "You Were Almost Like a Mother to These Kids. . . ."

Besides expressing the theme of the teaching career as a convenient parallel with raising one's own children, the retirees also held images of the teacher as a mother figure. One retiree remembered and reflected,

> The one-room school was more like a family atmosphere, a home atmosphere, you were almost like a mother to these kids, especially if you had been at the school very long and I had been there a long time. Some I had for seven years and you get very attached to these youngsters and they do to you too. And you are almost a mother to them. It was a nice family atmosphere. The older ones become like older brothers and sisters to the younger students. It was really a pleasure. I enjoyed it.

> I still hear from several of the kids at Christmastime who graduated from me. I think it's because you got close to them and they remember you kinda like a mother.

> Personally, I just love the children and they love me. I enjoy them tremendously. I want them to know I'm going to do everything I can

for them. Nurturing and caring is not only done at home. It's an additional part of education. When a child is comfortable, happy and being accepted, he'll learn more.

However, the mothering image also includes the image of the domineering matriarch whose main realm of power resides in a room filled with children. One retired teacher proclaimed that the image of schoolmarm caricature made teaching seem an unattractive choice. "I didn't want to be a teacher. I always envisioned a teacher as a tall skinny woman with her hair up with a knot on top . . . and I wasn't going to look like that."

But, she became a teacher. And the stern image that she at first rejected nevertheless influenced her behavior and her understanding of what it means to be a teacher:

> I used to scare my children half to death on the very first day of school. I'd say, "How many of you children have heard that Mrs. T. is really mean?" And they would look at you so funny, you know, and nearly all of them would say they'd heard that I was really, *really* mean. And I said, "You wanna know something? I am." And for six weeks I was really strict with those kids, until I got them in line . . . I think that in this day and age I probably would be considered an old-fashioned teacher, a strict disciplinarian, a not-smiling-until-Thanksgiving kind of thing. You set your expectations . . . and people live up to them.

A present-day teacher recognized herself and her acculturation into teaching in the retired teacher's description and found herself concurring: *"I'm reminded of my cooperating teacher when I was student teaching. One of the first things she told me was not to smile until Thanksgiving. And believe me, she practiced what she preached! I even find myself in situations today with inexperienced teachers and telling them, 'It's always easier to loosen up than to tighten up.' Pretty soon I'll have a bun on the back of my head!"*

I was fascinated by the frequency and strength of the mothering theme found in the interviews with the retired teachers. Here was the classic image of mothering: kindly, patient, nurturing—offering a sense of acceptance, approval, and belonging. So, too, existed the image of the mother providing discipline and order. Given the strength of this theme, it was all the more powerfully sounded when they spoke of their perceptions about how modern-day students are parented.

Conceivably, the image of the teacher as mother reflects the influences of images of schoolteachers in American culture on individuals, even on those who taught. Retired teachers appear to share many of the stereotypical images of teachers that we often see portrayed in television commercials, cartoons, and literature. And so we must wonder if the meaning of teaching stems from a familiar cultural image (mother), from advice handed down from colleagues (stern matriarch: "Don't smile until Thanksgiving"), or from teachers' understandings of the reality of their own classrooms.

---

### "Sometimes You Have a Needy Student ... and You're the Only Parent They Have."

As we listen to these teachers looking back, we detect a sense of affectionate nostalgia in their voices for the days gone by, especially as they make comparisons with their increasingly stark perceptions of contemporary days. In their view, American society certainly has changed. The retirees perceive the changes as disruptions of what is normal and proper for children, parents, and teachers.

> In those days, teaching was easy. It was fun. I always felt I had parental support. The children went home for lunch. There weren't as many separated parents. In the last few years that I taught there seemed always to be so many more social and emotional problems.

> The parents were very involved in those days. You never had to ask twice for room mothers or for anyone to come along to be in the classroom. Women did not work as much when I was first beginning so they were more free to come, I believe.

> At first, the parents were nearly always at home. Later on, both parents worked so the kid would come to school with the key tied around the neck. They would go home from school and there was nobody there. I think that made a difference. And you always found where the parents took an interest in the school, then the children seemed to take more of an interest too.

The emotional tones of the interview responses often conveyed moral judgments; the teachers blamed parents for letting teachers down; they insisted that schools and children had problems and that parents were at fault, particularly for the frustrations they felt in their later years of teaching. Thus, when asked what they thought was the most significant change that had occurred during their careers, the retired teachers' poignant criticism of parental attitudes emerged time and time again.

> At the start of my teaching career, parents were a little bit in awe of the teacher and when something happened at school, the teacher was right. It was felt that the teacher's solution was the correct one. Nowadays, you hear a child say, "My mother is going to sue you." I think you more often see mothers and fathers coming to school and being irate about what the teacher is doing. I don't think teachers have changed their methods that much. I think it's the attitude of

the parents, being a little more belligerent, more likely to have a chip on their shoulders, out to prove something by coming to school and berating the teacher. . . .

I had a lot of respect in the community when I first started teaching but at the end of the sixties it was starting to go in the other direction. That was one of the reasons I was ready to retire. It became a losing battle, just a losing battle. Even today I overhear things being said in the community about the school and the teachers in the presence of the youths, and it just makes my heart gripe because the children are the ones that suffer. They lose respect for teachers. This is not the way I was raised. This is not the way I was taught.

There are so many things that need to be taught in the home that they're not getting today. What bothers me is that the parents downgrade the school and the teacher and they let it be known to their children. The child shouldn't be exposed to criticism. If there is something to be corrected, it should be done between the adults and leave the child out of it.

The interviewer responded to this latter comment about parental criticism, saying: "*I agree. A child came in today and said that his dad said, 'This is dummy work that we're doing,' and I said, 'Your daddy should call me if he has a problem with what's going on in this room.'*" The retired teacher concluded, "I hate to say this, but it's ignorance; it's inadequacy on the part of the parents. What they don't understand, they find fault with."

The retirees also recounted their belief that parents today actually seem hostile to schools and teachers. In some emotionally charged interviews, indictments of parents were made. The retired teachers blamed parents not only for mothers absent from home and poor support of teachers and schools, but also for increasing hostility—manifest in strident competition between parent and teacher. They understood such negative parental attitudes as interfering with the education of the child, as overriding the authority and expertise of the teacher.

When I call the television repairman to come over to fix my TV, he tells me to leave the room and he fixes my TV. He gives me a bill for it. I think this is the thing about teaching. The teachers are the experts. Not that I don't want to involve the parents; I think they should be involved, but not to the point where they are dictating the curriculum and all these other things that are happening in schools. It doesn't work. The teachers are the experts. If they would give teachers a chance to do the job, I think the educational system would work.

Well, all you hear these days is that they need more money for education. That's just a lot of bunk. They just need to start in the home and straighten out the parents. I think most of the teachers today are doing the best they can, and it isn't the teachers' fault. It's just the training the children are getting in the home. The schools would be what they ought to be if the parents were doing their part.

Again the retired teachers returned to the issues of home and parenting. Many interviews portrayed the natural connection between the school and home within the limited number of occupations thought to be "women's work." For example, women became teachers first in their homes playing school with younger siblings, or they found in teaching a conveniently organized supplementary career to parenting, or they discovered in teaching a comfortable place to play the mothering role. "School is a home away from home," one retired teacher said. But it is significant that she then added, "in fact, I think some of the kids have more of a home life in school than in their homes."

The retired teachers saw this natural relationship between family and school as disintegrating. And that is the great irony: that the contributions teachers once felt themselves called upon to give are the very elements found to be lacking in the lives of the children they are now called to serve. In the views of these teachers, the gulf between the home and the school appears to be widening, and the mothering that these teachers provided no longer seems to be enough. These retired teachers seem to be saying that their way of viewing what it means to be a teacher is no longer sufficient. It's not enough to love children, to want to mother them, to be a good teacher and the classroom expert. It's not enough for today's children.

---

## "I Don't Think It's as Simple as That Anymore."

The image of the American schoolteacher appears to be undergoing some fundamental change, perhaps in response to the profound changes that are occurring in the larger society of which schools are just a part. Interviews demonstrate the teachers' beliefs that not only have parents changed, but also, for a variety of factors, so have the children.

> ... when I started out teaching, it was such fun. You didn't have to spend a lot of time on discipline or emotional problems in the classroom. Now I would say that it's at least a third of your kids. Maybe it was just more fun teaching then . . . and probably the response that you got from the children was more wholehearted. Now you have kids who have a lot of inhibitions, they have so many other problems, and they don't seem able to free themselves from some of these problems.
>
> You have to put yourself in the position of the child. The children we have nowadays are not coming from homes that are as stable as

they were thirty years ago. We live in a very transient society, and these children have to come in, and they have to learn your way of teaching, and then their parents pack up and leave, and they go to a new school, and they have to learn a whole new regime, all new friends, it's just too difficult.

I think the children of today [are changing] because of the media they are exposed to—movies and TV. I think they are more worldly than the children I had in second grade many years ago. If this is good, I don't know. But I think they have a wider knowledge than the kids did when I was in the classroom. Today the kids are used to having so much for themselves at home that when a teacher does some nice little thing for them, I don't think they appreciate it as much as they would twenty-five years ago. The children didn't get out in the world as much then as they do today. I don't think you get the reaction today that you did then. Most children have experienced a lot more things.

At first it was like a family and the children just loved to come to school. They didn't want to miss a day, even if they were sick, they didn't want to miss. And it seemed that they were anxious to learn, they wanted to do it to please you. I found, as time went on, that the kids didn't seem to care anymore whether they learned anything or not. I know they had a lot of outside interests too. You had TV and everything else that made a difference. But at first, the children just seemed to want to learn and to do well. They seemed to wish to do well.

Some of the changes in children and teaching that retirees alluded to relate directly to experiences or imagined experiences in urban schools. It must be remembered that nearly all of the retired teachers in the current sample are residents of suburban and exurban areas. Many had taught in these or nearby communities in earlier times, so in their own lives they have witnessed the movement from one-room schoolhouses in the farm communities of the not so distant past to the suburban age-graded consolidated schools of the present. Some had taught in the city and moved to the suburbs later. Some had gone into the city to teach for a year or two and returned to the outlying areas.

I wouldn't sell my childhood for anything. Living on a farm you know the sources of things. You know processes. You know cause and effect. You just get that in your living. And so I think I had many advantages. I wouldn't trade my farm experience for the city experience where many things aren't suited for the child. There, it's an adult world rather than a child's world, and they're trying to do away with childhood nowadays.

> In the beginning we were all farm families and we were all very closely related to each other and to the school. We were just like a big family. No problems . . . just nice kids. But then I went in to the inner city and I had kindergarten kids and they had a lot of problems. . . . They were much harder to teach.

Not all the retired teachers, however, attributed problematic changes to urban environments:

> When I was in Chicago, I had been teaching second grade. When I came out to suburbia I just took what I knew from teaching second grade and moved it down to first grade—the academic difference was horrendous. The children were a little more challenging out here. In the city the children were a little more appreciative, than when I came out here . . . maybe spoiled is the word. But then, my children were raised in the suburbs, too, so I have to say that I produced spoiled children compared to the children I worked with in the city.

Obviously, if the retirees believed that children have changed, so, too, had teaching. One former teacher explained:

> I just think it became harder as time went on. It is easier to get burnout today because it's harder to teach. It takes a lot more skill to analyze what's going on in these kids' heads and why they behave in certain ways and what you can do about it. It seems to me that if you were kind of a motherly person, and affectionate, and anxious for your pupils to succeed, that was enough. I don't think it is as simple as that anymore.
>
> The kids are not as attentive, they don't care as much as they used to. Cause now they have TV and they're entertained and they have all these activities. When I first started, kids just loved to learn, it was a pleasure, a real pleasure. And then it became harder and harder to keep getting their attention. That's how I think it has changed.
>
> [Children today] are bored in the classroom because of some of the technology or technical or mechanical things they have at home. They can manipulate those things, you know, at home, and how often can they do that in the classroom? They have to sit and listen. I think that children do not want to listen today. I just don't think most children can learn from listening.

The interviewer reacted to the retired teacher who was concerned that children can't listen by saying, *"Then you have to find a variety of ways to involve them."* The retired teacher answered back, "I think a teacher's job is to introduce material . . . and make it as interesting as possible to the kid, but I don't think that teachers today should have to really dwell on methods. I think they should be able to present the material and that's it."

I stopped the tape and rewound. This seemed a telling dialogue. I could almost hear the frustration in the retired teacher's voice as the present-day teacher called for a different kind of teaching. The interviewer does not have an image of herself elevated on a pedestal—dispensing knowledge to respectful students arranged below. Clearly, the present-day teacher sees her role differently; she is more willing to use what children like and what works for them. Perhaps she is less caught up in the material to be taught and more attentive to the children who are to be taught, perceiving that educational consumers are no longer as content with lectures. They want their teachers to be more active; they want to be more active, too. She realizes that good teaching means a changing set of challenges.

After listening to the taped conversation above, another present-day teacher responded:

> *That retired teacher described a fairly typical classroom of fifty, twenty, ten years ago, and I'm sorry to say, today. It's the type of classroom in which only a specific kind of learner does well. That's great for people like me, but not so great for all those other style learners out there. I hope that today we are starting to realize that there are many different ways to learn and our jobs as teachers is to accommodate* all *children. I don't want to be thought of as the expert by my kids. I don't know everything and certainly do not want to be viewed as if I do. If the children see you as a learner, they will view themselves as learners. That is, in essence, my job, sharing with kids how to learn.*

---

## "Hey, There's a Lot I Don't Miss at All."

Many retired teachers revealed their many complaints and concerns, one commenting, "Hey, there's a lot I don't miss at all." She went on to list them:

> A lot of the politics of the school system, I don't miss at all. I don't miss grading papers. I don't miss all the time in preparation, or all the hours of your own time outside of school that you have to put in. I don't miss the last day of school, or the last week, or the week before Christmas vacation, [and] the interruptions at school . . . there wasn't enough time in the day to teach as it was, and then to have it disrupted for a million reasons was terrible.

From hearing the interview tapes, we can add parent conferences and testing to this "not missed" list.

Other interviews disclosed the sad realities of teaching for several of the retirees. One said:

> The only thing that ever bothered me about my teaching was that we were locked in. You teach, you get tenured, you get your insurance, you get your years of seniority, and you can't move around from one school to the next. As a result, you are locked into a principal and to a school that you're not always happiest at.

This particular interview provoked a response from me. Teaching can be an isolating job, as the research of Johnson (1990) has shown; she contends that "strong norms of autonomy and privacy prevail among teachers" (p. 179). Teachers live professional lives largely apart from one another in separate rooms, separate buildings, separate districts. There is a certain irony in this because so many come to teaching with a perception of the family, of belonging, of mothering, of filling the image of the caring helper. Instead, many wind up feeling isolated, cut off from the children and each other. Particularly for urban teachers, it may be just too difficult to maintain the "family" in a large, bureaucratic school system. Perhaps the image of "teacher" is dependent on a societal framework or context to such a degree that the *teacher*, as a *person*, is in danger of being lost.

I also felt the pain of the retired teacher who bemoaned the loss of close relationships with children when she was asked what did she miss about teaching:

> I felt that inasmuch as I had ceased to have a homeroom, I didn't have the close contact with the children anymore. I had 125 children coming through my classroom and I was teaching reading and science all day long. I felt that was a negative thing in retrospect. At the time I felt it should be that way.

I was particularly intrigued by her answer because she said that it was only in retrospect that she realized how much she missed having better relationships with the children. How ironic this seems to me, that many of the retired teachers said that they went into teaching for the love of children, that the one quality needed above all else was the ability to love the kids. And here is a retired teacher—thinking over her career—and the one thing she realizes is that she increasingly missed having these very relationships with children and didn't even know it at the time! What happens in schooling that pulls us away from savoring such pleasures?

It seems fitting to end this section with the advice of a retired teacher to an imagined aspiring one:

> If I met a young teacher who was struggling, would I have any advice? Well, if I could help them in any way, I would. If they are absolutely against it and absolutely miserable, I'd say, "Get out." If

they are miserable, they are going to make the kids miserable. And that's not what we're here for.

---

### "Every Day I Discover Something New about Myself."

Although many depictions of teaching given by the retired teachers were supported and affirmed by their interviewers, the present-day teachers, through their responses, also demonstrated that they have different things to say about what it means to be a teacher. Clearly, the contemporary teachers seem more flexible, see more possibilities in teaching, are more reciprocally child-centered, and have a greater sense of themselves. I am impressed by their comments such as: *"You have to draw on your own resources and come up with something that works. If something doesn't work, you don't throw out the kid."* Or, *"it's not what you are teaching, it's who you're teaching."*

For these current professionals being a teacher means searching within oneself to give children what they need and to respond to each child as an individual person. A present-day teacher described the teacher's response to children as *"snowballing: you have ideas, the kids have ideas."* She understood that, in the process of teaching, teachers can become human and share in the discovery.

These contemporary teachers demonstrated an awareness of societal and educational changes that affect the work they do and the lives they live. It seems clear to these teachers that, although children appear to be different and parents create more challenges, a teacher in a classroom can discover a way of being which meets the children's and her own needs. Teaching also means being more sensitive to the adult imposition on the child. *"What it means to be a teacher is a level of trust—when they start doing it for themselves—when they will let you in."* Or, *"What it means to be a teacher is the ability to allow them to let you into their lives."*

These interviews and the responses to them reveal several foundations that undergird many teachers' sense of themselves. The retired teachers have indicated the significance of community, of family, and of respect as they generate images of teaching. Present-day teachers have expanded those reflections to encompass a contemporary world where such values are not necessarily universal or taken for granted. The teachers in classrooms today are moving beyond the definition of "teacher" which has served effectively in former days of schooling and are now expanding the breadth and variety of their conceptualizations.

Such a rethinking of our profession suggests that the teacher as a person need not be lost. In fact, being a teacher today may require a more personal ownership of the process of growing and learning, one that embraces the student not just as a consumer but more fully as a collaborator. Both can own what is made in the classroom.

It seems important that the teacher not just create information, or merely impart it to children, but also participate with the students in the reciprocal process of learning. As these teachers so aptly explained:

> A teacher is first of all a learner. A teacher who really loves to learn will be able to inspire the students to love learning.

> Every day I discover something new about myself, about them, and about my world—every day! I like to share it too. What it means to be a teacher is sharing, is discovery.

> Sometimes it is necessary to step out of the curriculum as established in some far away place and use the best that is in us—to draw upon our imaginations at our deepest level and respond as human beings. We must do the best we can, but it really must be the best. The children will respond and the teacher will grow in ways perhaps unimagined.

Perhaps "the best we can do" is in fact to join in the process of learning something new for ourselves, while making that process visible to our students as well and drawing them along. In this way learning can become knowledge lived, not merely displayed, in our relationships with one another. I believe that this process—of sharing, wondering, and questioning—is part of a newer image of what it means to be a teacher.

## NOTE

Thanks to the teacher-researchers who were my collaborators: Nancy Brankis, Bruce Cramer, Sue DeVeirman, Rose Filkowski, Helen Gebler, Jean Glenn, Barbara Halsey, Jill Hancock, Kay Handcock, Sally Henderson, Dean Hirshman, Karen Kaiz, Gail Kapp, Roberta Kerr, Linda Koolish, Lori Krupka, Tamara Lowy, Annette Lubkeman, Linda May, Barbara Modica, Richard Moon, Jayne Pedersen, Barbara Phillips, Charlotte Renehan, Mary Seaver, Karen Shinners, Phyllis Steffan, Teri Stone, Laura Wiza, Jill Wolf, Ruth Woodruff.

## REFERENCES

Johnson, S. M. (1990). *Teachers at work*. New York: Basic Books.

Lortie, D. (1975). *Schoolteacher*. Chicago: University of Chicago Press.

Van Manen, M. (1990). *Researching lived experience*. Albany, NY: SUNY Press.

Weiler, K. (1992). Remembering and representing life choices: A critical perspective on teachers' oral history narratives. *Qualitative Studies in Education, 3*(1), 39–50.

# 5

# Good Women and Old Stereotypes

## Retired Teachers Talk about Teaching

Nancy Green

Mary Phillips Manke

S eeking to understand more fully the images of teachers which have prevailed in this century, we went to teachers themselves. In this gendered profession, how do women interpret their role and their work? We looked for the answer to this question in the images a group of twelve retired women teachers had of their lives and careers. We begin with the biographies of the teachers interviewed for this chapter arranged by their birthdates in order to give our readers some grasp of the personalities, motivations, and choices of these women within social and historical contexts.

All these women were elementary-school teachers who taught in the Chicago or Milwaukee area. (We contacted them through currently working teachers and through the Chicago Retired Teachers' Association.) They were not selected systematically, except that we chose equal numbers of African-American and white teachers. They did, however, share a number of characteristics. All but one were in the first generation of their families to be educated beyond high school. (This is not surprising, as it would be today; they were born during the years in which high school attendance became common in the United States and college attendance was still relatively rare.) All held bachelor's degrees, although three earned them during their careers, having attended one or two years of normal school before beginning to teach. Three had earned master's degrees.

Most spent their lives and taught in the same city or community where they were born. All but one were married, and eight of the twelve had children. Three of the teachers began teaching in rural schools in an area outside Milwaukee that became suburban/industrial during their careers. The others taught in the city schools of Milwaukee and Chicago, in working-class, immigrant, poor, or lower middle-class communities.

Beyond these demographic facts, we found few generalizations that could be made about them. Placing them in categories, such as "the rural white teachers" or "the older African-American teachers," seemed unproductive to us. We could only say that, as a group, the twelve women displayed great similarity in their images of themselves as teachers. This similarity, which seems to transcend economic, racial, and demographic backgrounds, reflects pervasive cultural expectations of women in a woman's field.

**Leo Sparks,** born in 1910, is an African-American teacher from Carbondale, Illinois, and is the only one of our teachers who had a parent who was a college graduate. Her mother was a teacher; her father was "the only black contractor in Carbondale." She graduated in 1932 from Indiana State Teachers College at Terre Haute and came to Chicago looking for work as a teacher. Regulations limited elementary teaching positions to graduates of the Chicago Normal School, and as an alternative she worked as a playground supervisor and taught adult evening classes. She was assigned to the first of three all-black elementary schools in 1950 and taught until 1975. Fiercely independent and not reticent about her conviction that she was a "born" teacher, Leo Sparks stressed the importance of love and involvement with children's families, as well as having high standards for children's work. (All the teachers in this chapter are referred to by pseudonyms, except for Leo Sparks, who preferred that we use her actual name.)

**Emily Downer** is an African-American, born in 1911, whose family was "poor as Job's turkey" but strong, united, and devoted to reading. After graduating from Chicago Teacher's College in 1932, in the depths of the Depression, she waited six years for a permanent placement in a city where black teachers were allowed to teach only in all-black schools. She taught for thirty-five years, first in primary grades, then as an elementary librarian, and then again in primary grades. She retired in 1971 because her principal moved her to the eighth grade. One of the oldest of the teachers we interviewed, Emily Downer emphasized most strongly the importance of order and of "sticking to the curriculum."

**Martha Corey** was born in 1914 in Morgan Park, Illinois, an African-American community on the edge of Chicago. She still lives there in the house where she grew up. Her father worked in the post office, and all the members of her family were great readers. She graduated from Illinois State Normal College in 1937, one of the few African-Americans in her class. Because of Chicago's policy of hiring only Chicago Normal School graduates, in effect until the late 1940s, her first position was as a substitute at DuSable High School. Later, she taught physical education at two all-black elementary schools, and finished her thirty-year career in the central office in the research and evaluation department. Martha Corey was an avid student who completed forty hours beyond a master's degree and calls herself a "pseudo-intellectual." She retired early, in 1972, frustrated by cutbacks in programs she believed were effective and the uselessness of the compliance evaluation work she was doing.

**Pat Barnes,** a white Chicago teacher, was also born in 1914 and graduated from high school during the Great Depression. She took care of children in people's houses for five years, and then married and attended Chicago Teacher's College, graduating in 1943. She began to teach only after her son began kindergarten in 1949. For most of her thirty-year career she taught at just one school, on the southwest side of the city. At first, her pupils were from European immigrant families; later, her classes included children from Latino and Arab families. She particularly enjoyed the experience of teaching in a small school, where teachers supported one another and could teach as they wanted to. She retired in 1976.

**Sally Tate,** a white teacher, was born in 1914 in West Bend, Wisconsin. She attended a county normal school for one year, and began teaching at age 18 in a one-room school. She taught for four years before marrying. She had three sons, and it was to "do things for them" that she returned to work when the oldest was ten. She taught in a two-room school and studied at night and in the summer for a bachelor's degree. After five years in a two-room school, she moved to four-room Amy Bell School, where she remained for twenty years as the school grew to be a large modern elementary facility. Sally Tate retired in 1981 because of her husband's illness; after his death she substituted regularly for several years and still does so on occasion. She now volunteers regularly in the classroom where her granddaughter is the teacher.

**Georgia Tunney** had the most varied career of all the teachers we interviewed. Born in Alabama in 1915, she moved at age 6 to Pasadena, California, where she was the only African-American child in her elementary school. She was sent on a scholarship to both high school and college at Spelman College in Atlanta. After earning a master's degree in early childhood education from Atlanta University, she taught in Thomasville, Georgia, and in Indianapolis before settling with her husband in Milwaukee. She taught first grade and kindergarten in the Milwaukee Public Schools. After a few years as a professor of education at the University of Wisconsin at Milwaukee, Georgia Tunney returned to begin the Head Start program in Milwaukee, and eventually to direct it. Retired in 1979 after forty years as a teacher, she continues to be active as a volunteer and community leader.

**Ellie Varney,** an African-American teacher, was born in Springfield, Missouri, in 1918. Although she had not expected to go to college, a New Deal program, the National Youth Administration, gave her the opportunity to attend Lincoln University in Jefferson City. The program ended before she graduated, but with help from her soldier brother she was able to graduate in 1946. She began teaching in the high school she had attended in Springfield, Missouri. Urged by friends who had moved to Chicago, she joined them after three years of teaching, substituting during the day and taking courses at Chicago Teacher's College at night. Her first regular assignment in an elementary school began in 1951. Taking a two-year leave when her son was born, she was assigned to Shoup School in Chicago, where she remained for twenty-six years until she retired in 1981.

**Cora Ulm,** a white teacher, was born in 1922 in a rural area north of Milwaukee. She studied two years at Dodge City Normal before teaching for four years in a two-room school. Married to a returning soldier after World War II, she raised her children until 1962, when she returned to teaching. She took a job at Amy Bell Elementary School, near the family farm where she still lives. The school grew as nearby Germantown changed from agriculture to industry and suburban residences, and finally there were enough children for a graded school. From then on, Cora Ulm taught third grade. She earned a bachelor's degree in 1968 and retired in 1986.

**Dot Miller,** another white teacher from Amy Bell Elementary School in Germantown, was also born in 1922. She had two years of normal school before beginning to teach in a one-room school in Golden Dell, Wisconsin, where she remained for seven years. After one year at a bigger school, she married but continued to teach until her first child was born. Taking off only a year and a half with her first child and less than half a year with her second, Dot Miller taught a total of forty-five and a half years before retiring. Once Amy Bell had become a graded school, she taught either second grade or 1–2 / 2–3 combinations. Like Sally Tate, she took courses at night and in the summer to complete her bachelor's degree in 1957. She retired, reluctantly, in 1991.

**Norah Krupar,** a white teacher who was born in 1928, grew up in a poor Chicago neighborhood. She attended DePaul University, graduating in 1955. She was recruited by an elementary principal for his school in a poor neighborhood near the County Hospital. She enjoyed teaching there because she believed that, having grown up poor, she could relate well to the children she worked with. She took off seven years to have two children of her own and then returned in 1967 to teach in another working-class school, this time working with "brain-injured children." The designation was later changed to learning disabled, and Norah Krupar earned a master's in special education. She stayed in the same classroom for nearly twenty years but was forced to retire in early 1986 because of illness.

**Kate Turner** was born in Chicago in 1929 and attended first a junior college and then Chicago Teacher's College. Hearing that jobs were available in Milwaukee, she moved to the city and began a kindergarten teaching career of thirty-four years. She began as the first African-American teacher at a mostly white school and taught at a total of four schools in the city, including one for twelve years and another for eighteen. Kate Turner earned a master's degree at the University of Wisconsin at Milwaukee in 1977 and had to retire in 1989 because of arthritis.

**Frances Schmidt,** a white Chicagoan, was born in 1929 and graduated from Chicago Teachers College in 1950. She says proudly that her class was the last of the selectively admitted classes in the college; after that, the rules were changed in order to get enough teachers to serve the first of the baby-boom children. She taught first at a school on the West Side, then at Pasteur School, and finally, for twenty-two years, at Seward School in the "Back of the Yards" neighborhood, where she taught primarily children from Mexican immigrant families. Like Pat Barnes, she enjoyed the experience of teaching in what she said was "like a small country school." Teachers shared and supported one another, especially in minimizing any discipline problems that might arise. Like Kate Turner, she retired because of arthritis, regretfully, in 1991.

## Methodology

The interviews with these teachers, which were tape-recorded and later transcribed, were conducted in an unstructured manner, usually in the homes of the teachers. We began by describing the nature of the project and our wish to focus on the images people have of teachers. The first question we asked called for the teacher to give us a history of her career, including how she chose to become a teacher and what were the schools and settings in which she taught. When this "tour" (Spradley, 1979) of her career had been brought up to her retirement, we used a list of questions to elicit information that had not already been discussed.

Our questions focused on the teachers' changing images of their profession, as well as their beliefs about what others thought. We also asked whether they believed they were typical teachers and whether they would recommend that a young person today become a teacher.

After the interviews had been transcribed, we read and reread them, eventually beginning to name the themes that stood out for us. Drawing on principles of ethnographic research, we tried to let the concerns of the retired teachers surface, with a minimum of shaping on our part. As we began to focus on the cluster of themes that are central to this chapter, we also began to articulate and discuss their interconnections and what we believed they meant.

## Themes

Looking back on careers that began between 1930 and 1955, the teachers told us of their personal histories, the children and parents they had worked with, and their concerns about teaching and schools. As we read through transcripts of these interviews, we looked for themes that were common to many of them.

Our search revealed three interrelated themes that appeared in almost all the interviews. The first of these, the importance of *dedication in teaching,* arises from questions we asked about images of exemplary teachers. "Dedication" is a word that some of the teachers used more than others, but all agreed that the desire to serve was vital in the lives of teachers. Most emphasized the caring, loving side of service; others stressed commitment and hard work in the service of students' learning.

The second theme that emerged was that of the many *intrinsic rewards* which the teachers gleaned from their work. Again and again the interviewees mentioned the satisfaction, the excitement, the positive human relationships that arose from their work as classroom teachers.

The third theme involved the *financial rewards* of teaching. This theme raised more questions for us and quite possibly for the retired teachers than the other two. The retired teachers' understanding of the place of monetary rewards in their lives and those of their fellow teachers revealed ambiguities in our cultural expectations of schoolteachers and in their own expectations of themselves. Although they did expect to be paid reasonably well for their work, they expressed dismay at the existence of teachers who were "in it just for the money." Some said that teaching is not a well-paid profession; others mentioned that in some communities the public feels that teachers are paid too much; and still others had the impression that as salaries rise, dedication declines.

These three themes—dedication, intrinsic rewards, and remuneration— are closely linked to one another. There was a clear connection between the first two in particular. The greater one's dedication to teaching, the greater the intrinsic rewards one gains from it. However, remuneration does not seem to be linked to dedication, or even to the other rewards. Do these themes suggest that financial security in a profession is incompatible with more intangible rewards such as positive human relationships? Do women feel less capable of demanding satisfactory remuneration and remain content with intangible compensation? These interviews suggest that the question of rewards in a "women's profession" merits further consideration by researchers and by teachers themselves.

### Dedication to teaching

Almost all the teachers used the word "dedication" in describing teachers whom they admired, and its absence was what they most condemned in teachers they criticized. As aspects of dedication, they emphasized willingness to work hard, love of children, commitment to children's learning, and concern for children's needs—whether academic or emotional. In reflecting on the hard work involved in being a teacher, Norah Krupar said, "We used to laugh. We would say teachers are like bag ladies. They are always carry-ing something to the classroom or carrying something home. I think for anybody that tries to do a decent job it really isn't a short hour job, because it's a lot of preparation time. A lot of time and thought go into it." Describ-ing one of the schools where she taught, Frances Schmidt said, "There were about twenty-one on the faculty, and they were all such hard workers, such dedicated teachers. My husband used to always say to me, 'Why do you bring so much work home? I don't see anybody but you bringing all this work home.' That isn't true. Over there everybody brought work home."

In some cases, this hard work may have had an unintended consequence in teachers' own families. Two of those we interviewed commented on their own children's attitude toward becoming teachers. Frances Schmidt said, "I'd like to see my daughter get into teaching. She doesn't want to, and I think I may have spoiled it for her, because she says, 'Mom, I see you staying up at night working on lesson plans and marking papers and doing all this . . .' " Cora Ulm also mentioned that "You'd get home and of course you'd always have school work to do—I think that's why none of my children are teachers—you know, Mother always had so much homework. It was kind of a standing joke; none of them ever wanted to be a teacher."

But from the perspective of their own student days, these teachers saw hard-working teachers as worthy of emulation. Looking back on her early observations of teachers, Martha Corey said, "I began to recognize that the people I admired most were the teachers who gave of themselves and who went the extra mile." Thinking back to her teachers as she was growing up, Ellie Varney can't remember them ever missing school, except "maybe some teacher whose mother died or something like that . . . I am sure they must have had some illnesses, but mostly they were there. They were there, and they were kind and dedicated and loving."

In fact, love and care for children stand out as the most important reasons for all the hard work the teachers described. Norah Krupar said, "It is because you have that feeling for the child that you are there, because there is a lot of work in special ed." Leo Sparks's words profoundly reveal the deeply caring involvement that characterizes the images of these teachers' lives and ca-reers: "I love my [students'] parents, and my parents love me, and my kids love me, and my kids would [say], 'We belong to Miss S., and she calls us her babies, and she tells us she loves us. So you can't tell us anything.' "

Georgia Tunney echoed the theme of loving but revealed a universal kind of love that transcends love of individuals or even of children: "All my life I've tried to help somebody. I did not do it for recognition, I did it because I wanted to be of service, and because I feel that love goes beyond sexual love. Love is love for humanity."

The teachers' view of the importance of loving children came out strongly in the teachers' response to the question, "Would you advise a young person today to go into teaching?" Kate Turner replied, "The ones that love the kids I'm not really too worried about." Leo Sparks answered,

"Of course, if they love themselves and if they love children, if they love people. Unless they feel in here, feel that this is their purpose in being on this planet is to be a teacher. . . . Love is a prerequisite for teaching. That is the reason a whole lot of people have no business there." Cora Ulm explicitly connects love of children with the desire to help them learn. "If [a young person] likes to work with children and be around children, I would say yes. The schools need teachers who are caring and concerned and want to help kids learn."

"Helping kids learn" is, of course, implied in teaching, but some teachers stressed the academic side of teaching more than others. In describing a much admired teacher from her own high school days, Frances Schmidt said, "She tried so hard to have everyone pass her class and really come out with something. . . . I knew right away that this is what I wanted to do, too."

Academic weakness could even be turned into a strength; Kate Turner claims not to have been a good student in high school, but she thinks that made her a better teacher. She remarked, "Because I wanted children to love to learn, because I feel like if you love to learn on your own, if you can get that across, everything else sort of falls in place." Leo Sparks said, "I would tell them, 'You bring what you know to the table. I'll bring what I know. We put it together, and we all learn together, because you know things I will never know, and I know things you will never know, but if we put them both together, look how much we can know.' And they loved it."

Emily Downer was unusual among the teachers we interviewed in that she stressed the importance of "covering the curriculum." In fact, she would not now advise a young person to go into teaching because of what she sees as a "flimsy course of study. . . . It is not concrete enough. There isn't enough of 'this has to be done, and that has to be done.' [In earlier times,] from September to June, you were supposed to accomplish a great deal."

Dot Miller put concern for the children's learning in more individual terms. In describing the characteristics of a great teacher, she said, "They certainly have to motivate, and also follow through on that. They have to be willing to go that extra mile, and if you see someone is having a problem, don't embarrass them, but maybe call on them oftener and maybe take them aside and show them how to do things, and say, 'There's something I'd like you to do at recess time for me,' and 'Oh, by the way, you didn't get this, let me show you,' things like that."

For these teachers, sensitivity to the nonacademic needs of children is also an aspect of dedication. Pat Barnes said, "Sometimes things bother children. For example, one boy left the room one day, and I went to see what was the matter, and I think he was embarrassed, because his father was going to the hospital, and he viewed that as sort of a bad thing. Of course, you want them to learn, to achieve the goals they are supposed to for that grade, but I think you have to have a little empathy with certain individuals."

Leo Sparks recounted an experience with some neglected children. She and some other teachers had been feeding them before school.

As the weather got cold, when we drove up, those babies were there. I would unfreeze those hands and feet. I would take their socks off, take them down to the janitors to dry out and put the socks on the wall, so they would be dry and let the children sit there with newspaper under their little feet until they could move after I massaged them. I would tell the children, "I am your daytime mama. Whatever is wrong, whatever is bothering you, tell me." I said, "That is why my shoulders are broad." I said, "My lap will hold you."

One might wonder whether contemporary teachers feel a similar degree of dedication as that expressed by these retired teachers. Does a teacher today view herself as a "daytime mama"? Does society expect teachers to cast themselves in this light? What does this suggest about the nature of parents and parenting in American society?

The comments of these retired teachers who seem to view teaching much more broadly than mere instruction in academic areas, and who appear to see schoolteaching as a profession demanding dedication far beyond the realm of a "nine to three" day, remind us of the complexity of rewards, incentives, and gratification in this helping profession—both now and then.

### Intrinsic Rewards of Teaching

In most cases seeing themselves as models of the dedication they looked for in their colleagues, the teachers we interviewed had gained rich rewards from their years as teachers. The aspects of teaching which they found rewarding were closely related to what they saw as constituting dedication. Much of what they found rewarding came from working with, helping, and doing activities with children. Hard work and deep involvement in their jobs translated into pleasure in their autonomy, variety in their daily work, and opportunities for creativity and problem-solving. They also found rewards in relationships. They enjoyed their contacts, often over the long term, with parents and other teachers, and were delighted when children, growing up, remembered them over the years. Some of them found that their position as teacher brought them status in the community.

Most of the teachers found their work so rewarding, in fact, that retirement was a painful process. Dot Miller, after forty-five and one-half years as a teacher, said she would not have retired if her husband had not taken her by the hand to the district office to do so. Leo Sparks was still angry that her age had forced her to retire, especially since the rule was changed, shortly thereafter, to let teachers continue to age 70. Two teachers had to retire early because of arthritis in their knees; both of them said they were sorry to go. Another teacher went from her classroom to the hospital and never came back to get her teaching supplies because it was too painful. Only one retired early because changing times had robbed her of the satisfaction she had formerly received from teaching.

Teaching is working with children, and Dot Miller said, "To this day I love little kids, they're great. . . . And if you love to work with children, there's nothing else that compares with it. . . . You get so much satisfaction out of seeing what they do and all, and then seeing what they've done." She also spoke of the sense that she had helped an individual child or group of children: ". . . and if you have a little one there that, you know, is having a hard time at home, and divorce or something, if you can make that child smile and feel secure for the six hours she's in school, that's good."

Kate Turner agreed: "It's like the little pebble in the water. You know, you're touching so many children, and one person who's going to do a good job, it's very good."

Some of the teachers seemed to have derived great enjoyment from the special activities they did with children on a regular basis and from the children's response to those activities. Said Cora Ulm, "They loved to act out things—I remember one time they acted out a wedding. They brought stuff and they acted out the bride and the groom."

Pat Barnes told us that she and the children worked with clay once or twice a year and that the children loved it and remembered it years later. "You'd think that we had done this all the time instead of arithmetic or reading or something." She also said that she read aloud to the children: "Well, that is encouraging if the children go to the library and they want to get that book [that you read aloud] and they want to read it, or else sometimes they would want the same story read over."

Many of the teachers described what might be thought of as the intellectual rewards of teaching as well. Teaching provided room for their autonomy and for creativity. The job had variety; solving difficult problems was satisfying. Said Kate Turner, "We were coming up with an awful lot of ideas, and I had a friend at that time who could draw, and . . . he'd draw it for me and I'd have the idea and you know I had a lot of fun." Or, as Emily Downer said, "At that time if you wanted a good job, an interesting job where you are learning all the time, being a teacher was it"; for Frances Schmidt, "every year is different, and every year you come up with new ideas and new enthusiasm." Finally, Dot Miller spoke of the "satisfaction of solving behavior problems and getting the class to help you with that."

Some of the teachers recalled that their schools had offered them the rewards of community—of joint effort and of positive relationships. Frances Schmidt recalled: "It was like a family. We were like a family, and it was a lot of sharing of things, and we never, never had any discipline problems there. If on occasion we did—we kind of helped each other. It was fantastic." This was also true of relationships with parents. Dot Miller reported that "the parents showed a lot of respect to this day. They call and I've gotten beautiful things from the parents. A lot of things in this room are from parents. Beautiful things." Frances Schmidt stated that at her school, "if you did anything that was extra, the community, the parents really appreciated it."

One of the most powerful long-term rewards, mentioned by several of the teachers, was the continuing relationships they had with their students. According to Kate Turner, "I have one child [who] was in my first kindergarten, and she still keeps contact with me. She called me in the hospital . . . and she's brought her children over. She looks just the same." Emily Downer described her meeting with a former student after he had returned from medical school: "I hadn't seen him for years, and I hadn't forgotten him—and he said 'Well, I just had to come to tell you what I did and what I am now, and I also wanted to tell you that you were the best teacher I ever had, barring none.' " Similarly, Martha Corey observed: "Such a pleasure now . . . I meet so many of my former students who are all in different fields. Some of them are principals who have asked me to come and substitute in their schools." Leo Sparks spoke of these continuing relationships with special joy:

> I had a girl call me the other day to thank me. I had her in second grade at Forest School 38 years ago, and a bunch of those second graders have stayed together as friends, and they meet once a month. And she says, "You can't guess what we talk about—Miss S." Because when she called she said, "Miss S., you don't remember me, but I will never forget you. You will never know how much we loved you, still do, and how much you had to do with our lives." And I was on cloud, what, two hundred ten for a couple of weeks.

Many of our interviewees had continuing relationships with other teachers as well. Pat Barnes noted: "We still get together after all these years . . . just for lunch or something; and it was one of those situations, where it isn't a racial problem . . . but we always seemed to have such nice relationships." Referring to a school where she began teaching in the early 1950s, Frances Schmidt said, "To this day I have kept up with that friendship. We meet once a month, very nice ladies."

For many of those we interviewed, teaching was an occupation that carried high status. Dot Miller, a white teacher who began her career in a rural setting, said, "When I started teaching you were something in the community." This theme was even more prevalent in the interviews with African-American teachers. Of course, at the time these teachers entered the field (1930–1950), few white-collar jobs were open to African-American women. Kate Turner, a light-skinned African-American woman, obtained a white-collar job in Chicago after graduating from junior college. But she soon learned that her employers had assumed she was white. She told us, "Being a teacher probably meant more in the black world than in the white because it was considered a much better job in the black world."

Georgia Tunney, who first taught in rural Georgia, said, "The teacher in African-American culture was really very important. We gave respect; we respected the teacher." She added that respect for elders was also an important feature of this culture. Another African-American teacher, Martha

Corey, broadened the significance of this theme: "A person of my age would come to the teaching field thinking it was a privilege to be a teacher and thinking of the responsibility that we had as teachers and that we had this opportunity to change lives." Making a difference, witnessing change, being a part of something valuable within a social system—these were the rewards for intelligent, motivated women of past generations who had limited options in other professions for creativity or recognition. Teaching seems to have been a gratifying avenue for empowerment and self-expression—and a logical choice.

### The Financial Rewards of Teaching

Our interviews did not explicitly raise the question of the remuneration of teachers. In reflecting on this fact, we have considered the possibility that we ourselves share some of the same reservations about financial rewards for teaching that came to light among the women we interviewed. Still, a number of them did raise the issue in interesting ways, and a certain ambivalence about payment for "women's work" emerged. On the one hand, the teachers took it for granted that, although, of course, they were dedicated, they in fact worked for money.

On the other hand, one of the worst things these teachers could say about a teacher was that "she's in it for the money." This ambivalence was expressed by Ellie Varney, who said, "I think most of [the teachers] really loved their work. It wasn't a matter—well, it *was* a matter of a job, and of course, as you know, the pay was lower than most professions, but I think most teachers are very dedicated."

Some of the teachers mentioned in passing, perhaps because it was obvious to them, that they needed to work and to earn money. In describing how she returned to teaching while her children were still young, Norah Krupar said, "A friend died, and left her young children, and she didn't do for them what we had hoped to do for our children. So I said to my husband, 'I have to go back.' I wanted them to have lessons and everything." And Sally Tate observed, "Of course, we didn't have very much money, and the three boys, so I went back to teaching when they were old enough to go to school."

Dot Miller said that one reason she went to normal school was that she saw that young women who were teaching had clothes that farm girls just didn't have. Kate Turner was divorced after her children were born, and she depended on her salary to support herself and them.

Most of the teachers did not mention as a positive change that teachers are better paid now than in the past. On the contrary, many of them brought up concerns that higher salaries had had a negative effect on the profession. None mentioned higher pay as an indication of higher status or as recognition of professional expertise. While they were grateful for the salaries they earned toward the end of their careers, and for their pensions, these teachers worried that higher salaries were bringing people into teaching (or keeping them there) who lacked the dedication that defined teaching for them.

The teachers' ambivalence about the effects of higher salaries on teachers' dedication also touched their beliefs about the public estimation of teachers. They felt that people expect teachers to work for low salaries and don't respect them when they earn a higher salary. This ambivalence seemed to reflect a class difference that may also influence public perceptions on this issue. On the one hand, Ellie Varney told about a young woman she had been trying to persuade to go into teaching. The young woman and her mother had said, "There's not much money in it." But if some prospective teachers feel salaries are too low, the teachers told us that in some communities teachers' salaries are seen as too high. As Kate Turner said, "Much as you like having that money, it keeps people in there for the wrong reason." And Norah Krupar noted: "I think some of the people who are in teaching now are only there for the salary they think they can get. I'm sorry to say that. They don't seem to care that much about the children."

Some teachers, especially Emily Downer, mentioned a loss of a serious attitude about the work to be done in teaching.

> For example, I would buy professional books, and one of the younger teachers would say, "You will never catch me spending my money like that," but anything that most teachers felt they could do that could help them do a better job, I think they were willing to do it. I don't even know how to describe the feeling that many teachers have now, but I'm afraid that in many instances the attitude is, "This is a job. This is a job." I was surprised to find that. They seem to think, "If the children get it by the end of the term, fine. If they don't, so what. . . ." I think it is just one of the general things that is happening in—I started to say civilization, but no, in the United States.

All these teachers share a feeling, perhaps common to many older people, that things were better in their youth. Yet they do acknowledge that selfishness and bad teaching have always been present. Leo Sparks remarked that she had seen uncaring teachers throughout her career: "They didn't care, and some of them were bold enough to say it. 'I got mine. You get yours the best way.' That is the worst thing."

Most of the women we interviewed taught in communities that could be characterized as blue collar, immigrant, poor, or lower middle class. A number mentioned the feeling in their communities that teachers are paid too much. It should hardly surprise us that people who are insecure about their own future, and whose salaries are relatively low, might see teachers as better off than they are. As Dot Miller said, "Now teachers are starting to earn more than the factory workers. . . . I think when I started, you didn't get an awful lot of money. . . . But now, hey, teachers are earning, are in it a couple of years, they're earning 35, 40 thousand. Secretaries don't earn that. . . . So they're being paid more than many people now."

In response to a question about public attitudes toward teachers, Norah Krupar talked about how little she was paid when she started teaching in 1955: "People had the attitude that if you were a good person, you were dedicated to teaching, and you didn't need money. I think that is what their attitude was. You know those old stereotypes." The "old stereotypes" of teachers as selfless and above personal ambition not only kept community members from envying any privileges that teachers might have, but also granted them the respect due to "good women," who performed the nurturing tasks of the society without challenging a social order in which women had little public influence.

In an interesting reversal of the usual complaint that in our culture respect is based on income, Kate Turner said: "I think you got more respect because it's almost like volunteer work. When you're volunteering, you know people appreciate you so. But when you're getting all this money they resent you, especially when the tax payers are paying, but when I was making $3000 a year, people were grateful." Norah Krupar summarized this point of view and expressed a certain nostalgia for a time when, she felt, teachers were more respected. "I don't think people have as much respect for teachers as they had when I first started, and I think part of it has to do with the salary."

## Questions Raised by These Interviews

It has been particularly interesting to us to understand the interviews in light of the findings of several contemporary studies of the teaching profession. Several conclusions raised by Lortie in *Schoolteacher* (1975) and by Lieberman and Miller (1984) in *Teachers, Their World and Their Work* appear less prominently in our research or perhaps are even somewhat contradictory to the unifying themes of our study. Thus, at several points we pondered the changing structures of schools, society, and the teaching profession over time.

For example, the pronounced themes that emerged from our interviews differed from those that were found by Lortie (1975) whose study was conducted during the last several years in which these women were teaching. Lortie, viewing teaching from the perspective of sociological studies of professions, found the salient aspects of schoolteaching to be *presentism* (the lack of emphasis on long-range commitment to career), *conservatism* (based on the recruitment of people who are comfortable with existing systems of schooling and who have only limited interest in changing the career of teaching), and *individualism* (reflecting classroom isolation and preference for singular autonomy). While elements of these attributes are reflected to some extent in the teachers we interviewed, Lortie's themes did not emerge as the core meanings of teaching from the retrospective and subjective thoughts of the retired schoolteachers.

We also noticed that the twelve retired teachers emphasized issues other than those raised by the teachers Lieberman and Miller (1984) interviewed. Our interviewees first and foremost emphasized their interest in affect (the emotional development of children) above either intellectual achievement or discipline, issues that teachers in the 1980s (in the Lieberman and Miller study) accentuated, although the retired teachers certainly strove for discipline and intellect in their classrooms. Lieberman and Miller identify as the greatest problem of elementary-school teachers the difficulty of fitting everything they are expected to do into the time allotted. Only a few of the teachers we interviewed mentioned this problem, and then usually in the context of describing problems experienced by younger teachers. This may be due to the increasingly external nature of school requirements and mandates. It may be that teachers who taught thirty to forty years ago set their own daily and weekly expectations rather than adhering to standardized scheduling as many teachers feel they must do today. Furthermore, in the Lieberman and Miller study, the elementary teachers believed that the only significant rewards of the teaching profession lay in the students' "words, behaviors, expressions and suggestions" (p. 2). Our teachers found numerous other rewards, including relationships with other teachers and with parents. They also emphasized the social relationships among teachers and other adults in a school community. Thus, we imagine that in earlier decades schools seemed more collegial and teachers felt more in harmony with parents and their communities.

In addition to our interest in comparing our interviews with the two studies discussed above, we looked at the internal logic of the narratives of these retired teachers and reflected on them within a context of historical and recent inquiry and interpretation.

Most strikingly, as we thought about how the three themes of dedication, intrinsic rewards, and remuneration overlapped, we saw that there was a missing connection. Dedication and the intrinsic rewards of teaching are clearly related. The retired teachers definitely believed that the more dedication you showed, the more of those rewards you would receive. For example, when teachers displayed dedication by "going the extra mile" for their students, they also felt satisfaction in their students' success and in strong relationships with them.

The teaching profession, however, seems structured to provide no connection between dedication and monetary rewards. With few exceptions, teachers retain their jobs and move up the salary scale without regard for the level of dedication they display. None of the teachers expressed a desire to be rewarded with extra pay for extra dedication. Norah Krupar remarked, "I feel that in the Chicago public school system, you earn every penny you get, whether you are real conscientious or not."

In fact, as we indicated earlier, many of the retired teachers we interviewed clearly connected interest in financial rewards with *lack* of dedication and commitment. They believed that increased pay has not produced better teachers, but rather has led to a decline in commitment on the part of younger teachers. Common wisdom holds that increased salaries will lead to greater professionalism, which is considered desirable for teachers. However, there is an evident tension in these teachers' thinking between the concepts of professionalism and dedicated service.

Historically, professionalism has implied exclusive rights to a body of knowledge that is not shared by clients of professionals. It has been associated with male dominance of an occupation, as well as with hierarchical relationships between professionals and their clients. It may be said that this masculine construction of professionalism is in essence self-centeredness disguised as wisdom.

Service, on the other hand, implies a selflessness that is an essential component of the traditional stereotype of women's work. The person rendering service, usually a woman, has had a supportive role rather than being in a decision-making or controlling position. The ambivalence these teachers express about the relationship between remuneration and respect may reflect this cultural attitude.

Like many other women of their generation, they seemed to accept assigned gender roles without much question. They were aware, for example, that they could not do some things that men *could* do, but they did not protest at the time or complain even now. When we asked them what alternatives to becoming a teacher they had considered, they mentioned being a nurse or a beautician or a social worker, all careers that fit into traditional gender stereotypes. Only one mentioned a somewhat less sex-stereotyped profession. She said that she might have been a journalist, since she had been editor-in-chief of her college newspaper. Similarly, they accepted stereotyped notions of the meaning of work for women. Their central goals were caring, dedication, and service rather than financial rewards. In fact, they almost seemed to feel that money was corrupting and would subvert the more important rewards they sought.

Interestingly, Lortie notes the same aspect of the culture of teaching but—amazingly, from our 1990s' point of view—makes no connection to gender expectations. For example:

> The culture of teachers and the structure of rewards do not emphasize the acquisition of extrinsic rewards. The traditions of teaching make people who seek money, prestige, or power somewhat suspect; the characteristic style in public education is to mute personal ambition. The service ideal has extolled the virtue of giving more than one receives; the model teacher has been "dedicated." (I suspect that these values are linked to the sacred [religious] connotations of teaching in early American history.) (Lortie, 1975, p. 102).

These retired teachers seemed singularly unaware that cultural values might be imposed on them. Other chapters in this book, such as Joseph's essay on teacher education textbooks, or Trousdale's analysis of the representations of teachers in picture books, suggest that it is the larger society that establishes expectations for the behavior of teachers. Most of the teachers we interviewed seemed to identify the locus of these expectations as within themselves. They saw themselves as wanting to, or choosing to, be dedicated, rather than as having that required of them. And in no way were they apt to connect this expectation with their gender. Overall, they seemed to construct themselves as free agents rather than as subjects of imposition.

Although our teachers did not seem to be conscious of the imposition of cultural expectations, some of them were aware of and in one way or another had resisted imposition of control from the school system. Three teachers (Pat Barnes, Frances Schmidt, and Emily Downer) spoke warmly about their work in small schools where teachers essentially ran the show and there was a "family atmosphere." Although this was not precisely a case of resistance to imposition of control, in that it was by chance that they were teaching in those particular schools, it stands as an ideal of teacher control in the minds of some who experienced it.

Michael Apple has written about the ways—not necessarily linked to "militance and clear political commitment" (Apple, 1986, p. 48)—in which teachers have sought to control their work. Three of the teachers we interviewed spoke fervently of the ways they had resisted change imposed by their superiors. One stuck to her academic standards, resisting what she saw as their dilution; another drew the line at changes she felt limited her ability to respond to the emotional needs of students; a third, being "more of a rebel than some of 'em," as she put it, refused to use the workbooks that were assigned for her first graders.

Emily Downer was outraged when the idea of "social promotion" was introduced in the Chicago Public Schools in the late 1940s and recalled: "I simply did not pass [children who had not completed the work for the grade] and then other teachers would say to me, 'Oh, you are going to have your efficiency grade lowered.' I said, 'Well, that may be. If the efficiency grade is lowered, they are going to have to tell me why.' I was sure that no one was going to say it was because you didn't pass everybody, because to me that was ridiculous."

Leo Sparks was above all else committed to the emotional well-being of her students. She said:

> I am not afraid for the children to touch me and never have been, and even today if they say don't, I do. The people that are making these rules are not human. I don't care how many degrees they have. I used to not allow them in my room if they came and said, "I am doctor so-and-so." I said, "Get out. There is the door. Get out. I don't need you." I even put my principals out. They came up with

those initials. I said, "Don't say EMH or LD or whatever it is. Don't say it. Tell me there is a child that has a problem." I will not accept that label.

Sally Tate, the self-described "rebel," was expected to use twelve workbooks with her first grade students, and found that the whole day was, "Well, get out your language book, or get out your math book." She "managed to eliminate them one at a time; nobody ever noticed." Then there was time to do the kind of teaching she thought was best for the children.

It apparently did not occur to any of these teachers to join forces with others of like mind; their resistance was a matter of individual conscience and individual action.

Perhaps the most common form of resistance an individual can offer to an apparently unchangeable system is simply to leave. Two of our teachers took this option. Emily Downer left because her principal required her to teach a grade level with which she was uncomfortable, whereas Martha Corey resigned because the successful federal programs in which she had been working were terminated and she was left with unsatisfying work.

As Apple (1986) points out, women's resistance to control may have contradictory results. Teachers' responses may represent a victory of principle over policy, yet at the same time their actions may represent a defeat in leaving the system exactly as they found it, or, in the case of teachers who quit, depriving children of good teachers. Apple believes that "the important question is how the elements of good sense embodied in [resistant] teachers' lived culture can be reorganized in specifically feminist ways—ways that maintain the utter importance of caring and human relationships without at the same time reproducing other elements on that patriarchal terrain" (p. 52).

In more general terms, we noted that the teachers we interviewed did not look beyond their individual classrooms and schools to see themselves as part of a larger culture. Their focus on the emotional well-being and enjoyment of their students, though admirable, precluded their thinking about how what they taught the children contributed to the larger society. Like the teachers interviewed by Lortie (1975), the teachers in this group concentrated their attention at the classroom level. Though retired, and therefore possibly in a position to take a broader view, they continued to focus on the personal and individual in the educational endeavor. At its best, as they saw it, teaching represents personal commitment to the welfare of a particular group of children.

As a result of this rather narrow vantage point, when some of these teachers tried to explain what they understood as a decline in the dedication and caring of younger teachers, they looked within the profession itself for an explanation, rather than considering larger shifts in cultural values or economic realities. The one exception was Emily Downer, who linked a change in teachers' attitudes with a general decline in the work ethic in the

United States. For many others, higher salaries, with their hint of selfishness, were the villain. We might suggest that resistance to exploitation in the name of womanly values, positive concern for one's emotional and physical health, the increasing number of single mothers in the workforce, or an increasing emphasis on acquisition of material goods were social causes of the changes these teachers were seeing. Yet awareness of such perspectives were not expressed in our interviews.

Given teachers' inward-turning focus as suggested by these interviews, as well as their ambivalence about the relationship between remuneration and service, we believe that the teaching profession could benefit from the insights that might arise from a feminist analysis. On the issue of caring and compensation, Noddings (1990) has described how feminist theories of nursing have confronted the dilemma of maintaining the service ethic of nursing while retaining nurses' rights to respect for individual judgment and to adequate remuneration. Discussion of this dilemma is muted in the case of teaching because, although women predominate as teachers in elementary schools, men have typically spoken for teachers—as principals, as leaders in teachers' unions, and as researchers. A stronger voice for women as framers of the larger issues in teaching could change the meaning of professionalism in the field.

We believe that the themes that surfaced in this study of retired teachers have significance for teachers who are entering the profession. As future teachers think about their careers-to-be, do they see dedication as an important aspect of their work? Will they judge themselves and others in terms of dedication or lack of it? And what rewards do they envision themselves as obtaining from their teaching careers? What personal needs do they expect to fulfill in teaching?

We would also hope that teachers and prospective teachers might seek a wider perspective on education as a profession than we found in the retired teachers we interviewed. What role do cultural gender expectations play in teaching? How can teachers take into account changes in society without using them as excuses? How can teachers work together to gain greater control over how and what they teach? How can teachers give themselves to their particular students and classrooms without losing sight of their larger ideals for society? These are the questions that the words of twelve retired women elementary school teachers raised for us.

## REFERENCES

Apple, M. (1986). *Teachers and texts: A political economy of class and gender relations in education.* London: Routledge & Kegan Paul.

Lieberman, A. & L. Miller (1984). *Teachers, their world and their work: Implications for school improvement.* Arlington, VA: ASCD.

Lortie, D. C. (1975). *Schoolteacher: A sociological study.* Chicago: University of Chicago Press.

Noddings, N. (1990). Feminist critique in the professions. In C. B. Cazden (Ed.), *Review of research in education* (vol. 16, pp. 393–424). Washington, DC: AERA.

Spradley, J. P. (1979). *The ethnographic interview.* New York: Holt, Rinehart & Winston.

# 6

## A Mosaic

### Contemporary Schoolchildren's Images of Teachers

W. Nikola-Lisa

Gail E. Burnaford

W e believe that one of the most important sources of images of the teaching profession, and the acts of teachers in particular, comes from the perceptions of schoolchildren. Children have a unique set of experiences through which to inform us about the teaching profession and teachers themselves. In this chapter we have tried to capture children's voices as they react, respond, and reminisce about the teachers in their lives.

We think that these children have much to tell us; they give us a living reflection of who we are and what we mean to young children as one of their unyielding "significant others." When we listen to the children, we hear the voices of immediate experience. Children live with teachers daily; they watch, they hear, they absorb how teachers are in the "dailyness" of school life. The children's images of teachers are meaningful because they are both honest and playful. They are important because they come from those most affected by the images of teachers—the children.

But what meaning can be made of these images, these fragments of children's views of teachers and teaching? We must give credence to the immediacy of present experience but also look beyond it, realizing that children's images of teachers also reflect the symbolic cognitive and emotional world of children, the lore of the past in the memories of others, children's natural struggle for autonomy, and children's interpretive framework for describing and reacting to social realities.

It is quite possible to conjecture that the images conveyed in the discussions and stories captured here reflect the same archetypal patterns we

116

find in fairy tales and folklore from around the world. Teachers, much like the adult characters frequently found in classic fairy tales, are either symbolic of all-encompassing warmth and goodness—eternal mothers, fortresses against the evil outside world—or they are tyrants, giants, ogres, or witches who must be vanquished in order for the innocent child-protagonist to prevail.

That children use the landscape of traditional folk literature should not be too surprising. As Jane Yolen reminds us in *Touch Magic* (1981), a compendium of essays on fantasy and folklore, one of the most basic functions of myth and folk literature is to provide "a landscape of allusion." This landscape, however, is more than just a patchwork of odd creatures, haunting images, and bizarre stories; at its heart it offers a structure on which young children build their belief systems. This structure, the metaphoric equivalent of the perilous journey that the child-hero often undertakes in classic literature, is both pervasive and eternally optimistic: the child *always* returns victorious and assumes his or her identity as an older, though not quite fully grown, human being (Griswold, 1992).

Life does not always imitate art, however; children growing up in American schools do not necessarily emerge victorious. There are real consequences of meeting a teacher who is as oppressive as a witch, as frightening as an ogre. There are real consequences of being treated unfairly, of being humiliated in front of one's peers. Jack Zipes (1979), a literary critic specializing in European folk literature, sees the content of folk stories less in terms of abstract archetypal patterns, and more in terms of the underlying "social realities" they express. Ogres, witches, and giants represent real forces of evil in society (both personal and bureaucratic) that subvert, thwart, and destroy individual ambition and initiative.

We are not surprised that the children we interviewed appropriated terms, images, and even story structures from the landscape of folk literature because it is this expansive landscape that enables children to voice their strongest opinions and deepest fears—often quite candidly—about important and pervasive personal experiences. As Geller (1985) notes, children frequently use language constructions drawn from folklore, for example, riddles, jokes, puns, and rhymes, to say publicly what they would not dare to say otherwise.

But not all images of teachers come from this universal source. These children come to school, too, laden with the lore of teachers and teaching passed down to them from parents, grandparents, and older siblings. In turn, the adults children encounter in schools are laden with the reputations awarded them by family members and by society. The youngest travelers in this journey sift through what they have learned about teachers from such external sources and what they have experienced firsthand. They even try on some of the adult roles for size as they ponder what it means to be a teacher, thereby assuming some of the very characteristics they seem to abhor. "If I were a teacher, I'd boss them around all the time, and give them tons of work and they would always have to read when they were finished," a young writer declares.

Such flights into fantasy provide more than just role-playing opportunities; they provide an additional clue to understanding the "social realities" that children live daily in American schools. Whether children see teachers as tyrants, witches, ogres, victims, friends, or mother-figures, they see themselves, nonetheless, as smaller, less significant entities caught in a web of power relations. The young child's hypothetical statement, "If I were a teacher, I'd boss them around" is an expression of the powerlessness children often feel in school. This terse, spontaneous expression signifies the deeply held wish to throw off the teacher-as-oppressor. Like her literary counterpart, the child-hero who fights against tyranny at the hands of a larger, stronger enemy, the young child often sees herself as weak, and the wish to "boss them around," as Bettelheim (1977) has shown, is compensation for the insecurities of the child's inherited role as student.

This stated need for increased independence and autonomy is perhaps the most common thread found in these collected narratives. It parallels closely tales of separation and newly found identity commonly found in children's literature, in such diverse sources as *Heidi, The Secret Garden,* and *A Little Princess* (Favat, 1977). As we have noted above, children's remarks about teachers often include comments on the distribution of power—what belongs to the children and what belongs to the teacher. Challenging this distribution, and creating fantastic stories that transfer most of the power to the child, may be a satisfying means of settling the question of who is in charge, at least for the present. "Mrs. Mezzlre was a new teacher here at scoohl. we tat her evrething she nedid to know. She was a good teacher," one second grader reports.

In related fashion, the stories these children have told appear to have strong themes of justice and fairness in them. These themes are very serious to young children and are inextricably linked to images of adult authority. Teachers who mete out punishment, work, and reward fairly are described as somewhat heroic, regardless of age, gender, or personality characteristics. Those who deliver edicts without regard for individual equity and justice are portrayed as tyrants, witches, or fools.

In this aspect, the writings and discussions of the children seem to deviate from what may be termed classic children's literature. In literature, what is perceived as fair and just is often defined so by the adults. "The laws of the world are the laws of the adult," Favat (1977, p. 34) claims; these laws must be learned and obeyed. Often a moral lesson is learned in classic fiction for children, which serves to socialize the young to the norms of the older generation. Child-characters in classic literature tend eventually to accept these social laws and use them to achieve their ends or complete their journeys.

The children we spoke with offered their own concept of justice, which was at odds with the adult version. This suggests that the voices of children in schools are not often heard or heeded. A third grader states: "There is one thing I don't like about teachers—they yell all the time. They yell at the buses and in the classroom." The images these children convey are important; they are worth listening to and they are worth heeding. And, quite possibly, they hold within them a vision of just, humane teaching.

In such a vision of justice, there is room for Miss Smith, who helps the class make decisions about their new pet turtle, and Miss Bear, who holds class meetings to help children learn to work together. There is less room for teachers who yell all the time, who deny permission to use the bathroom, and who discipline with extra homework. The voices of these children may in fact help us as adults to shed the stereotypical images of teachers that we hold in our own memories and through the depictions of popular culture, revealing life-affirming ways of looking at what it means to be a teacher.

In the end, we have collected these stories not only for you to read and ponder, but for you to act upon as well. We hope that this mosaic of children's images will propel you into the classroom to inquire more about the images students hold of teachers. As the groundswell of reception theories touch our classrooms, imploring us to consider the "child's point of view," we must become motivated by more than just personal interest: we must take it as part of our professional responsibility to move into the child's world and listen with interest and respect.

## Data Collection and Reporting

The children in this study, attending kindergarten through sixth grade, reflect a variety of school and socioeconomic conditions. Thirty-two classrooms from public and private schools in both urban and suburban areas are represented. Since the sample population was drawn from the Chicago metropolitan area, no rural schoolchildren are included.

The suburban and private urban school setting represented a predominantly white, middle-class population, whereas the urban school setting represented a more heterogeneously distributed population. In the final sample presented here, we aimed for a balance in socioeconomic, cultural, and racial backgrounds.

Although we approached our task as researchers intent upon methodology, we wanted the children to enjoy and feel playful with their assignments; we tried to capture the children's responses in as informal a setting or climate as possible. In most cases we knew the classroom teacher personally, and at times we had even visited the classroom on previous occasions.

For the most part, we were the primary facilitators of data collection in the classroom, and, normally, the cooperating teacher was not present during data collection visits. On several occasions, and by special request, the cooperating teacher was asked to facilitate the collection of children's responses. These usually took the form of individually written responses that were collected by the cooperating teacher and forwarded to us.

In these special cases, great care was used in discriminating between those samples that had been contaminated by the presence of the classroom teacher. For instance, one first grade classroom's responses were all orchestrated in "personal letter" form. Each response began "Dear Mrs. . . . " and continued with a profusion of eulogizing statements. We found these responses less valuable than responses that were gathered in a more open-ended format allowing for a diversity of responses.

With regard to our data collection procedures, we aimed primarily for variety: whole group, small group, and individual students were solicited to participate in the study, and both repeated and single-classroom appearances were utilized. In some cases, followup interviews with either selected individuals or small groups of children were conducted.

In all the classes we visited, we tried to maintain an open-ended, informal question-and-answer format. At times, when appropriate, we either shared our own personal memories of teachers we had had, or used an age-appropriate children's book that had a teacher as its central image to further stimulate classroom discussion. Our primary aim, however, was always to step out of the way in order to enable students to reveal their own experiences and impressions.

Student responses took many forms. Often responses were tape-recorded; these usually involved class discussions, story responses, or student interviews. With younger children, a language experience approach was utilized to capture their discussion or group story on large chart paper. Individually written responses usually involved a response to a leading question, "What do you think makes a good teacher?"; a sentence completion, "If I were a teacher . . ."; or an open, creative response to a remembered personal experience. Several children illustrated their written responses as well.

After the raw data were accumulated, each of us read the data separately, noting images and patterns that seemed important and recurrent. Then, the two of us sat down and compared our notes to look for the overlap. Surprisingly, there was an overwhelming overlap of categorical perceptions.

Our study of the data led to the construction of ten distinct categories, nine of which arose owing to recurrent images or patterns, and one which was formulated structurally by the manner in which we asked one of our questions, that is, "What do you think makes a good teacher?" A brief annotation of the ten categories follows:

**Teacher as Novice.** This category reflects accounts that chronicle the dilemmas many new teachers (either first-year teachers or teachers new to a particular setting) face. Often these accounts focused on the beginning of the school year and specifically the first day of school.

**Teacher as Pushover.** The teacher as pushover depicts teachers who, for whatever reason, cope with the pressures of teaching by serving the impulsive interests of their students. In striving to befriend their students, they often lose sight of their own goals and engage in activities they believe will please their students. This is often at the expense of their students' respect.

**Teacher as Tyrant.** This category surfaced as many students perceived their teachers to be dictatorial or compulsively tyrannical. Teachers falling into this category often appeared to work their students very hard, assigning inordinate amounts of homework and dispensing odious punishments for misbehavior.

**Teacher as Incompetent.** This category relates to both the novice and pushover, but goes beyond both to capture student perceptions of their teachers as bumbling incompetents. Although only a few responses indicated this perception, they are graphic enough to warrant their own category.

**Teacher as Mother.** Students often responded that their teacher was just like a parent—usually like a mother to them. Although both male and female teachers are represented in the total sample, all the responses in this category portray only female teachers as being suitable parental models. Males, typically gym teachers, fit more the "big brother" or, if you will, "sports idol" rather than the father image.

**Teacher as Witch.** Although there may seem to be some overlap with the "teacher as tyrant" category, what distinguishes the two is that the witch image is tied into very distinct imagery about the "meanness" or "wickedness" of the teacher's personality in question. The "teacher as witch" is literally described like that—as a mean, vile witch. As such, an aspect of both physicality (appearance) and personality (temperament) delineates this category.

**Teacher as Friend.** This category represents those student views that regard the teacher as someone who can be confided in: someone who is reasonable, fair, and compassionate. The teacher described in this section is a human being with a full range of emotional responses and intellectual curiosity.

**Teacher as Problem-Solver.** This category represents student responses that view the role of the teacher as primarily one of maintaining order. Students were very explicit in stating that the role of the teacher was to solve problems—to reestablish order in the classroom. The problems, moreover, tended to be of both a personal and social nature.

**Teacher as Victim.** Whereas most of the above categories arose in the process of sorting the data, this category surfaced after the data had been sorted for some time. A sizable amount of data lay dormant until it fell together into what we here call the "teacher as victim." In essence, this material tends to portray the teacher as being somewhat trapped—a victim—by his or her own particular circumstances. The teacher is primarily "reactive" when it comes to student behavior and, although he or she may fall into incompetence or tyranny, the teacher never quite escapes from a heightened sense of entrapment.

**The Good Teacher.** One goal for this project, at least initially, was to get at the phenomenon of a "good" teacher. Consequently, we asked point blank, in a variety of situations and group mixes, the question, "What do you think makes a good teacher?" We left the qualifier "good" open to interpretation. Although many of the responses are predictable, even stereotypical, we gathered enough uniquely meaningful student responses to warrant this concluding section.

We arranged each individual category or section primarily by a factor of "readability." Thus, we chose to sequence each section according to how the section read overall, rather than by grade level or school organization. We deleted material that was excessively repetitive or either vague, incoherent, or otherwise unreadable. Both the sound of the children's responses and the individual content expressed guided our decisions. We perceived this piece as a literary document first; we wanted the poetry of the children's voices to speak clearly and to have each section, in effect, tell its own story represented by diverse verbalizations.

Despite listing only the first names of students, we still made some changes. In cases in which there were questions of either confidentiality or inaccuracy (where the taped recording was inaudible), we fabricated a name as a place marker. In addition to the students' first names, we also included a grade-level designation. All personal names, especially teachers' names mentioned in the body of a child's response or story, were changed for reasons of confidentiality.

Regarding the editing process, we attempted to present the original version of each student response. Under certain conditions we changed spellings and punctuation marks—typically, when the original meaning of the students' response was obscure. Quotation marks, in particular, were added when students used them inconsistently or in an improper way that made the reading difficult. Young children's responses that contained no quotation marks at all were left untouched for the most part and thus are printed here with original spelling.

Having said that, we leave you with a mosaic of children's voices.

### Teacher as Novice

Tom (grade 2): Once there was a teacher named Sarah. She was a new teacher and she liked kids. But she didn't now [know] alot about kids. And the kids had to teach the teacher. One day the teacher didn't tel them anything to do. After 4 minutes a big green monster came to the classroom and all the kids ran home and the teacher got eatin and when the kids got home they all had pet monsters.

Lindsey (grade 2): Mrs. Mezzlre was a new teacher here at scoohl. We tat her evrething she nedid to know. She was a good teacher.

Carly (grade 2): Ond day Mrs. Pop came into school. She did't no eney buty. One day a little girl came up to her and said what is your name. My name is Mrs. Pop. What is yours. My name is Emily. My class needs a new teacher because are old teacher left.

Elaine (grade 2): Once ther was a new teacher named Mrs. Meyer, it was the first day of school. Mrs. Meyer didn't know what to do. but the kids new what to do. Mrs. Meyer said my name is Mrs. Meyer. Do you know what to do? Yes. Becky made a list.

Collaborative Story (grades K–3): Miss Julie Crimsdale walked carefully into school on the first day. She opened the door. She was very frightened and very nervous. She asked the children what they wanted to do. They wanted to do spelling. She went to the spelling drawer to get the papers. A big bullfrog jumped out. She jumped back. She turned out the lights and it was dark and spooky! She was scared and turned the lights back on.

She didn't know where the frog was and she sat on the frog. Her dress got slimy! She screamed and fainted. The principal called a mean substitute and she was mad. The substitute was strict. She told the kids to get to work. Miss Crimsdale got up. The children learned not to play tricks on the teacher.

Collaborative Story (grade 2): Mrs. Johnson walked into her class and said "Good Morning." The class said, "Good Morning, Mrs. Johnson." She said, "Right now, starting with the day, we will start with science."

After they were done, it was play time, then center time. Then Mrs. Johnson ran out of ideas. She didn't sleep all night so she went to her desk and then she just fell asleep. The kids screamed out loud and she woke up. She then fell back asleep again. The kids snuck out the door. She woke up and she went looking for them. The kids went home and the mothers said, "Why are you back from school so early?" The kids said, "Because school ended early today." Then when the kids went back to school, they could not find their teacher because she was out looking for them. Ha. Ha.

### Teacher as Pushover

Katherine (grade 6): I think most kids my age think of teachers as people who are to be pushed around, not listened to, and disobeyed.

Katie (grade 6): I think most kids my age think of teachers as useless.

Dail (grade 6): If I could choose my teacher, it would be someone who gives grades easily and gives you A+'s when you really deserve a C.

Luke (grade 3): Once a new teacher came. His name was Mr. Buzz. He was nice. First we had spelling. Second we had reading. Then we had

**A child's-eye view of the classroom.**

lunch. Mr. Buzz said we could eat in the class room. Then we went out for recess for 30 minutes. When we came in it was time for math. After that we had gym at 12:45. It was 12:30. He said we could get are gym shoes on for gym. After gym we had a project. It was a kite. Then we got to go out side to fly them. When we were done it was 2:00. Mr. Buzz turned a boom box on. And turned it on loud. Then it was time to go home.

Jesse (grade 5): We were waiting for our new teacher. Then our teacher came in. He said, "I am your new teacher." He had a pair of wings and feathers. He was from duck land. The rest of the day was fun.

Tim (grade 3): Once there was a teacher named Mr. Hall. He would let you goof off and let you listen to rock music. He would snek out of class with the kids and run around the block. He would give a kid $60.00 to stay and talk. One day he let us stay in gym; he gave the gym teacher $80.00 so we could. He would not let the music teacher in the room. We never had to do work. We would just play. No one ever went to the prinsabols office. A kid asked if we could go on the roof and we did. One day we had a subsditout. She was so mean we ran away to are real teacher's house. He got so mad at that teacher he maid her go home and never teach agane and from then on we never had a subsditout.

Heather (grade 3): Once my mom walked me to school on my first day with my dog Bula. I met my teacher and so did my mom. Her name is Mrs. Goodkind. She's nice. She lets us do anything we want. Mrs. Goodkind won't give us work. She lets us draw if we want. She won't even send us down to the office.

Lizzy (grade 2): A new ticr [teacher] was coming. Her name was Mrs. Monson. She is very nice. We got to go to resess an hawr arly. We cod chow gum in class. We cod go to lonch arly. We had 18 pets, 5 dogs, 8 cats, 2 hamst, and 3 rabis. The kids tot she was great!

Aimee (grade 6): Most kids expect teachers to give them what they want, not give any work, and give them parties all day long and everyday.

Rachel (grade 6): Most kids expect teachers to let them goof around, party, and have the time of their lives.

Brian (grade 4): I'm going to tell yu how a good teacher is. A good teacher does not give you homework!!! She lets us go out side and play kick ball. She let us play checkers and play on the computer. The best teacher would let us play a base ball game. We would decide what to do. That's the teacher I would like.

Collaborative Story (grades 2–3): One day a stranger walked into the classroom. Who could it be? He talked to Mrs. March and she had a sad expression on her face. Mrs. March said she had an announcement to make. I will be in a meeting until lunch time and this will be your substitute. The new teacher says, "Hi everybody!" We're going to have a party. "Ok, agreed the class,"

Collaborative Story (grade 2): Mrs. Granolabar walked into her second grade class and said, "Good morning, class. How are you today? Do you want to work?" The class said, "No!" Then the teacher said, "What do you want to do?"

"Go out for recess!"

Mrs. Granolabar asked, "What do you want to do out at recess?"

"Play soccer, kickball, and freeze tag!"

"How about instead we party?" the teacher said.

"Yeah!" yelled the kids.

The teacher said, "Let's get some pizza!"

It got real wild. The principal came in and said, "Stop! What were you guys doing?"

Then one of the kids threw a piece of pizza at him. Then he threw a piece of pizza at them. The principal yelled at them. When Mrs.

Granolabar walked to the sink to get a glass of water, she walked between a student and the principal and got hit with two pieces of pizza. She joined the food fight.

Josh (grade 6): If I were a teacher I would only give a little homework, and a lot of recess. I would only teach 3 subjects. If a student was bad, I would send them out in the hall, but only for a little while. When they think that they can calm themselves, they can come back in. If I were a teacher I would let lunchtime be an hour long. I would also let the students work together, when ever they want to.

Billy (grade 2): If I was a teacher I would let the kids do anything!! I would have games and partys all day long!! I would have ten frogs!! I would let the kids bring movies, popcorn, juice and posters. I wuold be the nicest teacher in the whole world! And there will be no work!!

Mike (grade 4): One day are teacher was fird be cos of a cas of drok [drunk] driving. A new teacher came to are classrome the next day. She was older thene are other teacher. The new teachers name is Miss Believable. She believes overthing we sa. Wot wer Miss Dot's rules for the room? After ever sudjeet we go outside for reses. and not vary much homework and on the end of the yere we have a party. Hold it, are you telling me the troth? No! Do you have a lot of homework? Yes! And do you go out for reses after avey subject? No! And do you have a party at the end of the yere? No! But do you have a birthday party? Yes!

Brian (grade 2): I am Mr. Noe. I am teaching 8th grade. And I am a very nice teacher. I have an awesom class to teach. I got to let them put heavy metal on. I even let them go crusin! When they go crusin I will. One day I had a bad class. They were throwing stuff at me. I was going to say go to the Priceable [Principal], but I was too nice. I got mad, then I blew up. Then I teached anther class and I said noway!!! I don't want to blow up again!!! I gave them too much hard stuff. Maybe that's what a teacher does. And I became a gym teacher. I teached basketball.


### Teacher as Tyrant

Kristin (grade 2): If I were a teacher I would make every kid write a hundred sentences every day, make them read a hundred books every day, make them do a hundred math problems every day, then do only 99 science pages, 90 social studies pages. I would only let them see one movie every day. I would let them do as many skill packs as they wanted but they had to give them to me. I would only let them be at one center. I would make them clean the floor every day. I would make the girls go to the gym every day. I would make the boys clean the girls' desks and clean the rooms and the whole school, even ours.

Tammy (grade 3): If I were a teacher I would like to teach forth grade. I would like to teach math, reading, spelling, social studies, and science. If a child was bad I would say, "If you don't stop it I will send you down to the principal's office." If a child did not do their homework, I would tell him to stay in for recess.

If a child got into a fight I would give him a detention. If people were playing tackle football, I would say, "You can't play football for two days." That's what I would do if I were a teacher.

Jamy (grade 3): It was the first day of school. I hadn't met my teacher yet. When I got to school I had Ms. Bankly, the meanest teacher in Lake Vuco. The first day we had for homework page 1–66 in math, page 1–90 in language, page 1–80 in readin and page 1–100 in science, and it was do the next day. The next day I had it doon but I had to work on it from 2:30 p.m. to 12:30 a.m. Then we had twice the amount the next day. That day I snuk in her files. She was from the siko ward at the hospital. I told the prinsable. He fired her.

Student Interview (grades 2–3):

*Interviewer:* Do you think teachers have as much fun as you do?
*Fraizer:* No, because all they do is sit there and watch you.
*Interviewer:* Oh, they just sit there and watch you. Do you think that's part of their job to sit there and watch you?
*Fraizer:* All they do, they don't play or anything. Like at recess we play but they just stand there and (makes facial expression).
*Interviewer:* They just kind of stare ahead and don't have as much excitement or fun as the kids do?
*Douglas:* They have fun because when we're working they're laughing.
*Interviewer:* So when you're working, they're laughing. What do you think they're laughing about, Douglas?
*Douglas:* I don't know.
*Colin:* Cause we're slaving.

Scott (grade 6): I think most kids my age think of teachers as mean people, always on your back about stuff, and never saying things good about you.

Jessica (grade 2): I wish my teacher would not give us a lot of work.

Sarah (grade 2): If I were a teacher, I would give them 60 pages of math and let them read, then I would make them count 100 marbles, and if your math was not done you couldn't go outside for recess.

Chad (grade 2): If I were a teacher, I would teach them math. I would send them a ton of homework. Then I would teach them social studies.

Aimee (grade 6): I think most kids my age think of teachers as mean people who give lots of homework, yell at you for no reason, and are stupid.

Jennifer (grade 6): I think most kids my age think of teachers as robots that are so mechanized that they *only* teach or do what is expected and/or appropriate—without bending any rules.

### Student Interview (grade 6):

*Ylla:* I had an awful experience taking a math test. I had to go to the bathroom really bad and the teacher would not let me go to the bathroom, ok. And I go up to her and I go, "Can I go to the bathroom?" And she said, "No." And so I sat back and took the math test and as I finished I peed my pants. I got up and there was a puddle and stuff, and I was really upset and she kind of made me mad.
*Interviewer:* What did the teacher do? How did she react?
*Ylla:* She sat me down. She didn't do anything. She told me just wait until I go home.
*Interviewer:* What grade were you in?
*Ylla:* First.

Frazier (grade 2): Sometimes teachers boss you around too much. They overwhelm you with too much stuff and you can't remember it all.

Renee (grade 2): If I were a teacher I would boss them around all the time, and give them tons of work and they would always have to read when they were finished. But I would give them so much work that they would never get done and on the computer they would only get two problems and I would scream at them. They would have lots of homework to do and on the quiz they would have to say it 100 times, and they would never sing or go to gym, music and art and only the girls would sit by each other.

Adam (grade 6): Most kids expect teachers to give a lot of homework.

Mark (grade 6): Most kids expect teachers to be industructable.

John (grade 6): If a kid was bad, I would send him or her out into the hall. If things were really bad, I would send them to the principal. They would miss any fun activity that I had planned. Depending on how bad that student was, they would have to write "I will never again bother the class." It would be from 25 to 100 times.

Carrie (grade 4): If I were a teacher I would be sturn but kind. Mean but then sweet.

Kevin (grade 1): If I was a teacher I don't want my children to play a lot. I want them to learn a lot of stuff.

Student Interview (grade 5):

*Lisa:* I know a teacher. He never graded on how the person really did.
*Interviewer:* How did he grade?
*Lisa:* He graded on how he liked them.
*Interviewer:* Oh.
*Lisa:* And I know I tried as hard as I could and I never did better than a lot of other people, and I know that I tried a lot harder than other people, but he'd have me lower—I don't know why he didn't like me.

Sarah (grade 5): I had a teacher for only two classes, but like if you have a question, she usually said "You figure it out yourself." Sometimes if you tried and tried and still couldn't quite get it, she still made you do it and it was really hard to understand.

**One child's image of the contemporary teacher.**

### Teacher as Incompetent

Jennifer (grade 2): Dear, Mrs. Warren. I like you very much as a second grade teacher. I like Mrs. Freeman too but not as much as I like you. She is nice to me but she keeps on calling me Christine.

Collaborative Story (K): Mrs. Gerrard walked into her kindergarten classroom and said, "Good morning, class." The class was a mess. "Class, clean this mess up." The teacher was so mad that she wanted to quit. She told the principal she wanted to quit. "I'm never going to come back again."

She started to get mad and called her husband to pick her up.

The children had an idea. They cleaned the room up. The next morning she walked in. She was so happy. She decided to stay. The kids were proud. They were so happy she came back. If she ever wanted to quit, then her husband will be the teacher for her.

Collaborative Story (grade 3): Miss Prichard walked into her third grade class and said, "Oh my goodness! Where are all my kids? Mabey they're gone because my car broke down." She looked under her chair, couch and desk. "I will go to the art room to look for them." They were out on the playground.

When the kids knew that Miss Prichard was looking for them, they went to Chrissy's house. Miss Prichard went running after them. They ran too fast for her and got away. She said, "Oh, I give up." She met Miss Gooblegoo as she was leaving to go home. She walked past her classroom and saw her class was in there.

Aaron (grade 5): When I was in 4th grade I had a teacher Mr. Lewis. He was nice but not all that smart. One time he lost a homework sheet that I had turned in to him, so he kept me in for ressecs. While he was contimplating nature (in other words he was in space) I looked in his brief case I found my homework I gave it to him he said "What is this?" I said, " My homework." Then he said "You didn't turn in today's homework." I said, "No, this is yesterday's. I found it in your brief case and you did not assign homework for today."

### Teacher as Mother

Vicki Kim (grade 2): Dear Mrs. Stanford I like you a lot. You are so nice that you make me feel like I'm at home.

Tanya (grade 2): It's like being a mother sort of to the kids.

Thomas (grade 2): If I was a teacher I would be a good teacher. I would take care of my class and be useful and do my best. I would do my very best in being a teacher. Even if I could not make it to school I would try to. I do like my teacher she helps me with some of my work and when I grow up I will thank her for that. She is just like my mom.

Stephanie (grade 3): She cares for everybody in the class. She loves us like we're her own children.

Jennifer (grade 6): If I could choose my teacher it would be someone who can explain thoroughly, understands what it's like to be a student, and realize that there's more than one relationship between teacher-student—there can also be a parent to child, friend to friend, etc.

### Teacher as Witch

Collaborative Story (grade 1): Once upon a time, there was a first grade teacher named Mrs. Red. She was a mean teacher. She would give us lots of work. She didn't look red. She looked green. She has blond hair.

Adam (grade 3): One day I went to school and I saw the uglyest woman in the whole world. I couldent believe what I saw. She had a pimple and a wart on her cheek it was deskusting. She said "I'm a new teacher. Who are you?" "Just a brat," said Mark. "I'm Miss Goble," said the fat stupid teacher, and I said "buy," laughing at her pimple, and I said in the hall, "she's ugly, I hope she's not mine."

Jennifer (grade 6): Most kids expect teachers to give lots of lectures and make many points . . . they might even expect the teacher to be child-hating. Expecting teachers to look at only their point of view on one side of the argument and not the students. Looking at a teacher's perspective, I'd expect the kids to think I am strict and mean . . . and also that I have a job only to teach subjects . . . *that's it.*

Attren (grade 6): When I was in 3rd grade I had a teacher named Mrs. Kitts. I hated her! It seemed like she teacherd just for the fun of imbarasing and getting people in trouble. One time some body's locker got robbed and I got blamed. First of all I didn't do it and second there was no proof I did it. She clawed me with her nails and literally dragged me to the office. She was a terrible teacher. Whenever someone asked a question, she would answer, "That's not my strongest point in knowlege. Ask another teacher." In my point of view a good teacher is anyone but her.

Cheryl (grade 3): There was a new teacher in our school and her name was Ms. Stricked. Every one thought she was mean because of her name and she looked like a witch.

Mandy (grade 6): When I was in nursery school most of my teachers were mean. One especially, her name was Rhonda. She had brown curlye hair. She wouldn't let me suck my thumb, and she made me eat my mash potatos, eeew! During nap time I used to talk to my imaginary friend, Bobio, and sing to him. She would yell at me and make me go to sleep right next to her. That didn't stop me from talking though. She also told my mom that I was stupid because I didn't know how to count. I was only three. I hated that teacher.

Kurt (grade 6): I think most kids my age think of teachers as either a witch, an acquaintance, or a friend.

Daniel (grade 6): I was with my mother in the store when I saw my old teacher from 1st grade. I was imbarised and fritened. I didnt want her to see me. I kept on goin from ill to ill [aisle to aisle] trying to get out of her sight. Somehow she just kept showing up where I was, my mom and I findly left. Luckily my mom and I never got into a conversation with her and I was glad.

Sarah (grade 6): John walked into the room, he was the first one. He sat down in his desk and thought, "What if the new teacher is mean? What if she hates me from the start? Will she give a lot of homework? Will she be wierd?" It ended up that John was right about most of the things except, that she wasn't wierd. However, it all worked out.

Matt (grade 6): If I could choose my teacher it would be someone who is *young and nice*. I think most kids my age think of teachers as *old, grouchy ladies*.

Adam (grade 6): I think most kids my age think of teachers as mean, old, and oglie [ugly].

Collaborative Story (grade 1): Once there was a teacher and she was strict. She never let you have fun. And at snack time she would say, "Silence!" She would never let you write a story. Her name was Miss Crummy. One of the students put a cake on her chair. She sat on it. Then she got mad. And then she had a heart attack.

Brad (grade 3): Once there was a new teacher named Mrs. Wart. When she walked into school one day a new kid was there. When Mrs. Wart walked in he started to laugh. Mrs. Wart was embaressed. "Wait until you hear her name," a kid said. Mrs Wart said, "Now be quiet!" You should behave better." The hole day we had recess until a kid yelled at Mrs. Wart. She got real mad and said, "I'll give you one more chance, your lucky I didn't send you to the principal but you don't get recess tomorrow."

The next day Tom (the kid that got in trouble) snuck out and started fighting. Mrs. Wart didn't see it until someone started crying. "That was your last chance Tom!" Mrs. Wart said, "down to that office," she also said.

Student Interview (grade 2):

*Emily:* My teacher is a devil. She orders us around. She uses thought control over us.
*Interviewer:* What do you mean by thought control?
*Emily:* Like she makes you think what she wants you to think.

George (grade 6): If I were a teacher, I would give a lot of recess to all the kids in my class. If they were very rude to me, I would be rude to them, and teach them a lesson. I would only give them lessons, no work. For example Billy didn't listen to me. He was rude to me, so I was rude to him, and I talked to him about his behavior.

Dave (grade 6): I think most kids my age think of teachers as mean, rotten, spoiled people who hate kids.

Jigar (grade 4): If I were a teacher I would let my students have so much fun. I would take them out for recess. They would have a lot of fun. I would also help them with their homework.

If they were bad I would give them lots of homework. I would give them a Pop Quiz! They wouldn't get any recess, I would give them detention and expell them.

No, I wouldn't do that. I would be even meaner. I would tell there mom and dad to take them home from school. I would kick them out the city.

Mandy (grade 6): It's boring to color in a brontasauras, I think I'd rather talk, and draw at the same time. I'm in kindergarden, and my teacher's name is Mrs. McGregor. She's real mean. She's kind of boring actually. I don't see the point to coloring in a dinosaur. Especially green. Green's boring.
"Mandy!" Mrs. McGregor yelled at me, "Color now! Stop talking!"
"I am coloring." I said timidly.
"If you are coloring that in, so good, then I'd like to see the green!" she yelled.
Then she put up a board and told me I couldn't talk to any one, She said I had to color in every single spot. She said, "If I find one white speck you'll be sorry!" I hated that experience.

### Teacher as Friend

Cindy (grade 4): I will always remember my third grade teacher, Mrs. Schram. When my aunt died she was comforting, understanding and helpful.

Mason (grade 6): My favorite kind of teacher would have many great features. She would be nice and teach with enthusiasm. She would be energetic and always explain everything and not always be in a hurry. She would think of fun exciting things to do which would be new for me, I wouldn't even have heard of it. The topic would be something that I had very little knowledge of before, but she taught with such enthusiasm that I would enjoy it a lot. My teacher would always be relaxed and not yell! She would be so kind that I wouldn't be afraid to talk to her because I know she wouldn't mind. She would answer all my questions without any kind of agrivation, and I would always be happy in her classroom. When she taught she would do creative things so her class would never be boring. This is my favorite teacher.

Mike (grade 3): One day the first day of school I was in third grade and my teachers name was Mr. Jonathan. He was a very nice teacher, friendly, and open to all are questions. He was the nicese teacher in the school. Then one day he came to school he was grochy because he stad up all night grading papers. But the next week we help him grade papers during the day so for the rest of the year he was nice.

Abeeda (grade 1): A teacher would never break their promises.

Jean (grade 6): If I could choose my teacher it would be someone who *listens to me.*

Katherine (grade 6): If I could choose my teacher it would be someone who cared about people's rights and feeling and who liked books. Most kids expect teacher to see something the kids way and not one adults way.

Meredith (grade 6): I was in a play called "Mr. Scrooge" and I had lost my science log book. My science teacher (who is also my advisor) was very supporting. He told me that I didn't have to recopy anything until the play was over. After the play he said he would get together with me and talk about it. A day before we talked I found my log book. It was in my friend's bag.

Student Interview (grade 6):

*Interviewer:* Can you think of a teacher that stands out in your mind?
*Ylla:* The teacher I really liked was this year, but she left. She was our social studies teacher and she was just fun to be with and she joked around with us and she understood us.
*Interviewer:* She tried to be like you?
*Ylla:* Yeah. She wasn't relating to us as a teacher like I'm higher than you.
*Carrie:* Or, I work here, I know more than you do.
*Ylla:* She's kind of good.
*Interviewer:* She treated you like a friend, like an equal?
*Ylla:* Yeah.

Molly (grade 4): The teacher that gave me the fondest memories was Miss Franz, excuse me, I mean Miss O'Fabolous. She was great she would play games with us and her imagination was out of this world you should have seen her calender it wasn't a calender it filld up the bulletin board and on the 100th day (we kept track on the bulletin board) we had a party, a cuckoo party everybody had to dress weird it was fun that day we went to Mr. Hynals room and his class judged us and I won. She was very fun, creative, imaginative and hilarious she'd make you laugh so hard.

Aimee (grade 6): If I could choose my teacher it would be someone who could be my friend as well as my teacher. Also would be nice, friendly, and would listen to what I have to say. And not favor anybody.

Sarah (grade 4): I'll always remember Mrs. Smith. She is a very sweet teacher. She is very funny and makes me laugh. If I had a chance to pick a teacher for all times I would pick Mrs. Smith.

   I remember when someone was going to get in trouble and everyone thought he was going to get in trouble. But Mrs. Smith just let out a sigh and gave him a sad look and that was it.

Thomas (grade 3): My teacher is very nice and she even helped me. Before I got in her class I was helpless. She even tought me how to spell. So now you know why every body loves her.


### Teacher as Problem-Solver

Sally (grade 3): One day one of the girls in Miss Bear's class came up to her because she was upset because the girl that sat next to her was mad at her for some reason or another and she was going around saying stuf about her and everbody for some reason dident like her. So the teacher said to the class I want to have a talk with you about some things. First of all, we're going to talk about what things we do like and what things we don't. Then we're going to talk about why everybody in this class is ganging up on Meg. So they had their talk. They won the best class award for working together. Thanks to Miss Bear the Best.

Jennifer (grade 3): Miss Smith took her class to the pet store to get a class pet. After a little while the class decided to get a turtle. The class also decided to get a baby turtle so it would last longer. The next day, Alice asked if they could name the pet Patty. The teacher said yes and asked the students if it was okay. They all said yes except Jason. He said the turtle's name schold be Scott. The teacher setled it and said, I think the turtle's name schold be Patty-Scott. Everbody agreed and they lived hapily ever after.

Elene (grade 3): Hi! I'm Mr. Carlson I am a teacher. I teach 2nd grade. All my students are very smart. Janina is my smartest student in the class. I never have to yell at my class. They always listen to me. Today we are going to the zoo on a fieldtrip. Almost all my class is going to the zoo except Mary, Elenore and Kerensa. They were being mean to each other. Now we are there. Two of my kids start fighting about a rock. I said, "That is not a good reason to fight." I took the rock and gave it to Nattiline. She was the nicest kid in the class.

Eric (grade 2): I'm Mr. O'Lankford. I teach 9th grade. Its fun but some times its not because kids come to me and they have problems. I have to solve the problems with the other kid at the end of the day. I am glad I go home to take a shower and be at my dinner. I watch tv. Then I get into my night clothes and go to bed.

Christina (grade 6): Most kids expect teachers to listen to them and also help them with their problems.

Stephanie (grade 3): Mrs. Macron is always there when you need her. And she listens to your school problem and she's nice to the class.

Phil (grade 6): If I could choose my teacher it would be someone who listens to oppinions and runs a democracy if the suggestions are reasonable.

Greg (grade 6): If I could choose my teacher, it would be someone who understands children and listens to their problems.

### Teacher as Victim

Priyestt (grade 4): I am Mr. Dowd. I am a gym teacher. They are making big noises and fighting. I was teaching them how to play basketball. But they wer still fighting now the fighting was over because another teacher was coming in the gym. Being a gym teacher is hard. The kids are making noises. I can't even think about what I am doing. Then I forget everything and I get a headache. Being a teacher is hard work. Any teacher will not think it is so easy.

Matthew (grade 4): I think the day of a gym teacher is very hard. The kids act like brats to the gym teacher. The kids also act like it's recess. They give the teacher a very hard time and never do what they are told to do. The kids always talk about them behind the teachers back. The teacher always has to yell and tell the kids to sit in the corner. The gym teachers day must be so frusterating that's the way I think the day of a gym is like.

Tony (grade 1): My teacher runs around busy all day.

Hiromitsu (grade 2): Dear Mrs. Sloan, Thank you for teaching a lots of things. Like math, arts, soshal studies and reading. Everyone is speeking too loud and you have to scream or yell. So I think you are tired of yelling to your class. If you are tired you will make chatter box. And write the name in the box of the person who talked. I like you Mrs. Sloan!

Jill (grade 3): There is one thing I don't like about teaching they yell all the time. They yell on buses and in the class room. If they are not good I will not take them on the field trips so they better be good.

Gwen (grade 4): A Day of Life Being a Teacher

Once there was a teacher and her name was Miss Haplan. Her day started like this.

September 1, 1990 Miss Haplan was getting things set up for her new class. Everybody started talking when they came to school. She was worried.

Some kids were coming into the classroom. Soon everyone came. Mr. Cline, the principal said, "Welcome to Riley School."

First they started on math, reading and then spelling. Towards the afternoon the kids were wild. The morning was o.k. Afternoons aren't good. She was worried. Miss Kaplan said, "Be Quiet." Everyone stopped acting wild. "Now I want you to write a nice paragraph about dogs," said Miss Kaplan. Soon it was *Gym* time. Which was boring. Then it was time to leave. "That was a not so good day," said Miss Kaplan. That was the day.

Jeremy (grade 4): Day one, all the students were like animals throwing paper planes at me, spiting on the floor, kicking lockers doors, flooding the bath room.

Day two, they improve a little because of a huge lexer [lecture] I give them yester. now they don't spit on the floor or flood the bathroom. All I have to stop them from kicking lockers. I hade an idea how to stop them from kicking the lockers Ill double there home work. lets see how it works

Day three, no one kicked there lockers at all or paper air planes at all. Thank god now everthing is normal now. I can teach very well.

Michelle (grade 3): My name is Ms. Knight. I'm marred to Jordan Knight. He is on New Kids. I'm also a teacher. I'm also only 19. It's difficult but I manage. I'm an art teacher. It's hard because I have to make up all the crafts and buy all the stuff. By the end of the day I'm pennyless. I also have a sore throat from trying to yell out directions over all the kids screaming children. So at the end I have a sorr throat, sore ears, and a headache. I feel like I could just die.

Joey (grade 4): One day I got up and then I got dressed and then I ate and I went to school. I was a teacher and when I got there I was teacheing my kids how to do adding and subracting. And they drive me nuts! They say "Mr. Calomina Mr. Calomina" and they throw stuff. And then someone was yelling and then he went to the corner and I want to quit this job and so I did. I was a police man. I like this job so much. I am so happy now.

Nicole (grade 3): One morning I woke up and I get dressed then I went to school. I was the teacher. I teach gym. I let the kids play scooterholsey. The one boy came up to me and said that the other boy cheated. I said I did not see him, and the two boys got into a fight. I had a horrible day. Then I told the boy's if they are going to fight go to the princabbals office.

Gayle (grade 4): Dear Diary,
    Today was awful! Next year I'm not going to teach forth grade. It all started getting nuts at about 11:30 a.m. at math. I had to go to the washroom so I asked Geta Grossman to take names, boy-was that a mistake. When I came back there were paper airplanes flying around, spitballs on the ceiling, and people were passing notes. Everyone got a detention.
    At recess Ben Gardner started a fight with a first grader. He was suspended from school for 1 week because that's the third fight this week.
    From 2:15 p.m. on it got worse! As usual a few kids were unprepared. When I turned my back in science, David Kreslins and Stephanie Green, the two bullies of forth grade, started swearing at me. They were sent to the office.
    Fortunatly, the day got better and until the end of the day everything was beck to normal. I hope tomorrow is better.

Antonia (grade 3): I am Mr. Rios. I work in school. The name of the school is Grant School. I teach 5th grade. I like teaching them. They all like me. But what I don't like is when they go outside and come in with a lot of trouble. When all the kids came in they start. He was fighting with me the other one said no I didn't. then one kid came and said he was jumping on the swing. I said everybody quiet and sit down and do your work. Everybody did that.

Alexis (grade 5): If I were a teacher, I would ecxpect a well behaved class. I would give an assingment for each subject. They would just get one resses. If they were good they may get an ectra resses. After they would come in and get to work right away. Every month they would get popcorn. If they were bad they wouldn't get popcorn and they would be in for lunch for ten minutes. I would have helpers to grade papers. I would trie to be nice and not yell but if they yell they will be in trouble. Some students want to lern and some don't that makes teaching so hard.

Kelli (grade 3): If I were a teacher, I would teach sixth grade because the students would probably be mature.

Mike (grade 4): If I were a teacher I would teach second grade because the kids aren't smart enough to play brilliant pranks.

### The Good Teacher

Mike (grade 6): A good teacher is a teacher that does stuff that catches your intrest. Sometimes you start learning and you don't ever realize it. A good teacher is a teacher that does stuff that makes you think.

Sevan (grade 4): The best teacher would give us no homework at least three times a week. The best teacher would also let us have art and gym every day of the week. She would let us play games for the whole afternoon every day. She would let us go outside any time we wanted to go outside. My teacher's name would be Mrs. Perfect. Mrs. Perfect would be the best teacher in the whole world.

Frank (grade 6): A good teacher is a teacher that isn't mean to you and doesn't say your stupid. A good teacher is also a teacher that doesn't judge you. A good teacher is a teacher that doesn't always give punishments to you. If they do punish a lot of people, then you wouldn't want to talk to them because your nervous.

Katie (grade 6): A good teacher will go one on one and help people that need help. Once I really did not understand one math unit, and the test was that day. I went in early in the morning and we reviewed for the test. Then I did good on the test. If it wern't for Mrs. Morris I would have flunked the test.

Lee (grade 6): A good teacher would be a smart, well educated one. Someone who would be nice but would still teach (just in a fun way). Someone who would reward students for good work. Someone who would bring in many interesting things to show. Someone who would be fair and not put people down at anytime.

Student Interview (grade 3):

*Interviewer:* What makes a teacher a good teacher?
*Abeeda:* A good teacher would let you do whatever you want.
*Interviewer:* A good teacher would let you do whatever you want. Anything else?
*Abeeda:* She wouldn't ever order you around.
*Interviewer:* If you were the teacher, what would you do with your classroom?
*Abeeda:* Party all day.

Ian (grade 6): A good teacher: Imagination, challenge, a sense of humor, interaction, original, understanding, exciting.

Brandon (grade 6): A good teacher is a nice understanding teacher who gets the point across without homework.

Steve (grade 6): A good teacher has to be fun. They have to use creative ways to get the information in your head. They should be sort of strict.

Carrie (grade 6): He's a great teacher! He's strict. I really like him and he's got a good attitude and what he does it's kind of like, he gives us a problem and makes us figure it out. He doesn't give us "Don't do this, don't do that." We have to do it for ourselves. He makes sure we're doing everything, and it's kind of fun because then we don't have a teacher saying, "Do this, do that." And he's not ordering us. He's just being there.

Mary Jane (grade 2): All teachers are very nice pepole. Everybody should like teachers. Teachers are pepole to help you learn so when your a grown person you have lot of things to tell your children. That's why teachers are here to help you learn. If teachers were not here you would not learn things as your learning things now.

Nicholas (grade 3): A teacher is someone who passes on what they have learned. But also teachers teach you what to learn.

Josh (grade 6): A teacher shouldn't be mechanical. She should have a personality and think of interesting things to do instead of doing what the text book says to do.

Collaborative Response (grade K): They teach you how to be real, real quiet. They bring treats. They teach you how to be nice and not punch anybody. If you make a mistake they would say it nice.

Collaborative Response (grade 1): A good teacher wouldn't scream a lot. Take it easy on the marks. Try to understand the person. Make it fair.

Collaborative Response (grade 2): They give you rewards. They give you treats. They will let us eat in the room. They take you places.

Collaborative Response (grade 3): A good teachr is a responsible person. Smart. Interesting, sometimes fun. Thoughtful, sometimes mean, sometimes a little bit grumpy, grouchy.

Collaborative Response (grade 4): They give you time . . . to do the stuff . . . to finish. They will be nice to you. They don't give you a lot of homework. They don't give you the answer, they help you understand, but they don't give you the answer. They would pick up the classroom. A good teacher would listen to your school problems, like if a bully were picking on you or something. Understands you.

Collaborative Response (grade 5): I like a teacher who gives you a challenge, not just everything that's so boring. A good teacher is strict, but not overstrict, and nice is good too. A good teacher gives you work that you can handle, and she isn't somebody who just rates you on your math skills, or something like that. A good teacher should go deeper. They should be caring and considerate. Loving.

Collaborative Response (grade 6): Good teachers make you want to learn. They listen. They let students help with the discussion. They let you do projects, like art and stuff. They let you work in groups. They give you rewards. There are books to read and they tell you what the words mean in the books.

Jessica (grade 6): This is the profile of a great teacher.

Kathy Houston truly cares about not only her students, but everyone and everything. She will stick up for you even if she does not agree with you. For instance, there is a high-school girl (she teaches high school) that is either anorexic or bulemic. One day the girl came into English looking like she was going to pass out. Mrs. Houston noticed this and talked to her. She found out that she has a lot of personal problems and is currently helping her.

Every night, she works hard on her lesson plans, and it shows. She will test you to make sure that you are doing your work, but if you keep up, you have nothing to worry about.

She is kind, caring, and supportive, the perfect teacher.

## REFERENCES

Bettelheim, B. (1977). *The uses of enchantment: The meaning and importance of fairy tales*. New York: Alfred A. Knopf.

Favat, F. A. (1977). *Child and tale: The origins of interest*. Urbana, IL: National Council of Teachers of English.

Geller, L. G. (1985). *Wordplay and language learning for children*. Urbana, IL: National Council of Teachers of English.

Griswold, J. (1992). *Coming of age in America's classic children's books*. London: Oxford University Press.

Yolen, J. (1981). *Touch magic: Fantasy and faerie and folklore in the literature of childhood*. New York: Philomel Books.

Zipes, J. (1979). *Breaking the magic spell: Radical theories of folk and fairy tales*. New York: Methuen.

# Continuing Dialogue

1. You have read of the various images of teachers held by children and teachers themselves—teacher as parent, as storyteller, as friend, and even as iron butterfly. Write about the image or metaphor of "teacher as . . ." found in this text that seems the most engaging to you. Consider why this image attracts you. Also try to invent your own metaphor if you already are or will be a teacher. Reflect on the experiences and ideas that seem to have influenced your construction of this metaphor.

2. Interview school administrators, and ask them to create metaphors for teachers. Also try this question with school board members.

3. Interview the parents of schoolage children. What are their memories of their own teachers when they were children? What are their expectations for the teachers of their children? Encourage them to construct metaphors for past and contemporary teachers.

4. Comment on the concept that there are "ideal" images of teachers and "real" images held by teachers themselves, prospective teachers, the public, and students in classrooms.

5. As Fischer and Kiefer suggest in Chapter 2, a teacher has a *presence*. Interview schoolteachers (or people becoming teachers) about their understanding of their "presence" as teachers, about their visions and concerns for themselves as teachers, and their perceptions of their images in the communities in which they work or live and in American society.

6. Interview retired teachers, drawing on the questions used by interviewers in the chapters and employing an oral history research genre. Ask them to reveal memories about their decision to become teachers, considering especially whether social class or environments (e.g., urban, suburban, rural), and gender influenced their decision. Encourage them to construct metaphors of their teaching. Moreover, ask them what advice they would give to new teachers.

7. Consider the responses, attitudes, and perceptions of the two groups of retired teachers interviewed in Chapters 4 and 5. What similarities and differences do you find? (In one situation, currently employed teachers contacted and questioned the interviewees with the researcher editing, and in the other, the researchers themselves selected the interviewees and did the interviewing.) How did the different research methodologies affect your impressions from these interviews?

8. Write a letter to a retired teacher who feels frustrated or inadequate at the thought of teaching in classrooms today.

9. If you are a teacher or planning to become one, ask someone (perhaps another teacher, a retired teacher, or a classmate) to help you with your assignment to interview *you*. Beforehand, encourage the interviewer to elicit responses from you and engage in dialogue with you about such issues as how children learn, how teachers teach, and your own personal memories and perspectives on teaching. Record the interview; replay the tape and reflect on your own.

10. Read a fairy tale involving the life of a child. In what ways do the adult villains, heroines and heroes, and nurturing characters correspond to the categories of images constructed by Nikola-Lisa and Burnaford in their chapter about children's images of teachers?

11. Interview children and adolescents about their portrayals of teachers, perhaps encouraging them to use art work and cartoons to capture their images. (Consider asking them: What do teachers need to do and need to know? What makes a "good" teacher? How would you describe a "not-so-good" teacher?) You might also want to ask your interviewees to write a letter of advice to someone entering teaching.

# III

## Screen and Song

# 7

# A Teacher Ain't Nothin' But a Hero

## Teachers and Teaching in Film

William Ayers

Curled up in a well-worn seat in a large dark theater, wrapped around a box of stale popcorn, and illuminated by the eerie flicker of moving pictures across a silver screen, I search in shadows for images of teachers and teaching. This is a private screening, a lonely marathon of movie madness, and my mind and body begin to ache. But I am an explorer, I remind myself, and even bruised or battered I must go on. *Blackboard Jungle* blinks off and *Stand and Deliver* starts to roll.

I feel punchy, and I begin to wonder what a visitor from outer space would conclude if the dozen or so films I subject myself to were her only point of reference. Without experience or memory, prior knowledge, or teacher autobiography, this visitor would be in an interesting position to help me get beyond my own distorting spaces, to read what the moviemakers—these "writers with light"—make of teaching, to see what is actually there.

What is actually there? To begin with, the movies tell us that schools and teachers are in the business of saving children—saving them from their families, saving them from the purveyors of drugs and violence who are taking over our cities, saving them from themselves, their own pursuits and purposes. The problem is that most teachers are simply not up to the challenge. They are slugs: cynical, inept, backward, naive, hopeless. The occasional good teacher is a saint—he is anointed. His job—and it's always *his* job because the saint-teachers and most every other teacher in the movies is a man—is straightforward: he must separate the salvageable students from

147

be saved before it's too late, before the chosen few are sucked irredeemably back into the sewers of their own circumstances. Giving up on some kids is OK, according to the movies, but the bad teachers have already given up on *all* kids. That's their sin.

---

## Blackboard Jungle

These themes are articulated in a very loud voice in Richard Brooks's 1955 classic, *Blackboard Jungle*, a film that manages to exploit perfectly the tinny patriotism and surface smugness of its era while reflecting and, in a sense, prefiguring the underground conflicts and tensions about to burst to the surface. *Blackboard Jungle* says it all. Beginning with its title, it taps into deep racial stereotypes and captures the sense of civilization doing battle with savagery, of white chalk scraping along a black surface. It plays excitedly to all the received wisdom of teaching and schooling, as well as to the wider fears—racial and sexual—of a precarious middle class. Its portrait of the idealistic teacher struggling to save the delinquent boy with the good heart is imprinted on our collective consciousness; it is a major myth. Much of our cultural common sense, as well as every popular film since, is in a sense derivative. The fact that the police were called in to control violence in theaters across the country when it opened (a first) set a pattern that has also become a cliché.

*Blackboard Jungle* opens with a straight-laced, if disingenuous, apology read against a military drumbeat:

> We in the United States are fortunate to have a school system that is a tribute to our communities and to our faith in American youth.
>
> Today we are concerned with juvenile delinquency—its causes—and its effects. We are especially concerned when this delinquency boils over into our schools.
>
> The scenes and incidents depicted here are fictional. However, we believe that public awareness is a first step toward a remedy for any problem. It is in this spirit and with this faith that *Blackboard Jungle* was produced.

But the filmmakers don't mean it. The moment passes, and we are thrust into an urban schoolyard where tough-looking youngsters jitterbug and jostle one another to the pounding rhythm of Bill Haley and the Comets' "Rock Around the Clock." It is sexual and chaotic, and the audience is whiplashed, threatened.

Enter Richard Dadier (Glenn Ford), wide-eyed, shy, a young Korean War vet looking for a teaching job. Dadier, to his delight and surprise, is hired quickly, but he turns to the harsh and aloof principal with "just one question: the discipline problem." His voice trails off uncertainly, but the response is loud and clear. "There is no discipline problem—not as long as I'm principal." We are not reassured.

The teachers mimic and mock the principal's bravado: "There's no discipline problem at Alcatraz either"; "You can't teach a disorderly mob"; "They hire fools like us with college degrees to sit on that garbage can and keep them in school so women for a few hours a day can walk around the city without being attacked." Dadier is awed, but he can't resist the rookie's question, "These kids . . . they can't *all* be that bad . . . ?"

Oh no? Opening day is anarchy. The new teachers sit blinking at the barbarians, while the tough assistant principal snarls and cracks the whip. The auditorium pulsates—kids fighting and pushing one another, smoking and shouting. It is a mob scene. When the innocent Miss Hammond is introduced, the crowd goes wild, and with the camera playing on her ass, everyone leers. The film is ambivalent about the attack that follows later: she really shouldn't dress that way, it says, or look that way . . . but at the same time, these boys are clearly animals—can't they draw the line between wolf whistles and rape? All of Mr. Dadier's students shun him for his heroism in saving Miss Hammond and capturing her attacker.

Mr. Dadier struggles on. He means well, of course, and he cares. Within a certain framework, he even tries. He shows his students a cartoon to accompany his homily on thinking for themselves; he encourages them to see the importance of English if they want to become a carpenter or a mechanic. He encourages Gregory Miller (Sidney Poitier), the good delinquent ("a little smarter, a little brighter") to play the piano and to sing in the Christmas show. This is, of course, all part of the Hollywood dream: Blacks sing and dance, aspirations for working-class youth are appropriately low, and white liberals are loved for their good intentions. There is no hint that the problems facing these young people include structures of privilege and disadvantage, social class, racism, or the existence of two societies, separate and unequal. In fact, Mr. Dadier tells Miller to get the chip off his shoulder, that racism is "not a good excuse" for failure. . . "Dr. Ralph Bunche proved that."

Here is a short list of what Mr. Dadier endures: he is mugged and badly cut in an alley by a group of delinquents; his best friend on the faculty has his priceless collection of jazz records smashed up by the kids; he (Dadier) and his pregnant wife are almost killed by youngsters who are drag-racing; he is accused of racial prejudice after attempting to teach the ignorance of "name-calling"; his wife goes into labor prematurely as a result of anonymous notes and phone calls indicating that Miss Hammond and Dadier are having an affair. Dadier bends, but he never breaks; he perseveres. At his lowest point (with a new job offer in hand), his wife reminds him that "kids are people . . . most people are worthwhile. We all need the same things: patience, love, understanding." Her list is, of course, missing other possibilities: justice, power, and collective solutions.

Mr. Dadier is wide-eyed much of the time, unable to believe the depths to which humanity can sink. About to give up, he revisits his old professor and seeks advice. It is pure corn: with the "Star Spangled Banner" playing in the background, Dadier watches well-mannered students attending well-run classrooms; he questions how he can teach "kids who don't want to learn," have "IQs of 66" and act like "wild animals." The sage old man reminds him that most people want to be creative and that Dadier has been called to "sculpt minds" in a school where he is badly needed. "For every school like yours, there are a hundred like this. This school could use you; your school needs you." Dadier and the professor join in the last lines of the national anthem, and as he prepares to leave, Dadier thanks his mentor: "I think I'll take another crack at my jungle."

Back in the jungle, Dadier's efforts are paying off. He works on Miller, urging him to use his influence ("I've been looking at your file, and you're a natural leader") to break the grip of the gangs, and especially the power of the disturbed Artie West (Vic Morrow). When West pulls a knife on Dadier, Miller backs his teacher. The tide turns. One student breaks West's knife, while another pulls the American flag from its wall brace and knocks West to the ground. West and his gang are finished. Dadier exhorts the whole class to take them to the principal: "There's no place for these two in our classroom." With the bad delinquents gone, the good delinquents can get on with the serious business of learning: copying sentences from the board and so on. Miller gets the last word: "Everyone learns something in school . . . even the teacher."

---

## Conrack

Fast forward to 1974. In Pat Conroy, the teacher as savior—the "Christ complex"—is fully realized. Based on *The Water Is Wide*, the movie *Conrack* (directed by Martin Ritt) is billed as a "true story"—an account of Conroy's one-year sojourn as a teacher on the sea islands off South Carolina in 1969. It is, of course, true in the sense that the later *Lean on Me* and *Stand and Deliver* are true—a few ready-made verities, a handful of simple formulas, a couple of slogans thrown out and passed along. It is a comfortable kind of truth, a painless and uncomplicated romance, an easy belief.

The film opens with the humane and gentle Pat Conroy (Jon Voight) waking up in his comfortable and vital home, feeding his fish, birds, and plants, and gathering his belongings to venture across the wide water to awaken his black brethren on an isolated island off the coast. As the titles roll, the islanders too awaken but in poverty, simplicity, suspicion, and backwardness. But Conroy is coming: he is the missionary, full of light and love.

False prophets are everywhere. The white superintendent, Mr. Skef-fington (Hume Cronyn), who "never accepted Appomattox," preaches that the important things are "order, control, obedience," and he urges Conroy to beat the children: "Just milkin' the rat." "Mad Billy" (Paul Winfield) raves about the dangers of white folks. And the dreadful principal, Mrs. Scott, tells Con-roy, "You're in a snake-pit, son. Treat your babies tough. Step on them. I know colored people better than you." But, of course, she doesn't. Later, she tells him she's "making 'em tough, because it is tough. What do you know about it? You got that thin white skin. I don't have your advantages."

Conroy believes he has a direct line to the light, and he's not listening to blasphemy. He knows better. "We're off the old plantation, Mrs. Scott," he tells her, all shiny and smiling (a model for Bill Clinton, Al Gore, and the "new South"). True enough, the plantation days *are* gone, and instead of overseers, the field is crowded with self-righteous, self-important, self-anointed professional saints. Pat Conroy, sugary and sweet, is the model.

*Conrack* reflects the deficiencies we create in education with danger-ous generalizations, and then reveals how we compete for resources based on the case we make for the recipients' deprived and degraded condition. The object of everyone's ministrations has no name; it is simply a condi-tion. Professionals—saints and otherwise—need clients. In fact, profession-als invent clients who become defined by their weaknesses, their deficits, their shortcomings. In *Conrack*, only Conroy has a name, although no one is smart enough to get it right. (Mrs. Scott calls him "Mr. Patroy" through-out, and the kids slaughter his name consistently, calling him "Conrack.")

If the indistinguishable mass of youngsters has any name at all, it is "Ignorance." Conroy initially asks the kids what country they live in. Blank stares. "Come on gang, What's the name of this little red, white, and blue country of ours? Land of the free and home of the brave?" Nothing. "Honey," he turns to one of the girls. "How much is two and two?" There is nothing there. Conroy's heart is breaking as the scene fades.

Here are some of what the kids living on this island don't know: they don't know how to cook or make biscuits, they don't know how to play games of any kind, they don't know how to differentiate foxfire from baby's breath from Queen Anne's lace, they don't know the name of their island, they don't know how to build a fire or how to camp out or sing. They've never been in a boat or in the water. It's amazing they can even get up in the morning—they are that backward.

It never occurs to Conroy, of course, to find out if they have their own names for Queen Anne's lace or for their own land. He knows best. And so instead of assuming an intelligence in the youngsters, instead of investigat-ing and questioning as a step toward authentic teaching, he launches a campaign of cultural literacy that would make Allan Bloom proud. "Who's the home run king? . . . Babe Ruth." "Who led the barbarian hordes? . . . Attila the Hun." And so on.

## *Teachers*

Next, we jump to 1984 and the film, *Teachers*. Here is the inheritor of *Blackboard Jungle*. Although the corny sincerity and idealized chivalry of 1955 yield to a kind of hip idealism, the messages are intact. Take the question of women. In glaring contradiction to reality, the teachers in the movie are men. The occasional woman teacher is a prop—something to look at or rescue. "Bright kid; great ass"—thus, the sensitive Alex Jerrel (Nick Nolte) describes one of his favorite former students (Jobeth Williams) in Arthur Hiller's star-studded film. The student is grown up now, and being a modern woman she's got it all—a law degree and a great body. The line back to *Blackboard Jungle* is direct: only this time the hero-teacher can go ahead and fall for her; they can hop in bed, and together they can fight for school reform. The hero again rescues a woman in distress, only this time, it is a student (Laura Dern) suffering abuse from a teacher, and the rescue involves a trip to the abortion clinic. The more things change, the more they stay the same.

Or take the question of barbarians at the gate. *Teachers* opens with cops literally unlocking gates and unruly kids swarming into school. Once again, chaos. The principal hides in his office, teachers (one of whom is the school psychologist) go nuts fighting each other over the mimeograph machine, one child sits bleeding in the office waiting for someone to call an ambulance, the union rep is making some inane point not to report at 7:35 A.M. and the necessity of holding out until 7:38 A.M., and the assistant principal (Judd Hirsch), desperate for substitutes, tells his secretary to "scrape the bottom of the barrel."

Alex's phone rings. He stirs slowly, hung-over and partied out, picks up the receiver, and is summoned to school. The woman with whom he is sleeping is incensed to discover that he's *only* a schoolteacher, and she dresses hurriedly. This is apparently Alex's life: drinking, carousing, losing women (in one drunken scene he tells a friend that his wife left him because she wanted more than a teacher can provide—"food, clothing, shelter"), and dragging himself to school.

Alex battles a rogue's gallery in the school: a frightened principal, a union hack, incompetent colleagues, mindless bureaucrats, one teacher called "Ditto" who passes out work sheets and sleeps behind his newspaper (dying one day and no one notices), another who appears as a popular and creative history teacher but in fact has recently escaped from a mental hospital, and an old friend (Judd Hirsch) who once shared Alex's zeal but burned out long ago . . . ("We are not the bad guys; we do good with what we got").

As in *Blackboard Jungle* where there is "no home life, no church life [and] gangs are taking the place of parents," Alex must do hand-to-hand combat with the putatively pathological parents. At one point, he explodes, "The parents and the system so fucked up this kid that I don't think I can ever reach him!" And at another, he asks a mother, "Don't you care about your son's education?" She replies, "Isn't that your job, Mr. Jerrel?" Alex's project is Eddie (Ralph Maccio), the bad kid who will come around in spite of the lure of the streets and his parents' indifference, in spite of the official judgment that he's a lost cause. Only Alex cares, and when he's called crazy, he responds, "I can't help it . . . I'm a teacher."

---

### Lean on Me

Connections, connections. *Lean on Me*, the 1987 film—which made Joe Clark, the baseball bat-toting, bullhorn-exhorting, real-life principal of Eastside High in Paterson, New Jersey, the most famous principal in the world—opens to the pounding hard-rock rhythms of Guns N' Roses "Welcome to the Jungle." Again the montage of open drug deals, of teachers being assaulted, of a woman's clothes being ripped from her body. Again the barbarians at the gate. Again our hero saving kids from their parents. ("Why don't you get off welfare? Why don't you help your kids with their homework?") And again Morgan Freeman—in *Teachers* he was a toady lawyer for the superintendent; here he is the strutting Saint Joe.

Joe Clark harangues, batters, and bullies everyone around him—but for a purpose. Clark cares in his megalomaniacal way. He tells the kids that the larger society believes they are failures—"a bunch of niggers and spicks and poor white trash"—but that society is wrong. "You are not inferior," he insists. And this is his appeal. When Joe Clark says, "If you do not succeed in life—I don't want you to blame your parents, I don't want you to blame the white man . . . I want you to blame yourselves," it resonates quite the opposite from Richard Dadier's invocation of Ralph Bunche. One hopes at this point that Clark is going to organize the youngsters to overthrow the system that perpetuates their oppression or that he will at least find some way to unleash their energy and intelligence. Alas, he urges them to do a better job on the standardized tests.

Clark begins his tenure with the famous event that frames his career. He assembles "every hoodlum, drug dealer, and miscreant" on the stage of the auditorium and, in front of the whole school, expels the bunch. "These people are incorrigible," he shouts above the din. "You are all expurgated, you are dismissed, you are out of here forever." He turns then to the remaining students: "Next time it may be you. If you do no better than them it will be you." It's dramatic—an attention-getter. But the drama is repeated one way or another in every popular film on teaching.

Joe Clark is at war as "a way to save 2,700 other students." He's in the trenches, on the front lines, fighting man to man to save the good ones. He doesn't want to hear about the miscreants; let them go to hell, let the liberals bleed for them. The film ends with his vindication: the school retains its accreditation because the kids pass a basic skills test. In the final analysis, we never really learn how many kids drop out before graduation, and how many more are pushed out by the principal. The message seems to be we can believe in some kids, but the rest are indeed trash. Say it isn't so, Joe.

## Stand and Deliver

*Stand and Deliver* (1988) is "based on a true story," too—this time the story of Jaimie Escalante (Edward James Olmos), the renowned math teacher from Garfield High School in Los Angeles. Escalante battles the ghetto, the gangs, the low expectations. He teaches pride—we get glimpses of the Che Guevara mural and of graffiti proclaiming "Not a Minority," and we hear him tell his students that "your ancestors, the Mayans, contemplated zero . . . math is in your blood." He also teaches *ganas*—desire. "You already have two strikes," he says, "Your name and your complexion. . . . Math is the great equalizer. . . . I don't want to hear your problems. If you have *ganas* you can succeed."

Escalante chases the bad delinquents away, humiliates them, drives them from his class. Angel (Lou Diamond Phillips) is the good delinquent to be saved. Escalante gives him a set of books to keep at home so that his gang-banger pals won't know he's studying. Angel cares for his sick grandmother who has no idea of the importance of school to him. Other parents are worse: one student has to stop studying when her mother comes home from work; another is pulled from school to become a waitress in the family-owned restaurant; a third is told by her mom that "guys don't like it if you're too smart."

Escalante fights the parents' ignorance, and he aims to turn the school around. His strategy is "to start at the top." (Perhaps the trickle-down theme of social improvement is one reason why the Reagan–Bush administrations embraced this film so wholeheartedly.) He wants to teach advanced placement calculus. The principal laughs, and the chair of the Math Department scoffs, "Our kids can't handle calculus." But they can, and they do, and Escalante practically kills himself making it true.

Unlike Joe Clark, whose wife divorced him, Escalante's wife dutifully tolerates his obsession. Escalante works sixty hours a week, teaches ESL at night, and never takes a vacation. Like all the saint-teachers, he has no life. He is never learning something new, coaching Little League, making art, pursuing political projects. He doesn't need to reflect or consider or weigh or wonder—he's living an irrational life with a powerful pull. He is sacrificing himself for his students alone. Whereas Clark casts himself as crucified for his commitment, Escalante is downed by a heart attack only to rise again in order to inspire his students to win their confrontation with the test.

From *Blackboard Jungle* to *Stand and Deliver*, these popular teacher films are entirely comfortable with a specific common stance on teaching. This stance includes the wisdom that teaching can occur only after discipline is established, that teaching proceeds in states: first, get order; then, deliver the curriculum. The curriculum is assumed to be stable and good—it is immutable and unproblematic; it consists of disconnected (but important) bits and pieces of information. The movies assume that anyone with any sense would agree, and so they toss off the familiar phrase, and we can add phrases of our own: don't turn your back on the class; don't smile until Christmas; if you can't control them, you can't teach them; establish authority early; survival in the trenches requires good classroom control; and so on. Everyone believes it—experienced teachers mimic it—and so, beginning teachers grasp for anything that will help them with "classroom management," the assumed first principle of teaching.

The only problem with this prime piece of received wisdom is that it is not true. In fact, real learning requires assertion, not obedience, action, not passivity. It is an intimate act, an ambiguous and unpredictable act. It is deeply human. Teaching demands some connection between the knowledge, experiences, and aspirations of students, and deeper and wider ways of knowing. Teaching is intellectual work—puzzling and difficult—and at its heart it is ethical work. It is idiosyncratic, improvisational, and most of all relational. All attempts to reduce teaching and learning to a formula, to something that is easily predictable, degrade it immeasurably.

Concerns about classroom management must be reconsidered in light of concerns about curriculum—about what knowledge and experiences are of most value—as well as concerns about students as whole people with their own minds, bodies, feelings, spirits, hopes, and dreams. This is a complex process, and it involves our learning how to see beyond the blizzard of labels and stereotypes—how to embrace students as dynamic beings and fellow creatures. It requires building bridges from the known to the not yet known. And it demands liberating schooling from its singleminded obsession with control, obedience, and hierarchy—and everyone's place in it. Alas, the movies are of no help in this regard. On the contrary, the ready-made clichés and empty repetitions feed our collective powerlessness and manage our mindless acquiescence.

Common sense can be more dogmatic than any political party, more totalizing than any religious sect; it is insistent in its resistance to contradiction or even complexity. It wants to be taken on faith—there isn't room for either reflection or objection. Take it or leave it. Films on teaching fall into step. They are all about common sense, and they immunize against a language of possibility—for students, teachers, parents, and the public.

Becoming an outstanding teacher is exceedingly difficult work. The first step is a commitment to teach all children, regardless of condition or circumstance. Movie-star teachers make no such commitment. They invest themselves in some youngster or another and are willing to drive away many more. A second step is to find common cause with youngsters, their families, and their communities. Again, movie teachers despise families and can barely tolerate communities. The common wisdom is that children of the poor are lost in islands of nothingness and that school will lead them into the human family. So too, in many real-life schools, nothing about the presence of poor youngsters—and especially African-American youngsters—is considered valuable or important; their presence is conceived as a problem, an encumbrance, a deficit, an obstacle. Contempt, fear, and condescension are not a strong foundation for real teaching.

Outstanding teachers need to question the common sense—to break the rules, to become political and activist in concert with the kids. This is true heroism, an authentic act of courage. We need to take seriously the experiences of youngsters, their sense-making, their knowledge, and their dreams; and in particular we must question the structures that kids are rejecting. In other words, we must assume an intelligence in youngsters, assume that they are acting sensibly and are deriving meaning from situations that are difficult and often dreadful—and certainly, not of their own making. In finding common cause with youngsters, we may also find there our own salvation as teachers.

**NOTE**

Thanks to Zayd Dohrn, Lamya Khalidi, Craig Segal, and Yolanda Wilson for sneaking into the movies with me.

# 8

# Just Fun—Dreams of Revenge

## Images of Teachers in the Lyrics of Rock, Pop, and Folk-Protest

Fletcher DuBois

When I am with a group of teachers, guitar in hand, singing songs that portray school life or depict the rituals of escaping from its confines and contradictions, I inevitably end up apologizing. This is particularly the case when I get 'round to singing my song, "The Prison of Geometry," which is about a high school math teacher and the strained and fearful atmosphere in her classroom. The song has lines that are meant to be sung with an edge in the voice that conveys what verges on sadistic satisfaction with having power over students: phrases like "time's up now, all papers please" and "the question is whether you can answer the question" are meant to be cold and controlled and controlling. The profuse apologies made to the teachers present and not a little embarrassment on my part are the result of my not having other songs to offer them that balance this kind of critique and honor their efforts.

Some time ago I first posed the question to myself, neither academically nor calmly: "Why is it that the only song I've written about school is so negative?" I felt guilty toward some past teachers, the ones whom I remember both fondly and gratefully. Later, in the course of writing this chapter, I formulated that question less personally. Looking at examples of images of teachers in the lyrics of popular songs (popular here encompassing rock, pop, folk-protest, but avoiding other genres geared almost exclusively to an "adult" market such as easy listening or show tunes) has not solved my initial predicament, but it has helped me get a better understanding of what is involved in creating those images and what they might tell us about the process of teaching and learning.

157

There are a multitude of questions. For instance, when the commercial songs that do refer to teaching and school are listened to, where and how is this done and to what end? When kids write lyrics concerning teachers or learn them from their peers—participating in their own oral tradition—and when teachers take to composing their own songs about school, how do they use those images? Is it simply for enjoyment, done in the name of pleasure, or can it also be to depict, decipher, gain distance from, find strength for, or perhaps even in some small way bring about change in, the lives they lead?

In this chapter, the vital question is, to what extent do popular song lyrics reflect teacher imagery, and how do such lyrics correspond to our memories of teachers and classrooms? Hopefully, some of what can be found here will catch your fancy and take you back or forward in time to what it was, is, or might be like in school. "The question isn't whether you can answer the questions."

My aim in this chapter is to go somewhat lightly on analysis but to present enough varying material to induce a certain amount of confusion in myself and others, which can then give way to finding one's own order. The hope is that the process will shed some light not only on the medium of popular song in relation to schooling but also on what it means to be a student and what it means to be a teacher.

The "tracks" below are meant to be analogous to or reminiscent of tracks on a compact disc. The juxtaposition is not done without thought. Producers and artists spend a good deal of time arranging the timing and organization of tracks on a compact disc. But just as with a CD, with this text you make your own connections between the tracks and can jump around or even push "random" if you like. My attempt is to say something about the form of the medium in which most of these images appear by using a somewhat unconventional form myself. Making those connections while listening to the images may, to mix metaphors, bring some things into pedagogical focus.

At the risk of frustrating some readers, I don't offer any advance organizer to let you know what each of the tracks is about. Unless it's a collection of greatest hits, one doesn't know what's coming up on first hearing that new record or CD.

**Track 1:** Why? Intro-academico
**Track 2:** School days
**Track 3:** Just fun—dreams of revenge
**Track 4:** Two at the top of the charts
**Track 5:** R 'n' R to rap (day in school)
**Track 6:** Erotic sampler
**Track 7:** When cultures collide
**Track 8:** Why? Outro-aca (andnotso) demico

## Track 1: Why? Intro-academico

Why are images of teachers so seldom to be found in the lyrics of popular songs? And when they do appear, why are they almost always either unabashedly negative or peripheral, attesting to what seems to be the meager importance of that profession in the eyes of both the creators of those lyrics and those for whom they write, the potential listeners and customers? Shouldn't there be some songs somewhere that sing the praises of a particularly beloved teacher, standing as testimony to how she or he has helped young people live full and caring lives? I intentionally confined myself to forms of popular music that young people prefer or have preferred, and most of what I did find could hardly be classified as laudatory.

Teachers who appear in the lyrics of popular music are rarely commended, and if there is a positive tenor to what is written, it is usually due to the teacher's erotic appeal and has nothing to do with what is taught. Holm and Farber (1989), having reviewed the representation of education and schooling in rock music, agree. They base their research on the themes they have found in forty-five songs, songs which, for the most part, have been included in earlier studies. I am, however, less inclined than they are to seek to identify trends in this material. As I see it, there just aren't enough images to show major shifts in the depictions of teachers, especially if we take into account the concomitant changes in the media landscape in general (e.g., an expansion of what is permissible in the way of lyrics). Here, I have tried to extend the usual collection of songs by including some more recent and some unpublished material, adding songs by teenagers and teachers, and by paying attention to the folk-protest repertoire.

Those who have looked into the social scientific attempts to define just what "youth" is will know how little consensus there is on that subject. Chronological, psychological, socioeconomic, and subculturally oriented attempts to define this elusive phenomenon have not been very satisfying. Added to this is the gradual extension of the music market so that what was once considered strictly for "teenagers" may now have gained the status of "golden oldies." So what might have been protest may now have evolved or devolved into the realm of nostalgia. These considerations make a simple answer to the riddle of the dearth of positive images—namely, that young people have to identify themselves as separate and different from their parents, guardians, and other "grown-ups," and consequently can't tolerate such images in their music—just a little too simple.

### Track 2: School Days

I did have teachers that I found inspiring. They were the exception to the rule. So instead of trying to write a song about one of the wonderful schoolteachers I have had—Ms. Bozzo, Ms. Webster, Ms. Thompson/ Larsen—to name one teacher from elementary, junior and senior high, respectively, when I wrote a song about school, I took it upon myself to write one more protest song. Was it because there was an available tradition I could tap into? My song may in fact remind a listener of Pink Floyd's "Another Brick in the Wall" with its most famous of all rock's condemnations of schooling, "Hey teachers, leave the kids alone." I believe the particular teacher I had in mind while writing my song was someone who in no way conveyed the beauty of mathematics or life or learning and how they all connect, and I too just wanted to be left alone. This teacher, with her timidity toward life and her humorlessness in the classroom, "inspired" my song:

> *Triangles drawn with a compass and rule*
> *Where the sum of the angles is always the same*
> *Axioms, Theorems, the terrors of school*
> *Where everyone's forced to play in the game*
>
> *Now a collection of points, we will call that a line*
> *And when three of these are joined at their ends*
> *That makes a triangle and so it is defined*
> *And what we've defined never breaks never bends*
>
> *One angle's measure and two lines are given*
> *The question is whether you can answer the question*
> *No excuses now, like I forgot*
> *Either you know it . . . Or you do not*
>
> *The answer remember is to be expressed in degrees*
> *Time's up now, all papers please*
>
> *While handing them back they are always face down*
> *So that no one can see what the other receives*
> *Between them and the triangle some lost that round*
> *Their averages plunging from "C's" down to "D's"*
>
> *But the bells finally rung*
> *And they're finally sprung*
> *From the prison of geometry.*

The song was written more than ten years after I'd graduated from high school, and to be honest, I also remember liking to solve theorems. There was something calming about it when it wasn't done on a test or quiz. (There was one of each every week in that teacher's class.) Moreover, I do notice that I remembered enough of geometry to write the song and that that particular teacher's class left some indelible memories.

There is another song, also written by a student of that same teacher. The student is someone I have known for years since we grew up together in the same neighborhood. It was a different school, eighth instead of tenth grade, and probably beginning algebra, not geometry class. But most importantly, this song was not the product of hindsight. Sung to a familiar tune, it is critical to the point of being cruel, mentioning physical characteristics over which the teacher had no control, and almost in the same breath she seems to single this teacher out as being "the best." Why? Because she was perceived to be dedicated to her job, because she demanded more of her students than many other teachers? Or is it the kind of praise that comes out of fear?

When I interviewed this anonymous lyricist more than thirty years after she wrote the following lines, she characterized how she felt about the teacher in question: "Ambivalent is too weak a word, it was torn right down the middle between trembling admiration and absolute terror." She remembered times when that teacher would humiliate students and smash a ruler on a desk to waken those who dared to doze in her class:

> *Oh, salute the old guard*
> *Though her face is pocked and marred*
> *Though her nose is twisted*
> *And her work is hard*

> *Oh, salute the old guard*
> *She's the best teacher yet*
> *Though she drives like fury*
> *And her ways are set*
> *Cold and efficient*
> *Efficient and cold*
> *You'd better do as you are told*
> *Hard as a rock and twice as old*
> *That's the old guard.*

As adolescents, or through our adolescent memories, our songs parallel the medium of youth—rock music. This medium has often been seen to function as a demarcation line, situating youth on the one side and parents and members of the establishment on the other. It is not surprising that there seems to have been so little room for favorable depictions of the teaching profession. Unlike TV or film which include, though often romanticized, almost heroic images as well as highly derogatory ones, pop and rock music seem to have an unwritten law prohibiting any form of praise for teachers as people who help others learn. Even though they may in fact transmit some kind of information, they reign with terror and youth pay the price.

---

## Track 3: Just Fun—Dreams of Revenge

Recently, while doing a session with teachers about the topic of school as depicted in song, one of the participants mentioned that her 14-year-old daughter's repertoire of songs kids sing in and about educational institutions was much greater than her own. Later her daughter, Ashleigh, and two of her classmates kindly made a tape for me of several of those songs. I talked with Ashleigh about their project and in particular about one of those songs. She remembered having learned it when she was in either the second or third grade simply by hearing it sung by other kids. According to Ashleigh, she stopped singing it around the time she was in the fifth grade. She sang it because it was "fun," not out of any animosity toward teachers. The song itself is so extravagantly violent and includes such mythic elements (the teacher is 40 feet wide) that one cannot suspect any of the young singers of actually having any real malice. The song is evidently quite widespread, for the two other girls also knew the text from their childhood which they spent in parts of the country far from where Ashleigh lived.

> *On top of old Smokey all covered with sand*
> *I shot my poor teacher with a red rubber band*
>
> *I shot her with pleasure, I shot her with pride*
> *I couldn't have missed her, she was 40 feet wide*
>
> *I went to her funeral, I went to her grave*
> *Some people threw flowers but I threw grenades*
>
> *I blew up the city, I blew up the town*
> *I shot my poor teacher right out of the ground*
>
> *I looked in her coffin but she still wasn't dead*
> *So I took a bazooka and blew off her head.*

Is this the verbal revenge of the powerless, or is it an example of what some have seen as typical for elementary school-aged kids, namely, a reveling in stories about, and identifying with, figures who embody extraordinary powers? Or are those two possibilities somehow related? Here the teacher may be called poor, but she exhibits mythic qualities of persistence—she is nearly indestructible.

I wonder when and where second and third graders sang/sing this and other rebellious ditties. Not in the auditorium at school functions where parents are invited to attend, and not within earshot of the not so mythical teacher they see every weekday, that seems certain. And when they are sung, is it done with the excitement of performing something that is forbidden? Is it the verbal equivalent of pointing the toy gun and saying, "bang you're dead"? Are these songs just as necessary for young kids as some say fairy-tales are with their built in opportunity to identify with giant-killers and tricksters who overcome incredible odds? The oral tradition among young children is a fascinating topic, as is the notion of young children defending themselves against totally succumbing to the power of a near total institution by subversive singing. But then someone else will come along and offer an analysis of how such songs actually ensure that children do not then or later seek to change those institutions. So it goes.

Given enough time and an atmosphere that isn't threatening, teachers will, I have found, start to remember not only the formal school songs they once sang—those slow-paced, solemn alma maters sung at official occasions—but also songs like the one above where the teacher or the school meets some harsh fate. Another example is set to the tune of the "Battle Hymn of the Republic." After the teacher hits the child with a ruler, either revenge is had comically ("I hit her in the bean with a rotten tangerine") or drastically ("I stood behind the door with a loaded forty-four"). As a rule, well-known songs furnish the framework for such compositions. There is something of the campfire mentality about these songs; they are jolly, meaning no one harm. But underneath there must be some memory of what forced attendance meant and the blessing of a "snow" day. The pressure and the fear of humiliation are buried somewhere in our bodies. I don't believe, however, that these songs are what will necessarily trigger such memories, but they may have helped to make bearable what caused the memories in the first place.

When I asked some teachers once to write their own songs about school, one small group wrote their own version of "Old Smokey." They came up with a vendetta aimed at a principal. It begins

> On top of our desk all covered with work
> There lies our dead principal, oh what a jerk

One might think that since the principal is already dead the teachers are creating a milder version than the one they probably knew as kids where a representative of their own profession is blown away. But no . . . their song continues:

> Poor man was a loser right from the start
> So we all decided to rip out his heart

Another verse mentions his "last rites" and the fact that he had "failed his own test." The burial motif may be a carryover from the other earlier song. Extreme violence seems to be part of this genre, as does the idea of putting the person in power out of commission. But again the nonrealistic images of brutality make the song somewhat akin to a "B" grade horror movie one can laugh at because the special effects are so obviously just that. Still I am left with another question: Is it the hierarchical structure of school that fosters such a need to vent anger in a way that defuses it?

As a sign of exasperation with a part of the administration, a song like this may offer a little comic relief but the entrenched view of the implacable administrator will not in the long run permit the kind of change that I presume some of the teachers who wrote those lyrics would like to see. The song seems to be saying that the only way to improve things would be to get rid of the principal. If so, is this not tantamount to an admission of defeat in advance and thus an alibi for not attempting to seek change here and now?

One standard song that has been remodeled to serve other purposes is Merle Travis's "Sixteen Tons." Soon after it appeared, according to the folklorists Edith Fowke and Joe Glazer (1973), a number of versions depicting the plight of the overworked teacher were heard. One of them, reprinted in their *Songs of Work and Protest*, mentions overcrowded classrooms, inattentive pupils, too many papers to grade, and the results of physical violence, black eyes, and being lame ("I turned my back and then came the chalk"). Again this is meant as hyperbole. Written by an anonymous woman who taught in Arkansas, the text takes on new meanings in the 1990s where comic exaggeration turns out to be reality.

---

## Track 4: Two at the Top of the Charts

In the beginning of March 1992, "Shadow" Stevens, a top forty DJ, gave the introductory information about the number one single in typical riddle fashion: "This young 18-year-old had her first hit rise to Number One and stay there for five weeks! More than twenty years ago another teenage girl also had a hit stay for that long at the very top of the charts . . . ironically both that singer and the present one are known only by their first names."

Lulu's hit in 1967 was "To Sir with Love." Here my ears perk up, knowing that song to be one of the very few songs sung in honor of a teacher. I also know that song to be the exception to the rule, having been, I assume, written for the film of the same name. In the movie Sidney Poitier plays Mark Thackeray, the black West Indian engineer turned teacher, who overcomes all odds, flaunts curricular convention, and wins the admiration of his students. Lulu appeared in the film and sang the song at the end of a school party where Thackeray is moved to rethink his decision to quit teaching.

For an English audience the reference to "sir"—the form of address used for male teachers at that time—would have been clear. Although the movie has a British flavor to it, I believe it deserves mention in a discussion of American images of teachers owing to the film's and song's popularity in the United States during the sixties. I remember having been intensely embarrassed at Lulu's performance of the song in the film when I saw it not too long ago; this may have been partly due to my finding the scene "dated" and unrealistic in the extreme. (The sixties attire amused me as well.) But more importantly, I surmised that the song was the product of the medium of film and was hardly representative of teacher songs in the rock/pop genre. When Holm and Farber cite John Sebastian's "Welcome Back" as the great exception where a teacher is depicted positively with regard to their profession, they fail to note that this song was used as the music for a TV series about school which had "welcome back" in the title. My working assumption here is that the general rule of excluding positive references to teachers in song can be overlooked if that music is used primarily as the vehicle for film or TV. Those media, their own specific characteristics and catering to the audiences they seek to attract, provide other kinds of rules.

Then the new song sung by Shanice comes on. I haven't heard it before. And there it is right before my ears—the typical school reference. The song starts out with the singer describing how she is "drifting away" in the classroom, gazing out on to the "windows of the world." She is not paying attention. She sings, "I can't hear the teacher. His books don't call me at all." She is so involved in something else that she has tuned the teacher out. After a few more lines we know why. It's because, as the title of the song says, "I Love Your Smile." The smile of the person she's in love with is vastly more worthy of her attention than anything the teacher might possibly say.

The whole song does not take place in school; the second verse actually centers on her workplace and on what she wants to buy. Her boss is "lame," that is, another person in power who is not worth listening to, and thus perhaps, like the teacher, is peripheral. The verses take twenty seconds apiece. They are greatly outweighed by the instrumental refrain and, in some versions, the rap portion of the song. When I was taking down the words, I found that at first I couldn't understand what followed "I can't hear the teacher." Is this form mirroring content, or is it simply a coincidence? In any case, most of the lyrics here are probably far less important to the success of the song than the buoyant easy-to-remember refrain and arrangement. To really find our way into these texts, we would have to continually keep the music in mind. Lyrics to songs aren't poems; they are meant to be sung, and what gets lost on the printed page can hardly be overestimated.

The video of Shanice's song also underscores how inessential the school reference is. The visuals center around Shanice being photographed by a young man, the one with the smile, while singing either before an old-fashioned microphone or in modern landscapes, neither of which is in any way associated with school. At the very end of the video, the tables are turned and she finally photographs him. The subtext is definitely erotic, not academic. The shifts in the video, from black and white to color, from photo session to a family gathering outdoors, from thirties imagery to the present, are done (as is typical for music video) rapidly. In effect, it must not be boring and slow as the pace of the classroom is portrayed. The written and spoken pedagogical word cannot measure up to the visual, tactile, and auditory combinations offered up in video or romance.

In the song, there is something, not someone, that actually is said to teach. Time has "taught" her that she can "be better" because of this new-found love. And this is a lesson she is more than willing to learn. The classroom teacher isn't the *real* teacher; real lessons are learned out of school.

## Track 5: R 'n' R to Rap (Day in School)

In some songs schooling is the focus of the lyrics. The classic is Chuck Berry's "School Day." It begins with getting up to go to school and ends after three, when you are finally able to put down your "burdens" (the textbooks) and head for the haven of the juke joint where you get to choose what you want to hear by putting the coin "right into the slot" and can do what you've been longing to do all day—dance. In between, Berry describes the trials and tribulations of just getting through the day in school. The kid is "hoping to pass," working hard but distracted by the guy behind him who won't let him be. There is a hectic overcrowded lunchroom, and there is not really enough time to eat.

When the classroom scene resumes, replete with opened books, there comes the withering observation, "Gee, but the teacher don't know how mean she looks." I consider this to be a truly brilliant line that conveys the gulf between the teacher's conception of who she is and how she is perceived by students. (It has so much packed into so few words, and it attests to Berry's brilliance.) It does not totally condemn the teacher, for she is not aware of her effect and does not intend to seem cruel. But it is perfectly clear how she comes across to her students.

This is the one teacher during the day that is described in visual terms. The teacher at the beginning of the song is simply fulfilling the require-ments of rhyme by "teaching the golden rule," and she functions generically. It is the intimidating teacher that actually has an individual part to play in the song. This teacher who is introduced with the imperative "open your books," is someone who is in a position to command and does so. There is not the slightest indication that what she is telling them to read is important enough even to be mentioned. What is important is that she can make them open those books and close them.

It is not irrelevant that the teacher is female and that the student (at least in the original) is male. This is part of the high school drama. Today when the process of identification is being questioned and the notion of role models is being glorified, it is perhaps a useful experiment to change the gender in the song and see if it makes a difference to its dynamic.

Berry did not write the song as a description of his own schooling but rather as an attempt to reach the market of white kids that, up until that time, had been denied to him and his music. His idea, according to the interview in the film documentary on him, *Chuck Berry, Hail! Hail! Rock 'n' Roll,* (Hackford, 1987), was to write simply about what most young people experience. One of those things is school. Earlier in a *Rolling Stone* interview (Salvo, 1972), Berry makes a point that he wrote the song as an adult in a hotel, not as a teenager in school. What he does convey—with a great economy of words and a wonderful sense for the hidden/implicit curriculum—is the feel of the rhythm of high school, the hurry, the shifts of masses of young people all at one time, and the stress of trying to survive and pass against the odds of distractions, unsympathetic teachers, and the power of a much greater priority, namely, one's libido.

The song comes toward the end of the documentary on Berry. It is the grand finale of the live concert footage. A red convertible is brought on stage with Berry standing up in it, and he begins the number from the automobile. Berry urges the audience, which is almost exclusively white, to chime in only after the scene has shifted from school to the juke joint. The song is used then as a hymn to rock and roll sung by the audience that claps, sings along (a few dance), and celebrates the sensuous musical pleasure that is found outside the confines of the classroom, school, and whatever else has been weighing them down.

A much more recent depiction of school, a rap number by Young M.C., has the same structure—morning, lunchroom scene, and afternoon—with the emphasis on the erotic, as does Berry's classic. This time the student is the narrative voice. He gets to school late again, hearing the sound of his own "sneakers and the scratching of chalk." He receives a sarcastic greeting from his first period teacher who, when he asks to go to the bathroom, "got upset and screamed out 'no.' " This refusal leads into the recurring punch line which includes the title of the song: "It's off to the principal's office you go."

There are humorous moments: the gum stuck to both him and the seat of his chair, the applesauce that is so old it breaks his front tooth, and the late pass the nurse finally gives him which he wears "like a gun on my hip."

The bitter climax comes in the afternoon when he is passing notes, and his love letter is intercepted by the teacher, who reads all of it aloud. For a third time he is sent to the principal's office, but this seems far less important than the fact that his friends and even his girl had laughed at his letter. The conclusion, said as an afterthought, is that all this will be nothing compared to what happens when report cards come out.

The teachers in Young M.C.'s rap are not unaware of what they can do. They are malicious. Here there is no mention of the golden rule, or anything that the teacher teaches. (Berry's American history and practical math or any other subjects are absent, although the rapper does unsuccessfully try to copy another student's notes.) The student/hero seems to be caught up in an institution where the teacher's role is reduced to that of being a disciplinarian. The adults seem to have one common task: to send people to the principal's office—the seat of power and punishment. Here, too, it is not the teacher who is in the spotlight but rather the student who is trying to negotiate his way through one more day at school. It is an example of that typical tension between the kids and the older people who wield institutional power or at least are taken as symbols of a way of life not worth imitating. The song has a male protagonist making do, surviving the onslaughts that are to be expected when one bucks the system and refuses to conform to adult expectations.

How real live students actually make do is dependent on what they think school holds for them and what they have experienced in the way of success and failure in educational institutions. This varies, of course, according to social and economic class and gender.[1] But neither Berry nor Young M.C. is engaging in sociological study of adolescent behavior; they are evoking—with humor—pictures of the hurried, harried, hassled, and nevertheless undaunted young hero (where are the undaunted heroines?) for whom the operative words are more likely to be "dance" or "romance" and the all-important activities are apt to happen after school.

## Track 6: Erotic Sampler

If one wanted to present a new number constructed by sampling a variety of songs that deal with education and eroticism, the greatest choice would be among those songs that depict students and their dating rituals. But there is a much smaller collection of songs that involve a teacher-student connection. Abba sings about "The Day I Kissed the Teacher" in which the student admits that she taught her math teacher "a lesson or two." There is Elton John's atypical declaration of desperate devotion, "Teacher, I Need You," in which he tries to look like he is learning and intelligent merely in order to impress her. There is also Van Halen's much more aggressive "Hot for Teacher," where the implication is that the teacher, too, is interested in having the student stay after school but not as a punishment. Here there is a collage of spoken references to school and some off-color metaphors meshed with a heavy metal vocal and instrumental where the student sees what he has missed and realizes that "homework was never like this." In these three songs we run the gamut of supersweet to raging sound.

Sting's "Don't Stand So Close to Me," which was a hit for The Police, is one of those songs in which many people know the refrain but very few have any idea of what the rest of the text is about. The refrain, besides being a perfect example of incremental repetition, is apparently the only one from a hit song that is sung from the teacher's point of view. The teacher has become the subject of a student's romantic fantasy, and he is sorely tempted to reciprocate. The verses deal both with the hardships for the girl (the "teacher's pet"), who has to put up with the jealousy among her girlfriends, and with the frustration and recriminations that he has to bear. The refrain is a demand or plea for physical distance. But it seems to no avail. He "sees her" and ends up like a character in one of Nabokov's novels—meaning, I presume, that their romance is like that of Lolita, a very young girl, and a much older man.

Sting's own experience as a teacher of teenage students was limited to a brief period. In the few years that he actually was employed as a teacher, he taught 10 and 11 year olds (Sellers, 1989), so the song is not, he maintains, autobiographical. He seems to have dissociated himself from the profession, saying that he assumes the children he taught learned very little from him but that he gained experience in being able to stand up before a group and stay in control. In Sting's song what is learned is not subject matter, but how fellow students and colleagues react to the possibility of a forbidden affair that blurs the lines between what should and shouldn't be and how hard it is to try to put out the flame once it is burning.

A more recent example of the erotic connection is by Extreme, a heavy metal group that is currently quite popular. Their song, "Teacher's Pet," appeared on their first album as the track immediately following their "Mutha (Don't Wanna Go to School Today)." While "Mutha" presents the teacher as "always looking down," frowning and telling the student to find some place else to doze (school is confinement contrasted to the preferable "going out to play"), "Teacher's Pet" has the teacher as the object of sexual lust. The song contains a multitude of sexual innuendos: a reference to "oral examination," puns on the word "body," as in the student body or in the suggestion that the teacher can only get through to her students by means of "body chemistry." The topic of what they call the "teacher-student relation" and academic details can be dealt with in this song precisely because this is done while at the same time breaking taboos. The song functions as a provocation to the educational apparatus, which leaves no place for libidinal pleasure.

Much of the content of these songs is meant to goad the potential adult (who is not listening) and to be provocative. The young student (in Abba's song, a female; in Van Halen's and Extreme's, a male) is the one who makes advances and brings the sought-after teachers into a position where they could be embarrassed. The sexual realm, when it is equated with pleasure and not propagation, is suddenly the student's domain. This area is quite banned from school. The curriculum does allow for information about the possible risks associated with sexual contact (notions of love and commitment, perhaps, the biological facts of birth, certainly), but never, never does it celebrate sexuality as something that feels good. The teacher's professional role bans any display of sexuality. Since one of rock's prime subjects *is* sexuality, the teacher can only be depicted as unnatural and foreign to the world of young listeners.

## Track 7: When Cultures Collide

What happens when cultures collide? Do some lyrics portray what it is like to be forced to attend an institution that does not reflect one's own cultural identity? Joan Baez has written extensively about her own growing years, detailing her dislike not only of formal education, but also of teachers who have made a difference in her life. In *A Troubadour as Teacher, The Concert as Classroom* (DuBois, 1985), I have dealt at length with her depictions of schooling in a variety of media and with her own efforts to motivate young people to learn about nonviolence as a way to create social change. But what is relevant here is Baez's ethnic background, specifically her having a Mexican father and a mother who is Scotch/Irish and how that affected her experience at school. On several occasions, she has described how her dark skin, coupled with her inability to speak Spanish, isolated her from both fellow Mexican students and whites. Her song, "Honest Lullaby," which is about how she survived the hard junior and senior high years with the help of her singing and of her mother's honest caring, alludes to the competition centered around wearing the right clothes, to the mixture of various cultures at her school ("yellow, brown, and black and white"), to the energy it cost to remain a virgin, to her experiences in other countries and her not being honored by those in the town where she lived, and much more. But there is not a word about a teacher.

Although in her autobiography Baez recalls a teacher's misguided and racist attempts to make her feel good about her Spanish heritage (Baez, 1987), here in a musical idiom the all important thing is social life in school, the struggle for status: "Early, early in the game, I taught myself to sing and play and use a little trickery on kids who never favored me." It is the peers who are all important here. My point is that what Baez chooses to relate in song may be influenced by the nature of the medium and its ability to bond young people together for however brief a time.

One of the most bitter attacks on formal schooling in song form was written by another woman who rose to fame in the early sixties folk revival, the Native American Buffy St. Marie. "Suffer the Little Children" does not, however, deal solely with the predicament of Native Americans being forced into a classroom that does not reflect their traditions or fulfill their needs. (Other of her songs adamantly point to the injustices perpetrated on Native Americans by whites, e.g., "Now that the Buffalo's Gone.") The text of "Suffer . . . " is ironic and the music dissonant. The main culprit is the mother who is determined to have her sons be doctors or lawyers. Fathers and daughters don't appear. School has nothing to do with truth and everything to do with the breaking of spirits. There are images of lambs and slaughter. The performance is one of high-pitched anger. Her final indictment is in the form of an injunction: "teachers of the world teach them to fake it well."

Joan Baez quit college after only a few weeks of attending classes but later found her own alternative educational institutions and received several honorary doctorates. Buffy St. Marie, who disliked school, was nevertheless quite a successful college student. Baez is aware of how Chicanos have been disadvantaged by the school system and St. Marie, who is a full-blooded Cree, is all too aware of how formal educational institutions have harmed fellow Native Americans. Both of these singer-songwriters are highly critical of the institution called school, but what they choose to comment on in these two particular songs couldn't be more different. In the one song the mother is the person who helps the child survive the vicissitudes of school, whereas in the other the mother drives the child relentlessly, deifying the goal of academic success.

Two final examples of cultural conflict in schools come from Willie Dunn, a singer-songwriter and filmmaker who works in Canada. The songs deserve mention even though Dunn is Canadian and his songs are not particularly familiar to a U.S. audience. He belongs to the Micmac/Metis tribe (in Restigouche, Quebec) and writes songs about Native Americans. His "School Days" likens his years spent in the classroom to a prison sentence. The teacher reads the charge, and the principal sentences him for having been "at large" for five years and for having demonstrated ingenuity, creativity, spontaneity, and curiosity. He is also guilty of catching bees and climbing trees. The sentence adds up to the number of years one has to spend in school. The accusation is sung to a cheerful hoe-down square dance tune that, at least for me, takes on the function of musically portraying the freedom he has finally gained; he is finally out of there. The teacher is seen as only one part of a structure that systematically stifles real interests and inflicts pain.

Another of his songs, "Charlie Wenjack," recounts the true story of a 12-year-old boy who ran away from the reservation school in winter in order to find his father. The boy walks a long way before finally dying from the cold and exhaustion. In spite of the quite lyrical presentation, this song is no less powerful. Where were the real teachers who do not represent something foreign to Charlie Wenjack and his father and why have they not reached the young boy? Sometimes school kills.

----

### Track 8: Why? Outro-Aca (andnotso) Demico

There are many songs about school that I have not mentioned. Other works can serve as a resource for those who want to find more songs on the subject of schooling (see Butchart & Cooper, 1987; Holm & Farber, 1989) or to read and reflect more broadly on the role of popular music in youth culture (e.g., Lull, 1987, or Kotarba in *Youth and Society,* June 1987).

Despite format radio stations and the necessity for advertisers to know their market (despite the existence of subcultural styles), I believe it is getting harder and harder to identify the market for specific types of rock/pop music. Can this be due to a blurring of age divisions which may in part be traced to what Meyrowitz (1985) calls "the impact of electronic media on social behavior"? Does this mean that, in the future, images of teachers in song will change because lines of demarcation are no longer feasible? Will compact disc and music video pave the way for different images of schooling, and if so what will they be like?

I still have not come to a real understanding of why it is so hard to write about good teachers in the medium of song. There is the aspect of a ritual division of youth from the adult world, but those lines may be getting blurred as more and more former acts of rebellion become "golden oldies." Perhaps the wounds of what happens at school call out more to be exorcised through song. Perhaps it's pure economics and the topic just isn't commercial, or then again the task of convincingly portraying a great teacher in three minutes of song text may just be too overwhelming.

Years ago when I tried to capture in song the impact one college professor had (and still has) on my life, I ended up describing a jade Buddha statue I'd seen. Although later I was able to write about him and how he teaches (DuBois, 1988) in song, I had to mythologize to convey what having a real teacher meant to me. In the process I did not use the word "teacher" once in the text. The first verse goes:

> The man of jade has eyes that laugh
> The man of jade who is first and last
> Who loves the ancient words for what they mean
> Who moves as the clouds move reflected in a stream
> Who comes to your memory like a morning dream
> The man of jade

Toward the end of the song we are assured that "his shadow casts a light on the darkest path." So there are teachers who do help one see more and care more and make it through hard times. I wonder how many other song texts there are where the positive references to the teacher remain hidden.

**NOTE**

1. See Frith, 1981, for a particularly insightful treatment of "youth, leisure, and the politics of rock 'n' roll" in Great Britain, and Roe, 1987, for a Swedish study that claims that school achievement determines musical preference and shows how this preference is mediated by adolescent peer groups.

## REFERENCES

Baez, J. (1987). *And a Song to Sing With*. New York: Summit Books.

Butchart, R. E. & Cooper, B. L. (1987). Perceptions of education in the lyrics of American popular music, 1950–1980. *American Music*, Fall, 271–281.

DuBois, F. R. (1988). The true teacher, Rabindranath Tagore and Martin Buber. In A. Koepcke-Duttler (Ed.), *Buber-Gandhi-Tagore Aufforderung zu einem Weltgesprach* (pp. 172–195). Frankfurt/M. Verlage fuer Interkulturelle Kommunikation.

DuBois, F. R. (1985). *A troubadour as teacher, the concert as classroom?: Joan Baez—advocate of nonviolence and motivator of the young. A study in the biographical method*. Frankfurt am Main: Haag & Herchen.

Fowke, E. & Glazer, J. (1973). *Songs of work and protest*. New York: Dover.

Frith, S. (1981). *Sound effects: Youth leisure and the politics of rock n' roll*. New York: Pantheon Books.

Giroux, H. A. & Simon, R. I. (1989). *Popular culture, schooling, and everyday life*. New York: Bergin & Garvey.

Holm, G. & Farber, P. (1989, October). Rock around the school: An examination of the representation of education and schooling in contemporary rock and roll music (1960–1989). Paper presented at the American Educational Studies Association Annual Meeting, Chicago.

Kotarba, J. (Ed.) (1987) Adolescents and rock 'n' roll (issue). *Youth & Society, 18*(4).

Lull, J. (Ed.). (1987). *Popular music and communication*. Newbury Park, Calif.: Sage.

Meyrowitz, J. (1985). *No sense of place*. New York: Oxford University Press.

Roe, K. (1987). The school and music in adolescent socialization. In J. Lull (Ed.), *Popular music and communication*. Newbury Park, Calif.: Sage.

Salvo, P. W. (1981). Chuck Berry, 1972. In *The Rolling Stone Interviews 1967–1980*. London: A Rolling Stone Press Book, Arthur Barker Limited.

Sellers, R. (1989). *Sting*. Frankfurt am Main: Moewig.

### Film

Hackford, T. (1987) *Chuck Berry Hail! Hail! Rock 'n' Roll*. MCA Home Video 80465

### Songs

"Another Brick in the Wall" (Columbia 11187) Pink Floyd
"Charlie Wenjack" (Trikont US 32), Willie Dunn
"Don't Stand So Close to Me" (A & M 2301) The Police
"Honest Lullaby" (Epic/CBS83474) Joan Baez
"Hot for Teacher" (Warner Brothers 92–3985–1) Van Halen
"Getting Better" (Capitol SMAS 2653) The Beatles
"I Love Your Smile" (Motown MC 530 0077) Shanice
"The Principal's Office" (on "Stone Cold Rhymin" Island A2 91039) Young M.C.
"Man of Jade" (Stechapfel MC K00–6) Fletcher DuBois
"Mutha (Don't Wanna Go to School Today)" (A & M CD 395 2382) Extreme
"Prison of Geometry" (Stechapfel MC K00–5) Fletcher DuBois
"School Day" (Chess 1653) Chuck Berry

"School Days" (Trikont US 32) Willie Dunn
"School Boys in Disgrace" (album) (RCA LPL1–5102) The Kinks
"Suffer the Little Children" (Vanguard GH 852) Buffy St. Marie
"Teachers Lament" printed in Fowke & Glazer (1973)
"Teachers Pet" (A & M CD 395 2382) Extreme
"To Sir with Love" from the film of the same title, Lulu

# 9

## From Our Miss Brooks
## to Mr. Moore

### Playing Their Roles in
### Television Situation Comedies

Ken Kantor

A s a member of the baby-boom generation, I can recall our family's first television set in the early 1950s and evenings spent watching shows like Milton Berle's "Texaco Hour," Ed Sullivan's "Toast of the Town," Sid Caesar's "Your Show of Shows," and the "Colgate Comedy Hour," often featuring Dean Martin and Jerry Lewis. My family and I enjoyed watching these early variety shows, for they brought us together in the living room at night and helped to relieve the tensions of our work or school days.

An especially popular genre at this time was the situation comedy. To many people, shows like "I Love Lucy" or "The Honeymooners" come first to mind. But as a preadolescent middle-grade student, two other sitcoms held a special fascination for me because they had to do with schools, kids, and primarily teachers. The first was "Mr. Peepers," about a mild-mannered high school science teacher, played by Wally Cox. The humor was gentle and warm, much of it revolving around Mr. Peepers's shyness and self-effacing manner. Of particular interest was his courtship of the school nurse Nancy Remington; their eventual wedding was a major event for us. The other show was "Our Miss Brooks," about which I'll have more to say later in this chapter. What is significant here is that each of these programs presented teachers in funny but authentic ways. And each depiction ran counter to gender stereotypes, as Mr. Peepers was timid and withdrawn, and Miss Brooks assertive and outspoken. I can remember wishing that my own teachers were more like them.[1]

When I myself became a teacher in the 1960s, I thought about these shows and others that took place in school settings, and how they matched

175

with my experience. In a sense, television shows about schools are potentially occupational hazards to those of us who have worked in schools. If a
show attempts to reflect reality, we tend to be more critical, as we compare it
with our own knowledge and experience. For example, classrooms with ten
to fifteen well-behaved and attentive students who raise their hands politely
when they wish to speak can easily be classified under the heading of fantasy. At the same time, if the tenor of the show is sincere, and people in
schools are treated respectfully, we may overlook some inaccuracies. And if,
in addition, the intentions are largely comedic, and we like the style, the
exaggerations may be part of what works for us in the show.

As an example from a related context, a friend of mine is an attorney
who dislikes the currently popular television show "L.A. Law" for what he
considers to be its inaccurate representations of legal situations. At the
same time, he often enjoys the show "Night Court," which depicts wildly
improbable courtroom scenes. The difference? "L.A. Law" is a drama, with
some comedic elements, while "Night Court" is essentially a comedy, with
some dramatic elements. The one pretends to be authentic and, failing to be
so, is pretentious, while the other makes few claims to authenticity, other
than in its humorous spirit.

Our response to humor is also closely related to our current sensitivities
to stereotype. One-dimensional or disparaging images of professionals that
we may have found funny at one time may not seem so funny today, as we
are more alert to such manipulations. At the same time we recognize that
exaggeration is an essential aspect of what makes comedy effective. As an
illustration, educational administrators may object to negative portrayals of
school principals as narrow-minded, bombastic, and authoritarian. These
depictions play effectively, however, into society's generalized views of administrators (or perhaps examples of one or two such individuals from our
own experience). They are also necessary as foils to the more sympathetic
teacher protagonists in those shows. To put it bluntly, the sensitive and
capable principal may in actuality be the rule rather than the exception, but
in the eyes of television comedy writers (as well as many viewers) simply
isn't very funny.

In this chapter I am interested specifically in portrayals of teachers in
situation comedies during the period of time (1950 to 1990) that television
has extended its influence in our lives.[2] To illustrate these images, I want to
consider single episodes of each of four sitcoms: "Our Miss Brooks" (early
1950s), "Leave It to Beaver" (mid-1950s), "Welcome Back, Kotter," (late
1970s), and "Head of the Class" (late 1980s). Of these four shows, "Leave It
to Beaver" did not have a teacher as its primary character, but the depiction
of Miss Landers was revealing of a conventional image of female teachers.
Some other shows like "Mr. Novak," "Lucas Tanner," "Room 222," and "The
White Shadow" have had teachers as main characters but would not qualify
as sitcoms because of their generally dramatic intent. Because of my interest here in exploring specific aspects and dilemmas of comedy, I have not

included these more dramatic shows as points of focus. They are important, however, in comparative and historical terms, especially during the period of heightened social and political consciousness in the 1960s and 1970s.

## "Our Miss Brooks"

Connie Brooks, as played by Eve Arden, was an independent-minded, wisecracking high school English teacher who had to suffer others less competent—students like the dim-witted Walter Denton or the blustery principal Mr. Conklin. She also spent much time and energy pursuing the handsome but naive science teacher, Mr. Boynton, a confirmed bachelor who was oblivious to her advances. She lived as a boarder in the home of the older and somewhat daft Mrs. Davis. Miss Brooks was portrayed as a kind of knowing spinster, an intriguing combination of intelligent skeptic and hopeless romantic.

In this particular episode, the French teacher Mr. LaBlanche has proposed marriage to Miss Brooks in French; she believes that he was speaking for Mr. Boynton. The truth is revealed to her by Harriet Conklin (the principal's daughter), who translates Mr. LaBlanche's "pitch" and describes him as "swoonbait." In a later scene, Miss Brooks visits Mr. Boynton in the science lab, where he is attending to his pet frog Mac. When Boynton worries that Mac has been lethargic of late, Miss Brooks suggests that perhaps he's lonesome. Mr. Boynton says that's why he likes to spend as much time as possible with his frog, to which Miss Brooks replies, "Maybe he's got a friend for me?" Boynton doesn't get the hint.

He then tells her he has been saving money by making his own sandwiches; she intimates that when one does so, two can live as cheaply as one. Once again he misses the point. She reminds him that he's invited to eat dinner that evening with her and Mrs. Davis, and asks if he has any preferences for what is served. He says that he'll love whatever she puts on his plate, to which she replies, "Fine—I'll be on your plate."

Often when Miss Brooks made comments like these, she turned to the camera, as if addressing the audience, since no one else was getting the joke. We might protest the sexist image in the line "I'll be on your plate," but we also recognize that Miss Brooks remained the much superior one, with the dense Mr. Boynton and others as the targets of her jokes. Unfortunately, however, Miss Brooks was still trapped in the stereotype of the single female teacher who would be incomplete until she was married.

The show did depict Miss Brooks's relationships with her students, but primarily as individuals and outside the classroom; she carpooled, for example, with Walter Denton. We gained little sense of her teaching methods, other than by seeing something like a traditional grammar lesson written on the blackboard behind her. But her students did speak to her in personal ways, and we saw that she did have a life outside the school (a revelation about teachers to many of us in grade school at the time). And because she spoke to us so cleverly and forthrightly, we felt that she was indeed *our* Miss Brooks.

According to Mitz (1980), some teachers objected to what they perceived as unfavorable images of teachers and administrators in the show. Eve Arden defended her character, however, as one who cared about her students and her profession, despite some of the foolish predicaments in which she found herself. Arden also questioned whether anyone would be entertained by a show that depicted schools as they actually were.

Perhaps Arden was referring specifically to schools of the 1950s (like the ones I attended) which mirrored the cautious postwar mentality of the Eisenhower era. Stability and the status quo were the watchwords of the time; conservative values were preeminent. For many of us in schools, this meant a dull and uninspiring curriculum, in contrast to the excitement of rock and roll music or for that matter many television shows (Kantor, 1991). And women in particular, if they were not to be housewives, had limited career options. Teaching was, of course, one of those choices and gave women some opportunity to use their intellectual capacities. They were expected, however, to uphold and transmit the values of white middle-class society; Miss Brooks was ultimately no exception.

---

## "Leave It to Beaver"

A further example (though considerably less interesting than Miss Brooks) was Miss Landers, a continuing character on the popular show "Leave It to Beaver." She was a pleasant and attractive young teacher who managed a classroom of only slightly rambunctious preadolescents. She curbed their enthusiasms largely through gently disapproving looks and guided them along lines of middle-class propriety. She acted in loco parentis—the teacher as "mom" away from home. For the central character Theodore Cleaver ("the Beaver") especially, she reinforced the values of his parents.

The episode I've chosen begins with Miss Landers announcing in a saccharine voice to her class that they're about to begin one of their "interesting civics projects," a commemoration of Fire Prevention Week in which the students are to elect a "Junior Fire Chief." Harry, the chubby student at the front of the class, raises his hand and when called on stands up—this was typical classroom behavior in the show—to ask whether this will be like the lessons on erosion in which they "looked at dirt." Miss Landers assures him that this project will be different, and Harry sighs with relief. Penny, the one girl in the class with a speaking part, then asks in a sarcastic tone whether a girl can be elected Junior Fire Chief, or whether it's "just the *boys*." Other students laugh, but Miss Landers does not respond. Beaver wants to know if they'll "get to go to fires and junk," to which Miss Landers replies that they will be concerned with *preventing* fires. Richard announces that his grandfather was in the San Francisco fire; Miss Landers brightens and says that he must have had some interesting stories. Richard responds that his grandfather "croaked" before he knew him. Again, more laughter from the class (and the laugh track), and another disappointed look from Miss Landers.

As we would expect, Beaver is elected Junior Fire Chief, after a conspiracy by the boys to shut out the girls. When the winner is announced, Richard mimics a fire engine siren; Miss Landers tells him that's "enough enthusiasm." She then issues manuals on fire prevention and instructs the students to hand out violation slips to those responsible for potential fire hazards. Gilbert wonders if this means they'll get to "squeal" on their parents; Miss Landers admonishes him for not having quite the right spirit. After she informs the class of their upcoming visit to the Fire Department, Whitey asks whether if they see a fire, they should notify her or the fire department. At this point, Miss Landers's voice becomes stern, and she asks Whitey if he would like to have a note sent home to his parents. Whitey backs down quickly and sheepishly.

The students go out to conduct their projects, and Beaver gets reprimanded by his parents for issuing too many citations. Dejected, he stops at the fire station to talk with Gus, an elderly fireman, who advises him on more diplomatic ways to deal with others on matters of fire prevention. In the final part of the episode, the students give their reports, taking pride in the number of citations they have given out. Penny claims that she was in a horse show over the weekend, and her mother said she had too many things on her mind to complete the project, so that she will have to turn it in tomorrow. Annoyed, Miss Landers replies that she'd appreciate that. When she calls eagerly on Beaver to give his report, he reveals, to her surprise, that he gave no violations. When asked to explain, he states his discovery that a good fireman "doesn't go around yellin' at people," and that you have to treat others in a nice way. Miss Landers affirms that he seems to have learned quite a lot, to which Beaver responds that Gus the fireman "learned me most of it." Taking the opportunity to correct his grammar, she says that everyone is proud of what Gus *taught* him. She closes the lesson and the episode by telling the class to copy down an arithmetic assignment.

Like Miss Brooks, Miss Landers was young, attractive, and unmarried. The similarities ended there, however, for Miss Landers was largely one dimensional; we had little awareness of her life or personality outside the classroom. In fact, we never even learned her first name. Again, though, the show was primarily about the Beaver; Miss Landers was only a tangential character. If we presume that we were looking at school experience largely through Beaver's eyes, it's not surprising that he would see her as existing only within the classroom walls.

Although Miss Landers never raised her voice, she acted in quietly authoritarian ways. Through voice and facial expression she pulled the reins at those moments when boys would be boys and occasionally, as in Penny's case, when girls could be difficult. She served as only one of several teachers instructing Beaver in the superficial ways of middle-class morality. Ironically, in this episode the most significant teacher was Gus the fireman; Beaver's encounter with him was conveniently serendipitous. Miss Landers concurred with the lesson Gus had taught Beaver, but failed to acknowledge the flaw in her own assignment or her evaluation of it. The most important ethical influences for Beaver, however, were his parents (and to some extent his brother Wally); Miss Landers made relatively small contributions, for example, in correcting his grammar usage. In a lighthearted family situation comedy of the 1950s, she was largely decorative. At the same time, her character reflected widespread images of female teachers at the time, and to a lingering extent today.

---

## "Welcome Back, Kotter"

Since there is nearly a twenty-year span between "Leave It to Beaver" and "Welcome Back, Kotter," it is necessary to document the intervening changes in television programming, especially during the tumultuous period of the late 1960s and early 1970s. Perhaps the most significant situation comedy was "All in the Family," followed by shows like "M.A.S.H.," "Maude," and "Good Times." These programs addressed social and political issues particularly related to civil rights, the women's movement, and the war in Vietnam, and thus redefined the nature of the situation comedy. Two dramatic shows of the 1970s about schools—"Room 222" and "The White Shadow" (the latter of which premiered after "Welcome Back, Kotter")— dealt with questions of sexual relationships, drug use, racial prejudice, and students' attitudes toward school in more direct ways than did previous such programs. They also portrayed teachers and administrators who worked with culturally diverse groups of students and who served as positive role models for them. This was also true of the lighter sitcom "The Bill Cosby Show" (1969–1971), featuring Cosby as a high school physical education teacher and coach named Chet Kincaid. It depicted genuine interactions not only between Kincaid and his students, but also with members of his family, serving as a kind of precursor to the successful "Cosby Show" of 1984–1992. Noteworthy here is the shift of focus to the *male* teacher as the primary character, particularly as adult mentor to students struggling with the difficult problems of adolescence.

The increased attention to societal issues and realistic dilemmas as well as the male teacher image engendered by the 1960s was certainly reflected in "Welcome Back, Kotter," the hit television sitcom of the late 1970s. In this show Gabe Kotter acted largely as entertainer and sometimes friend to his group of "Sweathogs," academically unmotivated but often clever students from various ethnic backgrounds. The actor and creator Gabe Kaplan patterned the show after his own earlier experience as a student in remedial classes in an urban school and after a teacher who inspired him. Like Miss Brooks, Kotter was quick with witty comments and anecdotes, mostly in the vein of Jewish vaudeville (particularly Marx Brothers) humor, but he also served as advocate for his students' rights and guide to their future success.

This particular episode begins with a visit to Kotter before class by Charlie, a kind of "mad scientist" chemistry teacher. Charlie reminds Kotter that the assistant principal Mr. Woodman is observing in classes this week, and cautions him to keep his students quiet and busy. Kotter protests that he has recently been trying some experimental methods, urging his students to think for themselves rather than simply memorize facts. Charlie leaves the classroom with a few skeptical words.

Five of the Sweathogs then enter performing a current dance routine. Kotter responds by doing the Twist, and the nerdy Horschack tells him that he's an "oldie but goodie." Vinnie Barbarino, the handsome and slow-witted student played by John Travolta, then asks if they are going to "rap" like the day before. Kotter agrees to this and has them take places in a circle on the floor, informing them that the circle represents the oldest form of education, and encouraging them to talk about whatever they wish to. Extending his arm with his familiar cry "Ooh! Ooh! Ooh!" Horschack proudly announces that he watched *The Wizard of Oz* the previous night, for the fourteenth time. Kotter asks the students what they think the movie was about, to which the Puerto Rican-Jewish Juan Epstein, in his best Chico Marx style, replies that it was about two hours and twenty minutes.

Freddie "Boom Boom" Washington, a black student, then enters the conversation, complaining that *The Wizard of Oz* is simply a movie for kids with a lot of "made-up junk." Kotter argues that the characters in the film represented real people, the scarecrow looking for brains (the Sweathogs all point to Horschack), the tin man in search of a heart (they point to Epstein), and the lion needing courage (everyone points to Kotter). Kotter then does his impression of Bert Lahr as the cowardly lion; Horschack calls this "very impressive." In summary fashion, Kotter asserts that the characters were all going after something they already had but didn't realize. Vinnie reacts, "Boy, were they dumb!"

Still unconvinced, Freddie argues that the movie isn't "cool." When Kotter asks if it's important to him to try to be cool, Freddie answers in street talk style that he doesn't have to try; he *is* cool. Verna Jean, the one female student in the inner Sweathog circle, interjects that if you turn the lights down, Freddie will heat up. Kotter suggests to him that you've got to be a cool "something." Freddie reveals that he plans to build the tallest building in the world, Kotter asks whether it will be called "Washington Heights," and Freddie, feigning laughter, says it will be called the "Boom Boom Building."

About this time Mr. Woodman enters the room unnoticed. Continuing the discussion about future goals, Epstein claims that he wants to be a "typhoon." When everyone looks puzzled, he clarifies himself—"a restaurant typhoon" specializing in Puerto Rican-Jewish delicacies. Tapping his pen like a cigar and exploiting the ethnic stereotypes further, Kotter refers to Epstein as "the refried matzo ball king." At this point, Mr. Woodman asks Kotter in a critical voice what he is doing. "Groucho" is the immediate deadpan response. Kotter then informs Woodman that he's trying something new and that watching it might be the high point of his day; the administrator replies sharply that his day has no high points. Kotter further explains that they are rapping; Woodman wants to know "wrapping what?"

Kotter then turns to Barbarino, asking him what he wants to be when he grows up. Vinnie answers, "Marlon Brando," relating his intention of being discovered in a drug store. "Wearing a tight sweater?" retorts Kotter, playing on the famous Lana Turner story. Disgusted, Woodman steps in again, demanding to know when Kotter is going to begin class and why he's not using the textbook. Getting up from the floor, Kotter tells him that the textbook is the "pits," with no relevance to his students' lives; the Sweathogs are "forgotten people." He then cites passages from the American History text, which supposedly states that the railroad will soon span the country, Texas is the largest of the thirty-eight states, and television will be invented. Woodman still doesn't get the point and orders Kotter to come out into the hall.

Outside the classroom, Woodman angrily chastises Kotter for his foolish methods and reminds him that social studies consists of memorizing names, places, and dates. Kotter argues that such an approach is only reciting; learning, on the other hand, involves discussion and dialogue, like that of the ancient Greeks. When Woodman questions where the ancient Greeks are today, Kotter jokes that they're all in a restaurant on Ninth Avenue. His anger increasing, Woodman claims that in school, teachers talk and students listen; that was the way he taught, and that's the way Kotter has to teach. Kotter responds that he doesn't wish to harm his students by following outmoded rules. Woodman decides that he will have to bring Kotter up on charges before the Teacher's Review Board. When Kotter suggests that he must be kidding, Woodman answers that he never kids, since he has no sense of humor.

The second half of the episode consists of the hearing, at which Kotter is accused of not using the textbook or following the prescribed curriculum. Shortly after the hearing begins, the Sweathogs enter through the window, dressed as painters in Marx Brothers fashion. They have come to testify for Kotter, which the review board officer, Ms. Riley, allows them to do despite Woodman's protestations. It turns out that the Sweathogs have been to the library to look up legal precedents; Ms. Riley is impressed with their willingness to conduct research. Although their testimony consists mostly of one-liners—at one point Kotter and Epstein lapse into a Groucho and

Chico exchange—they do make a few serious points. Freddie, for example, commends Kotter for encouraging students to ask their own questions; Horschack says that prior to Kotter's class, going to school was like being vaccinated, but now they are expected to learn. And Kotter, speaking on his own behalf, contends that the Sweathogs aren't incapable, but need nontraditional teaching approaches to help them learn how to learn and gain future success. Lest things get too serious, though, he concludes by saying "copies of the speech can be obtained from . . ."

Ms. Riley acknowledges that Kotter's methods are unorthodox, but says she supports the rights of teachers to teach, and she praises the students for their initiative. She insists, however, that Kotter use the textbook, and she leaves the room doing her own pen-tapping Groucho joke. In the final scene back in the classroom, Kotter places the textbooks on the heads of his students, ostensibly to help teach them good posture.

Like "Our Miss Brooks," "Welcome Back, Kotter" was controversial, for many educators objected to the images of the permissive teacher and the cavalier, disaffected Sweathogs. Of particular concern was racial and ethnic stereotyping—Washington's strutting and jive talking, Barbarino's macho posturing, Epstein's hustling and con games. At one point the National Education Association (NEA) appointed an adviser to the show to protect images of teachers and students. (In contrast, the NEA gave commendations to "Room 222" and "The White Shadow" for what it identified as presenting positive teacher images.) Not surprisingly, Gabe Kaplan disdained this action, citing it as unnecessary censorship (Mitz, 1980).

Despite the comedic format, the show explored serious themes, not the least of which was the idea of a teacher giving something back to his school and community. Kotter did indeed defend his students, and he challenged traditional teaching approaches involving transmission of factual information, use of outdated texts, and conventional seating arrangements. In the circle, the students related *The Wizard of Oz* to their own lives, which was apparently difficult to do with their archaic textbook. But any possible depth of discussion was short-circuited by the vaudeville structure. As in the Marx Brothers movies, nothing could ever get too serious; anything substantive was quickly undercut by a joke, usually involving word play or sight gags. The heart of the show was in what is known in the comedy business as "shtick." Again, the foil was provided by Woodman, who admitted he had no sense of humor. And although Kotter, like Mr. Boynton, was sometimes the object of the joke, he was more often than not, like Miss Brooks, the creator of the joke. As writer and lead actor, Gabe Kaplan left little doubt as to who was in charge of the comic enterprise.

As with Miss Brooks and Cosby's character Chet Kincaid, we did gain entry into Kotter's personal life, particularly through his relationship with his wife Julie. The Sweathogs themselves paid frequent visits to Kotter's home; Julie sometimes expressed her resentment at the intrusions. Later in the show's run, the Kotters had twins, and they struggled with the tension of raising children on a teacher's salary. Generally, however, episodes began or ended, in egocentric male fashion, with Gabe telling Julie a joke about a member of his family; she listened appreciatively and always laughed at the punch line. He was first and last the stand-up comic; social commentary had to take a back seat to entertainment.

Lest we assume, however, that issues were insignificant, we should recognize that the show, and this episode especially, did confront central questions of teaching, learning, and curriculum. Kotter's defense of his methods and his critique of outdated textbooks were much in keeping with the 1960s ideas of "relevance," as quaint as those may seem to us today. Perhaps most importantly, he argued for his "Sweathogs," the victims of the self-fulfilling prophecy for whom schooling was "the pits." Implicitly if not explicitly, "Welcome Back, Kotter" commented poignantly throughout its television run on the negative effects of tracking and the importance of respecting all students as capable of learning.

---

### "Head of the Class"

Similar to Kotter, though less casual, Mr. Moore of the late 1980s show "Head of the Class" was a knowledgeable, innovative, and politically liberal teacher of a group of high school students identified as gifted (not unlike the Sweathogs in their cleverness). He acted as a role model, mentor, and even guru to these students who required outlets for their creative energies and talents. And like Kotter, he provided wisdom and guidance about choices related both to present and future directions.

At the beginning of the episode described here, Mr. Moore is talking with his students about those who have inspired famous people. Alan, a preppie type, asks "Who cares?" Sounding like Kotter, Moore reminds them that history is not made up of places and facts, but of people. "Who made Jack Kennedy into John F. Kennedy?" he asks. Dennis, the class cynic, wonders "who made Michael Jackson into Diana Ross?" Moore argues that everyone was inspired by someone, and Maria asks about who inspired him. He tells them wistfully about his Uncle Charlie, a vibrant and funny manager of a traveling carnival who encouraged him to get out of Wheezer, Idaho, and into the world. He begins to picture Uncle Charlie, dead now for some twenty years, standing outside the hall window, until one of the students jolts him out of his reverie. He then gives an assignment to the students to look up thirty famous people and find out who inspired them, and how. The students object vehemently, claiming that they have tests to study for. Mr. Moore is unsympathetic, telling them that he's assigning it, so they get to do it. The bell rings, and they leave the classroom grumbling.

Back at his apartment, Moore again envisions his uncle and complains to Charlie that he has not been reaching his students as he feels he used to. He expresses his temptation to get out of teaching. The "apparition" of Charlie asks if he realizes what will happen to the students if he leaves the school, and Moore replies that he's just one of many teachers, with only limited influence. Charlie suggests that he and Moore find out by visiting the class at their tenth reunion.

At this fantasy reunion, Mr. Moore sees his students in various kinds of decline. Maria, talking to Arvid, looks and sounds cheap, having spent her time getting divorced and shopping. She claims that life lost its meaning after Mr. Moore departed. Arvid, once the class genius, reveals that he was similarly affected and left the space program to start a butcher shop. Another student says that she met a fortune teller who told her she had no future. At this point the school secretary, a romantic interest for Moore, steps in wearing a nun's habit, and says "I guess we all change." Two of the students have gotten married; the wife complains that her husband won't write any more and that since she became pregnant she had to give up mud wrestling. Still another female student in ragged clothes asks plaintively if anyone wants to buy a chicken farm. Seeing Dennis seated on the floor looking degenerate and wearing a "Help Me" sign, Mr. Moore comments that somehow that makes sense to him. Alan is talking to a young woman with a blonde wig and heavy makeup who has replaced Vanna White on "Wheel of Fortune." Suddenly the principal, a blustery Mr. Woodman type, rolls into the room in a wheelchair with a blanket covering his lap. He is shocked at what has happened to the students and calls them bums. Still skeptical, Moore tells Charlie that it would never happen like this. When the students do a conscientious job on the assignment, however, he reconsiders and decides to stay in teaching.

Perhaps more so than with other television sitcom teachers, we gained a sense of Mr. Moore as a person with a number of dimensions. He wanted students to see history as exciting and get beyond their narrowly academic views. He strove to set an example of thinking critically, being goal oriented, and making the most of one's talents and abilities. In a sense, he was the teacher as intellectual and visionary, who motivated students to expand their own intellects. Ironically, somewhat like Miss Landers, he didn't in this instance recognize the narrowness of his assigning students to gather factual information about famous people; the task seemed inconsistent with his emphasis on critical thinking. The episode also played into cause-and-effect conceptions of the teacher as the single most powerful inspiration in an individual's life, although many have attested to one teacher having had just that kind of influence. Perhaps most problematic here are questions of gifted education, or the other side of the "Sweathogs" coin. If the kind of learning in Mr. Moore's classes is best for "gifted" students, is it not also best for "average" or "low-achieving" students? What kinds of lessons did the students in his class learn about distinctions between themselves and students in other classes? Should not all students derive the benefit of having an inspirational teacher like Mr. Moore? Intriguingly, the similarities between Kotter and Moore and their students seem to outweigh the differences, which seem to be more a matter of comedic style than substantive approaches to teaching and learning.

Finally, if Miss Landers represented the surrogate mother in the classroom of the 1950s, Kotter and Moore represented the substitute fathers, both in and out of the classroom, of the 1970s and 1980s. In the latter situations, while references were sometimes made to relationships with parents, students were often seen turning to their teachers for help with personal problems or counsel on their life's directions. To some extent, Miss Brooks was a confidante for students like Walter Denton and Harriet Conklin, but we never gained a sense that she was assuming roles traditionally ascribed to parents. With the recognition that many families were not like the idealized Cleavers came an expanded view of the teacher in loco parentis, especially in terms of a perceived need for strong male figures in young people's lives.

Situation comedies have therefore capitalized on varied images of the teacher, as spinster or bachelor, mother or father, entertainer, missionary, moral example, rebel, provocateur, idealist. Administrators are often depicted as pompous, dictatorial, old-fashioned, but rarely sympathetic; and students as variously dim-witted, mischievous, manipulative, innocent, resistant, apathetic, hip, motivated or unmotivated, cooperative or uncooperative. Sometimes conventions are critiqued, as with Kotter's or Moore's departing from traditional methods or curriculum. But ultimately the comedic form seems to require playing to rather than debunking stereotypes. If the challenge goes too deep, the show runs the risk of losing its audience, who after all tune in to be entertained and not preached at. There is also the constraint of the half-hour limit; problems must be quickly identified and even more quickly resolved. Only now and then is the dilemma sustaining enough to necessitate a "to be continued" episode. General tensions can be maintained from week to week, but specific problems need to be fixed.

So, good situation comedy can make for shallow depictions of teachers and teaching. Even teachers like Kotter and Moore who show concern for the intellectual and emotional growth of their students replicate some of the very approaches they are supposedly battling against. Each sets his own agenda and controls students' behavior, Kotter through his joke telling and Moore through reverting to busywork assignments.

Do we see any changes in the images of teachers in television shows of the 1990s? Teachers have been depicted more authentically on "The Wonder Years," as when a math teacher helps Kevin Arnold (the main character) learn a valuable lesson about intellectual honesty, and a young English teacher encourages her students to question assumptions and think critically about values in literature. In keeping with the tenor of the show, however, these examples are sentimentalized and serve primarily to influence Kevin's development, as Miss Landers did in a more superficial way with the Beaver. Social issues and teacher-student interactions are dealt with more realistically in the recent Canadian productions of "Degrassi Junior High" and "Degrassi High School," but again, the chief characters are the students rather than the teachers, and the shows are more dramatic than comedic in nature.

We might indeed question whether the sitcom *can* deal with substantive issues with greater insight and sophistication. Certainly shows like "All in the Family," "M.A.S.H.," "The Mary Tyler Moore Show," "Good Times," and "The Bob Newhart Show" set higher standards and paved the way for current shows like "The Golden Girls," "Cheers," "The Cosby Show," and "Murphy Brown." Of these shows, the one that dealt most closely with educational questions was "The Cosby Show," in which Cliff and Clair Huxtable acted as wise and caring guides to their children's development. Although some have criticized the show for its middle-class and unrealistic portrayal of black family life (making it seem little different at times from "The Donna Reed Show" or "Leave It to Beaver"), others have praised the show for broadening our perspectives on African-American people and presenting parents as strong role models and teachers of young people.

Much has to do, I think, with what we expect from a television situation comedy about teachers. If we're looking for paragons of excellence, realistic treatment of dilemmas, penetrating analyses of teaching and learning, or progressive social values that go beyond mere dichotomizing, we're likely to be disappointed. On the other hand, there is often something in the comedic spirit that is uplifting and even liberating. A teacher I know told me that she was a beginning teacher at the time of the original airing of "Welcome Back, Kotter," and she looked to it as a release from the daily pressures of her work. She knew from her experience that the situations in the show were improbable, but she appreciated the opportunity to laugh about otherwise serious matters. Humor, especially the Jewish-style humor reflected in "Kotter," has been and continues to be a source of philosophy and indeed survival.

We also need to reject a monolithic view of what defines comedy. The shows described here reflect a range of types of humor, from lighthearted whimsy to broad farce to sardonic wit to social satire; sometimes they contain several of these elements. Again, our response is related to what we expect. If, for example, we anticipate an episode of "Welcome Back, Kotter" to give us an in-depth and realistic view of contemporary pedagogy, we'll find that it doesn't measure up; such insight doesn't come with the territory.

Even given a certain generosity, though, humor can be offensive. Comedy that exploits racial, ethnic, gender, religious or regional stereotypes can be detrimental, as it reinforces ignorance and prejudice. The depictions of Freddie in "Welcome Back, Kotter" or J. J. in "Good Times," for example, may be little better than the caricatures of black people in "Amos 'n' Andy."

In contrast, Mr. Moore's gifted class is made up of students from various racial and economic backgrounds, making the point that academic ability is not reserved to middle-class whites. The problem then becomes one of avoiding stereotypes about gifted students, or about students not in gifted classes. So the results are often mixed; the paradox of humor is that it can be both funny and offensive at the same time. Laughter usually comes at someone's expense; when the object of derision becomes a particular group of people, the effects are potentially harmful.

Particularly distressing is television's treatment of women, and specifically the lack of strong and captivating images of female teachers in sitcoms. The woman principal in the popular "Parker Lewis Can't Lose" is in the Mr. Conklin/Woodman mold, an autocratic, vengeful administrator who is constantly hoodwinked by students. And she bears the additional burden of being depicted as the sex-starved unmarried woman, a virtual object of misogyny. Women in sitcoms fare much better if engaged in professions like news reporting (Mary Richards or Murphy Brown) or law (Clair Huxtable) or even bartending (Rebecca Howe in "Cheers"). So while leading characters like Kotter and Moore provide positive images of male teachers (far cries from the impenetrable Mr. Boynton), the omission of correspondingly strong female teachers perpetuates the disrespectful view of teaching as insignificant "women's work."

In a sense, the timid Mr. Peepers provided an expanded model of the male teacher, as he displayed the gentler side of human nature. And ironically, Miss Brooks, despite her foolish pursuit of Mr. Boynton, gave us an image of an intelligent, articulate, independent, and genuinely funny female teacher, in my opinion a character matched since that time only by Murphy Brown. The creators of these early sitcoms seemed more willing to play against stereotypes than to exploit them. Certainly, with respect to creating a positive, sympathetic, authentic, or appreciative image of a woman as teacher, television situation comedy writers and producers have been wandering for forty years in the desert.

## NOTES

1. This chapter is dedicated to the memories of actors Eve Arden and Wally Cox, whose humanity was revealed in the goodness of Connie Brooks and Robinson Peepers.
2. For background material on these television shows, I am indebted to Rock Mitz's *The Great TV Sitcom Book* (1980) and, to a lesser extent, to Tim Brooks and Earle Marshe's *Complete Directory to Prime-Time Network TV Shows 1946–Present* (New York: Ballantine Books, 1985). I also wish to express my appreciation to the Museum of Broadcast Communications in Chicago for providing me access to videotaped episodes of "Our Miss Brooks" and "Leave It to Beaver."

## REFERENCES

Kantor, K. (1991). "Deliver me from the days of old": Rock and roll (etc.) as liberation. In G. Willis & W. H. Schubert (Eds.), *Reflections from the heart of educational inquiry: Understanding teaching and curriculum through the arts* (pp. 168–173). Albany, NY: State University of New York Press.

Mitz, R. (1980). *The great TV sitcom book*. New York: Richard Marek Publishers.

# Continuing Dialogue

1. Imagine a screen play for a movie that will be commercially popular in which a teacher is a main character, and write a brief outline and character sketch of that teacher. Explain why you think your film would be popular with commercial audiences.

2. View a movie specifically filmed for adolescent audiences, for example, *The Breakfast Club* or *Ferris Bueller's Day Off.* Describe the portrayal of teachers in such movies and consider whether those images are similar to the ones you had of teachers who taught you when you were an adolescent. Also, try viewing a movie specifically filmed for adolescent audiences *with* teenagers. Ask them what they think about the depictions and roles of the teachers in those films. What messages about the image of the teacher are being conveyed? What relationship do these films have with real experiences?

3. View *Dead Poet's Society,* a film in which the hero in a private school teaches adolescents from upper-class backgrounds. Consider how the teacher in that film compares to Ayers's description of teacher heroes in *Blackboard Jungle, Conrack,* or *Stand and Deliver.* View the film or read the book *Up the Down Staircase* by Bel Kaufman (1964). Does the main character characterize her role as heroic (again using Ayers's characteristics of teacher heroes)? Would you consider her a heroine?

4. Interview a small group of children (perhaps fourth-grade students) and invite them to sing songs they have heard on the playground about schools or teachers. (These songs might include jump-rope jingles, chants, or limericks.) Be ready with a tape recorder to record their songs. Ask them the following questions: Where do these songs come from? What do the songs mean? And why do children sing them? Try the above interview with adolescents and adults, inviting them to share their memories of such school songs and their old records or tapes which may include songs about teachers.

5. If you have an opportunity to speak with children and adults who went to school in countries other than the United States, ask them about the songs concerning schools and teachers they remember from childhood. Also, if you have an opportunity to hear (and understand) the rock and roll lyrics from other cultures, note if there are any striking differences from the schoolteacher lyrics used in American music.

6. On your own or with others, write lyrics about some school-related topic. You can use a familiar tune or make up your own melody.

7. Watch a major television network channel for two to three hours on a Saturday morning. Note the references, images, and dialogue related to teachers and schools in programming and commercials. Reflect about your observations and their implications for the teaching profession in American society. Try this activity in the company of a child. Encourage the child's responses to the images of teachers portrayed.

# IV

## Literature and Textbooks

# 10

# Teacher as Gatekeeper

## Schoolteachers in Picture Books for Young Children

Ann M. Trousdale

F or many children, starting school is the first transition from the known, secure world of home and family into a larger, unknown world. What will school be like? What do people do in school all day? Will I be able to learn what I'm supposed to learn? Will I make friends? What will the teacher be like? Dispelling such anxieties and answering such questions is the concern of a number of picture books for young children. In many of these books, the teacher plays a prominent role in determining what the school experience will be. Other books represent the ongoing school experience, dealing with issues that arise later in the primary years. Again, the teacher is often a critical factor in the child's experience of school.

Books for preschoolers tend to portray the teacher in a positive light, as a sympathetic, understanding, nurturing individual who makes the child's entry into the world of school safe and secure. Positive images of teachers continue to predominate in books for the primary grades, with several noteworthy exceptions. Some books present a negative picture of the teacher, portraying the teacher as overly rigid, incompetent, or, in some instances, actually abusive. Altogether, the image presented of teachers is a surprisingly complex one, with no one stereotype prevailing.

The books analyzed and discussed in this chapter are fictional picture books for young children, published between 1960 and 1990. They include, quite simply, all the fictional picture books on the topic I could locate, a total of forty-six books. I have not included works of nonfiction or chapters in books, although analysis of those books would doubtless be informative.

## Teacher as Ally and Comforter

In the books that provide positive pictures of teachers, the teachers tend to be both the children's ally and a source of comfort. These teachers are also competent classroom managers. Thus, the classroom is a safe, secure environment in which the children will meet new friends, enjoy their learning experiences, and find sympathy and understanding when anxieties or embarrassments occur.

Twelve of the books in the sample are about a child's first day at school (Berenstain, 1978; Carruth, 1985; Cazet, 1990; Cohen, 1967; Hamilton-Merrit, 1982; Jackson, 1985; Quackenbush, 1982; Relf, 1981; Schwartz, 1988; Tester, 1979; Thaler, 1989; Wells, 1981). The clear intent of these books is to alleviate children's anxiety about going to school. In Mike Thaler's *The Teacher from the Black Lagoon* (1989), for example, a child's fearful fantasies about school are explored and then dispelled. The young protagonist imagines the teacher as a green, scaly, fire-breathing monster who eats students who misbehave—or turns them into frogs. It turns out that the real Miss Green is young, pretty, and quite pleasant.

Jane Hamilton-Merrit's *My First Days of School* (1982) is most obvious in its intent to inform and reassure children about school. It is unusual in its use of photographs of real people in a real school as illustrations, but it is not presented as a photo-essay or an informational book. It is presented as a story; its point of view is manipulated to be that of a first-grade child; the use of the child's voice is clearly intended to say, in effect, "See? School is going to be okay!"

While making new friends and being accepted by peers seem to be the major concerns of the young protagonists, the teacher is central to both instilling and allaying the child's fears. Most of the books about entering school are serious in tone, but two give teachers or school officials humorous treatment (Cazet, 1990; Thaler, 1989).

Among books about first grade, Miriam Cohen's series about a first-grade class (Cohen, 1972, 1980a, 1984, 1985, 1988, 1989) provides a bellwether case of the teacher as effective ally and comforter. This rounded, full-breasted, pleasant teacher is the quintessential nurturing female. She is wise, perceptive, and gentle. She does not have a name, and her age is indeterminate; she could be any age from 30 to 60. (See Figure 10-1.)

Without fail this teacher finds ways to ameliorate childhood woes: the death of a pet (Cohen, 1984); insecurities and problems with self-esteem (Cohen, 1980b, 1988); the need to feel an important part of group activities (Cohen, 1985, 1988); anxiety about leaving the security of the known to venture into the unknown (Cohen, 1989). This teacher effectively "mothers" her class without "smothering" them with her care; she does not attempt to make her children dependent on her. Indeed, at the end of the year, she

All the kids and the teacher were smacking George on the back and hugging him.

**Figure 10-1**   (Illus. Hoban, in Cohen, *It's George!*, 1988)

gently pushes them out of the first-grade nest, encouraging them to test their wings in second grade (Cohen, 1989).

In Judy Blume's *The One in the Middle Is a Green Kangaroo* (1982), the teacher understands and compensates for parental lack of attention, again without encouraging the children to form any inappropriate ties to herself. Freddie Dissel is a middle child who feels neglected at home. It is his teacher, Miss Gumber, who arranges for Freddie to try out for a part in the school play. She continues to support and encourage him right through to the performance, thereby helping Freddie find recognition and a sense of accomplishment.

Other teachers who are particularly sensitive to children's needs are found in Patricia Relf's *The First Day of School* (1981); Syd Hoff's *The Horse in Harry's Room* (1970); Joanne Oppenheim's Mrs. Peloki series

(1980, 1987); and Sylvia Root Tester's *We Laughed a Lot, My First Day of School* (1979).

Books dealing with the grades beyond first grade tend to move away from an idealized picture of the teacher to a more complex perspective. In Harry Allard's Miss Nelson books (Allard, 1977, 1982, 1985), Miss Nelson herself represents such a transformation. Miss Nelson actually bears a physical resemblance to Cohen's first-grade teacher: she is soft, blonde, rounded, and gentle. In the first book of the series, *Miss Nelson Is Missing* (1977), the children in her class take advantage of her good nature and misbehave. (See Figure 10-2.) One day, however, a substitute teacher appears: Miss Viola Swamp. Miss Viola Swamp is dressed like a witch. (See Figure 10-3.) She lays down the law. No one gets away with anything. She burdens the children with lots of work, until the children wish for Miss Nelson's return. When she does return, the class is so glad to have her back that no one misbehaves. Little do the children know that in Miss Nelson's closet at home is the black dress worn by Miss Viola Swamp.

In the two sequels, Miss Viola Swamp reappears to take care of school crises. In *Miss Nelson Is Back* (1982), she restores order to Miss Nelson's class when the school principal proves to be inadequate as a substitute. In *Miss Nelson Has a Field Day* (1985), The Swamp takes over coaching the losing football team, whips them into shape, and thus restores the flagging school spirit.

Miss Nelson and several other teachers in the sample are portrayed as individuals who have the imagination or flexibility to handle unexpected events or crises (Cazet, 1990; McCully, 1987; Parish, 1969; Thaler, 1989). Miss Nelson is unusual among them in that she apparently has access to—and uses—two sides of her nature: the soft, gentle, blond nurturer and the angular, harsh, dark enforcer. She is both mother and military commandant.

## Teacher as Adversary or Buffoon

Seven books in the survey contained negative images of teachers. Some are more humorous treatments, such as Mrs. Stanley, in Trinka Hakes Noble's *The Day Jimmy's Boa Ate the Wash* (1980), who is simply not able to control her students during a calamitous field trip. Mr. Quackerbottom in James Howe's *The Day the Teacher Went Bananas* (1984) is a rather befuddled but innocuous teacher who is confused and ineffectual enough somehow to be "sent" to the zoo rather than to school—and who goes there—while a gorilla is sent to the school.

Mrs. Shelbert, in Steven Kellogg's *The Mysterious Tadpole* (1979), can function only in predictable situations; when the unexpected occurs, she loses control of the class. When Louis's "tadpole" grows beyond conventional

They were even rude during story hour.

**Figure 10-2**   (Illus. Marshall, in Allard and Marshall, *Miss Nelson Is Missing*, 1977)

size, she simply asks him to stop bringing it to school. It is the librarian who helps Louis with his problem.

Other books level more severe indictments against teachers. Serious pedagogical limitations are presented in Tomie de Paola's *The Art Lesson*

**Figure 10-3**    (Illus. Marshall, in Allard and Marshall, *Miss Nelson Is Missing,* 1977)

(1989) and in Miriam Cohen's *No Good in Art* (1980b). In both books, the young male protagonist suffers from inept art instruction, instruction that stifles the imagination while promoting conformity. In de Paola's book, neither the regular classroom teacher nor the art teacher has any idea what art is, what it requires, or how it should be taught. Their interest is in inhibiting artistic expression and enforcing uniformity. Were it not for the proper kind of example and encouragement that he receives at home, young Tommy's interest in becoming an artist would clearly be frustrated. De Paola's book smacks of autobiography, and yet one has the sense that it rather pulls its punches. The compromise reached in the end of the book is not a truly satisfying one; a great deal more anger toward these teachers is justified than the book communicates.

In Cohen's book, the kindergarten art teacher criticizes and corrects Jim's drawing, convincing him of his lack of ability in art so that he enters first grade sure that he's "no good in art." The understanding first-grade art teacher appreciates the children's imagination, encourages Jim, and rectifies the situation. Thus, the same book presents dichotomous images of teachers: teacher as wounder and teacher as healer. Cohen seems to be making two statements in this context. One has to do with the profound influence teachers have on students, to hurt or to help. The other implies that the teaching profession contains a diversity of human beings—and offers the hope that one sensitive and imaginative teacher may repair the damage done by a callous or repressive one.

Another strict, unimaginative, and authoritarian teacher is presented in Marc Brown's *Arthur's Teacher Trouble* (1986). Mr. Ratburn is so rigid in his approach to teaching and so ambitious for one of his students to win the school spellathon that he overloads them with work and has them do tedious seatwork while other classes have more engaging learning experiences. Young Arthur complains but conforms—and at the end his compliance is rewarded: he wins the spellathon and earns Mr. Ratburn's approval.

A strange and very negative picture of a teacher is presented in Patricia Giff's *Today Was a Terrible Day* (1980). Ronald Morgan is having a terrible day at school, and his teacher, rather than mitigating his misery, exacerbates it. She is sarcastic, ridiculing, and fault-finding. She embarrasses him on four occasions. Curiously—and inexplicably—she gives him a note to take home and read, in which she sympathizes with his "sad day" but assures him that the next day will be a "happy day" because it will be *her* birthday. This teacher is so self-centered that she assumes that her birthday will be a happy day for everyone. The ending of the story illustrates young children's need to love and be loved by their teachers: despite his teacher's self-centeredness and cruelty, Ronald's response to this note is to want to buy his teacher a birthday present.

This teacher's attitude and behavior indicate a serious character disorder, but the tone of the book is in no way critical of her. It does not seem to consider such teacher behavior as out of the ordinary. The acritical stance taken toward the teacher's behavior suggests that such behavior is familiar enough to be recognized and accepted without question. Yet it must raise questions for educators: How common indeed is this kind of abusive behavior? Can it be eradicated or remediated? What is its effect on children? Child victims of abusive parents have been the subject of much study; is there a need for studies of child victims of abusive teachers?

Giff's book may be contrasted with Judith Viorst's book about a similar problem, *Alexander and the Terrible, Horrible, No Good, Very Bad Day* (1972). In Viorst's book, episodes at school are simply a part of a day that starts off badly when Alexander awakens in the morning and continues horribly until he goes to bed at night. Mrs. Dickens, the teacher, is pictured as a normal, pleasant young woman who does correct Alexander when he makes a mistake and who generally does not take any nonsense from her students, but she clearly likes them and is amused by them. She is in no way abusive.

## Teacher's Power and Use of Power

Issues of the teacher's power are raised in many of these books. Is the teacher able to provide a safe entry into the new world of school? Can the teacher protect the child from negative or frightening experiences? How does the teacher use his or her own power in the classroom, to stimulate and encourage the child, or to dominate and control? And how powerful is the teacher in the larger context of the school or society?

Many of these books present an image of the teacher as an extension of mother, as a nurturing, protective, and caring person who is indeed able to provide a secure environment. These books tend to be about kindergarten or first grade. There is no confrontation between the teacher and the children; the teacher is their advocate and protector.

Other books are concerned with power struggles between the teacher and the students. The teacher who completely loses control of the students is made to appear ridiculous (Noble, 1980); at the opposite end of the spectrum, the teacher who dominates and oppresses the students is also viewed negatively (Brown, 1986). Most of the books that deal with power issues fall somewhere along the spectrum between these two extremes and provide various perspectives on how power and control are negotiated in the classroom.

The central conflict in Harry Allard's Miss Nelson books (Allard, 1977, 1982, 1985) is the power struggle between teachers and students. The kind and gentle Miss Nelson is ineffectual in establishing classroom order; it takes the intervention of the harsh, unattractive, unpleasant Miss Viola Swamp to bring the children into line. While the subject is treated in a humorous way, the implication seems to be, first, that teachers must exercise control over their students, and, second, that that can be done only through intimidation and domination. Once the students are intimidated, the teacher may revert to being pleasant and mild-mannered.

Other books give the power shifts between teachers and students a gentler treatment, implying that students will naturally misbehave if and when they can get away with it, but that teachers are able to function within that tension. In these books, extreme measures are not found to be necessary. In Emily Arnold McCully's *School* (1987), for example, the students misbehave at their desks when the teacher is writing on the chalkboard, but they behave themselves when she turns around to the class.

Mrs. Peloki (Oppenheim, 1980) faces a crisis that threatens her classroom order: a snake has been seen in the boys' bathroom. She screws up her courage to go in to catch the snake but is not able to master her fear and runs back out when she sees it. The little boys are also afraid of the snake; it is a little girl who goes in and catches it. The relationship between Mrs. Peloki and her students is so obviously a positive and respectful one that when she is not able to handle a crisis, the class does not fall apart. Instead, a member of the class comes to the rescue. On the other hand, when Mrs. Peloki is ill and a substitute arrives (Oppenheim, 1987), the class pulls every trick in the book!

Humorous comments on teacher power are made by James Marshall and Robert Munsch. In Marshall's *The Cut-Ups Cut Loose* (1987), inveterate pranksters Spud Jenkins and Joe Turner return to school in the fall ready to play more practical jokes, but the new principal, Lamar J. Spurgle, is on to them and puts an end to their shenanigans. Spurgle, however, has his comeuppance at the hands of Sister Aloysius, a teacher at the local Catholic school; Sister Aloysius was once Spurgle's own teacher and she still intimidates him.

In *Thomas' Snowsuit* (Munsch, 1985), both the teacher and the principal are seen as ineffectual against a young child's refusal to put on his new snowsuit. The first skirmish ends with the teacher in the snowsuit and Thomas in the teacher's dress. The principal intervenes but has no better luck. Finally, Thomas's friends call him to come out to play, and he puts on the snowsuit and runs outside.

Examples of a teacher misusing power in the classroom are found in Marc Brown's *Arthur's Teacher Trouble* (1986) and Patricia R. Giff's *Today Was a Terrible Day* (1980). In Brown's book, Mr. Ratburn is a strict taskmaster who overloads his students with work in order to win a school competition. Miss Tyler, in Giff's book, uses sarcasm and ridicule to embarrass and control young Ronald. Ronald's undiminished desire to please his teacher makes a poignant end to the story. Again, there is no indication that the author sees anything amiss in the classroom scenario she has described.

The great majority of the books treat the classroom as a world of its own, establishing little connection to or relationship with the larger context of school or society. However, several books in the sample raise the question of the teacher's relationship to power from outside the classroom.

In Miriam Cohen's books about first grade, the teacher is the unshakable source of comfort, wisdom, and encouragement. She provides significant learning experiences for her students. She seems to be able to handle any hurt or altercation or crisis that occurs. However, she is not able to protect her students from a mandated situation that she recognizes as harmful to them: standardized testing (Cohen, 1980a).

The teacher realizes that the test questions are silly, that they do not measure the students' knowledge, and that the result of the testing is to stratify and label the children. When the negative effects of the testing are apparent, she affirms the students in the important knowledge that they do have and is able to restore the positive learning environment that characterizes her classroom. Yet she has been powerless to stop this meaningless and harmful intrusion into her class. She accepts it and then ameliorates its negative effects the best way she can.

Relationships of power between teachers and school principals are represented in several of the books. In every case but one (Cohen, 1988), the teacher is a female and the principal is a male. While the positions of political power tend to be gender-specific, the representation of who has effectual power varies widely.

A traditional view of female-teacher and male-principal relationships is seen in Jane Hamilton-Merrit's *My First Days of School* (1982). The male school principal pays a visit to the classroom—"to say hello," according to the child-narrator. The principal is smiling and relaxed. The teacher, Mrs. Vanderlip, however, is standing stiffly and looks a bit tense. One wonders whether the purpose of the principal's visit is really to "say hello," or is this simply the child's assumption? Why is the principal so relaxed and the teacher so tense—pleased, but anxious? (See Figure 10-4.)

In *Thomas' Snowsuit* (Munsch, 1985), the male principal attempts to intervene when the female teacher cannot handle a seemingly simple classroom situation, getting a child into his snowsuit for recess. Both principal and teacher turn out to be equally ineffective, but it is the principal who is so undone that he quits his job and moves "to Arizona where nobody ever wears a snowsuit."

In *The Cut-Ups Cut Loose* (Marshall, 1987), the principal who is clever and resourceful enough to outwit the young pranksters is in turn cowed by his (female) former teacher. It would seem that the story represents a shift in power, from male principal to female teacher, but this is no adult-to-adult relationship. The humor of the story rests on the fact that the teacher's influence over the principal derives from her having intimidated him as a young child; he has not outgrown his early awe of her. This grown man is a little boy before his former teacher.

In Denys Cazet's *Never Spit on Your Shoes* (1990), the illustrations provide the commentary on administrative control and importance. The teacher in this book is pleasant and competent, if a bit traditional in her approach to teaching. She takes her students on a tour of the school, past the principal's office. Hanging on the doorknob is a "Do Not Disturb" sign; snoring sounds emanate from the office.

In the two sequels to *Miss Nelson Is Missing* (Allard, 1977), it is the teacher who clearly has the real authority in the school. The principal, Mr.

While we are working, we have a surprise visit.
The principal comes to say hello.

**Figure 10-4**   (Hamilton-Merrit, *My First Days of School*, 1982)

Blandsworth, is an ineffectual, boring buffoon. It is Miss Nelson, in the guise of Viola Swamp, who must take charge and restore order where he cannot.

In the two books by Miriam Cohen (1984, 1988) in which the principal is a female, there is no sense of an imbalance of power between teacher and principal. Indeed, the female principal is as helpful as the teacher in seeing that young George receives the class recognition and acceptance that he so clearly needs; she enters the classroom to announce that George will be on the evening news. She and the first-grade teacher sit companionably side by side at lunch in the school cafeteria.

---

## Gender Differences among Teachers

The American schoolteacher population depicted in books for young children is predominantly female. Of the forty-seven teachers that appear in the sample, forty-one (or 87 percent) are female; and six (or 13 percent) are male. Ten of these books are animal fantasies with animal teachers. These percentages reflect the preponderance of females among the United States' public school teachers. According to the National Education Association, 68.8 percent of elementary and secondary school teachers are female (*Digest of Education Statistics,* 1989). Although no statistics were available for the elementary grades alone, these grades do tend to be even more female-dominated than the middle school or high school grades.

### What's in a Smile?

There is no physical stereotype of the teacher in these books, male or female. Female teachers come in a variety of body types. Some are slim; some are of average build; others are plump. Some are young; some are middle-aged; others are older. Some are arrayed in frilly, feminine fashions; others wear more tailored clothing. The only characteristic common to the female teachers who are given positive treatment is that they smile. They smile *a lot.* They smile almost continuously at their students, except when they are surprised or gently disapproving. The female teachers who receive negative treatment do not tend to smile at their students.

The male teachers are a bit more stereotyped—or at least they fall into more discernible patterns. Perhaps that is because there are fewer of them. The two male teachers who are presented in a positive light are young, and they dress casually (Schwartz, 1988; Tester, 1979). In contrast, the teachers who are presented in a negative light are older and are dressed more formally, in suits (Brown, 1986; Howe, 1984). Mr. Green (Tester, 1979) is more sensitive to his students' feelings than Mr. Blum is (Schwartz, 1988), and Mr. Green has more fun with his students. Neither, however, is the constant smiler that we see among the positive female teachers. Both Mr. Green and Mr. Blum wear pleasant expressions, often half-smiles, and Mr. Green makes funny faces when he reads a book about clowns. But the male teachers do not constantly show their teeth. (Interestingly, it is the rigid Mr. Ratburn in *Arthur's Teacher Trouble* [Brown, 1986] whom we see smile. He ordinarily wears an expression of distance and mild disapproval, until Arthur wins the spellathon; then he smiles. His smile clearly is provoked only by his student's victory in the school competition; his approval is clearly conditional.) In these books, male teachers who are treated positively are well disposed toward their students and are at ease with them, but they do not smile at them constantly.

What does a smile signify? Surely the female teachers' smiles are intended to indicate good will, a lack of threatening intent. But a smile, as it is often unconsciously practiced by females, also signifies a lack of threat that may be interpreted as a submissive attitude, a desire to please. Why do the male teachers not need to smile so continuously? Does this reflect male and female socialization, and if so, what does it mean for the role of female teachers both in the classroom and in the larger contexts of school and society? (See Figure 10-5.)

### Establishing Boundaries or Bridges

Among the female teachers, a positive image is established through their great sensitivity to students' needs and an impulse and ability to cover embarrassment or chagrin; but the books show no such pattern for the male teachers. Mr. Green in Tester's book is quite sensitive to Juan's insecurity, but Mr. Blum in Schwartz's book seems utterly oblivious to Annabelle's series of embarrassments. He corrects her mistakes and lets her endure the laughter of the other children. If he is aware of her feelings—and there is no indication that he is—he chooses to ignore them and to let Annabelle get along the best way she can. And yet no criticism of him is implied; he is a pleasant young man. At the end he lets Annabelle be milk monitor, and thus her self-esteem is restored. But he does not bestow this honor in an effort to include her or to restore her self-confidence. It is an honor he gives to any child who can count the milk money; Mr. Blum himself is surprised that Annabelle can count that high.

With the exception of Mr. Green in Tester's book (1979), the male teachers in these books are not perceived to be as empathetic with students or as eager to soothe hurt feelings or to mend relationships as their female counterparts. These tendencies have been identified as broadly gender-related. The male teachers assume, or foster, boundaries between their students rather than bridges; they encourage independence, autonomy, competitiveness. To what extent is this representation of male primary-grade teachers accurate? Surely the implications for children's experiences of the primary grades are significant. Is it necessary or desirable that primary-grade teachers manifest the classic female tendency to nurture, to establish and maintain relationships, to promote cooperation rather than competition? To what extent should children be left to deal with their own hurts; to what extent should competitiveness and emotional independence be encouraged?

**Figure 10-5**   (Schwartz, *Annabelle Swift, Kindergartener,* 1988)

### *The Nameless Female Teacher*

In sixteen of the forty-six books in this sample, the female teacher has
no name (Carruth, 1982, 1985; Cazet, 1990; Cohen, 1967, 1972, 1980a,
1980b, 1984, 1985, 1988, 1989; Gross, 1982; Hoff, 1970; McCully, 1987;
Munsch, 1985; Wells, 1981). That is, in 38 percent of the books with female
teachers, the teacher is nameless, but in the remainder of the books, the
students do have names. In thirteen, the young protagonist is a male, with a
name. (McCully's book is a wordless picture book; none of the characters has
a name. In two others—Cohen, 1980a, 1989—the story is about the entire
class, with no one student being the protagonist.) In contrast, every male
teacher has a name—including names made up for humorous effect, such as
Mr. Quackerbottom (Howe, 1984) and Mr. Ratburn (Brown, 1986).

These observations raise some disturbing questions. Here immature males are individualized, but mature females are not. Is this simply an oversight? Given the care and deliberation that go into writing and publishing books, that seems unlikely.

Is it unconscious sexism? Overt sexism? This namelessness indicates that female teachers are perceived as lacking in individuality and force of personality. Is even the mature female to take a supportive back seat to a male child, fading into the background so that he might stand out? Is the namelessness an indication of, or a justification for, the low esteem in which teachers are held in American society? Or the low esteem in which women in general are held?

One might suppose that this namelessness suggests that the teacher archetype is so familiar that she needs no name; we know her, named or not. Many of these nameless female teachers are presented in a positive light; they nurture and care for their students (and particularly for the young male protagonist); they support their students' growth and progress; but they themselves remain nameless. Yet no archetypal teacher prevails among the nameless ones. There are those who are inept and insensitive (Cohen, 1980b; Munsch, 1985) as well as those who are competent and sensitive (Carruth, 1982, 1985; Cazet, 1990; Cohen, 1967, 1972, 1980b, 1984, 1985, 1989; Gross, 1982; Hoff, 1970; Wells, 1981). The namelessness of these female teachers remains a puzzling and disturbing question.

Five of the sixteen books in which female teachers have no names are animal fantasies, in which the teacher and the students are animals (Carruth, 1982, 1985; Cazet, 1990; McCully, 1987; Wells, 1981). Again, in all but one (McCully, 1987, the wordless picture book), the children do have names; even among animals, it is the adult female who has no name. In each of these books, the nameless female is presented in a positive light. In only one animal fantasy is the teacher a male, and he is given a name: the strict Mr. Ratburn in *Arthur's Teacher Trouble* (Brown, 1986). In over one-third of the books in this sample, then, the female teacher is nameless, and is the only nameless person among a classroom of named children.

## Members of the Mainstream Culture

Thirty-three of the thirty-seven human teachers in these books—or 92 percent—are white. (Ten books are animal fantasies with animals as teachers.) Two teachers—or 5 percent—are black; one dark-skinned teacher (Cohen, 1972) is of uncertain ethnicity. These books present an even more nearly all-white schoolteacher population than that which actually exists in American public schools. According to the National Education Association, 89.6 percent of American schoolteachers are white; 6.9 percent are black; and 3.4 percent are of other ethnic origin (*Digest of Education Statistics,* 1989).

The dark-skinned teacher in Cohen's *The New Teacher* (1972) leaves school to have a baby. (See Figure 10-6.) She is replaced by a nonpregnant, blond, white female. Thus is one of the few minority teachers—who may be viewed as the stereotype of the sexually active, fecund dark-skinned woman—replaced by a member of the white mainstream.

The names of the teachers as well as their skin color suggest that they are representatives of the mainstream culture. Of the thirty-one teachers in the sample who have names, two-thirds (23) have Anglo-Saxon names, such as Mrs. Dickens, Miss Bird, Mrs. White, Miss Tyler, Miss Gray, Mr. Smith, and Mrs. Jones. Only a few teachers have names that suggest ethnic or geographic origin other than Anglo-Saxon or Western European: Mrs. Peloki (Oppenheim, 1980, 1987), Mr. Blum (Schwartz, 1988), Sister Aloysius (Brown, 1986). Even the two black teachers have Anglo-Saxon names: Mrs. Ford (Relf, 1981) and Mrs. Becker (Lasker, 1980). Cohen's dark-skinned pregnant teacher has no name. There are no explicitly Hispanic or Asian-American teachers in these books.

The predominantly white teacher population represented in picture books for young children reflects, and even exaggerates, the current state of affairs in American education. In addition, the books do little to address the

The teacher went away to have a baby.
Everybody in first grade loved her.
They didn't see why she needed a baby
when she had the whole first grade.

**Figure 10-6**   (Illus. Hoban, in Cohen, *The New Teacher,* 1972)

problems inherent in such a situation. As the student population among minorities grows, there is little commensurate growth among minority teachers. Many educators are concerned about an increasing gap between teachers' and students' sociocultural backgrounds. These books do not address the potential for tensions and misunderstandings arising from sociocultural differences; indeed, the student population is itself predominantly white. Only one of the books in the sample even mentions sociocultural or ethnic influence in the child's attendance at school. In Sylvia Root Tester's *We Laughed a Lot, My First Day of School* (1979), Juan, a first-generation Mexican immigrant, is the first member of his family to have the opportunity for schooling that living in the United States affords. It is with great pride and hope that his parents send him off for his first day at school. The teacher, who has an Anglo-Saxon name (Mr. Green), looks as if he too could be Mexican-American, but apparently he is not. He makes Juan feel at ease in school and helps him get off to a good start. (See Figure 10-7.)

Anna-Maria is the token dark-skinned student in Miriam Cohen's books. She is the brightest student in the class, and she has some conflicts with her classmates, but they are not due to ethnic differences. Her blonde, white teacher treats her with the same tact and sensitivity with which she treats the rest of the class. In neither Cohen's nor Tester's books is there any indication that ethnic differences could be a problem.

Generally, these books ignore the growing disproportion between student and teacher ethnicity in American schools. None of them treats multiculturalism. Indeed, where ethnic diversity is represented, it is a token matter. The school is represented as a melting pot, where the mainstream culture prevails.

Of course, the apparent purpose of many of these books is to assuage children's anxieties about school, and so it perhaps would be surprising to find such troubling issues addressed. Yet for many nonwhite children, cultural differences are a problem. It is doubtful that these books accurately reflect the experiences of minority children in American schools. The question must arise: To what extent do these books which introduce children to school subtly introduce them to a world that is nearly all white, Anglo-Saxon, and female? To a world that offers employment predominantly to Anglo-Saxon white females? To a world that assumes the dominance of mainstream culture, a world that is not multicultural but rather one in which the few minority teachers and students that are represented are assimilated into the mainstream?

The books included in this sample indicate that picture books for young children present a wide spectrum of images of schoolteachers, ranging from the sensitive, nurturing teacher with whom the child can feel secure to the insensitive or authoritarian teacher who is a threat to the child's development or sense of well-being. The teachers at this end of the spectrum tend to be driven by a particular, limited curriculum, or to be self-serving in their motivation. Teachers at the other end of the spectrum, whose images have

**Figure 10-7**   (Tester, *We Laughed a Lot My First Day of School,* 1979)

been described as "positive" in this chapter, range from the rather traditional to the more flexible in their classsroom management, but generally
they tend to be more child-centered in their attitude.

The largely all-white, Anglo-Saxon, female population of teachers in
these books is of particular interest in a nation whose student population is
increasingly nonwhite and in which male student dropout rates are high.
The body of literature about school available for young children does not
suggest that minority children can expect to find a place in this seemingly
all-white world unless they are simply assimilated into the mainstream. It
does not suggest that male children can expect to find male role models in

school or that school is a place where males are employed to any significant extent. The question is raised: are children's perceptions of the teaching profession subtly shaped to view the teaching profession as a profession for white, mainstream females? Other disturbing questions are raised as well, questions that have to do with the negative perceptions of teachers reflected in these books.

Educators, like people in other professions, have tended to look toward one another for self-definition. Our sense of our profession is shaped largely by the examples, perceptions, or descriptions of others in our field. It is helpful—and healthy—to look beyond our own self-definitions to consider how we are perceived by others, by members of our society who have spent years in classrooms with schoolteachers and who now write about the perceptions they gained there.

Given the power of literature both to reflect writers' perceptions of reality and to shape readers' perceptions of reality, such works cannot be read acritically. They beg for attention, analysis, reflection, and discussion. Those books that raise the most disturbing questions may prove to be the most helpful to educators, providing we indeed pay attention to them.

## REFERENCES

Allard, H. (1985). *Miss Nelson has a field day.* J. Marshall, Illus. Boston: Houghton Mifflin.

Allard, H. (1982). *Miss Nelson is back.* J. Marshall, Illus. Boston: Houghton Mifflin.

Allard, H. (1977). *Miss Nelson is missing.* J. Marshall, Illus. Boston: Houghton Mifflin.

Berenstain, S. & Berenstain, J. (1986). *The Berenstain Bears' trouble at school.* New York: Random House.

Berenstain, S. & Berenstain, J. (1978). *The Berenstain Bears go to school.* New York: Random House.

Blume, J. (1982). *The one in the middle is the green kangaroo.* L. Axeman, Illus. New York: Dell.

Brown, M. (1986). *Arthur's teacher trouble.* Boston: Little, Brown.

Carruth, J. (1985). *First day at school.* T. Hutchings, Illus. New York: Modern Publishing.

Carruth, J. (1982). *The lucky glasses.* T. Hutchings, Illus. New York: Modern Publishing.

Cazet, D. (1990). *Never spit on your shoes.* New York: Orchard.

Cohen, M. (1989). *See you in second grade!* L. Hoban, Illus. New York: Greenwillow.

Cohen, M. (1988). *It's George!* L. Hoban, Illus. New York: Greenwillow.

Cohen, M. (1985). *Starring first grade.* L. Hoban, Illus. New York: Greenwillow.

Cohen, M. (1984). *Jim's dog Muffins.* L. Hoban, Illus. New York: Dell.

Cohen, M. (1980a). *First grade takes a test.* L. Hoban, Illus. New York: Greenwillow.

Cohen, M. (1980b). *No good in art*. L. Hoban, Illus. New York: Greenwillow.

Cohen, M. (1972). *The new teacher*. L. Hoban, Illus. New York: Macmillan.

Cohen, M. (1967). *Will I have a friend?* L. Hoban, Illus. New York: Macmillan.

de Paola, T. (1989). *The art lesson*. New York: G. P. Putnam's Sons.

*Digest of Education Statistics*. (1989). Washington, DC: U.S. Department of Education.

Giff, P. R. (1980). *Today was a terrible day*. S. Natti, Illus. New York: Viking Press.

Gross, A. (1982). *The I don't want to go to school book*. M. Venezia, Illus. Chicago: Children's Press.

Hamilton-Merrit, J. (1982). *My first days of school*. New York: Simon & Schuster.

Hoff, S. (1970). *The horse in Harry's room*. New York: Harper & Row.

Howe, J. (1984). *The day the teacher went bananas*. L. Hoban, Illus. New York: E. P. Dutton.

Jackson, K. (1985). *First day of school*. J. E. Goodman, Illus. Mahwah, NJ: Troll.

Kellogg, S. (1977). *The mysterious tadpole*. New York: Dial.

Lasker, J. (1980). *Nick joins in*. Chicago: Albert Whitman.

Marshall, J. (1987). *The cut-ups cut loose*. New York: Viking Kestrel.

McCully, E. A. (1987). *School*. New York: Harper & Row.

Munsch, R. (1985). *Thomas' snowsuit*. M. Martchenko, Illus. Toronto: Annick.

Noble, T. H. (1980). *The day Jimmy's boa ate the wash*. S. Kellogg, Illus. New York: Dial.

Oppenheim, J. (1987). *Mrs. Peloki's substitute*. J. A. Zarins, Illus. New York: Dodd, Mead.

Oppenheim, J. (1980). *Mrs. Peloki's snake*. J. A. dos Santos, Illus. New York: Dodd, Mead.

Parish, P. (1977). *Teach us, Amelia Bedelia*. L. Sweat, Illus. New York: Greenwillow.

Parish, P. (1969). *Jumper goes to school*. C. Szekeres, Illus. New York: Simon & Schuster.

Quackenbush, R. (1982). *First grade jitters*. New York: J. B. Lippincott.

Relf, P. (1981). *The first day of school*. D. DiSalvo, Illus. New York: Golden.

Schwartz, A. (1988). *Annabelle Swift, kindergartener*. New York: Orchard.

Tester, S. R. (1979). *We laughed a lot, my first day of school*. F. Hook, Illus. Chicago: Children's Press.

Thaler, M. (1989). *The teacher from the black lagoon*. J. Lee, Illus. New York: Scholastic.

Thaler, M. (1981). *A hippopotamus ate the teacher*. J. Lee, Illus. New York: Avon.

Viorst, J. (1972). *Alexander and the terrible, horrible, no good, very bad day*. R. Cruz, Illus. New York: Aladdin.

Wells, R. (1981). *Timothy goes to school*. New York: Dial Press.

# 11

# Personal Memories and Social Response

## Teacher Images in Literature for Older Children

Gail E. Burnaford

> *Mrs. Gorf had a long tongue and pointed ears. She was the meanest teacher in Wayside School. She taught the class on the thirtieth story.*
>
> *"If you children are bad," she warned, "or if you answer a problem wrong, I'll wiggle my ears, stick out my tongue, and turn you into apples!" Mrs. Gorf didn't like children, but she loved apples* (Sachar, 1978, p. 11).

lthough Mrs. Gorf, from Louis Sachar's fantasy *Sideways Stories From Wayside School,* is a caricature who reminds us of the wicked witch figure in any well-known fairy-tale, she may also represent an image of a teacher in some classroom in our own school history. She amuses, yet horrifies. She is silly, yet terrifying. Where did she come from, and why does she have a place in the imagery of teachers?

Adult readers of this fiction may find themselves scanning their memories to call up the figures of such teacher-tyrants. Are there Mrs. Gorfs in our past who abhor children so much that they wish to "eat" them up? Or perhaps our fantasies lie in the vein of Stanley Kiesel's novel, graphically titled *The War Between the Pitiful Teachers and the Splendid Kids* (Kiesel, 1980). In Kiesel's work, the teachers are less than terrifying; in fact, they are so hopelessly incompetent and boorish that the children are successful in taking over the school and running it themselves.

Both Kiesel's and Sachar's novels about teachers and students in schools reflect a social context in which school reform is an issue for discussion in the media and in the boardroom. The novels also suggest through hyperbole the attention currently being paid to teachers—their working conditions, their preparations, and their reputations—in the worlds of adults and children. Teacher images are being explored in this fiction as its primary readers experience schooling firsthand.

In analyzing this literature written for older children, we must use a double lens—that of an adult who may also be a teacher and that of a child-reader. Such multiple perspectives, at times admittedly conjectural, may provide some glimpses of the increasing complexity of teacher imagery as children progress in their schooling. All readers bring to the texts the sum of their own experiences and interactions with teachers in and out of schools.

Stanley Fish notes that when works of literature are analyzed, the *reader* is often forgotten, left behind, or ignored, while the literary critic becomes enmeshed in the text itself (Fish, 1980). Instead, Fish suggests inviting the reader to become an "actively mediating presence" in the analysis—one whose sensitivity and experiential background cannot be neglected in the name of objectivity (p. 23). Thus, adult readers cannot and should not ignore their recollections of teachers, but rather may enrich the reading by embracing those memories, while attempting to see through the eyes of a child-reader. Ideally, one should talk with young readers of these texts as they read and write about them, gathering a sense of how they perceive these teacher-characters in the novels and how such characters may contribute to their image of a teacher.

Our society often trivializes the word "image." We say someone is the "spittin' image" of his father. We speak in terms of a piece of photography capturing the image of a person or scene. The connotations of the word as used in these instances are physical, and they suggest likeness or sameness. For writers of literature, imaging takes on a different dimension, for it is closely related to the word "imagination." Books require readers to imagine or see with the mind's eye because actual visual images are absent. Imaging then is the exercising of the imagination in the written genre, and such imaging goes beyond the mere physical representation of such a person or scene. None of us has encountered a *real* Mrs. Gorf who is capable of actually turning children into apples. She is in fact a rendering of an image, albeit an exaggerated one. It may be that it is the literary artists of our time who are most capable of unveiling images of teachers, because it is they who challenge us to look behind the physical images to what lies in the realms of our imagination. It is that fictional teacher, created in a social and political context and nurtured by the imaginative reader, who is the focus of this chapter.

Herbert J. Gans (1974) in his analysis of popular culture notes that a society's art and entertainment do not develop in a vacuum. In fact, they tend to grow out of a society's values and the characteristics of its members.

A society's literature, as well as its visual art, television, and film, is in a very real sense its shared history. It is a public representation of those values and characteristics within a culture. What values and characteristics of school culture are embodied in the literature selected and read by young people? What can we learn about teachers and students by examining this literature?

I have read much of the contemporary literature for older children in order to explore meanings, understand the possible origins of those meanings, and gather some sense of the themes that surround images of teachers in these writings. Those potential meanings and themes may help us to discover a bit more of what it means to be a teacher in contemporary American society. I have explored chapter books written primarily during the 1970s and 1980s for intermediate and early adolescent children. Ten to fourteen-year-olds enjoy and understand contemporary literature, much of which focuses on scenes and events closely related to their own lives. The teachers in these texts are most often secondary characters; the main protagonists are the young people. The students often choose this realistic, modern fiction for their own independent reading. Therefore, this literature may let us enter into this world of teachers as they appear in print to young readers.

We can bring certain assumptions to this analysis. First, we can probably assume that our encounters with teachers in our own lives provide an appropriate setting for image-making through literature. Second, we can assume that all of us have been influenced by teachers either consciously or unconsciously, either immediately or long after the encounter. Finally, we can conjecture that all of us remember a teacher or teachers who have affected our lives, our livelihoods, and our sense of our own self-worth. These assumptions highlight the pervasive nature of imagery surrounding teachers. The imagery is embedded in our own experiences and school memories. The writers of literature with teacher-characters can depend on these shared experiences to help readers shape their own literary reflections on just who teachers are and how they may appear to be in fiction.

## Control and Authority over Images of Teachers

> *Do we have a fear of fiction . . . that it may be true? The story is the chief vehicle for truth. We search for truth through story. Objectivity is impossible; to look at something is to change* (L'Engle, 1990).

Barely one percent of children's hardcover books are written or illustrated by African-American authors (Creager, 1991). Although very recently some attention has been given to multicultural literature for children, African-American characters—as well as representatives of other racial/ethnic groups—are rare in the paperback series that are most popular with the intermediate/early adolescent age group. It seems that it is nearly impossible to publish "ordinary" books about children with minority experiences; yet the children's book publishing industry is thriving and prosperous. Publishers believe that minority children will read books about white children, but not vice versa (Creager, 1991).

Of the twenty-two books I used for this research—gathered from library and school booklists as well as award listings—only two featured African-American teachers. I could not locate books with other minorities featured as teachers. Only three books had male teachers, two of whom were removed from teaching for violating the moral values of the school and community in which they taught. The vast majority of teachers portrayed in the contemporary fiction surveyed were white females.

Clearly, the image of fictional teachers becomes a political, economic, moral, and social issue if we consider the origins, limitations, and profound messages inherent in the demography of children's literature. Spring (1990) refers to this scenario as the application of ideological management, or "the conscious exclusion or addition of information and ideas conveyed to the public" (p. 378). He contends that the control of ideas is in fact a source of power.

The publishing industry has unabashedly controlled the nature and number of books, particularly those in paperback, which are printed and distributed in major bookstore chains in this country. Publishers have identified the young reader market as being white, suburban, and middle/upper middle class. The result of such management is the dearth of books, outside of smaller, local ethnic bookstores, which reflect the multicultural environment in the cities and towns of the United States.

Teachers in these popular books for young readers are most often white, middle class, conservative, and female. While they are figures of control and authority over children, they are often safely and comfortably enmeshed within the cultural control of the community. If they reject the bounds of acceptable conduct, as deemed by the citizenry, they are dismissed.

Such is the case with Mr. Carroway, the drama coach in Asher's *Things Are Seldom What They Seem* (1983). He makes sexual overtures to 15-year-old Maggie and her best friend, Karen. The two girls report him to the principal, and Carroway is permanently removed from the teaching profession. The portrayal of this teacher lets the young reader reflect on a forbidden dimension of the teacher-student relationship. Issues of the boundaries of friendships as well as of teacher behavior are real ones; sexual harassment appears in the classroom where, if disclosed, there is no leniency.

Inherent in Carroway's story is the underlying fear of male teachers working with impressionable young females. Virile, handsome male teachers are purported to be difficult to control and sexually driven. Such an image is not consistent with the traditionally conservative image of an unmarried female teacher, who is constrained and contained by a supervising school board, and who is socially and morally proper.

This fear of the male teacher, which could contribute to our imagery surrounding teachers in society, reaches even greater proportions in the story *What Happened to Mr. Forster?* (Bargar, 1981). Mr. Forster, Louis's sixth-grade teacher, befriends the young man in a genuine way and sees promise in his journal writing. He encourages Louis to continue his writing. But parents in the community suspect that because Forster is not married and lives with another man, he must be homosexual. They protest and Mr. Forster is fired. The friendship that Bargar portrays between teacher and student is nurturing with no sexual overtones. Yet, the community fears any man who may challenge the conservative image of teachers. Current discussions of the propriety of disclosing one's sexual preference have yet to reach the school context, but Bargar's book does raise the question.

It would seem that contemporary literature for older children resists the portraiture of teachers within a diverse, pluralistic culture. Although there are signs that more writing for children will feature people of color and settings beyond white suburbia, it appears that the image of "teacher" is still firmly planted in the white, female, middle-class role that is a familiar staple in the current literature. Values are carefully controlled by the privileged, while the images of teachers remain quite traditional and unsurprising.

## The Creative Spirit and the Image of Teacher

Writers were once children in classrooms who were influenced by and in turn influenced teachers. The memories of these experiences often appear to affect the writing about teaching and teachers which these adults who are able to see through children's eyes undertake. Mollie Hunter begins her book for would-be fiction writers entitled *Talent Is Not Enough* with an anecdote featuring a teacher who informed her at an early age that she would be a writer. Hunter recalls her own amazing shock over that statement at the time and then expresses her thanks to the "strong-minded lady" who planted the seed that later became a reality (Hunter, 1976, pp. 4–5). She concludes her book with a story of a schoolmaster who loved words and respected language. It was from this real-life schoolmaster that Hunter learned that same love and respect for words. Thus, we have two teachers with enormous impact, two memories that become transformed and thus recreated in her autobiographical novel, *A Sound of Chariots,* in the characterizations of Mrs. Mackie and Dr. McIntyre (Hunter, 1972).

Similarly, Katherine Paterson begins her book about her life and writings, *The Spying Heart,* with her own memories of teachers. "The fourth grade was a time of almost unmitigated terror and humiliation for me. I recognize now that some of my best writing had its seeds in that awful year," she acknowledges (1989, p. 4). Then later in that text, she confesses, "Yes, I probably do still have lots of childhood goblins that need exorcising" (p. 78). Such "goblins" evoke images of Mrs. Gorf, who preys on our minds and our memories, turning us from children into apples, or perhaps just into dull-witted grown-ups.

Several of Paterson's protagonists in her fiction for young readers struggle with teachers who fail to appreciate and do not try to understand. Mrs. Myers, in *Bridge to Terabithia* (1979), pontificates rather piously on Leslie's essay written about her favorite hobby, scuba diving. Holding up Leslie's writing as a model for others to emulate, Mrs. Myers seems compelled to add that scuba diving is a very unusual hobby . . . for a girl (p. 33). Young readers can relate to Jesse's disgust and Leslie's bemusement at Mrs. Myers who is predictably chauvinistic.

Yet, Paterson's readers can also appreciate the impact that the music teacher, Miss Edmunds, has on young Jesse. Paterson helps her young readers reflect on how such positive relationships with students and teachers can be built. She does this in the book *The Great Gilly Hopkins* (1978) as well. Gilly, a belligerent young foster child, has faced a myriad of teachers who pity her because she has no parents and then frustrate her with inept attempts to reach her. Mrs. Harris, Gilly's new sixth-grade teacher, stands tall and proud, sensitive to Gilly's temperament, intelligence, and past frustrations. She serves as the ideal teacher who is savvy about learning and about children. She is fair, nonjudgmental, and thoroughly inspired in her teaching, and Gilly is bright enough to eventually sense her good fortune to be in her class. Gilly also faces her own prejudices as she becomes more comfortable with and trusting of Mrs. Harris, who is African-American. Paterson seems to illustrate that such friendships between child and teacher are possible, but they are not easy and they are not automatic.

Paterson's experience in the fourth grade finds a parallel in the story of *Anastasia Krupnik* by Lois Lowry (1979). Anastasia is a bright, creative child of an English professor/poet. She submits one of her original works for a poetry assignment to her teacher, Mrs. Westvessel, in celebration of Creativity Week at their school. Mrs. Westvessel applauds the children's poetry, all with nearly perfect aabb rhyme schemes, as they recite their works aloud. Then it is Anastasia's turn. She reads:

> hush   hush   the sea-soft night is aswim
>      with   wrinklesquirm creatures
>           listen (!)
> to them   move   smooth   in the moistly dark
>     here in the   whisperwarm   wet

(Lowry, p. 12).

Mrs. Westvessel responds: "Where are your capital letters, Anastasia?" "Where is the rhyme?" "What kind of poem *is* this, Anastasia? Can you explain it, please?" (Lowry, p. 12).

Of course, Anastasia cannot or will not explain her poem, and she is rewarded with a huge, red "F" on her paper. Such are the "childhood goblins" Paterson recollects, and such are the makings of image.

Children who grow up to become writers may have been artistic, creative, and possibly nonconforming in their early years. Tendencies to write from the heart, as Paterson advises, may exhume some memories in writers of teachers who did not perceive such creativity kindly (Paterson, 1989). Perceived reactions and responses by teachers to these potentially gifted writers may be responsible for some of these teacher images in the literature for older children. They also indicate the locus of power in classrooms where children are directed and teachers do the directing. Happily, in these books, the budding writer often finds a gifted teacher somewhere in his or her life to encourage the process. For Anastasia, it was her English professor-father who changed the huge, red "F" very deftly to an "A" when she brought her paper home from school. Paterson shows her reader that a teacher can be anywhere and that true teaching nourishes and nurtures.

Sarah Smedman examines the scenes in novels in which teachers, particularly if they are harsh, egocentric, and overly obsessed with discipline, play such disquieting roles that they remain indelibly in the readers' minds. According to Smedman (1989), that "these disturbing scenes of classroom drama etch themselves in readers' memories as enduringly as they do in the minds of their fictional students undoubtedly derives not only from the fact

*"I intend to be a writer someday, and you'll figure prominently in all my books!"*

**Figure 11-1**   (Frank Cotham, 1983)

that readers recognize from their own personal experience the teachers they meet in fiction, but also from the fact that the writers themselves have suffered under classroom tyrants as painfully as do their fictional protagonists" (p. 131).

One such unforgettable portrait is that of Miss Dunstan in *A Sound of Chariots* (Hunter, 1972). Miss Dunstan relishes the opportunity to use her red pen to purge students' writings of originality and correct the logic and language of budding authors. When young Bridie dares to argue about her red-penned changes, she receives a thrashing on the hands with a belt. Then when Bridie becomes angry and continues to resist, Miss Dunstan lashes her bare calves with the harsh, leather belt. How many young readers have experienced the emotional, if not physical, whippings of frustrated, angry teachers? How many more thousands of readers have felt the dismay and resentment from the exercise of the teacher's infamous red pen?

The misfit, the child who is different—are these recollections unique to artists, creative types who mature to be writers? They may in fact reveal a universal about being a young adolescent in this society. Probably all adolescents feel like misfits at some point. One must remember that in this literature written for young readers, it is not the teacher who is the focus of attention, but rather the child-protagonist. It is the child-character, the hero, with whom the reader may identify or empathize. Children in books who encounter injustice in classrooms are easily recognized by readers, who believe in a rather strict sense of fairness in all aspects of their lives. If a young protagonist is treated unfairly or unjustly and responds bravely, she or he is truly heroic.

## Teacher-Friend: Surrogates and Stereotypes

The strong, dominant images of teachers that tend to come to mind quickly seem to be the most pervasive in our culture. Tyrannical teachers who abuse and misuse their power over children are familiar figures in fantasy and contemporary literature for older children. Yet, even though these images assault us, they may not necessarily be the most influential or the most prevalent in this fiction. Interacting with the easy caricature of the apple-eating Mrs. Gorf may be relatively amusing and passively interesting for child-readers, but entering into a literary relationship or a dialogue with a more complicated, multidimensional adult who is also a teacher is an infinitely more active and engaging enterprise. Because these relationships are not often as dramatic, the child-reader's identification with them is perhaps more challenging. Similarly, because they are not as overtly compelling at first glance, adult readers may tend to underestimate their impact on the image of teachers which children hold as being middle-aged, white females who care for and mother children.

There is matronly Mrs. Goodwin in Susan Shreve's *The Flunking of Joshua T. Bates* (1984) who has Joshua in her third-grade class after he fails the grade with another teacher. Mrs Goodwin gives Joshua after-school reading lessons, complete with chocolate chip cookies and tea. He experiences success and is able to move on to the fourth grade just after Thanksgiving. Mrs. Goodwin is not a martyr; she is a caring, competent teacher who gives Joshua the chance he needs. She is a whole person as well; Shreve lets Joshua and the reader know that Mrs. Goodwin is experiencing a divorce during this school year. She, too, is needy and finds Joshua's companionship comforting. In every sense, she is a positive character with virtually no negative qualities.

Seventh grader Norman has a friend in his teacher, Mrs. Adelsack, in Ivy Ruckman's *What's an Average Kid Like Me Doing Way Up Here?* (1983). She's a home economics teacher who allows the seventh graders to make brownies, hero sandwiches, campfire pizza, and other goodies for their class assignments. Together, she and Norman organize a plan to save Fortuna Middle School from consolidation with a neighboring school. Norman tells us, "I liked having her treat me like an adult . . . I guess she'd forgotten I was just a punk kid in one of her classes" (p. 104).

The protagonist in Marilyn Sachs's *A Summer's Lease* (1979) tells the story of her summer spent in the mountains as a live-in sitter for one of her teachers. Mrs. Horne counsels and advises Gloria as she attempts to relate to her peers and the younger children. She is a mother-figure who nurtures, yet disciplines. " 'Oh, Mrs. Horne,' I wept, and snuggled up against her as if I was a little child. There was a warmth and a smell about her, a mother smell, that I'd nearly forgotten," Gloria remembers (p. 86).

Surrogate mothers abound in this literature for older children. It seems that even though 10 through 14 year olds are beginning to experiment with independence and autonomy, they still respond to an image of a teacher who reminds them of home and mothering. The image of a teacher who is supportive, collaborative, and helpful is perhaps reassuring to young readers who are facing the demands of their independence more and more often. Such a teacher-character enables the protagonist in these stories to grow and learn life's lessons. A child-reader focuses on the actions and reactions of the child-protagonist. The teacher becomes the supporting actor in the drama— necessary but not as important as the young hero.

Such a theatrical analogy seems appropriate in the societal realm as well. Teachers are seen as those who support others in endeavors. Their role is well-defined, if confining. We are comforted by their presence; they are often necessary to our success (though not always) and yet we seldom remember them as heroes.

Viewing teachers as surrogate mothers may be an extension of the familiar primary school stereotype of teachers as childcare-givers. For young children, a teacher's role involves a variety of tasks outside the academic ones, including the teaching of table manners, nursing hurt fingers, and comforting sobbing youngsters. Many such tasks are often associated with mothering as well. Such a characterization of a teacher is comfortable for children, parents, and the community. Children at the intermediate, early adolescent age are beginning to encounter teachers who may not be as interested in child development as they are in content areas and academic skills. The transition that many students face during this time can be unnerving and difficult. Teachers in the literature for this age group appear to support this change in attitude for young readers; they are more well rounded, having lives of their own and interests beyond the welfare of their students, but still they are often reassuringly matronly and comfortable.

## Teacher-Nonconformist: An Anomaly and a Reality

> *Miss Burger was the only one in school who didn't think I was a misfit. And she was the only high school teacher I had ever heard of who had a doctorate in Shakespearean studies. She was so brilliant, but I was the only one in her class who wasn't bored and didn't throw M&Ms or pennies at her when she read* Macbeth. *She told me things about myself I'll never forget—the kinds of things that changed my life. Until, finally, she had a nervous breakdown and they took her away* (Zindel, 1990, pp. 228–229).

Some heroes in the literature may be teachers. Surely the teacher described above was heroic in the eyes of a protégé and writer of adolescent fiction, Paul Zindel. Yet, Miss Burger is a tragic hero, perhaps even a bit Shakespearean, sacrificing herself, her sanity, for no ostensible reward, save the inspiration of a student. There are other such figures who are admired, if not exemplary, in this fiction for older children.

Ms. Finney, in Paula Danziger's *The Cat Ate My Gymsuit* (1974), is Marcy's favorite teacher. But she introduces herself as "Ms." and even uses her first name as she tells the class about herself. She asks her students to write about what they know in her English class. She goes beyond the curriculum by bringing in books from her personal library for the students to read; she starts an afterschool book club to encourage reading and discussion. She is an ardent believer in free expression and stimulates her students to believe likewise. But Ms. Finney makes a fatal mistake when she refuses to salute the flag during assembly. She has denied the authority code of the school, and she is dismissed. Marcy is incensed. She defends her teacher to her principal, to her parents, to anyone who will listen. But Ms. Finney does not return to school. Certain traditions cannot be ignored or defied.

The theme of the truly competent teacher who genuinely communicates with students and yet is removed from the classroom for some actual or presumed infraction of the rules is a familiar one. Consider the following exchange between two youngsters from the Kiesel novel (1980), *The War Between the Pitiful Teachers and the Splendid Kids:*

> —"Curly, you been in other schools. Did you ever have a good teacher?"
> —"Once. Miss Nagel. Room 11. But she got bumped—dismissed."
> —"How come?"
> —"Cause she didn't use the same readers the other teachers used. And she forgot to take her register with her out on fire drills. And she always had to be reminded to put her chairs on tables after school. Then they found out she let kids read comic books in class. We even made our own comic books. Mine was pretty good—*Sir Vanish, the Magician*" (p. 33).

Danziger's and Kiesel's portraits of teachers suggest that those who succeed in the system are those who follow the rules, who obey authority. Those who leave, either voluntarily or forcibly, are those who exhibit creativity and challenge students, thereby ignoring the regulations. Teachers can remain teachers only if they subscribe to the regimentation and routine. But there are always those who make an impression on the impressionable by breaking rank and reaching students. Both types appear in fiction for young readers.

Some teachers in the literature are untraditional to the point of eccentricity. Sometimes, they too are punished for being beyond the mainstream of society, despite the fact that they reach students who remember them and are inspired by them. M. E. Kerr's Miss Blue, in her novel, *Are You There, Miss Blue?* (1975), is a science teacher who dramatizes her lessons in order to make them meaningful for students. She relates scientific principles to what the young people know and experience in their everyday lives, and she does it with spirit and imagination. The young heroine Flanders reports: "I wasn't the only one under Miss Blue's spell in the classroom; most of us came away with the sort of full, silent feeling that you have after you've seen a really good movie and you have to walk back out into the real world again" (Kerr, p. 92). But, Miss Blue is a religious fanatic. She claims to have visited with Jesus in her room. Her fanaticism eventually becomes obtrusive to the authorities in the school, and she is asked to leave. Flanders notes that she loses track of her classmates and of her other teachers, but she never forgets Miss Blue.

Ms. Svetlana Ivanovitch, in Jamie Gilson's *Thirteen Ways to Sink a Sub* (1982) and *4B Goes Wild* (1983), is also an eccentric, but she manages to succeed in the world of schooling where Miss Blue and Ms. Finney in a sense fail. She folk dances with the children in gym, throws a mean snowball, and confesses to her students that she is a new teacher with much to learn. She often thinks aloud, questioning her actions and revealing her human foibles. The children begin by struggling with her odd-sounding name, her

outlandish dress, and her unconventional approach to teaching. They grow
to respect her and relish the time they spend in her classroom.

Ms. Frizzle is the height of eccentricity in the *The Magic Schoolbus*
series by Joanna Cole (1986, 1987, 1988, 1990, 1992). She wears dresses
with octopi and caterpillars on them and her shoes sometimes have frogs or
fish attached to them. She takes her students on wild field trips into the
center of the earth or into the city waterworks to learn concrete, hands-on
lessons about science and technology. Her bizarre appearance and her strategies for learning are strangely appealing. She is welcomed by the students,
as Miss Ivanovitch is, yet both in a sense challenge the mold of the teacher.

In these novels, a child-reader will most likely empathize with the students who champion the causes of their most admired teachers and with the
teachers who either maintain their individualism within the system or
leave it in order to retain their identities. In this sense, nonconformity,
defying the rules of expected teacher behavior, is celebrated. These books
may serve as stepping stones to the social reality surrounding the imagery
of teaching. We do live in a society where teachers are expected to conform to
patterns of conduct established by administration and community members.
Insubordination or alleged inappropriate demeanor is not tolerated. The
notion of teacher as servant to the taxpaying public is not far from the
surface. Children do appear to have definite expectations for the parts teachers play in the world, despite the reality that individual teachers are unique
personalities with their own personal lives outside the classroom. Yet, the
reader is sympathetic to heroic figures, both children and teachers, who
challenge the system.

Through the fictional image of a teacher who resists traditional norms
and behaviors, young readers can imagine what it is like to examine and
challenge the social system, even when such resistance results in negative
consequences. The harsh reality is that being a nonconformist can be punish-
ing and hurtful for these teacher-characters. Such an image of what it can
be like to be a teacher may stretch the definition in the minds of child-
readers. It also strikes a sympathizing chord in young readers who are
similarly exploring rebellion and nonconformity.

One such inspirational teacher who is actually otherworldly in his wisdom and depth of sensitivity is Mr. Blajeny in Madeleine L'Engle's fantasy
novel *A Wind in the Door* (1973). Mr. Blajeny, usually referred to in the
novel as "Teacher" with a capital T, extends the scope and breadth of school
and schooling with and for the children in the book. "Are you ready to
start—we will call it, for want of a better word in your language, school?" he
asks young Charles Wallace and his sister (p. 59). With Teacher, school
takes on new dimensions, for he does not ask the gifted Charles Wallace to
conform and adapt to his situations. Indeed, the sky is Mr. Blajeny's schoolroom, and he challenges Charles Wallace to expand rather than narrow his
world. Yet, Teacher does not impose his own perceptions. "I am only a
Teacher, and I would not arrange the future ahead of time if I could" (pp. 65–

66). Instead he helps the children to reject limits—to their imaginations, their beliefs, and their capacities to love.

Mr. Blajeny stands in marked contrast to the character of Mr. Jenkins, who is Charles Wallace's "earthbound" teacher in his real school in his own hometown. The dichotomy between inspiration and boorishness, between creativity and pedantry, is striking in L'Engle's novel.

The character of Mama in Mildred Taylor's *Roll of Thunder, Hear My Cry* (1976) is another such unconventional teacher-hero in the literature. But Mama is a character who works in the milieu of harsh reality rather than fantasy. Taylor's novel is one of the few widely distributed books by an African-American author focusing on an African-American family's struggles for respect and decency in the Deep South. Mama teaches history at the neighborhood segregated school. She openly teaches them about slavery, despite the fact that there is little mention of it in the texts handed down to them from the all-white school down the road. She makes a heroic stand in front of the County School Board superintendent and her students, and she is summarily dismissed. She is both a mother and a teacher; she is a role model and a symbol for the young storyteller, Cassie.

Once again, the child-reader encounters a maverick; her dismissal only elevates her heroic status and sets an example for her four fictional children and her readers to follow. Such teaching becomes a social stance, a philosophical position to uphold, not a role filled according to the demands of a society.

---

## Discussion

"Art is a means of seeing truth that cannot be observed directly" (Paterson, 1989, p. 102). Teacher as tyrant, teacher as friend, teacher as mother, teacher as maverick, teacher as eccentric, and teacher as hero—they all appear in this literature. But because these novels are about people, these images are often not orderly, neatly categorizable, or easily typed. What meaning can we then derive from our exploration which may reveal truths that cannot be observed directly but may in fact deserve deliberation?

Umberto Eco (1979) observes that, in a given literary message, there is both the sender and the addressee. That is, the adolescent is *in* the text with the writer and the story. If the writer of this fiction is successful, she or he has managed to see through the eyes of that adolescent or child. Such a writer must "see the world with double vision—both as the child he was and the adult he is now" (Zach, 1990, p. 426). In such a process, the child-reader and the adult writer become equals both immersing themselves in the text.

Young readers probably don't read fiction to find Great Truths about humanity and life. They may, however, expect to find themselves in the text, to encounter their own experiences, emotions, and expectations. Paterson states: "The story must ring true. It must tell us something we already know but didn't realize we knew" (1989, p. 62). That may be the truth with a small *t*. Truth becomes the truth of those young readers and not that of an adult reader who may eavesdrop on the conversations between author, story, and young reader. If this is not factual or objective truth, it may be the practical truth of shared experiences, perhaps summoned from memories of teachers we have encountered or from realities we have known in our own remembering.

Such a truth may not be explicit or simple to unravel. The images of the teachers we find in this literature are diverse, ranging from the stereotypical to the richly unique. These images invite all readers to search beneath the surface to inquire into the nature of human relationships between children and adults and to bring to light what may be missing and what appears to be present in these portraits of teachers. What is often missing from the teacher images in this literature is flexibility and diversity of color, race, gender, and class; what is present is an image of a teacher who conforms or risks dismissal from the system. What is missing is a consistent view of a teacher who represents a new way of looking at learning and teaching— beyond school walls and chairs with attached desks; what is present is the image of teachers reconstituted from our memories of traditional classrooms with authoritative teachers who directed teaching and learning from the front of the classroom.

In this fictional world, child-readers encounter a complexity that they did not find in the picture books or easy reader books of their younger days. Teachers in this world address issues with children such as human relationships, social values, and political agendas. Teachers are more often not portrayed as totally good or totally evil. Young protagonists in these novels have choices and decisions to make which affect their relationships with the people around them, including teachers. The interaction with these teachers is often complicated; teachers have lives outside of school walls which round out their characterizations and challenge readers to see them as whole persons. Images then evolve into a more intricate portrait of who teachers are or can be and what teaching is about.

The precise role of literature in creating or maintaining public images can only be conjectural. It does seem judicious to assume that some of the imagery surrounding teachers stems from the memories of all who have spent thousands of hours in classrooms with teachers. If, as some writers claim, their work contains a sense of truth, then we might connect our memories with the stories these youthful characters tell. It also seems essential to note that these images of teachers are grounded in a social and historical context of schooling.

Author-philosopher John Barth (1990) writes about the teacher: "The condition of the true artisan, perhaps, is most nearly akin to the gifted schoolteacher's: an all but anonymous calling that allows for mastery, even for a sort of genius, but rarely for fame, applause, or wealth; whose chief reward must be the mere superlative doing of the thing. The maker of stained glass or fine jewelry, however, works only with platinum, gemstones, gold, not with young minds and spirits" (p. 170).

Dialogue about teacher images in this literature may help us realize that the calling is far from anonymous; rather, it is an endeavor marked by relationships with young people who will remember their teachers long after their days in the classroom have ended. The reality of that memory is affirming for teachers, despite the absence of genuine fame, applause, or wealth in the profession.

Yet, that very absence of fame, applause, and wealth may deserve a second look. The view of teachers as subordinate—to the wills of school boards, community members, parents, and at times energetic students—is upheld in this literature for older children. The view of teachers as supporting players to young people's starring roles is also clearly present in this fiction. Perhaps what this exploration makes most clear is that imagery can be analyzed only within a setting and within an understanding of the roles of all the characters in the drama. Only by looking at images and expectations of students, administrators, parents, and society as a whole can we approach a meaningful rendition of teacher images in the literature.

## REFERENCES

Asher, S. (1983). *Things are seldom what they seem.* New York: Delacorte Press.
Bargar, G. W. (1981). *What happened to Mr. Forster?* New York: Clarion Books.
Barth, J. (1990). Teacher. In L. Rubin, Jr. (Ed.), *An apple for my teacher.* Chapel Hill, NC: Algonquin Books.
Cole, J. (1986). *The magic schoolbus at the waterworks.* New York: Scholastic.
Cole, J. (1987). *The magic schoolbus: Inside the earth.* New York: Scholastic.
Cole, J. (1988). *The magic schoolbus: Inside the human body.* New York: Scholastic.
Cole, J. (1990). *The magic schoolbus, lost in the solar system.* New York: Scholastic.
Cole, J. (1992). *The magic schoolbus on the ocean floor.* New York: Scholastic.
Creager, E. (1991). A black mark for children's books. *Chicago Tribune,* May 15.
Danziger, P. (1974). *The cat ate my gymsuit.* New York: Dell Publishing.
Eco, U. (1979). *The role of the reader: Explorations in the semiotics of text.* Bloomington: Indiana University Press.
Fish, S. (1980). *Is there a text in this class?* Cambridge, MA: Harvard University Press.
Gans, H. J. (1974). *Popular culture and high culture: An analysis and evaluation of taste.* New York: Basic Books.
Gilson, J. (1983). *4B goes wild.* New York: Lothrop, Lee, & Shepard.
Gilson, J. (1982). *Thirteen ways to sink a sub.* New York: Lothrop, Lee, & Shepard.
Hunter, M. (1976). *Talent is not enough.* New York: Harper & Row.

Hunter, M. (1972). *A sound of chariots*. New York: Harper & Row.

Kerr, M. E. (1975). *Are you there, Miss Blue?* New York: Harper & Row.

Kiesel, S. (1980). *The war between the pitiful teachers and the splendid kids*. New York: Avon Books.

L'Engle, M. (1990). Unnamed presentation. Wheaton College, Wheaton, IL. March 3.

L'Engle, M. (1973). *A wind in the door*. New York: Dell Publishing.

Lowry, L. (1979). *Anastasia Krupnik*. New York: Bantam Books.

Paterson, K. (1989). *The spying heart: More thoughts on reading and writing books for children*. New York: E. P. Dutton.

Paterson, K. (1979). *Bridge to Terabithia*. New York: Harper & Row.

Paterson, K. (1978). *The great Gilly Hopkins*. New York: Crowell Publishing.

Ruckman, I. (1983). *What's an average kid like me doing way up here?* New York: Delacorte Press.

Sachar, L. (1978). *Sideways stories from wayside school*. New York: Avon Books.

Sachs, M. (1979). *A summer's lease*. New York: E.P. Dutton.

Shreve, S. (1984). *The flunking of Joshua T. Bates*. New York: Alfred A. Knopf.

Smedman, M. S. (1989). Not always gladly does she teach, nor gladly learn: Teachers in Kunstlerinroman for young readers. *Children's Literature in Education 20*(3), 131–149.

Spring, J. (1990). *The American school 1642–1990: Varieties of historical interpretation of the foundations and development of American education* (2nd ed.). New York: Longman.

Taylor, M. (1976). *Roll of thunder, hear my cry*. New York: Bantam Books.

Zach, C. (1990). Double vision: A special tool for young adult writers. In S. K. Burack (Ed.), *The writer's handbook*. Boston: The Writer.

Zindel, P. (1990). Paul Zindel. In D. R. Gallo (Ed.), *Speaking for ourselves: Autobiographical sketches by notable authors of books for young adults* (pp. 228–230). Urbana, IL: National Council of Teachers of English.

# 12

## Opening and Closing the Door

### Urban Teachers in American Literature, 1900–1940

Rosalind Benjet

According to conventional wisdom, American schools, perhaps more than any other institutions, were responsible for the rapid assimilation of immigrants in the early part of the twentieth century. It was the task of the urban schools to impart American values, American morality, and American learning to a diverse group of children, many immigrants themselves, and others children of immigrants. Children spent five hours or more a day at school, and therefore certain assumptions about the schooling process seem logical. Teachers would seem to play an important role in the lives of their pupils; school itself would seem to be the focus of a child's life; and students would seem to model their behavior after that of their teachers. In order to study these assumptions further to determine just what the influences of teachers on their pupils were, I looked into both fictional and biographical materials dealing with the period between 1900 and 1940. Upon examination, the literature of the period dealing with teachers and schools follows none of the logic outlined above; instead, the reader most often finds polarized descriptions of teachers, either as menacing sadists or idealized do-gooders.

The urban classrooms of the period were usually arranged identically: rows of desks bolted to the floor facing the blackboard. Most teachers were female, and classrooms were constructed to accommodate forty to sixty students. Teachers were expected to cover ten subjects a day and, most important of all, to maintain order. Teachers often had little education beyond their own high school studies, so textbooks were relied on to shape what was actually taught. Pedagogical methods relied heavily on memorization and recitation drills; group instruction was the norm, and students who made errors were often punished. Small-group work was rare, and the teacher-centered classroom was the one most children entered (Cuban, 1984, p. 24).

Because of the teacher-centered atmosphere, students had time to study their teachers' idiosyncrasies, often finding them to be negative. Teachers who are partial, teachers who verbally abuse their pupils, and even teachers who physically abuse their pupils appear often in literature; yet just as often we encounter the teacher who nurtures and encourages students. Occasionally, writers recognize teachers as human, but more often the teacher is depicted as one dimensional.

Public schools had more on their agenda than merely the three R's for immigrant children. Selma Berrol (1982) assesses the function of the schools as one that would "uplift their [children's] morale, improve their manners, erase their first language, and make them into 'little citizens' as quickly as possible" (p. 33). Frank Thompson (1920) views Americanization and citizenship as the "usual resultants of school training" (p. 591). In the Boston public schools of Thompson's day, children of immigrant backgrounds would learn how Americans celebrated holidays and how 'real' Americans should behave. Berrol (1982, p. 36) adds that schools also assumed a social service function, teaching American housekeeping methods to girls, providing physical education, and teaching children about American sports like baseball. Some schools even provided vacation programs and medical examinations; one well-meaning institution arranged a mass adenoidectomy (enlarged adenoids were thought to prevent learning) until parents protested (Berrol, 1982, p. 37).

In *A Tree Grows in Brooklyn,* Betty Smith (1947) describes her heroine's school as overcrowded, with three thousand children in a building designed for a thousand (p. 134). She describes the schools as "brutalizing," and adds that "Child psychology had not been heard of in Williamsburg [Brooklyn] in those days" (pp. 134–135). As for the teachers in these schools, Smith claims that few were truly interested in their work, with most becoming teachers because it was one of the best opportunities for women at the time, because of the long summer vacation, and because of the pension they would receive at retirement. Women who married were not allowed to teach at that time, so "most of the teachers were women made neurotic by starved love instincts" (p. 135). She sees the "cruelest" teachers as those women who had risen from immigrant or poor backgrounds: "in their bitterness towards those unfortunate little ones, they were somehow exorcising their own fearful background" (p. 135). Smith concludes that those teachers who were kind and caring either married or left the profession for other reasons.

With stereotypes like Smith's as a model, it is no surprise that writers often see teachers as physically unattractive. In Michael Gold's *Jews Without Money* (1930) the hero hates school, preferring to spend his time on the street. He refers to his teacher as the "fat old maid" (p. 36). As a student new to American schools, Leonard Covello (1958) is surprised that his teacher is a woman; in Italy the teachers were men. His teacher, Mrs. Cutter, is middle-aged, has gray hair parted in the middle, and wears pince-nez type glasses attached to her blouse by a ribbon (p. 25). Rose Butler Browne (1969) describes the "typical schoolmarm" as wearing a large full skirt, and carrying keys attached to a tape sewn on her pocket. Her hair would be parted in the middle and swept back, and she would wear "no-nonsense" shoes (p. 93). Leo Rosten (1967) describes his seventh-grade teacher, Miss O'Neill, as a woman wearing a wig to cover her baldness, which the students attributed to her having been a nun (p. 167). In *Young Lonigan* we find a teacher referred to as "Battleaxe Bertha talking and hearing lessons, her thin, sunken-jawed face white as a ghost, and sometimes looking like a corpse" (Farrell, 1932, p. 4). In "You Will Wind Up in Sing Sing," Edward Silver (1967) depicts Old Lady Danford, a sixth-grade teacher at P.S. 164 in Brooklyn, who was fond of telling her students that they could "amount to something" but if they didn't behave they might "wind up in Sing Sing" (p. 17). Although Miss Danford was under 30 and attractive, he says: "If she were a man, she would have been a drill sergeant in the Marines. She took no guff from anybody, and if the occasion called for it she was fast and good with her hands" (p. 17).

There can be no doubt about the frequency of corporal punishment in these urban schools. Francie Nolan of *A Tree Grows in Brooklyn* tells us of a "lady principal" who "got recalcitrant boys into her office and made them take down their pants so that she could flay their naked buttocks with a rattan cane" (Smith, 1947, p. 134). Studs Lonigan of *Young Lonigan* reminisces about Sister Carmel, a fourth-grade teacher who "used to hit everybody with the edge of a ruler because she knew they all called her the bearded lady" (Farrell, 1932, p. 4). Continuing his discourse, Studs recalls another teacher, Sister Bertha: "She was old and crabby and always hauling off on somebody; it was a miracle that a person as old as Bertha could sock as hard or holler as loud as she could" (p. 5). Still another teacher, Sister Cyrilla, was known to hit Vince Curley, one of the local children: "[She] used to pound him on the bean with her clapper, and he'd sit there yelling he was going to tell his mother; and it was funny, and all the kids in the room laughed their guts out" (p. 5).

"School is a jail for children. One's crime is youth, and the jailers punish one for it," muses the hero of *Jews Without Money*. He remembers that at 6 years of age he shocked his teacher by using a dirty word. As punishment, she washed his mouth with soap and made him stand in the corner all day. His parents objected and complained to the principal, not because of the punishment, but because the soap wasn't kosher (Gold, 1930, p. 36).

Harpo Marx (1961) was equally vehement about the violent atmosphere in the schools of the time, declaring that he didn't get his education at P.S. 86 in New York because he left school in second grade after being thrown out the window. Miss Flatto, his teacher, predicted that he would "come to no good end." We are informed that he was thrown out the window by other children when the teacher was out of the room, but the teacher didn't believe him and sent a note to his mother, asking her to straighten out the child or "he'd be a disgrace to his family, his community and his country" (pp. 17–18).

The hero of "A Nice Old-Fashioned Romance with Love Lyrics and Everything" by William Saroyan (1983b) is a lad who receives corporal punishment from both his teacher and his principal. When he gets in trouble at school, he is sent to the principal's office, where he pleads his case vigorously but ineffectually: "The minute I got him cornered he got out his strap" (p. 150). Later his teacher, Miss Daffney, falsely accuses him of writing a poem on the blackboard that said she was in love with Mr. Derringer, the principal, so she hits him on the knuckles with a ruler. When he objects, she tells him to sit down. "She had me by the right ear, the one that was getting out of shape from being grabbed hold of by Miss Daffney and other teachers" (p. 151). When Miss Daffney tells him to hold his tongue, he sticks it out and gets hit on the nose with the ruler. Finally, the boy is sent to the principal for punishment. This time Mr. Derringer says that he'll hit a chair ten times with his strap while the boy "howls" (p. 154). But Mr. Derringer's mercy seems anticlimactic in a sea of cruelty.

When Leonard Covello in *The Heart Is the Teacher* (1958) attends school on the first day, the other children tell him he is going to meet the devil (Mrs. Cutter) who wears skirts and carries a long stick. Indeed, Mrs. Cutter does carry a bamboo stick, and she wears a heavy gold wedding band; "suddenly her clenched fist with the ring came down on my head" (p. 26). She has punished the boy because his friends, knowing he doesn't understand English, have told him to recite "b-u-t-t-e-r" so she thinks he is poking fun at her. The child, of course, doesn't realize until much later exactly what "crime" he has committed.

No doubt some of these teachers were downright mean, but other punishment was likely given with discipline as a goal. M. E. Ravage (1917) tells us of a history teacher who was "helpless in the hands of his pupils." The boys of the class were disrespectful and threw chalk at the teacher, and one even got up and waltzed around the room. Ravage contrasts this with his physics class where the teacher required discipline and the same students "became meek as lambs" and paid attention (p. 183).

Corporal punishment was not unusual in schools of the early twentieth century, and stories of teachers striking students with rulers or sticks are not uncommon. Because the accounts we have seen are written by adults looking back on childhood events, the cruelty of the teachers seems magnified; the passage of time seems to make these episodes more disturbing than they probably were when they happened. Yet the images of corporal punishment are both graphic and numerous, and these images of the teacher appear all too often in the literature of the period.

As Betty Smith observed, the teaching profession seemed to attract some of those people who actually enjoyed tormenting their students. After a nature study lecture on items like bird's nests, cornstalks, and autumn leaves, Michael Gold's hero in *Jews Without Money* (1930) overhears his "old maid teacher" complain: "It was like lecturing a cage of young monkeys on the jungle joys" (p. 40). We can feel the boy's pain in an ode he composed in response to an anti-Semitic remark this teacher made to him: "O irritable, starched old maid teacher, O stupid, proper unimaginative despot, O cow with no milk or calf or bull, it was torture to you, Ku Kluxer before your time, to teach in a Jewish neighborhood. . . . O teacher for little slaves, O ruptured American virgin of fifty-five, you should not have called me 'little kike' " (pp. 36–37).

Rose Butler Browne (1969) tells of attending kindergarten at Rice Training School, a branch of Boston Normal School located in the heart of Boston. The children are making valentines to take home, pasting angel heads on a place mat. Whereas the other children have place mats on which the angel heads face each other, Browne's angel heads face the same direction. When she asks the teacher for angel heads facing each other, the teacher says, "You'll take these or none." She asks again and the teacher rejects the request. Browne, who is black, does not attribute this incident to racial prejudice, but merely to a teacher who is unkind (p. 69).

In *The Promised Land* (1912) Mary Antin, an ideal student and one who usually idolizes her teachers, observes: "The mean sort of teachers are not teachers at all; they are self-seekers who take up teaching as a business, to support themselves and keep their hands white" (p. 217). It seems clear that the teachers depicted in literature are representative of any large population group: some are interested in their students and what they learn, others are indifferent, and still others are actively hostile toward their students. Those who are hostile sometimes manifest their feelings by using corporal punishment and at other times by showing partiality to students because of race, ethnic background, or family status.

As a black child in an almost completely white school, Rose Butler Browne behaved in a way that the white teachers considered inappropriate: "The white teachers looking out through the school windows resented a little colored girl taking over the schoolyard" (Browne, 1969, p. 72). Later, when Browne ran for the position of secretary of the Civic League, the other students supported her, but the principal of the school told students that Rose's name must be withdrawn because she [the principal] "felt that this position belonged to a student in a higher grade since there was a large amount of outside correspondence to be handled." Browne herself did not attribute this remark to racial prejudice but to the "snobbish feeling that poor people should be kept in their proper social relationship" (p. 91). At a time when civil rights was not yet an issue, it seems that discrimination against race could be interpreted in the guise of discrimination against social class. While, as we will see later, this type of discrimination also flourished, because there were many other poor children in Browne's school, it would seem that race was indeed the principal's primary motivation.

Teachers exhibited not only racial prejudice, but also ethnic prejudice.

Some of this prejudice was rather harmless. Novelist Jerre Mangione talks about teachers in Buffalo who expected Italian students to be superior students in art and music. According to Mangione, these teachers were actually disappointed when the Italian students showed no signs "of becoming another Verdi or Da Vinci" (La Gumina, 1982, p. 69). La Gumina states that school administrators and teachers often had stereotypical expectations regarding the ethnic background of students. Jewish children were expected to learn quickly while Italian children were expected to do poorly in school. Therefore, homogeneous grouping put the Italian students in vocational-type courses where they received little extra help of any kind in their work. School administrators perceived that Italian families preferred manual jobs for boys, so that too much education would be deemed detrimental. "Education might have the effect of diminishing a boy's masculinity" (La Gumina, 1982, pp. 69–73).

Leonard Covello (1958) recalls a situation that occurred while he was a teacher in a predominantly Italian East Harlem neighborhood. A committee was formed to discuss the creation of a new high school in the neighborhood. He preferred a general high school, but others, including several administrators, favored an industrial school. Covello interprets the situation: "An industrial high school presumes to make trade workers of our boys. It suggests that the boys of East Harlem are not capable of doing academic work" (p. 181). For Covello, ethnic discrimination was not a new occurrence. His first American teacher, Miss Cutter, had suggested that he change his last name from Coviello to Covello because it would be easier for Americans to pronounce. Although the children wanted to change it so that they would fit in, their parents didn't always understand. Covello's father defended retaining the original name: "A person's life and his honor is in his name. He never changes it. A name is not a shirt or a piece of underwear" (p. 36). Covello later changed his name anyway. Similarly, Harry Golden (1969) recalled his eighth-grade teacher Mr. Ryan, who helped his students Americanize their names before they entered high school. At that time, Golden's first name was changed from Herschel to Harry (p. 47). He, too, showed no regret.

Teachers and schools discriminated not only against various racial and ethnic groups, but also against the poor as a class. Anzia Yezierska, herself an immigrant, describes the plight of many immigrant students. One of her heroines tells of being denied a diploma by a teacher because of her personal appearance. The girl worked in a laundry both before classes and until eleven o'clock at night. She described her feelings at the time: "The hate I felt for Miss Whiteside spread like poison inside my soul, into hate for all clean society" (Yezierska, 1984, p. 172).

Another of Yezierska's heroines enters an immigrant school full of hope of receiving an education and full of admiration for Miss Olney, a "tall, gracious woman" who "seemed to me the living spirit of America" (Yezierska, 1984, p. 279). All too soon, however, we learn that Miss Olney's school offers only vocational training; the girl can choose between being a sewing machine operator or a cook. Miss Olney says, "It's nice of you to want to help America, but I think the best way would be for you to learn a trade. That's what this school is for, to help girls find themselves, and the best way to do [that] is to learn something useful. . . . I think you will have to go elsewhere if you want to set the world on fire" (pp. 281–282).

Although the negative images of teachers are doubtlessly unattractive and even repugnant, we must remember that these reminiscences come from adults, not children. Some of the reflections may have become magnified with time, while others may have been accurate. Logic tells us that many kinds of people entered the teaching profession in the early part of the century: some were removed and cruel; others were sensitive and caring. Moreover, teacher preparation did little to familiarize new recruits with their immigrant charges. Teachers appeared to bring the biases of society into the classroom.

Teachers in this literature do demonstrate moments of compassion and humanity. In "The Death of Children" William Saroyan (1983a) tells us a story about a class during World War I. Miss Gamma's two brothers have enlisted in the army, and she "came to class with bloodshot eyes and a dazed expression on her face" (p. 78). She tried to carry on and then asked if someone would volunteer to lead the class in singing patriotic songs. Finally, a Mexican girl, who spoke little English, volunteered to sing "Juanita" in Spanish. The children recognized the teacher's apprehensions and were eager to make her feel better.

Sara Smolinsky, a character in *Bread Givers* by Anzia Yezierska (1925), has dropped out of school in order to work and help her family. She is forced to enroll in high school at night, going to school five nights a week "in a crowded class of fifty, with a teacher so busy with her class that she had no time to notice me" (p. 162). M. E. Ravage, who has been out of school for some time, returns and is asked by a teacher not much older than he to write an essay about school spirit. Of course, he knows nothing about the concept of school spirit and hands her a blank paper. This teacher, however, is understanding and allows him to write an essay on his choice of topic (Ravage, 1917, pp. 182–183).

It seems that writers do perceive teachers as sometimes being kind, perceptive, and especially encouraging to immigrant children. Harry Roskolenko (1965) remembers his teacher, Miss Gola, as a "grand lady . . . a beautiful woman who smelled of heaven, who had a soft voice and gentle hands, and who seemed much concerned with me." In fact, he believes that she "found facets in me that no one at home saw at all" (p. 8). Harry Golden, who lived on the Lower East Side of New York, tells us that teachers were his first real contact with Christians and that he found them to be "kind, gentle, and generous." When he was assigned chores like cleaning the schoolroom, the teachers left chocolate cake and coffee for the boy (Golden, 1969, p. 47).

When we read what many of these writers observe about the assimilation of immigrants into American society and the conflict between American and ethnic value systems, we realize that the multicultural issue is not a new one. Leonard Covello (1958) recognizes the dilemma faced by immigrants: "Our teachers impressed us mainly because they did not live in the neighborhood. They dressed better and spoke differently and seemed to come from somewhere beyond the horizon. . . . in trying to make a good impression on our teachers, it was always at the expense of our family and what was Italian in us" (p. 47).

The dominant cultural image of the era, however, was that of the melting pot, and that is what we most often see. Harry Golden remembers that children often taught new immigrants obscenities to respond to greetings like "Good morning." But the teachers in his school were tolerant, explaining the joke to the newcomers and even expecting this mischief from their students (Golden, 1969, p. 45). He adds that he felt that his teachers were "inspired" because they were able to take new immigrants and make them into Americans within a single generation (p. 47). Mary Antin (1912) repeats this sentiment when she concludes that a school does its job well when it makes immigrants into "good Americans" (p. 222).

Teachers not only played an important role in the process of Americanizing the immigrants, but they also helped the children of the poor to realize their potential. Again and again we are told of students who received encouragement and help far beyond the teacher's regular duties. Leonard Covello (1958, p. 44) recalls his teacher at P.S. 83 in New York, Miss Quigley, who tells the boy about the public library and how he can use it. Later she offers a prize (a biography of Abraham Lincoln) to the best pupil in the class, and he wins the contest. When he is in high school, Covello at first believes that he must go to work because he has no money to pay for college. His English teacher, Miss Harding, informs him about scholarship opportunities for college, but he has no confidence in himself. Finally, he changes his mind and asks Miss Harding if it is too late to apply for the scholarship. She smiles, says it is not too late, takes his arm, and they go to the principal's office to call about the scholarship (p. 62). Rose Butler Browne (1969) is also encouraged by her social studies teacher to attend college. Mrs. Bosworth inspires Rose to be a teacher; she takes a personal interest in the bright black girl, introducing her to a West Indian doctor, a trustee of Howard University, who visits Browne's home to encourage her to attend the university. But Browne and her parents reject this idea; they consider a black school something less than other schools like Wellesley where the doctor's own daughter had gone (pp. 94–95). Nevertheless, it is the teacher's personal interest that makes all this possible.

When teachers are understanding and provide comfort to their students, we see an ideal emerge, a leader and yet a friend, a role model and yet a sensitive human being. In Mary Antin's family, teachers were held in such esteem that she says of her father: "a school-teacher was no ordinary mortal in his eyes; she was a superior being, set above the common run of men by her erudition and devotion to higher things" (Antin, 1912, p. 217). No wonder that Antin formed a lifelong friendship with her teacher, Miss Dillingham, who became "so dear a friend that I can hardly name her with the rest" (p. 208). Miss Dillingham encouraged the young girl to write poetry, teaching her meter and introducing her to the poetry of Longfellow (p. 215). Their rapport was so special that Antin says of Miss Dillingham: "It was her way to say only a little, and look at me, and trust me to understand" (p. 213). Few of us can boast of having such a relationship with a teacher, but when it did exist, as it does for Mary Antin, it becomes a lifelong memory.

When teachers are perceived as friendly, interesting human beings, the reactions of their students contrast greatly with the negative reactions we have seen. In Anzia Yezierska's *How I Found America* (1984), the heroine's sister Bessie speaks about her high school teacher: "Miss Latham makes it so interesting. She stops in the middle of the lesson and tells us things. She ain't like a teacher. She's like a real person" (pp. 290–291). The unnamed sister later makes friends with Miss Latham, who cares about her students and their families and invites the girl to share confidences whenever she wants (p. 296). Writer Yezierska was aware that a kind, caring individual could have tremendous influence on students. In "America and I" a student describes a teacher in an English class for foreigners: "The teacher had such a good, friendly face, her eyes looked so understanding, as if she could see right into my heart" (Yezierska, 1991, p. 149). Another of Yezierska's teachers helped an immigrant child who entered the school a few weeks after the rest of the class. The student got excited and had trouble expressing her thoughts: "But the teacher didn't see my nervousness. He only saw that I had something to say, and he helped me say it" (Yezierska, 1984, p. 133).

Although Leo Rosten (1967) at first disliked his seventh-grade English teacher, his attitude changed later when she led him "into a sunlit realm of order and meaning" (p. 168). According to Rosten, this teacher was not aware of her influence on him; nor was she particularly interested in him. It was not her mission to make students like her. He says, "She concentrated on nothing more than the transmission of her knowledge and her skill" (p. 169).

When teachers are a source of both comfort and knowledge to their students, both student and teacher seem to benefit. Rose Butler Browne (1969) speaks of her second-grade teacher, Mrs. Vial, "a large stout woman possessed of much love and good humor" (p. 70). One day a thunderstorm interrupts their class and the teacher tries to calm the frightened students. Rose had been taught by her grandmother to be quiet during a storm or she would "anger the Lord," but instead, the child runs to her teacher for comfort and reassurance (p. 71). In order for this sort of situation to occur, teachers cannot all be the ogres that some writers portray.

Teachers can be powerful influences on their students, and at times students even see God-like qualities in them. In fact, the teacher's role often becomes central in shaping the lives of students. When such a situation exists, what students say about teachers becomes a series of accolades that few of us ever receive. In the eyes of Marya Mannes (1967), her high school English teacher, Miss Sweet, who encouraged students to write by asking them to write about "what delights you," is "immortal as all teachers who have implanted visions of worth and beauty in their pupils are immortal" (p. 192). Sara Smolinsky of Anzia Yezierska's *Bread Givers* (1925), now a teacher herself, reminisces about seeing her teacher when she was a child: "But more even than the music of the hurdy-gurdy was the inspiring sight of the Teacher as she passed the street. How thrilled I felt if I could brush by Teacher's skirt and look up into her face as she passed me. If I was lucky enough to win a glance or a smile from that superior creature, how happy I felt for the rest of the day!" (p. 269). Yezierska's teacher recalls M. E. Ravage's observation of people on the street in the Lower East Side of New York, including "the schoolteacher, with her neat figure and sweet smile, and a bevy of admiring little children always clinging to her skirts as she tried to make her way from the corner of Eldridge Street 'uptown' " (Ravage, 1917, p. 90).

Sometimes an even larger than life image is ascribed to teachers, possibly because for poor bright students, school and teachers were the true bright spots in a colorless existence. When the teacher is viewed in this way, we find almost religious overtones in the descriptions of teachers. In "The Miracle" Anzia Yezierska (1984) says, "My teacher was so much above me that he wasn't a man to me at all. He was a God. His face lighted up the shop for me, and his voice sang itself in me everywhere I went. It was like healing medicine to the flaming fever within me to listen to his voice. And then I'd repeat to myself his words and live in them as if they were religion" (p. 135). In considering the different kinds of teachers, Mary Antin (1912) concludes that "true teachers are of another strain. Apostles all of an ideal, they go to their work in a spirit of love and inquiry, seeking not comfort—but truth that is the soul of wisdom, the joy of big-eyed children, the food of 'hungry youth' " (p. 218). When both student and teacher are sensitive, this is the kind of relationship that can develop.

We cannot forget that some children like Mary Antin thrive in the educational atmosphere while others rebel. As Oscar Handlin (1982) points out in "Education and the European Immigrant," school was never the totality of the lives of immigrant children, but only a part. They learned from their family, the neighborhood, the workplace, and the movie houses as well as the school (p. 15). Because many children lived in cramped, unattractive quarters, they spent many hours in the streets, playing games and socializing with their peers. Not all parents valued education, and some merely needed the money that a working child could bring to the family. Other parents, burdened by large numbers of children, failed to provide individual attention or interest to each child, leaving the children to pursue their own interests. In these situations some negative images of teachers will inevitably develop.

In spite of outside influences, however, school was the focus of the lives of many children.[1] The successful alumni of urban schools are visible in virtually every profession, and for many this success would not have been possible without teachers and schools. For approximately six hours a day a child was exposed to an American school and an American teacher, and when everything functioned well, the school wielded an enormous influence in integrating immigrants into American society. It was indeed within the power of a teacher either to open or to close the door of education.

## NOTE

1. More modern American fiction clearly shows that the university teacher plays an important role in the imagination of fiction writers, if not their very lives. There appears to be a dearth of fiction which, in either profound or even superficial ways, deals with schoolteachers in American literature after approximately 1940, except for several books in which the authors themselves worked as schoolteachers. However, the last several years have witnessed a revitalized portrayal of the immigrant experience reflecting American population trends. We will need to see if the schoolteacher again figures prominently in the imagination of today's multicultural American writers as their voices become more present in the literature.

## REFERENCES

Antin, M. (1912). *The promised land*. Boston: Houghton Mifflin.

Berrol, S. (1982). Public schools and immigrants: The New York City experience. In B. J. Weiss (Ed.) *American education and the European immigrant: 1840–1940* (pp. 31–43) Urbana: University of Illinois Press

Browne, R. B. & English, J. W. (1969). *Love my children*. Elgin, IL: David C. Cook.

Covello, L. & D'Agostino, G. (1958). *The heart is the teacher*. New York: McGraw-Hill.

Cuban, L. (1984). *How teachers taught: Constancy and change in American classrooms 1890–1980*. New York: Longman.

Farrell, J. T. (1932). *Young Lonigan*. New York: Vanguard.

Gold, M. (1930). *Jews without money*. New York: Liveright.

Golden, H. (1969). *The right time: An autobiography*. New York: G. P. Putnam's Sons.

Handlin, O. (1982). Education and the European Immigrant. In B. J. Weiss (Ed.), *American education and the European immigrant: 1840–1940* (pp. 3–16). Urbana: University of Illinois Press.

La Gumina, S. (1982). American education: The Italian immigrant response. In B. J. Weiss (Ed.), *American education and the European immigrant: 1840–1940* (pp. 61–77). Urbana: University of Illinois Press.

Mannes, Marya. (1967). If you can't express it, you don't know it. In M. L. Ernst (Ed.), *The teacher*. Englewood Cliffs, NJ: Prentice-Hall.

Marx, H. & Barber, R. (1961). *Harpo speaks!* New York: Bernard Geis Associates.

Ravage, M. E. (1917). *An American in the making: The life story of an immigrant*. New York: Harper.

Roskolenko, H. (1965). *When I was last in Cherry Street*. New York: Stein & Day.

Rosten, L. (1967). Dear Miss O'Neill. In M. L. Ernst (Ed.), *The teacher* (pp. 163–170). Englewood Cliffs, NJ: Prentice-Hall.

Saroyan, W. (1983a). The death of children. In *My name is Saroyan* (pp. 80–82). New York: Coward-McCann.

Saroyan, W. (1983b). A nice old-fashioned romance with love lyrics and everything. In *My name is Saroyan* (pp. 150–154). New York: Coward-McCann.

Silver, E. (1967). You will wind up in Sing Sing. In M. L. Ernst (Ed.), *The teacher* (pp. 15–22). Englewood Cliffs, NJ: Prentice-Hall.

Smith, B. (1947). *A tree grows in Brooklyn*. New York: Harper & Row.

Thompson, F. V. (1920). The school as the instrument for nationalization: Here and elsewhere. In P. Davis (Ed.), *Immigration and Americanization* (pp. 582–599). Boston: Ginn & Co.

Yezierska, A. (1991). America and I. In *How I found America: Collected stories of Anzia Yezierska* (pp. 144–153). New York: Persea Books.

Yezierska, A. (1925). *Bread givers*. Garden City, NY: Doubleday Page & Co.

Yezierska, A. (1920/1985). How I found America. In *Hungry Hearts,* pp. 250–298. Reprint. Salem, NH: Ayer.

Yezierska, A. (1920/1985). The miracle. In *Hungry Hearts,* pp. 114–141. Reprint. Salem, NH: Ayer.

Yezierska, A. (1920/1985). Soap and water. In *Hungry Hearts,* pp. 163–177. Reprint. Salem, NH: Ayer.

# 13

# The Sentimental Image
# of the Rural Schoolteacher

Mary Phillips Manke

A deep and sentimental nostalgia for certain images of our national past is a recurring theme in American popular culture. Remembered settings are forever desired, forever recalled—yet hidden beneath a coat of sugary icing, concealing their reality. It is easy to call up some of these images: the warm kitchen of a prosperous farmhouse, filled with loving care and the rich aroma of apple pie; the summer days of a traditional country boyhood, quintessentially carefree and rebellious; the wholehearted patriotism of a small-town Fourth of July, glowing with pride and community solidarity; a legislature or constitutional convention of the early Republic, where wise and thoughtful representatives sat solemnly to weigh the needs of their neighbors and make rational decisions for the good of all. Another such setting is the one-room country school, home to happy, well-behaved children and the ideal teacher.

Before going on to a fuller discussion of our nostalgic memory of these schools, it is important to recognize how the coating of sentiment that overlays these images not only obscures the negative aspects of their reality but also makes it difficult to see what about them was both real and desirable, and might be revived or revisited to enhance our modern lives. For example, the life of the rural farmhouse was based on a level of physical work by both men and women that few would choose to undertake today, and it must frequently have been pervaded by sadness caused by the early deaths of adults and children. Yet the unity and continuity of family was often maintained there in the face of formidable obstacles. The boys we remember playing through the summer often worked harder than most adults do now, and grew up with little education or knowledge of the world outside their neighborhoods. Yet they probably did claim freedom from adult restraints during some part of their childhood, an opportunity that the fears and pressures of the modern world deny to most children today.

Those happy Fourths were founded on an unquestioned faith in our national rightness that is a luxury we cannot afford in these times, and the unified communities that celebrated it were likely to exclude from their membership those perceived to be "different" in religion, ethnicity, or values. Yet those communities did know how to celebrate their shared values and how to build bonds of care and concern among neighbors. Similarly, the remembered legislators were far from representative of those for whom they made decisions and were often narrow and exclusive in their views. Yet they did embody a belief in the obligation of service to the community that is far from pervasive among well-educated and successful members of today's society.[1]

As these images appear, bathed in a golden aura of nostalgia and sentiment, we fail to discern in them what was *not* good in our national past, what we want to leave behind us. Equally, because our cynical modern intelligences warn us that nothing lighted by that golden glow can be real, we are unable to find in these images of the past the benefits they might have for our present and future. This is particularly true of our image of the country school.

The popular American view of the history of schools has been characterized by nostalgia for the teachers, classrooms, students, and curricula of the imagined rural past. The continuing popularity of images created by Norman Rockwell and of reprints of the *McGuffey Reader* are two indications of this nostalgia. In a remembered golden age of American education, many believe, learning and teaching were successful enterprises conducted in country and small-town schools by dedicated, competent, and morally superior teachers who maintained discipline and passed on important knowledge to well-behaved and willing students. These beliefs have led to a persistent demand for a return to the education of the past; if the past was perfect, how could we *not* want to return to it?

## Sources and Methodology

This study began as an attempt to reconcile conflicting images of the early twentieth-century rural school which I had accumulated over a number of years. I was aware of a popular nostalgia for the schools of the past, especially for the version of the rural school presented by Norman Rockwell and the *McGuffey Reader*. Memories from my reading of early twentieth-century fiction seemed to contrast with this nostalgic image. Furthermore, many educational historians, such as Tyack (1974), presented an essentially negative view of these schools.[2]

In an effort to gain a better understanding of these images, I first returned to a reading of the kinds of novels I remembered, as well as some memoirs written by teachers from the period. Relying on the realistic nature of such fiction, I made notes of each incident that had to do with schooling and I began to see particular themes emerging from my reading. Later, seeking confirmation of the images I had found in fiction and memoir, I turned to texts that were intended to prepare teachers for service in rural schools, and I searched for material in those texts on the same themes as in literature.

Limiting myself to novels published in the twentieth century, I read *Rebecca of Sunnybrook Farm* (1903) by Kate Douglas Wiggin, now regarded as a "children's classic" but originally written for a general audience; and *A Daughter of the Land* (1918) by Gene Stratton-Porter and *Glenngarry School Days* (1902) by Ralph Connor, which are now read very little. I also included three of Laura Ingalls Wilder's "Little House" books, which have enjoyed continuing popularity as children's books since they were published in the 1930s and 1940s. *Farmer Boy* (1933), *Little Town on the Prairie* (1941), and *These Happy Golden Years* (1943) each contain considerable material on rural schools.

The memoirs I read include Mary Ellen Chase's *A Goodly Fellowship* (1939), Marshall A. Barber's *The Schoolhouse at Prairie View* (1938), and Marion G. Kirkpatrick's *The Rural School from Within* (1917), as well as the briefer reminiscences found in F. R. Donovan's sociological study, *The Schoolma'am* (1938), and in *Cloverdale: A Salute to One-Room School-teachers* by H. B. Christensen (1986).

The textbooks I read were written in the early 1900s; their dual purpose was to serve as texts for the short courses offered at normal schools to prepare rural teachers and as ready references on educational questions for those same teachers when they had returned to the isolated work of their rural schools. Of these I read M. Carney's *Country Life and the Country School* (1912), J. Kennedy's *Rural Life and the Rural School* (1915), H.W. Foght's *The Rural Teacher and His Work* (1917), T. J. Woofter's *Teaching in Rural Schools* (1917), F. J. Lowth's *Everyday Problems of the Country Teacher* (1936), and J. R. Slacks's *The Rural Teacher's Work* (1938).

Reading these quite diverse sources has led me to two general conclusions. First, the image of rural teachers and rural schools presented in them is far more varied than the common nostalgic and sentimental vision of rural schools. Most of the same problems that trouble schools today were actually part of daily life in the rural schools of the past. Many of the novels and reminiscences include passages that reveal what was difficult and daunting about the teacher's life in the rural school. More than that, the advice given in the texts, though phrased very positively, is evidently aimed at helping the teacher surmount these difficulties.

Second, it is remarkable to what an extent many of these writers, whether novelists, teachers, or textbook writers (usually instructors at normal schools), held as a positive value what the more modern thinker or scholar would call sentimentality. Not only is the rural teacher often sentimentalized—that is, painted with a rather sickly wash of one-sided praise and positive thinking—but the textbooks actually recommend the reading of sentimental novels of the schoolroom as ways to raise the tone of the teacher's mind and show her what she should try to achieve.

Perhaps this sentimental tone, common to all three kinds of sources— novels, textbooks, and memoirs—is part of the reason why we have remembered the "beautiful and good" dimensions of the rural school and forgotten the problematic.

I will consider four aspects of the rural teacher's image: her character, her concerns about discipline, order, and student behavior, her choice of curriculum and teaching methods, and her preparation to teach. These are discussed separately only for the sake of convenience. Clearly, the kind of person the teacher is and her own education are linked tightly to issues of her classroom management, subject matter, and instructional methods, especially when the teacher herself is likely to have received most of her education in a school much like the one where she would teach.

### The Character of the Teacher

The very use of the word "character" to describe what we might now call personality has its own set of connotations. Personality may simply refer to a set of individual qualities, innate or acquired through one's life experiences. Character is something to be created, worked on, developed, and judged. It is good or bad, strong or weak, and not simply (and less judgmentally) introverted or extroverted, friendly or quiet, as personality might be. The lengthy descriptions of the teacher's character found in the texts they were to use suggest that building a strong character for themselves was a vital task for which teachers were responsible.

In fact, Lowth (1936), who had been the principal of the rural teacher training school at Janesville, Wisconsin, suggested that teachers score themselves on various aspects of their character and work to improve their scores. Lowth wrote, "It would pay any teacher to make out a score card of say twenty-five personal qualities, and then check herself to see where she stands. Mark each attribute on the basis of one hundred. For example, a teacher might mark herself 100 on honesty but only 60 on initiative. She may be worth 95 in sympathy, but only 65 in accuracy "(p. 43).

Slacks (1938), who was professor of rural education at Iowa State Teachers College, gave a list of qualities necessary for the rural teacher which is representative of those provided in nearly all the texts encountered here. He called for the teacher to be healthy (and health is considered to be the result of good personal hygiene), enthusiastic, alert, consistent, self-controlled, fair, and good-natured; to have a well-modulated voice; to possess a sense of humor; to be hardworking, orderly, honest and sincere, and energetic; and to have sympathy and patience.

Some of the most sentimental statements about the desired character of the rural teacher are found in the texts intended for their use. For example,

Kirkpatrick (1917) declared: "The teacher who has drunk deeply from sorrow's cup, and is rich in experience that has left him not hardened and embittered against the world, but softened and sweetened with a charity that looks for goodness in all men and all women . . . has a preparation for a life work that has for its accomplishment the building of a citizenship based upon the love of man for man (p. 135)."[3] Woofter (1936) insisted on teachers' dedication: "Teaching is a great profession. . . . Human life is the greatest thing in the world, and he who is called to the training and development of human life has the greatest calling in the world. Only those who can so appreciate the greatness of teaching should enter the profession" (p. 25).

It seems a short step from the demand for such characteristics to the belief that teachers typically did possess them, especially when the texts that teachers studied recommended that they read sentimental novels, and model themselves on heroes and heroines possessing all these traits. Many of these novels are no longer to be found in libraries. Several lists name, among others: Elizabeth Enslow, *The Schoolhouse in the Foothills;* Bess Streeter Aldrich, *A Lantern in Her Hand;* Dan Stephens, *Phelps and His Teachers;* Edward Eggleston, *The Hoosier Schoolmaster;* W. H. Smith, *The Evolution of Dodd;* and Angelina Wray, *Jean Mitchell's School,* as well as Kate Douglas Wiggin, *Rebecca of Sunnybrook Farm* and Ralph Connor, *Glengarry School Days.*

According to Lowth (1936, pp. 52–53), Wray's novel "exemplifies the everlasting truth that the teacher's personality is by far the largest factor in the work of the school," while Eggleston's "sets forth some of those great and inevitable truths of our human relationships which all teachers need to know. The young instructor made good. Discover how he won out."

Teachers were told to read these novels, but not, it is important to note, to glean suggestions for teaching from the descriptions of schooling which they contain. In fact, Owen Wister's *The Virginian* (1917), which appeared on virtually every list, has as its lovely heroine a young teacher whose teaching is never described at all, but only acts as a hindrance to the development of her romance with the Virginia-born cowhand of the title. Reading this novel was recommended strictly as a guide to character development, particularly of that "womanly sweetness" and steadfastness of purpose that characterize the heroine.

The teachers described in the novels and memoirs read for this study, by contrast, are painted as quite ordinary persons, with characters no more or less "developed" than those of other people. Laura Ingalls Wilder, in her self-portrait in *These Happy Golden Years* (1943), is no paragon, but a young and inexperienced woman trying to survive her first teaching job from day to day. Although Connor's *Glengarry School Days* (1902) includes the portrait of one teacher who was well educated and of admirable character, other schoolmasters were not described so positively. One was portrayed as friendly and pleasant, but not remarkable, while another was weak and cruel, even sadistic.

Mary Ellen Chase, in her memoir *A Goodly Fellowship* (1939), told us that she approached her first teaching job, as a young woman of 18 or 19, with such fear that if possible she would "then and there have run for cover, leaving the Buck's Harbor School to whatever fate awaited it" (p. 37). She referred to the "mental and physical agility [rather] than mere knowledge" which the school required of her (p. 39). The difficulty of accomplishing the prescribed program for all the classes in the available time, together with her own "weakness" in arithmetic, left her little time to think about her character, although she noted an improvement in her ability to be well-organized and to keep her mind on what she was doing.

Similarly, the teachers interviewed by Christensen (1986) informed him about many aspects of their life and work in the schools, but at no time did they speak of their character or its development as important to their work. They liked teaching or they did not, they loved children or they did not, they found the conditions difficult or they did not, but if they rated themselves on a scale of 1 to 100 and tried to improve their characters, they did not remember doing so as important to their teaching.

### Discipline, Order, and Student Behavior

A second aspect of the image of the teacher is that of discipline or student behavior. In the nostalgic popular image, rural teachers were blessed with students who—unlike today's children—were well behaved and eager to learn. Perhaps some of the boys were a bit rambunctious at times, but serious difficulties with discipline were not part of the picture. Contrary to this sentimental image, both the novels and the memoirs used in this study paint teachers as having a major focus on maintaining discipline. Far from presiding gently but firmly over quiet and well-behaved students whose cooperation can be taken for granted, they are often shown as using, and needing to use, harsh methods to control their classes.

A vivid example from Wilder's *Farmer Boy* (1933) concerns the childhood of Wilder's husband, Almanzo Wilder. Almanzo was only 6 or 8 years old when a kind and weak-looking master taught the local school. All went well until the winter term, when there was little farmwork to do and the oldest boys came to school for the first time. Wrote Wilder: "These big boys were sixteen or seventeen years old, and they came to school only in the middle of the winter term. They came to thrash the teacher and break up the school. They boasted that no teacher could finish the winter term at that school, and no teacher ever had" (p. 46).

In fact, the last master to teach at the school had been injured so badly by the boys that he had later died. Little Almanzo was very much afraid of what would happen to the gentle schoolmaster in the inevitable conflict. He was surprised—as the big boys were—to learn that the master kept a blacksnake whip in his desk drawer and was ready to use it to drive his attackers out of the school.

Perhaps this was an extreme and unusual way to deal with such a problem, but the problem itself was by no means unique. Connor (1902) described discipline at the Glengarry School under two masters. The first, Archibald Munro, was respected by all and was "the only master who had ever been able to control, without at least one appeal to the trustees, the stormy tempers of the young giants that used to come to school during the winter months" (p. 14).

Munro was replaced by a new master who favored inflexible enforcement of numerous rules. He whipped so many of the smaller boys that the older boys left the school, considering it beneath their dignity to "carry [the master] out" (p. 118). However, a confrontation finally occurred when a little boy refused to put out his hand to be beaten, and the master believed that his "whole authority was at stake. 'I cannot have boys refusing to obey me in this school,' " he insisted, and treated the boy so brutally that the oldest of the remaining boys attacked him, knocked him to the floor, and were prepared to tie him up when they were interrupted by an adult (p. 118).

Mary Ellen Chase, later a novelist and an English professor at Smith College, was required by her father to teach school for a year after her first year of college. He left her on the steps of the schoolhouse where she was to teach with "no aid but a stout razor strap" (p. 36). She was afraid, so afraid that she raged at "certain boys of sixteen or older who otherwise might have been at sea," flourished the strap, and had no more difficulty that term. Later, she described a school in Montana and spoke admiringly of the principal, "She could use a wide leather strap across the knees of unruly boys, who sat calmly in the chair without the least outcry" (p. 186).

In other cases, gentler methods of gaining the cooperation of students came into play. When Laura Ingalls (Wilder, 1943) at the age of 16 went to teach her own school, she had trouble controlling the oldest boy and thought longingly of giving him the whipping he needed. She was too small to do it and had to find other ways to deal with him. When she asked her parents for advice, her father said, "Everybody's born free, like it says in the Declaration of Independence. You can lead a horse to water but you can't make him drink, and good or bad, nobody but Clarence can ever boss Clarence. You better just manage." And her mother advised her, "It's attention he wants, that's why he cuts up. . . . It's all in that word 'manage' " (p. 54). So, Laura shortened Clarence's assignments, commiserated with him on how hard it is to catch up once you are behind, and ignored his challenges. Soon he did the work and improved his behavior.

There were less successful stories, however. Laura herself had been the pupil of a new female teacher in *Little Town on the Prairie*. This young schoolteacher arrived in the school saying, "You must not look on me as a taskmistress, but a friend" (Wilder, 1941, p. 132). The young woman believed that there was no need to punish, and that she and the students could work together through love, not fear. But the students grew increasingly unruly, and in anger she began to make the students stand in the corner and

sent some home from school. Only a visit by members of the school board
enabled her to regain control of the school.

Some of the teachers interviewed by Howard Christensen (1986) said
they had few discipline problems and regarded the behavior of children they
had taught in the past more favorably than the behavior of today's children.
Others described the ways they enforced discipline:

> I guess I was known as a hard disciplinarian. I remember the kids
> in Glenwood used to like to make spitballs, and I made one boy stay
> after school, and I don't know how many I made him make, but it
> cured him. I was hard, let's say. I remembered my own teachers who
> had good discipline and were tough (p. 107).

> I had very little problems. Once in a while I would have somebody
> who had moved in from another district who would try to smart off a
> little at first, but once you got them corralled, it would be all right
> (p. 110).

> I can't remember there was any big problem. I suppose I hollered.
> You could touch them, but I can't remember that I ever did. Some-
> body said, "Boy, you were tough!" (p. 111).

The textbooks, too, contained many references to discipline and suggestions for controlling students' behavior. In his text, *Everyday Problems of the
Country Teacher* (1936), Lowth took a different view of the role of discipline
in the rural school. "There is something radically wrong with the teacher's
spirit, aims, and plans, if she needs to give much attention to order. In an
orderly school the children are busy of their own volition" (pp. 187–188). He
then characterized "disorderly teachers" as those who are "loud-talking"
and "irascible," and attributed disorder among pupils to lack of "proper
treatment and training." He held that it is "rare indeed to find a pupil who
persists in disorderly practices simply out of a spirit of meanness." He suggested that most problems with pupils could be solved by giving them appropriate assignments, and he described deprivation of privileges and "a private interview" as "drastic treatment" that would rarely be needed (p. 189).

Interestingly, however, Lowth deliberated further on the issues of punishment and discipline, implying that these *would* be issues of significance
for the teacher. He described the circumstances in which the teacher might
be forced to punish a student, but he ruled out as inappropriate such disciplinary tactics as threatening and nagging, sarcasm and ridicule, humiliation and physical punishment. Thus, the sentimental view of the firm and
friendly teacher working with cooperative pupils was placed next to—but
not reconciled with—the image of a teacher dealing with students who were
found to be "lying, cheating, [using] profane language on the playground,
marring furniture and outbuildings, and [giving] impertinent responses"
(p. 193).

Kennedy (1915), who was dean of the School of Education at the University of North Dakota, made no mention at all of either discipline or punishment, but instead wrote about "enlisting the cooperation of pupils. . . . All children . . . if approached or stimulated in the proper way—like to *do* things, to perform services for others. . . . A pupil will do anything in his power for his teacher" (p. 141).

Woofter (1917), dean of the School of Education at the University of Georgia, began the chapter on discipline in his teacher preparation text with the statement: "Discipline is the feature of the school which first puts the young teacher on trial" (p. 105). He proceeded to define the purpose of discipline as the production of "the harmony of life." Yet the twenty-seven pages of the chapter provide a wide range of suggestions to assist the teacher in controlling the behavior of students, including, in its final pages, the statement that "corporal punishment . . . should not be entirely forbidden" (p. 131). Although it is to be used as a next-to-last resort, expulsion being the only harsher penalty, some "offenders" will require it, at least up to the age of puberty.

What rules were the teachers enforcing with these methods of discipline? Some principal examples include: "No whispering permitted in school, and no fidgeting. Everyone must be perfectly still and keep his eyes fixed on his lessons" (Wilder, 1933, p. 8). And "no speaking in school unless you raise your hand for permission to speak; written excuses must be presented for absence or tardiness; no sound should be heard in the school" (Connor, 1902, p. 83).

Silence, immobility, and order were presented in these sources as essential to schooling, even though teachers must use strong disciplinary methods to achieve them. Laura Ingalls feared she would incur the wrath of her school superintendent if she allowed her students to warm themselves at the stove in her cold prairie school (Wilder, 1943, p. 80).

Woofter (1917) wrote that "Formerly, school government was one of repression. If a pupil was caught looking out of the window, he was called to book summarily, and if caught drawing pictures he might expect to have his ears boxed. 'Absolutely still' was the order" (p. 112). Woofter rejoiced in the more enlightened attitudes of 1917, but nevertheless delineated a formidable list of rules for good behavior that were to be developed as habits in children. They were to be prompt and regular in their attendance—"no lagging nor straggling." They were to be working busily at all times, often because the work was interesting to them, but sometimes simply because one must work. They were to produce only neat and orderly work. They were to keep silent, avoiding "whispering and other unnecessary communication." There should be proper times for interruptions, and pupils should be trained to wait for those times (pp. 111–114). Later, Woofter mentioned such offenses as "whispering, note-writing, leaving the room too often, and noisy walking" as reasons for punishment (p. 126).

Learning, like behavior, was considered a matter of discipline, and students who had not mastered their lessons were described as subject to whipping, shaming, and other penalties. Almanzo Wilder was very fond of the gentle master with the blacksnake whip in his desk because he "never whipped little boys who forgot how to spell a word" (Wilder, 1933, p. 5). By implication, other masters did so.

Laura Ingalls's (Wilder, 1943) difficulties with a recalcitrant pupil centered not on active misbehavior, but on his failure to learn the lessons she assigned him. As mentioned above, she would have whipped him if she had been big enough. Clearly, author and audience would assume that failure to learn is caused by laziness or idleness, both of them defects of character.

These sources do not support the image of the firm teacher, presiding over well-behaved and cooperative children. Teachers varied in their approach to discipline and found in their schools both children whose behavior enabled the orderly running of the school and those whose behavior made order difficult to maintain. Neither the disciplinary techniques they used nor the influence of their characters produced the well-disciplined and effective classrooms that the sentimental or nostalgic image of the rural teacher would imply.

### Instructional Methods and Curriculum

The teachers' views of learning and discipline were, of course, tightly connected to the instructional methods they used and to the curriculum that was taught. An important determinant of these methods was the structure of their schools. Since most of the schools described in these sources were one-room structures, and since children of the same age might have attended school for quite different numbers of years and perhaps mastered quite different skills or amounts of knowledge, it was customary to place the children at an appropriate point in the graded curriculum and allow them to proceed from that point.

When Mary Ellen Chase (1939) taught in her first school in Maine, she had forty-nine children ranging in age from 5 to 16 (as well as up to six "babies" between the ages of 2 and 4, who enjoyed watching the school's "furious educational progress," p. 44). These she sorted into a total of twenty-nine groups for arithmetic, reading, geography, history, and spelling. She taught grammar to the whole school. She learned to hear one group reading while another group was doing arithmetic at the chalkboard and the rest of the school was studying in their seats. Her day consisted of hearing all the arithmetic and reading groups before 10:30, then hearing four geography groups before lunch, and teaching grammar after lunch. Then she heard four history classes and finished the day with spelling. She comments that there was no time for music or art, and one readily believes it (p. 40).

At the school attended by Wiggin's Rebecca, "There were classes of a sort, although nobody, broadly speaking, studied the same book with anybody else, or arrived at the same proficiency in any one branch of learning" (p. 45). Rebecca was placed in the sixth reader, but was "threttened" with being put in the baby primer class in arithmetic because she could not say the sevens table (p. 39).

In these circumstances, rote and drill were the basic methods used by teachers. The pupil sat at her desk and read her lesson, either silently or aloud through a buzz of other voices reading their lessons aloud. Or she might use a slate to write out a lesson in spelling or arithmetic. When she was called up for the teacher to "hear" her lesson, she was expected to recite it verbatim, or to solve correctly the problems given in the arithmetic lesson. The established goal was to do these things perfectly and then to do them again for another lesson.

What could not be memorized was not taught and not learned. The teacher's task was to set the lessons to be memorized and then hear them to determine whether they had been learned. Geography was the locating of features and the "bounding" of states and countries, not the understanding of the world's cultures and economies. History was the memorization of events and biographies, not the exploration of historical processes. Reading was the correct oral reading of passages; comprehension was assumed to follow. Arithmetic was the successive mastery of more difficult kinds of problems by working examples and memorizing algorithms.

Teachers' efforts at enlivening the learning process are described in these sources. There seemed to be a need to add enjoyment or to relieve boredom, but apparently not to expand the scope of the curriculum. Both *Glengarry School Days* and *Little Town on the Prairie* contain colorful accounts of spelling bees that produced great excitement. In the Ingalls book, some of the adults in the community join in the competition. Competitive problem solving in arithmetic is also mentioned in Barber's (1938) memoir. Two of the teachers described held an annual public examination of the school, with prizes for the best performers (Wiggin, 1903 and Connor, 1902).

Some of the teachers allotted some time to activities that they and their students considered more pleasurable than routine studies. These often took place on Friday afternoons and were seen as a reward for hard work and good behavior. A teacher might play the violin (Connor, 1902, p. 261) or tell stories of shipwreck and pirates (Chase, 1939, p. 19). Such diversions clearly were not part of the ordinary work of the school.

### Qualifications of Teachers

A final, though somewhat equivocal, aspect of our image of teachers of the past is that they were well qualified for their work, perhaps more so than the teachers of today. We would like to think of them as well-educated teachers, passing down significant knowledge to students. Yet the teachers described in these sources were young and had little advanced education.

"Anyhow, she knows how to teach. She has a certificate" (Wilder, 1941, p. 125). This was the comment of an older child about a new teacher. The certificate, however, had been obtained by passing a test on the content of the graded school curriculum, which in many cases the new teacher had just completed herself. No added knowledge, either in the content areas or in pedagogy, was required.

When Laura Ingalls was finishing school, she went to town on Saturday and took a test for certification. Her score would be the only determinant of her qualifications (Wilder, 1943, p. 148). By this time, however, she had already taught a term in a country school. She felt perfectly qualified to do this, as she had always been a good student and had progressed further than any of the children (some of whom were older than she was) whom she was asked to teach.

In Stratton-Porter's *Daughter of the Land* (1918), two sisters who were teachers persuade their brother to teach school too. The girls have each had a summer at Normal School, where they reviewed the content of their years of schooling, but the brother has had no training at all. Stratton-Porter wrote, "Well, Hiram had taken the county examination, as all pupils of the past ten years had when they finished the county schools. It was a test required to prove whether they had done their work well. Hiram held a certification to teach for one year, given to him by the County Superintendent when he passed the examination" (p. 98).

Mary Ellen Chase was even less well prepared when she went to teach in a village school in Maine. As noted earlier, it was her father's view that a girl should teach school for a year or two before entering college or after her first or second year of college. Chase had always been a poor student in mathematics and did not know how to do all that she had to teach. Her first year of teaching found her "weeping at night over bank discount and compound proportion" (p. 43). Reminiscing about the pupils in her first school, she wrote, "Three of them are teachers who, I trust, have never emulated my desperate and stumbling efforts either at discipline or at instruction" (p. 45).

It was during the period described in these novels that teacher training began to be available and increasingly required, and that its length gradually became increased. For example, not until 1934 did Wisconsin require two years of training (Christensen, 1986). Earlier than this, however, at least some brief periods of training began to be required for the better teaching jobs. For example, in Stratton-Porter's Indiana at the turn of the century, a girl who wished to teach in a desirable school in the fall and who had finished her own schooling in the spring had to spend eight weeks of the summer at the normal school in the city (Stratton-Porter, 1918, p. 25).

In *Daughter of the Land,* one of the sisters helped her untrained brother get ready to teach. "He is brushing up a little nights, and I am helping him on 'theory' " (Stratton-Porter, 1918, p. 114). Presumably she learned the "theory" during the eight-week summer session of normal school which she had just attended.

Mary Ellen Chase counseled, thirty years after her first year of teaching, that a young teacher's best plan was to emulate her own instructors. Her common sense, initiative, and enthusiasm would then help her in solving any problems that might arise (Chase, 1939, p. 59). Thus, Laura Ingalls, opening her first school, "thought it best to maintain the routine of the town school and have each person come forward to recite" (Wilder, 1943, p. 18). She solemnly intoned, "Third Reading Group, come forward," and watched one little girl make her way to the front of the room.

Mabel Carney (1912), who was director of the Country School Department at Illinois State Normal University, said of these teachers: "It is true, as frequently maintained, that country teachers are young and inexperienced and poorly prepared for their work. But it is also true that as a group they are filled with a great sincerity" (p. 195).

---

## Discussion

The image of teachers presented in these sources, then, is far from the nostalgic one held by many Americans today. Rather than being competent, dedicated, and morally superior people who maintained discipline and passed on important knowledge to well-behaved and willing students, teachers are described as poorly prepared both academically and in pedagogical training, as struggling with disobedient students for the control of the school, and as using strictly rote methods to teach a limited and fact-bound curriculum. The historical reality of the rural school and the rural teacher was summarized by Mary Ellen Chase (1939):

> The schools of such a village were simply its schools. They were hewn out of respectability and governed by necessity. No one thought of them as either good or bad, and without doubt they possessed qualities of both (p. 5).

> The rural school has gone never to return, at least in its original state. It has become an outworn institution, to be regarded by those who knew it more with sentiment than respect (p. 52).

The nostalgic image of these teachers' character which comes across most strongly in the textbooks intended for their use is revealed as a product of the sentimentalism that shaped the views of professors of education and perhaps some earlier novelists, rather than those of the teachers themselves. Like teachers today, these rural teachers worked hard under difficult conditions. They were never the paragons we might like to recall.

Why, then, might Americans hold a sentimental and nostalgic view of our educational past? If there are two perspectives on history, one that sees its course as a progress toward a future golden age and one that traces its decline from a golden age of the past, the first has been central to American ideology. Americans have always claimed to be moving from less to more, from worse to better, fulfilling the country's manifest destiny. As de Tocqueville pointed out in 1840, Americans believed that in our nation human perfectibility is being enacted. However, this ideology leads to frequent frustration. What is one to believe when the looked-for perfection does not appear, when somehow the golden age does not arrive?

Perhaps it is in these moments of frustration and fear that we seek the golden age in our past, hiding in a cloud of sentiment the indications that it never existed at all. As we are increasingly bombarded with criticisms of our schools, our teachers, and our students, we feel more and more strongly the need to believe that once, if only in the past, our schools approached the ideal we set for them. If that ideal was achieved once, perhaps it can be regained. If it has never been achieved, then what we ask of our schools and teachers may be forever out of reach.

The task of searching the history of rural schools for what was good about them is beyond the scope of this chapter. Yet certain elements of the portraits of schools presented in these texts call for our consideration. The rural schools they describe are, as Mary Ellen Chase pointed out, very much part of the communities they served. The community and the parents were responsible to the school, and the school and teacher to them. The schools reflected what parents and teachers believed was right, rather than the views of educational experts, industrial leaders, or national politicians. Thus, the schools enhanced, rather than decreased, that liberty which seems an essential part of our heritage as Americans.

Tyack (1974) observed that this tight connection between school and community had both advantages and disadvantages. In a cohesive community, the school reaped the benefits of cohesiveness. Teachers, parents, and community members could work well together for what they all perceived as the welfare of the children and of the community as a whole. But if the community was at odds with itself, all would suffer as the school became a battleground on which community dissension was played out.

Today as this chapter is being written, the issue of transferring power over the schools from the educational experts and bureaucrats of the "one best system" to parents and communities is undergoing active debate. From large-scale efforts, like the Chicago school reform movement, to involving parents and community members in the governance of schools, to calls for voucher systems and individual parent choice of schools inside and outside the public sector—change in this direction is occurring and is likely to continue. It would seem to be a good time to take a careful look—not a sentimental or nostalgic look, but a realistic, critical one—at what the small community schools and teachers of the past were really like.

## NOTES

1. These ideas are discussed at length in R. N. Bellah, R. Madsen, W. M. Sullivan, A. Swidler, and S. M. Tipton, *Habits of the Heart: Individualism and Commitment in American Life* (New York: Harper & Row, 1985).
2. Larry Cuban (1984), in *How Teachers Taught: Constancy and Change in American Classrooms 1890–1980,* notes that some rural schoolteachers used innovative child-centered activities more often than their urban counterparts.
3. It is interesting to note the use of masculine pronouns to refer to members of a profession predominantly female, then and now.

## REFERENCES

Barber, M. A. (1938). *The schoolhouse at Prairie View.* Lawrence: University of Kansas Press.

Carney, M. (1912). *Country life and the country school.* Chicago: Row Peterson.

Chase, M. E. (1939). *A goodly fellowship.* New York: Macmillan.

Christensen, H. B. (1986). *Cloverdale: A salute to one-room schoolteachers.* Winona, MN: Apollo Books.

Connor, R. (1902). *Glengarry school days.* New York: Fleming A. Revell.

Cuban, L. (1984). *How teachers taught: Constancy and change in American classrooms 1890–1980.* New York: Longman.

De Tocqueville, A. (1835–40/1956). *Democracy in America,* Ed. R. D. Heffner. New York: New American Library.

Donovan, F. R. (1938). *The schoolma'am.* New York: Frederick A. Stokes.

Foght, H. W. (1917). *The rural teacher and his work.* New York: Macmillan.

Kennedy, J. (1915). *Rural life and the rural school.* New York: American Book.

Kirkpatrick, M. G. (1917). *The rural school from within.* Philadelphia: J. B. Lippincott.

Lowth, F. J. (1936). *Everyday problems of the country teacher.* New York: Macmillan.

Slacks, J. R. (1938). *The rural teacher's work.* Boston: Ginn & Co.

Stratton-Porter, G. (1918). *Daughter of the land.* New York: Grosset & Dunlap.

Tyack, D. (1974). *The one best system: A history of American urban education.* Cambridge, MA: Harvard University Press.

Wiggin, K. D. (1903). *Rebecca of Sunnybrook farm.* New York: Houghton Mifflin.

Wilder, L. I. (1943/1971). *These happy golden years.* New York: Harper & Row.

Wilder, L. I. (1941/1971). *Little town on the prairie.* New York: Harper & Row.

Wilder, L. I. (1933/1971). *Farmer boy.* New York: Harper & Row.

Wister, O. (1917). *The Virginian.* New York: Macmillan.

Woofter, T. J. (1917). *Teaching in rural schools.* Boston: Houghton Mifflin.

# 14

# "The Ideal Teacher"

Images of Paragons in
Teacher Education Textbooks
before 1940

Pamela Bolotin Joseph

I
f you had been a student in an American teacher education class (or a schoolteacher attempting to buy a book on self-improvement) during the first several decades of the twentieth century, most likely you would have been given a textbook that told you how to become *The Ideal Teacher* (Palmer, 1908/1910), *The Excellent Teacher* (Avent, 1931), or to succeed at *Getting Ahead as a Teacher* (Duke, 1923) or *Developing a Teacher Personality That Wins* (Sandford, 1938). Even if your textbook had a more negative approach—*Problems of the Teaching Profession* (Almack & Lang, 1925) or *Clarifying the Teacher's Problems* (Gist, 1932)—you would read about the authors' conception of a teacher paragon, an exemplary or ideal teacher.[1] If you had doubts about the qualities you would need, checklists of ideal traits could explicitly guide you (Charters & Waples, 1929; Overn, 1935; Sandford, 1938). (Figures 14.1 and 14.2 offer examples.) The textbook writers would not just explain about classroom management, school organization, or curriculum, but they would implore you to become an archetype of this virtuous profession. Paragons of teaching would be described with flourishing style or pedantic rhetoric, entreating or commanding you to make yourself into the image esteemed by the authors.

Because I wished to understand how teachers were acculturated into their profession, I decided to explore how teacher-educators described what it meant to be an ideal teacher. Unable to reconstruct lectures, supervision, or conversations between teacher-educators and their students, I sought images of exemplary teachers in the textbooks of teacher education. I wanted to know: How did textbook writers portray the characteristics of the excellent schoolteacher? What images did teacher educators create and sanc-

# THE TEACHER'S IDEALS

## TEACHER–RATING BLANK

Teacher.................Building...................Subject taught..........
Date.........................................................................

| DETAILED RATING | I V.P. | 2 :3 Poor | 4 :5 :6 Med. | 7 :8 Good | 9 :10 Ex. |
|---|---|---|---|---|---|
| **I. Personal Equipment** 1. General appearance.............. | | : | : : | : | : |
| 2. Health........................... | | : | : : | : | : |
| 3. Voice............................ | | : | : : | : | : |
| 4. Intellectual capacity ............. | | : | : : | : | : |
| 5. Initiative and self-reliance......... | | : | : : | : | : |
| 6. Adaptability and resourcefulness.... | | : | : : | : | : |
| 7. Accuracy........................ | | : | : : | : | : |
| 8. Industry......................... | | : | : : | : | : |
| 9. Enthusiasm and optimism.......... | | : | : : | : | : |
| 10. Integrity and sincerity............. | | : | : : | : | : |
| 11. Self-control...................... | | : | : : | : | : |
| 12. Promptness...................... | | : | : : | : | : |
| 13. Tact............................ | | : | : : | : | : |
| 14. Sense of justice................... | | : | : : | : | : |
| **II. Social Professional Equipment** 15. Academic preparation.............. | | : | : : | : | : |
| 16. Professional preparation........... | | : | : : | : | : |
| 17. Grasp of subject matter........... | | : | : : | : | : |
| 18. Understanding of children.......... | | : | : : | : | : |
| 19. Interest in the life of the school..... | | : | : : | : | : |
| 20. Interest in the life of the community. | | : | : : | : | : |
| 21. Ability to meet and interest patrons. | | : | : : | : | : |
| 22. Interest in lives of pupils.......... | | : | : : | : | : |
| 23. Co-operation and loyalty.......... | | : | : : | : | : |
| 24. Professional interest and growth..... | | : | : : | : | : |
| 25. Daily preparation................. | | : | : : | : | : |
| 26. Use of English................... | | : | : : | : | : |
| **III. School Management** 27. Care of light, heat, and ventilation.. | | : | : : | : | : |
| 28. Neatness of room................. | | : | : : | : | : |
| 29. Care of routine................... | | : | : : | : | : |
| 30. Discipline (governing skill) ........ | | : | : : | : | : |
| **IV. Technique of Teaching** 31. Definiteness and clearness of aim.... | | : | : : | : | : |
| 32. Skill in habit formation............ | | : | : : | : | : |
| 33. Skill in stimulating thought......... | | : | : : | : | : |
| 34. Skill in teaching how to study....... | | : | : : | : | : |
| 35. Skill in questioning............... | | : | : : | : | : |
| 36. Choice of subject matter........... | | : | : : | : | : |
| 37. Organization of subject matter...... | | : | : : | : | : |
| 38. Skill and care in assignment........ | | : | : : | . | : |
| 39. Skill in motivating work........... | | : | : : | : | : |
| 40. Attention to individual needs....... | | : | : : | : | : |
| **V. Results** 41. Attention and response of the class.. | | : | : : | : | : |
| 42. Growth of pupils in subject matter.. | | : | : : | : | : |
| 43. General development of pupils...... | | : | : : | : | : |
| 44. Stimulation of community.......... | | : | : : | : | : |
| 45. Moral influence................... | | : | : : | : | : |
| **GENERAL RATING** ................... | | | | | |

Rule for averaging: Place a check in the column representing your rating on each item. Give each check a numerical value equal to the no. of the column.
Counting from left, then average, e. g., 25 (10) = 250    400 ÷ 45 = 8.8
10 ( 9) = 90
10 ( 6) = 60
———
400

**Figure 14-1** (Gist, *Clarifying the Teacher's Problems*, 1932)

# QUALIFICATIONS FOR TEACHING

## A STUDENT SCORE CARD

| | Excellent | Good | Medium | Fair | Poor |
|---|---|---|---|---|---|
| **I. Physical Characteristics:** | | | | | |
| 1. Health | | | | | |
| 2. Appearance | | | | | |
| 3. Carriage—bodily poise | | | | | |
| 4. Walk | | | | | |
| **II. Use of Language:** | | | | | |
| **Spoken:** | | | | | |
| 1. Enunciation | | | | | |
| 2. Pronunciation | | | | | |
| 3. Quality of voice | | | | | |
| 4. Oral discourse | | | | | |
| **Written:** | | | | | |
| 1. Spelling | | | | | |
| 2. Handwriting | | | | | |
| 3. Sentence structure | | | | | |
| 4. Paragraph sense | | | | | |
| **III. Student Qualities:** | | | | | |
| 1. Interest in subject | | | | | |
| 2. Preparation for class | | | | | |
| 3. Sense of responsibility | | | | | |
| 4. Ability to think in class | | | | | |
| 5. Attitude toward class criticism | | | | | |
| 6. Original questions asked | | | | | |
| 7. Contributions made from knowledge learned elsewhere | | | | | |
| 8. Sincerity in class work | | | | | |
| 9. Honesty in class work | | | | | |
| 10. General attitude toward school | | | | | |
| **IV. Personal Qualities** | | | | | |
| 1. Mental alertness | | | | | |
| 2. Mental balance | | | | | |
| 3. Courtesy—refinment | | | | | |
| 4. Common sense | | | | | |
| 5. Dress—taste in | | | | | |
| 6. Forcefulness | | | | | |
| 7. Moral standards | | | | | |
| 8. Tactfulness | | | | | |
| 9. Truthfulness | | | | | |

THIS IS A SAMPLE OF A STUDENT-RATING CARD USED IN A TEACHERS COLLEGE. THE VARIOUS QUALITIES MENTIONED MAY WELL FORM THE BASIS OF THE "SELF-RATING" EXERCISES PROPOSED IN THE TEXT.

---

**Figure 14-2** (Bagley and Keith, *An Introduction to Teaching*, 1924)

tion in order to illustrate ideal traits? How did textbooks "school" young people into the profession of teaching?

This chapter explores these questions by examining predominant images of paragons in teacher education texts during the first several decades of the twentieth century. I chose to study teacher education textbooks before 1940 for several reasons.

Initially, I kept noticing dusty but beguiling volumes at university libraries when I was looking for more recent works about the teaching profession. I amused myself with wonderful and appalling bits of trivia for my department's bulletin board (e.g., tips on good grooming for teachers circa 1920). Increasingly, however, I became fascinated with book titles, advice, and their authors' charming and peculiar use of metaphors to describe teachers.

In addition, the idea of studying teacher education textbooks appealed to me because I frequently utilize textbooks in my teaching in order to communicate how schools teach values. Through analyses of textbooks for schoolchildren, my students and I have learned something about how we have educated our young. Images in texts—of children and adults, of males and females, communities and cultures—reveal what heroes (rarely, heroines) the authors revered, what behaviors they admired, and what values they cherished—all with the none too subtle message that children should copy the lives of the heroes and heed the morals of stories told.

Finally, I often need to study the past in order to learn about the present. This strategy allows me to stand back and view structures or images that I cannot see immediately, thus enabling new insight for application to current literature and discussion. Through historical inquiry, I believe I can view contemporary teacher education with fresh eyes so that I can better see issues and patterns in current practice. It is my hope that readers of this chapter will use the curious—sometimes bolder and simpler—lenses of the past in this study of teacher education textbooks in order to help them to better understand what in contemporary American textbooks is commonplace and thus unnoticed.

## Metaphors of American Culture

When I began reading the textbooks of the time period before 1940, I became intrigued by their authors' use of language to construct metaphors of teachers and teaching. Images of ideal teachers appeared to originate not so much from the textbook writers' ageless vision of superior teaching, but rather from their understanding of current customs and events in American culture and schooling. Conceptions of teacher paragons emanated in response to popular ideas and expressions of the time period. In order to communicate to their audience, textbook authors created images that would have meaning in the vernacular and, furthermore, would fit into then-current discussion about schools. Thus, I perceived predominant images of ideal teachers that exhibited multifaceted impressions of American culture over time. It came as no surprise that major groups of images reflected the military and World War I, factories and business, and, finally, the social and economic upheaval of the Great Depression.

The authors of textbooks writing after World War I portrayed ideal teachers through specific references to elements of the conflict among nations and to American war experiences. In demonstrating that the exemplary teacher must not be authoritarian, Winship (1919) proclaimed: "The sudden collapse of the Kaiser was at the same time the collapse of Germany, the collapse of autocracy everywhere, the collapse of bossism in school and out" (p. 47). Another author insisted that the ideal teacher must be a moral educator by admonishing, "If all teachers in all nations would only give proper emphasis to moral training, we would not have to worry over making the world safe for democracy" (Grant, 1922, p. 220).

Others writing in this time period conceptualized metaphors of teaching through images of war and soldiering. In *Education as a Life Work: An Introduction into Education,* Jordan (1930) asserted that teaching was not just women's work and tried to persuade males to enter the teaching profession by recruiting "a man who is looking for an opportunity for service, who wants to do a really big thing in life, a thing which calls for men of red blood, of tremendous vitality . . . to go into the world with those ideals and skills which will make them fit to maintain the glory of our country and to insure its perpetual prosperity. This is a real 'man's job' " (p. 28). Lee (1938) in *Teaching as a Man's Job*, thought that schools ought to place signs outside their doors that read "American Education Needs Men" (p. 11). Moreover, the same author compared the heroic "unknown teacher" to the unknown soldier (p. 10). Such metaphors of teaching obviously carried the message that to teach was patriotic, that although men could no longer serve their country in the battlefield, they could serve in the classroom.[2]

During the period of time examined in this study, however, the most prominent images of teachers related to American culture were formulated from the realm of business and industry. Teachers should "give a personal touch to customers," explained Milner (1912) in reference to teachers' relationships with parents (p. 68). "Education is a business enterprize," commented Walsh (1926).[3] Hines (1926) deduced that hiring a teacher was "in a limited sense a purely business transaction." Striving for "trained and informed intelligence" in order to save civilization, Bagley and Keith (1932) also described teachers using the metaphor of industry: "The teacher is actually and essentially a producer" (p. 3). Metaphors connoting management, productivity, sales, and customers in the business world were routinely applied to teaching in the literature of teacher education.

In particular, textbooks contained various references to products: education was a product, a child was product, and so, too, the teacher. "The public is not completely pleased with the schools and their products," wrote Palmer in 1914 (p. vi); or, "Parents can neutralize all the classroom products" (Dearborn, 1925, p. 27); "The world demands a better product," proclaimed an author arguing for better teacher training (Hines, 1926, p. 3); "We are striving to make the teacher a finished product," wrote a successful administrator in a chapter of advice to teachers (Duke, 1923, p. 24).

Not only was the school compared to business; writers also described schools mechanistically, fostering images of machines and automation—for example, "The school may be conceived as a factory" (Overn, 1935, p. 14). Furthermore, in order to run industry economically, one must get rid of waste or inefficiency; authors made similar statements about teachers and students. Because of the problem of teacher selection, "the causes for waste are perhaps more evident in teaching than in other professions" (Hines, 1926, p. 80). Or, "The teacher realizes that she has a responsibility to society in training childhood for the highest possible degree of efficiency" (Gist, 1932, p. 6).[4]

Limits of the applicability of the metaphor of industry to teaching were also noticed by some authors who wrote for teachers. Milner (1912) demonstrated her skepticism about education in America: "If, in the grinding process, a few grains of humanity escape, there are compulsory education laws and vigorous able-bodied truant officers to gather up the grains and return them to the mill" (p. 224). Others criticized the effect of schooling as an industrial machine on teachers, saying that "the classroom teachers feel lost in a machine-like organization" (Lewis, 1926, p. 13), and "little confidence has in the main been placed in teachers and their ability to direct their own activities" (Melby, 1937, p. 119). Although the opponents of the industry metaphor defended their positions eloquently, textbook writers who were comfortable with such imagery applied to teaching far outnumbered the critics.

The third pattern of metaphors alluded to the great economic and political changes (the Russian Revolution and the Great Depression) that influenced American thought and culture. Strayer and Engelhard (1920) warned that "If the school does not give the best and most extensive training possible to the intellectually capable, those children will . . . rise as leaders of social and economic groups which may be expected to be antagonistic to a social order whose advantages were denied them." (p. 377). Sandford (1938) urged educators to free themselves from old ways of thinking: "The willingness of most of our people to give drastic experiments in other fields a fair trial shows that they think almost everything better than the old order" (p. 48). Whether apprehensive or fearful, such writers encouraged teachers to possess more insight about the future.

Therefore, some authors urged teachers to think of themselves as leaders responsible for changing humanity—for "race betterment" (Gist, 1932, p. 6) or for social engineering (Davis, 1930, p. 66; Snyder & Alexander,

1932, p. 4). The economic and political crises of the 1930s prompted authors to urge teachers to bring about better conditions by creating better
citizens.

But how could teachers improve society by becoming social engineers?
Various paths were suggested: Teachers could influence "the social order of
the next generation" by exposing children to ideas and habits that would
eventually determine if society would become "competitive or cooperative"
(Snyder & Alexander, 1932, p. 4). Or, schoolteachers must appreciate "the
importance and dignity of their function in human society by building "character and morale in children" (Averill, 1939, p. 15).[5]

The images and metaphors of American culture utilized to describe
teacher paragons paralleled the social and educational ideas of the time
period; therefore, throughout this diverse rendering of images in textbooks,
I can find no constant of a teacher ideal. Metaphorical language leaves
fragmentary impressions of schoolteachers who should be producers or products, visionaries or mechanical underlings, dedicated idealists or participants in business transactions.[6] And yet—as the images projected the noble
teacher, the teacher as empowerer, and as a producer of order within a
regulated, mechanistic system—such metaphorical responses to events or
trends in American culture introduced certain predominant themes. These
themes permeated the literature of teacher education textbooks that did not
narrowly correspond to specific events or social-economic trends. Ultimately, images from American culture delineated the archetypes of teacher
paragons in teacher education textbooks throughout the first several decades of the twentieth century.

## The Noble Profession

One dominant image of the paragon schoolteacher made a continuous
and dramatic appearance in the textbooks of teacher education—teacher as
selfless altruist, dedicated soldier, patriot, saint, or redeemer. A striking
commonality of this literature was the theme of the intrinsic rewards of
teaching. "There is a free-will devotion which he puts into his work that
draws its own peculiar form of compensation," wrote A. C. Perry in 1912;
"teaching, like virtue, is its own reward" (p. 54). Throughout the time period
before 1940, textbook writers proclaimed this sentiment: "The excellent
teacher is 'forgetful of self' " (Avent, 1931, p. 158); "He thinks of others'
comfort first. . . . He is willing to labor on, spend and be spent, even to be
forgotten for the sake of *others*. . . . While others are practicing 'Safety first'
for themselves, his motto is 'Safety last' for himself" (Avent, 1931, p. 128).
Another author fervently noted, "She is so unselfish that any thought of
reward or personal consideration is usually far from her mind" (Milner,

1912, p. 17). Self-sacrifice gave teachers a gallant nobility, the textbook writers believed.

The authors aspired to depict teachers as professionals, but, clearly, the notion of professionalism evoked a selfless ideal. The criterion of a profession (in contrast to a trade), wrote Almack and Lang (1925), is that "monetary consideration is secondary. Unselfishness is one of its prime principles. Altruism is the prevailing spirit" (p. 59). Pulliam (1930) commented on "the disposition on the part of the professional man to place the service he renders to the public above the pay that he gets for it" (p. 371). "This is not to say that professional men are martyrs," added Edwin Lee (1938), "but they want, also, those personal satisfactions which are higher than and not represented in economic reward" (p. 67). Perry (1912) went so far as to write that money actually tainted the professional by not allowing him to perform to the fullest. For example, "the physician frequently gives his most devoted service when he has lost all thought of his fee . . . so does the teacher best serve the pupils before him when his service is unrelated in his mind to his salary check" (p. 54).

But schoolteachers had compensations, even if not financial ones. The writers frequently explained that teachers found reward simply by working with young people. Students were tonics; they could magically rejuvenate teachers. "Good teachers stay young through the very contagion of youth" (Bagley & Keith, 1932, p. 2); "Truly, to live is to grow. . . . It is the teacher's privilege to deal with youth, and youth enjoys life" (Marsh, 1928, p. 2); "The greatest social satisfaction of the teacher comes in his contact with youth. His own spirit draws refreshment from the spring of youth" (Snyder & Alexander, 1932, p. 58).

The teaching of youth also provides stimulation that would invigorate teachers. "The teacher has the pleasure of watching pupils' mental growth . . . Is not this a precious reward?" (McFee, 1918, p. 246); "There is something in the contact with childhood, something in the miracle of human growth . . . which soon interests the newest recruit at teaching" (Palmer, 1914, p. v). So, too, the teaching process vitalizes: "Another reason for the fascination of teaching doubtless lies in the new problems that it continually presents. . . . There is a never-ending variety in the human material with which the teacher deals, and this means a never-ending variety in the problems that must be solved" (Bagley & Keith, 1932, p. 2).

The texts also declared the nobility of teaching as service because of what teachers could do for young people. "There is no higher opportunity than that which comes to a teacher. She has an opportunity to give to many children many opportunities that a mother gives a few children" (Winship, 1919, p. 17). "To make even one pupil better may be a greater service to humanity than to amass a fortune; and you may make thousands better" (Wright, 1920, p. 4).

Several authors embellished the argument that the creation of better individuals would improve humanity. They gloried in the idea of teachers consciously working for humanity, for a better world (Lee, 1938, p. 11; McFee, 1918, p. 249).

Not content to imagine teachers serving humanity by working hard to bring about improvement, a few textbook authors compared teachers to holy men. Teaching, declared Averill (1939), "is a way of life comparable with the way of the preacher and prophet" (p. 136). Palmer (1914) advised teachers to realize that teaching has a "redemptive character." He added, "The scientific man and the artist are redeemers too, in their several modes. No less than we they would save mankind from a low order of living" (p. 19). And, comparing teachers with the wise men, Avent (1931) blithely maintained, "The excellent teacher has much higher ideals than people in general; otherwise he could not be excellent" (p. 284).

Only a few authors saw the dangers of such grand idealism. Palmer (1914) maintained that a person should enter teaching out of a desire to teach; "the notion of benefiting somebody comes afterwards" (p. 15). Averill (1939) cautioned teachers that their desire to help humanity must bow to patience; one generation cannot change humanity (p. 19).

Vehemently critical of the image of "self-sacrifice and nobility of the profession" (p. 34), Simon (1938) believed such an image was actually harmful to the teaching process. Furthermore, Simon urged teachers not to consider their pupils first in forming their rationale for personal interests and activities: "The teacher who visits a picture gallery or reads a book because he thinks he ought to do it for the sake of the little ones, might almost as well not do it at all. Your first duty is to yourself. Children instinctively react to vitality and will get its full benefit soon enough" (p. 42).

Florence Milner (1912) warned teaching candidates that they might not always feel rewarded, for students often do not appreciate or realize the teacher's contribution: "Let anyone who enters upon the teaching profession in the hope of these rewards pause before it is too late to turn aside . . . two things are as sure as death . . . the thoughtlessness of youth and its supreme selfishness" (p. 16). Occasionally, Milner noted, a teacher will receive a little consideration—"just often enough to renew your courage." But, she mused, "this is as it should be. Youth is and ought to be egoistic" (p. 16).

On the whole, the ideal of noble, selfless teacher permeated these texts and captured the writers' zeal. Less prominent, and certainly less passionately deliberated, was the issue of the effect of such benevolent nobility on the teaching profession. Raised often as an afterthought—in a hesitant or an apologetic manner—was the authors' proposition that the profession needed higher status, security, and even more money. A few urged teachers to form professional associations and demand better compensation (Almack & Lang, 1925, p. 64; Simon, 1938, p. 57), but militant unionism had no advocates. Most writers believed that teachers should overcome or ignore difficulties by living within their means, not caring about status, and delighting in the dignity of the profession: "There is . . . a security in one's task that transcends mere economic security, indispensable as the latter is. It is a security that comes from the awareness of social respect and esteem for conscientious and generous service rendered. In the fullness of satisfaction created by such a wholesome mental attitude as this toward one's task, there is no room for conflict" (Averill, 1939, p. 10). The noble teacher does not worry about reward; such concerns could only damage the profession and perhaps even do harm to the teacher's mental health. Repeatedly, the authors insisted that the problem of lack of reward and status did not lie within society or social values but within the teachers themselves. When teachers would become even more professional, more noble, more selfless, then society would honor and reward them properly.

## The Intellectual Teacher, the Empowering Teacher

Existing as a corollary to teaching as the noble profession (because of the reward of stimulation and vitality from working with youth) was the image of the schoolteacher as the dynamic teacher. This professional was a scholar, an open-minded intellectual, a leader, a scientist, and an artist. This teacher paragon existed as a model to students, enabling them to become scholars and analytical thinkers. Such vibrant images pervaded many teacher education texts either substantively or superficially. In some cases, such teacher paragons epitomized the authors' goals for teaching, whereas in others the authors paid lip-service to these images but gave otherwise contradictory counsel.

### Qualities of the Intellectual Paragon

How did textbook authors describe the intellectual schoolteacher? In *The Ideal Teacher*, Palmer (1908) stipulated that a teacher paragon must possess four characteristics: the capability of living with little reward, the ability and passion to create scholars, an accumulation of knowledge, and an active, open mind. To Palmer, the teaching profession—whether on the college or classroom level—was noble and self-sacrificing, and yet powerful, dynamic, and fluid. "A finished teacher is a contradiction in terms," he proclaimed; "our reach will forever exceed our grasp. . . . We can always be more stimulating, imaginative" (p. 29). Snyder and Alexander (1932) succinctly expressed Palmer's paragon: "There must be a thinking teacher before there can be a thinking child" (p. 56).

Several authors expressed Palmer's sentiments by using a plant metaphor to describe the teacher—as a "live tree that grows at every branch, not a petrified tree" (Marsh, 1928, p. 6; Winship, 1919, p. 64). Milner (1912) urged schoolteachers to make books "close personal friends" and to read different books because "in a growing garden the same flowers do not blossom day after day" (p. 13). Scholarship could bring delight to the teacher who grew intellectually along with the students (McFee, 1918, pp. 16, 245).

According to Grant, poor teaching occurs when the teacher does not grow, because of "mental crystallization, the inability . . . to act on new ideas" (1927, p. 243). Grant continues: "Twenty years after normal-school graduation some teachers are teaching reading in the same way that they did the first year. They secure what *they* call good results, and fight nothing but change" (pp. 245–246). As Milner (1912) explained, devotion to one's work alone does not make the excellent teacher: "A man once asked a teacher if she had read a certain book, mentioning one of excellent merit which was then attracting wide attention. 'No,' she replied, 'I haven't had time for twenty years to read anything but primers and first readers, and the nature book which I have to teach' " (p. 33). "If this woman were a good teacher in spite of this narrow, contracted, pitiful condition," Milner commented, "what a great teacher she might have been if she could have but climbed the hill-side ever so little a way" (pp. 33–34).

This crystallization is illustrated in the attitude of the schoolteacher and the use of the textbook in the classroom. "Many pupils have been advised to 'see what the book says,' until they have become dependent on the text. They have acquired the habit of believing all that is printed. Many teachers have taught the text and nothing but the text" (Grant, 1922, p. 129). Teachers' blatant dependence on the textbook limited both schoolteacher and pupil. Furthermore, because textbooks and teachers did not encourage critical thinking, wrote Zirbes and Taba (1937), "young people are denied the most invigorating parts of the thinking process" (p. 103).

Authors critical of schoolteachers for their lack of scholarly capacities and broadmindedness implied that teachers' inflexible personalities and their poor training prevented realization of the ideal of teacher as intellectual. Teachers had to rid themselves of their intellectual rigidity. The authors who portrayed schoolteachers as intellectuals insisted that unless teachers were scholars, professional growth was impossible.

### Teaching for Empowerment

The ideal teacher merely as a scholar did not complete the vision of this paragon; the teacher must also empower students. Rather than extolling the academician who could impart knowledge, most textbook writers sympathetic to Palmer's paragon understood scholarship as the catalyst for teaching. The teacher as intellectual depicted a powerful image of transformation, a professional who would not merely pour knowledge into a passive vessel but would learn along with the student. Colgrove (1911) poetically expressed this thought by writing, "The true teacher at work is a liberator" (p. 390).

The concept of student empowerment was closely linked to the teachers' social mission. The textbook authors wrote about their democratic vision in which students would become more informed, critical, cooperative and yet independent citizens (Bagley & Keith, 1932, p. 3; Strayer & Engelhard, 1920, p. 377; Zirbes & Taba, 1937, pp. 115–116). The teacher paragon could understand that, by enabling children to think, the independence and democratic vision of a future generation would be ensured because the "wellspring of democracy is the independent intelligence of its several members" (Valentine, 1931, p. 32). Some texts reflected George Counts's (1932) galvanizing belief that it was necessary for schools to "disturb the social order." According to Lee, "To a very large extent, the ability of any citizen to take part intelligently in his government depends upon the kind of education he has received. . . . To teach his pupils to think clearly, to criticize fearlessly and to judge intelligently—this is the great, the almost matchless privilege of the teacher in a democracy" (1938, pp. 18–19).

Thus, several writers wrote of the teachers' obligation not only to the students but also to society—including future generations. For example, wrote Watson (1937), "The chief responsibility of the teacher is to improve the quality of life in the coming generation" (p. 155). Only by enabling students to obtain "social insight to replace the blind prejudices which now so often rule" can the teacher so improve society (p. 155).

Ultimately, the schoolteacher—as scholar and intellectual—endeavored to help students discover "truth"—the greatest wisdom of the ages. Colgrove (1911) explained, "The child, like the primitive man, is the slave of ignorance, of fear, and of nature. It is the purpose of teaching to set him free" (p. 391). The emancipation of students meant the banishment of ignorance and prejudice and their recognition and acceptance of the most humanizing and ennobling ideas of civilization.

### The Teacher's Presence

Textbook writers who believed that educators should empower students urged teachers to convey their strong presence—the essence of their personalities and values—in order to transfer their own beliefs and behavior to their students (Colgrove, 1911, p. 391; Grant, 1927, p. 295; Snyder & Alexander, 1932, p. 4). Apparently, authors who imagined the teacher as liberator did not conceive of the educator as the facilitator of the student's fulfillment of unique potential or the giver of the child's freedom.

A few of the textbooks gave higher priority to the teacher's ability to empower the students than to the teacher's own intellectual capacities. "He may not be a great scholar," wrote Wright (1920) of the schoolteacher, but he still could make his students "wise and good men" (p. 45). So, too, could students be influenced by the teacher's presence as a human being—"his attitude toward life, his way of thinking, his friendships, his prejudices" (Simon, 1938, p. 40).

But role modeling fine qualities did not satisfy many of the textbook authors. The teacher should demonstrate tremendous leadership by influencing the child educationally and morally (Hines, 1926, p. 169; Winship, 1919, p. 142). Even those educators who were appalled by dogmatic teaching responded to critics of child-centered education (who feared that nontraditional education would create a totally unguided classroom) by insisting that the teacher could enable students by demonstrating strong direction (Zirbes & Taba, 1937, p. 108).

A minority of the textbook authors feared the strong presence of the teacher because a strong teacher personality could prevent the empowering of students. The harm to children could be seen when the teacher left the school or students passed on to another grade: "When that time comes, it is usually clear enough that the 'strong Personality' of the teacher has actually weakened the pupils. They have become so thoroughly dependent on this stimulus that they are unable to stand alone. The interest that they displayed in their lessons turns out to be only a borrowed interest" (Bagley & Keith, 1932, p. 339). However, as in the case of the teacher as selfless paragon, authors offered little criticism of the image of the teacher as dynamic leader. Forceful, magnetic personalities were envisioned for teachers, but the possible consequences for students were seldom contemplated.

### As Scientist and Artist

How could teachers become intellectual enablers? For the answer, many of the textbook authors turned to scientific knowledge of child development and pedagogy and finally to the educator's artistic conception of teaching.

Textbook writers recommended that teachers study not only subjects but also the interests and capabilities of the students themselves (Davis, 1930, p. 105; Grant, 1922, pp. 124, 129). The teacher must also look ahead and "chart the correct course" for the child (Milner, 1912, p. 228) or "knowing just where she is bound intellectually, the teacher can make adequate provisions for proper teaching equipment" (Holley, 1922, p. 59).

An intellectual teacher not only studied child development but also approached education scientifically. Perhaps no author stated that idea as clearly as Freeland (1925): "The teacher who advances in the profession uses his classroom as a laboratory. . . . Each day holds the possibility of a new discovery" (p. 7). Similarly, Melby declared that the teacher "must become a full-fledged practitioner in educational science. He is more comparable to the physician than to the nurse" (1937, p. 128).

Several textbooks introduced dual concepts of the teacher as scientist and as artist. "There is, in fact, a close kinship between the scientific discoverer, even in education, and the creative artist" (Valentine, 1931, p. 34). Excellent teachers develop their expertise through the laboratory of the classroom; what they achieve is an artistic expression of craft through "controlled experimentation" (Grant, 1927, pp. 246–247). "The true teacher is a combination of artist, scientist, and skilled craftsman," wrote Lee (1938); "like all artistic pursuits, the teacher's task is a creative one" (p. 38).

The empowering schoolteacher as a creative force—the artist–teacher— appeared often in the teacher education literature (Avent, 1931, p. 34; Grant, 1927, p. 244; Holley, 1922, p. 5; Valentine, 1931, p. 27). The admirers of this paragon maintained that, in stark contrast to workers in other occupations, only the teacher exhibits creative sensitivity to the individuality of the teaching process and the student. In this regard, Averill comments: "The teacher-operative is about the only artisan left in the modern world who still maintains the same relationship to her craft that the guild workers enjoyed centuries ago. The machine has not destroyed the unity of the relationship. The teacher continues still to work upon the totality of the raw material placed at her disposal, and continues thus in a position to experience the fullest pleasure and satisfaction at every stage and in every process" (1939, p. 6). Or, as Valentine ironically remarked, "No factory manager would employ a staff of artist-minded workers to turn out his product. . . . Standardization would be impossible. They would 'gum up' the machinery" (1931, p. 40). Similarly, Sandford (1938) warned that "present tendencies in education fail to create inspiration among teachers." The mechanistic school day would drain the energies of teachers; individuals with "initiative" could not survive the routine of the school system (p. 51).

Proponents of the paragon of teacher as artist feared that the modern school would not allow for creativity, that science could not be in harmony with art when it brought only standardization. The molding and vitalizing of students would be impossible because schools and classrooms modeled after factories would crush the teachers' artistic gifts and not allow them to evolve their own talents and intuition in order to empower individual students. Textbook authors who imagined the intellectual, empowering teacher believed in their vision of the teacher's potential power, but they had less faith that American schools would sanction the existence of this paragon.

## The Controller and the Controlled

Not all textbook writers envisioned teacher paragons as scholars who would cultivate their students' intelligence. Having little or no realization of the intellectual possibilities of the teaching profession for teacher or student, many of the authors portrayed the teacher as controller—the maker of order. Numerous texts emphasized order and organizing, control and discipline, authority and power. Examples of such sentiments include: "Order is heaven's first law, and it is scarcely more essential to the peace and harmony there, than it is to the happiness and success of a school" (McFee, 1918, p. 13); "There is, however, no exception to the principle that within the schoolroom the authority of the teacher is absolute" (Perry, 1912, p. 35);

"The teacher is the hub of the educational wheel, for he controls the immediate environment of the pupils" (Overn, 1935, p. 7); and "The last step in the transformation of the student into the teacher is the acquirement of power to bring things to pass. The teacher is not all instructor; he is organizer, ruler, and trainer" (Colgrove, 1911, p. 65).

Even if they proclaimed that teachers should be scholars, the authors generally did not envision how difficult it would be to serve at once as stimulator and controller. Few noted, as did Donovan (1938), that the requirements of schooling for discipline prevented the teacher from becoming the intellectual enabler: "The schoolma'am must constantly be two persons of opposite tendencies. She must be the one who sees and represses undesirable traits and unsuitable behavior; at the same time she must also be the one who stimulates the thinking and draws forth the expression from her pupils which means successful classroom procedure" (p. 16).

Pragmatically, the ideal teacher as an intellectual who empowers students could not be a successful teacher—one who keeps a job by continually enjoying the blessings of the administration and the community. In his *The Sociology of Teaching* (1932), Waller concluded that "the ability to discipline is the usual test" for teacher advancement. A teacher must "fit in" and have "a degree of dexterity in manipulating the social environment" (p. 30). In order to be successful, teachers had to control their classrooms and positively manipulate their own images within the community.

Thus, the expectations of those who hire teachers (administrators or boards of education) would influence the goals teachers set for themselves. As Grant (1922) emphasized, the attainment of order would preempt any other purpose for teaching: "No teacher can expect to succeed until she is able to govern her school. The first thing that patrons expect of their teacher is to 'keep order,' and the second thing they expect of her is to teach. If she can't do the first, she can't do the second" (1922, p. 95). Regardless of whether teacher-educators seemed genuinely excited about the teaching process and the development of children, the textbook writers counseled teaching candidates to be authority figures: "It is better to be inflexible than to be always undecided" (Wright, 1920, p. 39), or, "being a drill-sergeant is also better than being a dishrag" (Simon, 1938, pp. 83–84).

Waller (1932) also mentioned that teachers' personalities were influenced by the expectation that they must maintain order. He explained that "teachers fear two things above all others: the loss of control over their classes, and the loss of their jobs." These fears, in Waller's analysis, become "the central features of the personality" (p. 156).

If fear of censure from school officials or from citizens of the community was not enough to dissuade teachers from keeping unruly classrooms, textbook writers also insinuated that teachers who could not control their classrooms were incompetent, neurotic, or foolish. Furthermore, they cautioned that control of the classroom must originate from self-control.

> The teacher who is not complete master of herself will certainly fail to master others . . . if she finds she cannot exercise this self-control, she should seek other employment. (McFee, 1918, p. 13).

> The good teacher knows that temper begets temper, that noise begets noise, and that order begets order. She knows that the teacher who would control her pupils must first control herself (Grant, 1922, p. 96).

> Many of the serious problems that the teacher faces in her everyday work originate from her own personality. Three of the greatest maxims a teacher . . . can practice are those announced hundreds of years ago . . . "Know thyself." "Control thyself." "Deny thyself" (Lewis, 1926, p. 324).[7]

The textbook writers played on the anxieties of teachers and teaching candidates about losing control, threatening them with nightmares of chaos in the classroom and the ruin of their standing in their schools or communities.

Images of control were also fostered through descriptions of teachers' function in the order of the school and their place in the organization of the community. Prospective teachers were reminded that achieving authority in the classroom was somewhat symbolic, for administrators and community members would hold and grant the real power. Within a system of subordination to administrators and public opinion, teachers were shown their place (Sandford, 1938, p. 103; Walsh, 1926, p. 214). Thus, depictions of teachers in orderly classrooms were juxtaposed with images of the teachers' place in the order of the school system. The textbook authors created a tension between authority and submission; the image of the teacher as controller thus became connected with the image of the teacher as the controlled.

The implication that teachers must be submissive to the authority of others—and deny their own interests or opinions—became more explicit when the textbook writers discussed the teacher's relationship to the community. What did it mean to be a teacher in the twentieth century before 1940? Particularly in nonurban areas, textbook authors explained that being a teacher meant living in a fishbowl. Wrote Van Nice, "The teacher, because he is widely known, is a convenient topic for conversation. . . . Only the checking influence of numerous friends will keep those reports (that hint at questionable habits, tastes or judgment) down and prevent their gaining both weight and momentum as they go" (1929, p. 92). According to Simon, "A teacher's life is, in a small town, practically public property: almost everyone regards himself as a duly constituted censor of a teacher's behavior—not to mention his professional skill" (1938, p. 44).

Schoolteachers had to scrutinize their own behavior more than most other people not only because they were well known in the community, but also because they had to live according to a special code of conduct. As Davis (1930) wrote, "The teacher ought to know that it is the standard which the community sets for teachers that counts, not the standard which it may set for itself" (p. 59). Or, "Parents expect teachers to exemplify behaviors more worthy of emulation by youth than that of the parents themselves" (Knudsen & McAfee, 1936, p. 10). Furthermore, "Teachers in general are bound by a stricter moral code than other professional persons, ministers of the gospel alone excepted. Thus it follows that they are considered unethical if they violate the standards set by the community for conduct of the teacher, even though there be no real infraction of the broader moral code" (Jordan, 1930, p. 258).

Social scientists of that time period concluded that educators had a nearly unique position among occupations. Because teachers were thought to be able to influence the young, communities exerted strict control over schoolteachers. Parents and other community members feared that teachers could influence young people to adopt socially unacceptable opinions about economics or politics.

The profession endured scrutiny and repression from many sources. Elsbree (1939) believed that communities had shifted attention away from controlling the teachers' social relations and church attendance and towards the monitoring of teachers' political viewpoints (pp. 540, 542). Beale (1936) wrote that "in most communities this tradition means that the teacher shall not in thought or action violate the local mores and shall stand a more rigid test in the least common denominator of the dominant religious faiths than that required of most citizens" (p. 624). He also blamed the repression of teachers on administrators' conscious or unconscious behaviors and on "social forces for which no individual is responsible" (p. 13).

Most textbook writers confirmed the existence of social and political restrictions upon teachers but had varying responses to such repression, ranging from approval of the teacher's moral pedestal to despair over the effect of repression on the teacher's personality.

The authors who approved of the peculiar moral code for teachers and the limitations on social and political freedom presented several rationalizations for their position. "The excellent teacher," they maintained, would not "disregard local sensibilities; he adheres to the social code and complies with social conventions" (Avent, 1931, p. 246). An excellent teacher would not be interested in entertainments of which the community disapproved; therefore, some authors self-righteously wondered, why should a teacher paragon criticize limitations on freedom? (Pulliam, 1930, p. 437).

Some authors went so far as to suggest that this repression was a badge of honor, the sign of the community's respect for the teaching profession; the community did not care what amusements entertained the bank clerk and the stenographer (Knudsen & McAfee, 1936, p. 9). Other writers claimed that, although the standards were difficult to live up to, the teacher who lived in an exemplary fashion (morally and socially) would reap the reward of a "favorable reputation" (Marsh, 1928, p. 155).

Recognizing the strict social controls on schoolteachers, textbook authors gave advice about how to deal with communities' restrictions. Such advice can be summarized briefly: If you don't like the restrictions, don't take the job (Davis, 1930, p. 59; Weber, 1937, p. 34); "make do," but look for a new position for next year (Gist, 1932, p. 306); or, just sacrifice your own inclinations and don't offend the community (Carpenter & Rufi, 1931, p. 229; Jordan, 1930, p. 258; Snyder & Alexander, 1932, p. 58). In an earlier decade, Almack and Lang (1925) suggested that first the teacher should follow the "behavioral modes" of her new community, but later, after winning the community's confidence, she would have a chance to express her individuality (p. 295). Other writers thought that the teacher could influence the community's standards through education and through good example—not through criticism of the community (Carpenter & Rufi, 1931, p. 204).

Successful teachers were described as "people pleasers"; in their personal and professional lives they must modify their attitudes, values, and behavior to conform to those of the community. Thus teachers would become smoothly adaptable, never calling attention to themselves (Avent, 1931, p. 197) except when someone noticed their dependability and helpfulness, such as their availability to the community as Sunday school teachers.[8] Teachers could not call attention to themselves by letting community members or students know their political affiliations, and, assuredly, they did not dare to become involved with political campaigns (Davis, 1930, p. 53; Marsh, 1928, p. 166). Several textbooks that presented advice on pleasing a community gave counsel urging concessions that would restrict the teacher from friendship and intimacy. For example, teachers were warned to avoid intimate relationships not only because a love interest would attract attention to themselves, but also because an intimate friendship demands loyalty. According to Van Nice: "intimacy is dangerous . . . to enter into intimate friendships is to assume the enemies of those people" (1929, pp. 62, 104). "The excellent teacher" and "the tactful teacher" surrendered their own humanity for the sake of obliging the community.

A few authors worried about what effect such submission would have on the teacher's personality or character. For example, Valentine (1931) feared that the inhibited person could not be a creative, artistic teacher (p. 283). Simon (1938) had foreseen that social repression would create a "timidity and conservatism" in teachers: "In small towns particularly the teacher thus becomes not a courageous, independent thinker and an adventuresome person, as the leader of children ought to be, but a timid soul censored by a board and spied upon by everyone. Consideration of his every action is prefaced by those two hamstringing words, 'Dare I?' 'Dare I wear these clothes?' 'Dare I go to this restaurant?' 'Dare I be seen soon again with this young man or woman?' 'Dare I vote thus?' 'Dare I say this?' and finally, 'Dare I think so-and-so?' " (p. 44).

And yet, Simon did not forthrightly propose that the teacher must fight this repression. Rather, his advice was to "lie low" and first establish a good reputation. He recommended that the teacher ignore more trivial issues such as standards of dress (issues of "personal convenience") in order to "fight his real battles" (p. 47). Simon reminded the teacher "not to flaunt his disrespect for the conventions of his community in regard to symbols," but to care about more substantive issues that involved "principles much more far-reaching than your personal convenience" (p. 47).

Generally, in book after book, including texts advocating the empowering paragon and greater teacher professionalism and activism, the authors rendered images of the teacher as controller and controlled. They routinely advised teachers to give up their individuality—to adopt a dehumanizing conformity to local or popular customs. At best, these books taught teachers "how to play the game" in order to obtain a teaching position and keep it. At worst, they tried to persuade teachers to be submissive to an extent that only the most repressive societies could imagine. Clearly, ideal schoolteachers had to withstand close scrutiny and exhibit flawless behavior in all aspects of their lives. They had to demonstrate their ability to control not only the children but also themselves. What teacher education textbooks had in common was their advocacy of conformity to dominant community standards and their authors' perception of the coercion manifest in the community's relationship to the schoolteacher.

## Resisting Stereotype and Caricature

Still, it would be impossible to understand images of teacher paragons without recognizing that throughout the literature of teacher education, authors contrasted their impressions of ideal teachers with negative images that exhibited a variety of unattractive characteristics. Teacher-educators insisted that the ideal teacher should recognize and resist detestable stereotypes and caricatures of the profession that so provoked the authors' scorn.

Paradoxically, teacher-educators dared to encourage people to enter the profession, despite their communication of extremely negative stereotypes. The textbooks consistently juxtaposed reassurance with trepidation. A person should be "proud to be a teacher," expounded an author (Winship, 1919), but nevertheless, he commented, "there is often a disposition on the part of . . . some teachers to dread to be thought of as a teacher" (pp. 17, 18). Why should people dread to become teachers? We need look no farther than the textbooks themselves, which presented numerous caricatures of schoolteachers and contemptuous comments about them:

> There is no need of calling attention to the artificial attitude of a certain type of kindergarten teachers, to their affected tone of voice, their lovey-dovey manner, the smile that is lip service only (Milner, 1912, p. 47).

> Most of the disparaging jokes about teaching picture a meticulous prig, who is out of sympathy and completely out of touch with living men and women (Pulliam, 1930, p. 435).

> Though she may be thirty pounds overweight, popular conception sees in her a hard thinness of personality; although she has the curves of a houri, she remains a sexless human slab. . . . Her blouses may be entirely without collars but she wears a neckpiece that chokes her (Donovan, 1938, p. 14).

Textbooks for teachers thus portrayed schoolteachers as inhuman, unattractive, genderless prudes. The authors rendered these caricatures in their texts for various reasons.

In warning teachers to repudiate repugnant stereotypes, the writers used negative images to support their superficial recommendations or cure-alls. Sandford (1938) concentrated on the narrowness of teachers' interests: "For the enrichment of our own personalities we need to broaden our range of interests. . . . Our tendency to talk shop, in season and out, betrays us. Our paucity of interests outside of our work is apparent whenever we are in a social group that does not appreciate shop talk. To have some of our statements successfully challenged . . . will help us to escape the offensive air of finality so common to those who work with their inferiors" (Sandford, 1938, pp. 107–108). For his part, Van Nice called attention to teachers' traditionally poor grooming: "Many a teacher has remained low in the esteem of people because he or she failed to recognize the importance of personal habits of neatness and cleanliness. The race has long suffered from the consequences of untidiness, carelessness, and indifference. Whenever they appear they bring their heritage of annoyance and contempt" (Van Nice, 1929, p. 51). Such petty suggestions about socialization and grooming essentially conveyed the message that teachers must adopt the conversation and clothing of nonteachers. Clearly, passages such as these reflected the contempt textbook writers felt for schoolteachers.

Other authors suggested that teachers must become more attuned to their own interests and personalities in order to defy stereotypes in more than a superficial manner. Such changes in themselves included less preoccupation with "administrative detail" and more emphasis on intellectual stimulus (Davis, 1930, p. 336; Simon, 1938, p. 41). Teachers were admonished to examine the caricatures critically and to change themselves accordingly (Davis, 1930, p. 305). The authors implied that if candidates became stereotypical schoolteachers, they had only themselves to blame. After reading the textbook, the pitfalls of becoming a caricature—replete with repugnant habits of thought and behavior—had been brought to their attention.

The authors also had other purposes for writing about negative stereotypes: they wanted to introduce the problems of the teaching profession so that prospective teachers could realistically contemplate their vocational choice and prepare themselves to deal with difficulties. The writers instructed these prospective teachers to understand that no matter what their demeanor, the daily existence of teaching in schools as well as the expectations of communities and American society created stereotypes.

Textbooks that raised the specter of unattractive caricature frequently blamed the nature of the profession itself for molding teachers into the stereotype. Donovan (1938) lamented that the need to create classroom order eventually affects the teacher's personality. Teachers, she said, believe that in order to survive in the classroom they must dominate children. "All successful teachers acquire a dominating personality. Some conceal its outward manifestations better than others, that is all," she wrote (p. 18). Averill (1939) contended that, after years in the classroom, teachers "may lose their youthful outlook and grow stale and uninteresting long before their time" (p. 16); he attributed schoolteachers' "narrow, cranky and harsh attitudes" to "accumulating physical strain and fatigue that go with years of teaching" under unhealthy conditions, for example, unventilated classrooms (p. 16).

Some authors tempered the idea of the schoolteacher caricature with the thought that all professions naturally encourage certain behaviors or characteristics among their practitioners (Donovan, 1938, p. 13; Marsh, 1928, p. v). Conversely, Donovan questioned whether such caricatured behaviors actually existed or whether the popular image—the American cartoon—of the "schoolma'am" prevented people from responding to the teacher as a human being; Donovan wrote, "She is to the community not an individual but a teacher" (p. 14).

Others, however, affirmed that schoolteachers faced special circumstances that made them different because of the unusual characteristics of their work. "In his relation to others in the community, the teacher occupies a position different from that of any other worker," commented Walsh (1926). "This difference is most marked in the case of teachers in the elementary school, especially in the lower grades. The teacher's actual work is with the children and these have little to do with adult interests. Thus the teacher, by his very work, is often set apart from the actual affairs of life and from the activities that are occupying the minds of other adults" (p. 271). Similarly, Waller (1932), stated that the teacher lived somewhat apart from the community because of the nature of the child-focused vocation. In addition, the teachers' isolation was increased, Waller observed, because of their constant mobility which prevented their sustained interaction with communities (p. 49).

Both Simon (1938) and Waller (1932), however, implicated communities for encouraging the stereotype—for desiring schoolteachers who could impart little of their humanity. Communities hired and maintained positions for mundane personalities, Simon cautioned: "So you may fall into the easy temptation of the blameless, colourless, safe existence which most communities buy from their teachers with a sense of security" (p. 40). Using parallel reasoning, Waller explained, "The community can never know the teacher because it insists upon regarding him as something more than a god and something less than a man. In short, the teacher is psychologically isolated from the community because he must live within the teacher stereotype" (p. 49). From the standpoint of the sociologist, Waller perceived what teacher-educators inspiring young people to enter the profession could not see or would not admit: a circuitous state of affairs that would prohibit teachers from overcoming caricature. Despite the teachers' own interests and inclinations (and their awareness of the advice supplied by teacher education textbooks to refrain from caricatured behavior), they would be pigeonholed by the community and viewed in a stereotypical manner. Schoolteachers constricted by cultural images of teachers—as absurd prudes or pedagogues—would have had little chance of socially interacting with community members in order to repudiate such likely misconceptions.

## Contemplating the Ideal Teacher

The predominant images of ideal teachers in teacher education literature in the early twentieth century demonstrated the textbook authors' distinct and sometimes contradictory convictions about teaching and the roles of schoolteachers. Powerful images of teachers transforming students and society contrasted with conceptions of apprehensive employees warned against engaging in any activity that would make them visible to the community. Within the pages of these textbooks could be found illustrations of teachers as honored professionals countervailed by offensive descriptions of schoolteachers as priggish caricatures. Moreover, the textbooks reflected their writers' various intentions: to recruit teaching candidates by eulogizing the possibilities and the nobility of teaching, to prepare new teachers to cope with low status and even ridicule of the profession in the public eye, or to use these books as excuses for publishing patronizing "self-help" books for a large occupational audience.

Despite their multiplicity and contradictions, these textbooks uniformly portrayed the exceptionality of the teaching profession. The textbook authors conveyed the special nature of teachers' responsibility in the classroom and existence in the community, articulating the notion that—except for the clergy—working and living as a teacher was not comparable to the experience of other human beings. The demand for sainthood in both the teacher's impetus and personality, the high expectations for the teacher's positive influence on children and society, the stringent codes of conduct that had to satisfy dominant community groups, and the necessity of withstanding repulsive stereotypes—all made schoolteaching a singular occupation. In order to be an ideal teacher, it was not enough to work as a skilled and talented professional. Teacher paragons could not be merely excellent teachers; they had to be sublime.

## NOTES

1. I looked at textbooks written for teachers and teacher aspirants, books whose introductions or prefaces contained these sentiments: "The teacher who reads the different chapters should obtain a new insight into the problems of her profession and the place and importance of her work" (Almack & Lang, 1925, pp. vi–vii), or "This volume is dedicated to good teachers and to students who will become good teachers" (Knudsen & McAfee, 1936, Preface). I also looked at books about supervision and administration because they illustrated images of teachers and their authors urged teachers to read them.

   The textbook authors were, with few exceptions, teacher-educators; many were from state universities and normal schools, and less frequently from prestigious universities. Numerous writers held administrative or supervisory positions, several were sociologists, and rarely did they work as classroom teachers. A few authors retired from their professions in education but desired to share their experiences and wisdom, thus "devoting themselves to educational guidance and giving inspirational talks at all kinds of meetings" (Sandford, 1938, Publisher's Introduction). The vast majority of the authors were men.

2. I found no indication that the authors carried the comparison of soldiering and teaching to the extreme, viewing the classroom as a battlefield. Their apparent intention was merely to point out that schoolteaching was a service-oriented and vital profession, perhaps suggestive of the hymn, "Onward Christian Soldiers."

3. An extreme example of admiration for business is found in *Teaching as a Profession: Its Ethical Standards* by M. J. Walsh (1926). The writer criticized educators and praised businesspeople. He insisted that "in a rapidly changing social order in which other vocations, both business and professional, have caught something of the unselfish spirit of service and have realized the economic value of business integrity, teaching has lagged behind" in developing standards of conduct (p. v).

4. The phenomenon of describing schools in terms of efficient factories was by no means unique to teacher education literature. In the early decades of the twentieth century, many plans and studies for American schools dealt with such concepts as scientific management, cost efficiency, and standardization. Perhaps no better source of describing the business/factory mentality in American schools is Raymond E. Callahan's *Education and the Cult of Efficiency: A Study of the Social Forces that Have Shaped the Administration of the Public Schools.* (Chicago: University of Chicago Press, 1962).

5. Similarly, the metaphors of social vision and change correspond to a dynamic educational milieu in which educators and philosophers imagined the schools and teachers leading a new generation to a more equitable and democratic American society. A classic description of these ideas can be found in Merle Curti's *The Social Ideas of American Educators* (Totowa, NJ: Littlefield, Adams, 1935/1971).

6. I believe it is necessary and not too cynical to suggest that authors constructed images not only because the imagery seemed significant to them, but also because they sought to enhance the popularity of their textbooks by using the jargon of the times.

7. Although I have attempted to provide examples of ideal teacher characteristics that speak to both male and female teachers, advice about self-control appears to be aimed at female readers. Furthermore, knowing that some authors refer to

the teacher as "he," I examined advice about self-control in the male-oriented texts and found a switch to the plural, for example, Avent (1931), *"they* often take out their bad feelings on their pupils. *They* have no shame for show of temper" (p. 217, italics mine).

8. It seemed, however, that teaching Sunday school could be hazardous to one's job security. Various authors warned that Sunday school teaching could lead to controversy because if a teacher taught in a certain church, the members of other denominations might turn against the teacher for not teaching Sunday school in their church.

## REFERENCES

Almack, J. C. & Lang, A. R. (1925). *Problems of the teaching profession.* Boston: Houghton Mifflin.

Avent, J. E. (1931). *The excellent teacher.* Knoxville, TN: Joseph E. Avent, Publisher.

Averill, L. A. (1939). *Mental hygiene for the classroom teacher.* New York: Pitman Publishing.

Bagley, W. C. & Keith, J. A. H. (1932). *An introduction to teaching.* New York: Macmillan.

Beale, H. K. (1936). *Are American teachers free?: An analysis of restraints upon the freedom of teaching in American schools.* New York: Charles Scribner's Sons.

Carpenter, W. W. & Rufi, J. (1931). *The teacher and secondary-school administration from the point of view of the classroom teacher.* Boston: Ginn & Co.

Charters, W. W. & Waples, D. (1929). *The Commonwealth teacher-training study.* Chicago: University of Chicago Press.

Colgrove, C. P. (1911). *The teacher and the school.* New York: Charles Scribner's Sons.

Counts, G. (1932). *Dare the school build a new social order?* New York: John Day.

Davis, S. E. (1930). *The teacher's relationships.* New York: Macmillan.

Dearborn, N. H. (1925). *An introduction to teaching.* New York: D. Appleton.

Donovan, F. R. (1938). *The schoolma'am.* New York: Frederick A. Stokes.

Duke, C. W. (1923). *Getting ahead as a teacher.* Harrisburg, PA: Handy Book.

Elsbree, W. S. (1939). *The American teacher: Evolution of a profession in a democracy.* New York: American Book.

Freeland, G. E. (1925). *The improvement of teaching.* New York: Macmillan.

Gist, A. S. (1932). *Clarifying the teacher's problems.* New York: Charles Scribner's Sons.

Grant, E. B. (1927). Principles and characteristics of good teaching. In M. B. Hillegas & T. H. Briggs (Eds.), *The classroom teacher* (pp. 243–296). Chicago: The Classroom Teacher.

Grant, J. R. (1922). *Acquiring skill in teaching.* New York: Silver, Burdett & Co.

Hines, H. C. (1926). *Finding the right teaching position.* New York: Charles Scribner's Sons.

Holley, C. E. (1922). *The teacher's technique.* New York: Century.

Jordan, R. H. (1930). *Education as a life work: An introduction into education* New York: Century.

Knudsen, C. W. & McAfee, L. O. (1936). *An introduction to teaching.* Garden City, NY: Doubleday, Doran & Co.

Lee, E. A. (1938). *Teaching as a man's job.* Homewood, IL: Phi Delta Kappa.

Lewis, E. E. (1926). *Personnel problems of the teaching staff.* New York: Century.

Marsh, J. F. (1928). *The teacher outside the school.* Yonkers-on-Hudson, NY: World Book.

McFee, I. N. (1918). *The teacher, the school, and the community.* New York: American Book.

Melby, E. O. (1937). The teacher and the school system. In W. H. Kilpatrick (Ed.), *The teacher and society* (pp. 117–142). New York: D. Appleton-Century.

Milner, F. (1912). *The teacher.* Chicago: Scott, Foresman & Co.

Overn, A. V. (1935). *The teacher in modern education: A guide to professional problems and administrative responsibilities.* New York: D. Appleton-Century.

Palmer, G. H. (1914). *Trades and professions.* Boston: Houghton Mifflin.

Palmer, G. H. (1908/1910). *The ideal teacher.* Boston: Houghton Mifflin.

Perry, A. C., Jr. (1912). *The status of the teacher.* Boston: Houghton Mifflin.

Pulliam, R. (1930). *Extra-instructional activities of the teacher.* Garden City, NY: Doubleday, Doran.

Sandford, C. M. (1938). *Developing a teacher personality that wins.* Evanston, IL: Row, Peterson & Co.

Simon, H. W. (1938). *Preface to teaching.* New York: Oxford University Press.

Snyder, A. & Alexander, T. (1932). Teaching as a profession: Guidance suggestions for students. *Teachers College Bulletin, 23*(3), 1–69.

Strayer, G. D. & Engelhard, N. L. (1920). *The classroom teacher.* New York: American Book.

Valentine, P. F. (1931). *The art of the teacher: An essay in Humanism.* New York: D. Appleton.

Van Nice, C. R. (1929). *Tact and the teacher.* Lawrence, KS: Plainview Publications.

Waller, W. (1932). *The sociology of teaching.* New York: John Wiley & Sons.

Walsh, M. J. (1926). *Teaching as a profession: Its ethical standards.* New York: Henry Holt.

Watson, G. (1937). The economic status of the teacher. In W. H. Kilpatrick (Ed.), *The teacher and society* (pp. 143–173). New York: D. Appleton-Century.

Weber, S. E. (1937). *Cooperative administration and supervision of the teaching personnel.* New York: Thomas Nelson & Son.

Winship, A. E. (1919). *Danger signals for teacher.* Chicago: Forbes & Co.

Wright, H. P. (1920). *The young man and teaching.* New York: Macmillan.

Zirbes, L. & Taba, H. (1937). The teacher at work. In W. H. Kilpatrick (Ed.), *The teacher and society* (pp. 93–118). New York: D. Appleton-Century Company.

# Continuing Dialogue

1. Write a story for young children about a teacher in a classroom. Then reflect on the choices you made as you wrote your story—the kind of information about the teacher and the classroom that you gave young readers, the "drama" or conflict you portrayed, the depiction of the teacher's personality and teaching, and the relationship of the teacher to the children in the classroom and/or to parents and administrators.

2. In their chapters (Chapters 10 and 11), Trousdale and Burnaford both suggest that fiction for children tends to present the teaching profession as predominantly female, white, and middle class. Write a response to their analyses of the teaching profession and ask yourself these questions: What tensions or misunderstandings might arise when teachers and students come from different social and cultural backgrounds? Do you think that teachers respond differently to children from their own socioeconomic backgrounds than to children from backgrounds significantly different from their own? What do you think accounts for the namelessness of so many female teachers in picture books for young children?

3. Read a primary book to young children in which a teacher is featured as a major character. Ask them about their understanding of the teacher in the book. What kind of teacher is she/he? Is she/he a good teacher? How do we know? Would her/his classroom be a nice place to visit? Why? Relate in a journal what you have learned concerning these children's views of teaching, reflecting on the story you read, your response to it, and the children's responses.

4. Investigate literature for children written before 1970 which contains characterizations of teachers. Analyze the social context in which these works were written and explore how those contexts may affect the images of teachers therein.

5. Examine very recent literature written for children (written within the last five years). Are the images of teachers in this recent literature different from those in books written during the 1970s and 1980s? How are multiculturalism/diversity issues being addressed?

6. Refer to the chapter entitled "A Mosaic: Contemporary Schoolchildren's Images of Teachers" (Chapter 6), which presents the stories and discussions of children about real and imaginary teachers. How might you

describe the relationship between the images of teachers represented by those children and the images portrayed in the children's literature?

7.  Benjet (in Chapter 12) points out that she chose to focus on American literature before 1940 because of the dearth of schoolteacher characters in more recent novels. Write a response reflecting on why more contemporary novelists seldom portray schoolteachers. Also consider if you think that situation is likely to change.

8.  Interview teachers and retired teachers, asking them about their education that prepared them to teach—classes taken, books read, kinds of advice given. (Ask them to share with you any textbooks they might still own.) Also, ask them whether they believed that their teacher education textbooks, classes, teacher training instruction were meaningful to them when they first became teachers or after years of teaching.

9.  Interview students who are currently studying to be teachers, asking them why they want to become teachers and how they imagine themselves in their own future classrooms. Then refer to Manke's chapter (Chapter 13) about the sentimental image of the rural schoolteacher and compare your interviewees' responses with the romanticized notions of teachers as described by Manke. Do the students you interview reflect the romanticized or sentimental images Manke describes?

10. Read at least one teacher education textbook published since 1940. Consider these questions: What advice is given about becoming a teacher? Do you consider the advice realistic? If you read two textbooks, consider the differences and similarities of their advice, organization, and topics that the authors seem to consider important. Describe the historical events or the social, economic, and political contexts of American society when these books were written. Did these contexts seem to influence the textbook authors?

11. The chapter discussing the textbooks of teacher education before 1940 (Chapter 14) provides examples of scorecards that rate the traits or qualifications of teachers. Considering those examples, design a scorecard that you think might be applicable to an "ideal" teacher today. What are the advantages of a "scorecard?" What problems do you envision with such a system of teacher evaluation?

# Afterword
## The Dialogue Continues

This is the place where the authors traditionally sum up their most important ideas or render their final interpretation of "what it all means." We, too, share this temptation to tell you what really matters to us the most about these studies of teacher images. In our own thinking as editors and contributors, we could argue that there are many crucial conceptual strands that readers could "take away" from this book, notably the influence of culture and popular culture; the social-political context that shapes the creation of image and self-definition; the inherent symbols and conflicts within human development that envelop teachers because of the roles they play in their relationships with young people; or the personal meaning given to schoolteachers' lives and work as they construct images of themselves.

Within the structure we have given this book, however, it is our readers who have the last thoughts or words. What seems most sensible and right to us is the creation of an epilogue not by the editors, but by the readers. And so we conclude with questions that attempt to integrate your responses, interpretations, and reflections about images of schoolteachers in America into a conclusion that has personal meaning to you. We hope that your continuing dialogue on the subject will lead to more conversations with your colleagues:

1. What ideas presented in these chapters have been supported by your personal experiences as a student or as a teacher?

2. What ideas have allowed you to think about the question, "What does it mean to be a teacher?" in different ways than before you read this book?

3. Of the various influences or forces that have shaped the images of schoolteachers, what do you believe to be the most powerful and why?

285

4. How have the images of schoolteachers in America affected you as a community member, as a student, or as a teacher?

5. How can teachers, teacher-educators, administrators, students, parents, and the community shape the images of teachers?

6. What are your hopes for images of teachers in the twenty-first century? What are your expectations?

# Contributors

**William Ayers** is associate professor of education at the University of Illinois at Chicago. Before his academic career, he was an early childhood educator. He is the author of *The Good Preschool Teacher* and co-editor, with William Schubert, of *Teacher Lore*. He has published a chapter in *Reflections from the Heart of Educational Inquiry: Understanding Curriculum and Teaching through the Arts* (edited by George Willis and William Schubert) and articles in the *Cambridge Journal of Education, Action in Teacher Education,* and *Harvard Educational Review*. His scholarly and practical work centers on urban school improvement, teacher education, and the ethics of teaching.

**Rosalind Benjet** is a doctoral student in humanities at the University of Texas, Dallas. She formerly was an instructor of literature and composition at Oakton Community College in Illinois and a high school teacher of English, French, and Spanish. Her research interests are the uses of critical thinking in teaching composition, community college faculty, and Jewish-American literature.

**Gail E. Burnaford** is assistant professor in the Interdisciplinary Studies Department of National-Louis University in Evanston, Illinois, where she also teaches Literature for Children. She has taught both high school and junior high English and language arts and has also taught preschool. She formerly taught at Kennesaw State College and Georgia State University in Atlanta, Georgia. Her research interests include curriculum integration, middle school curriculum, and children's literature. She has published articles in *The Middle School Journal, Music Educators Journal, Best Practice* and *Research in Middle Level Education*.

**Fletcher DuBois** is a faculty member in the Interdisciplinary Studies Department of National-Louis University at Heidelberg, Germany. He formerly was a faculty member at the University of Heidelberg. His publications include *A Troubadour as Teacher, the Concert as Classroom: Joan Baez—Advocate of Nonviolence and Motivator of the Young* and *Buber-Gandhi-Tagore Aufforderung zu einem Weltgesprach*. He also is a folk singer.

**Sara Efron** is an adjunct faculty member in the Curriculum and Instruction and the Educational Foundations departments of National-Louis University and a faculty member of the Ann Blitstein Teachers' Institute for Women. Currently, she also works as a curriculum consultant and has been teacher and academic coordinator at Solomon Schechter Day School, coordinator at Kohl Teacher Center in Wilmette, director of a program for learning-disabled children at a summer camp, and a high school and junior high teacher of Hebrew language and literature. Her scholarly interests are moral education, curriculum, and literature.

**Joseph Fischer** is a professor and one of the founding instructors of the Graduate Field-Based Program in the Interdisciplinary Studies Department at National-Louis University. He has had a long relationship with the Chicago Public Schools and continues to be a consultant involved with staff development and literature. He has lived and studied for many years in South America and Germany. His research interests include teacher centers and comparative education.

**Nancy Green** is professor in the Educational Foundations Department of Northeastern Illinois University. She has a long involvement with the Chicago Teachers' Center, working with the Chicago Public Schools. Her scholarly interests include the teaching profession, gender issues, and the history of education. She has published in *The Journal of Teacher Education, History of Education Quarterly, Catalyst: Voices of Chicago School Reform,* and *Chicago History.*

**David Hobson** is associate professor in the Interdisciplinary Studies Department of National-Louis University. He was a founder and long-time director of the Graduate Center for Human Development and Learning at Fairleigh Dickinson University. As a former middle and high school social studies teacher, he has taught psychology and sociology to adolescents. He has published in the field of human development and social relations.

**Pamela Bolotin Joseph** is a core faculty member in the Graduate Programs in Education Department at Antioch University–Seattle. She formerly was assistant professor at National-Louis University and has taught at Northwestern University and Northeastern Illinois University; she has been a social studies and language arts teacher in high school and junior high. She has published in *The Journal of Moral Education, Social Education, Theory and Research in Social Education, The Journal of Teacher Education,* and *The American School Board Journal.* She has worked with various community organizations in support of public schooling and served on a board of education.

**Ken Kantor** has a joint appointment as professor in Curriculum and Instruction and Reading and Language Arts departments at National-Louis University; he has also served as director of the doctoral program in Instructional Leadership. He has taught English on the high school level and has been a faculty member at Bowling Green State University and the University of Georgia. He has published chapters in *Teaching and Thinking about Curriculum: Critical Inquiries* (edited by J. Dan Marshall and James Sears) and *Reflections from the Heart of Educational Inquiry: Understanding Teaching and Curriculum through the Arts* (edited by G. Willis and W. H. Schubert). He has also published in *The Journal of Curriculum Theorizing.*

**Anne Kiefer** is a faculty member in the Interdisciplinary Studies Department at National-Louis University, working both with teachers receiving master's degrees in curriculum and instruction and with teachers in interdisciplinary ESL programs.

She has been a teacher and high school principal, administrator of ESL and bilingual programs, and a project director of staff development and preschool Title VII programs. Her research interests include English as a second language, bilingual education, and teacher renewal.

**Mary Phillips Manke** is assistant professor in the Interdisciplinary Studies Department at National-Louis University—Milwaukee Center. Her research interests include the social foundations of education, qualitative research, and linguistics. She has published in *The Journal of Rural Education, Journal of College Student Development,* and wrote a chapter for the book, *Improving the Effectiveness of Teachers with Mainstreamed Learning Disabled Students* (edited by R. McNergney and D. Hallahan).

**W. Nikola-Lisa** is associate professor in the Interdisciplinary Studies Department in Curriculum and Instruction at National-Louis University in Evanston, Illinois. He is the 1990 recipient of the Ezra Jack Keats Fellowship, de Grummond Collection, University of Southern Mississippi, and the author of several books for children including *Night Is Coming* (Dutton, 1991) and *Storm* (Atheneum, 1993). He has also published author studies and critical commentaries on children's literature in *Children's Literature Association Journal, The New Advocate,* and *The Lion and the Unicorn.*

**Ann M. Trousdale** is assistant professor at Louisiana State University. She previously was a faculty member at Northern Illinois University and has taught elementary, middle school, and high school. Her research interests include storytelling, oral interpretation of literature, critical issues in children's literature, feminist and African-American issues, and images of schooling in the arts. She has been published in *Research in the Teaching of English, Language Arts,* and *The New Advocate.* She has also been a newspaper reporter, a photographer, and a potter.

**Acknowledgments** (continued from copyright page)

**Figure 14-1.** Reprinted with the permission of Charles Scribner's Sons, an imprint of Macmillan Publishing Company from *Clarifying the Teacher's Problems* by Arthur S. Gist. Copyright © 1932 Charles Scribner's Sons; copyright renewed.

**Figure 14-2.** Reprinted with the permission of Macmillan Publishing Company from *An Introduction to Teaching* from "American Teachers College Series," by William C. Bagley and John A. Keith. Copyright © 1924 by Macmillan Publishing Company.

# Name Index

Abbs, P., 55, 56
Alexander, T., *See* Snyder, A.
Allard, H., 198, 199, 202, 204–205
Almack, J. C., 258, 265, 266, 275, 280
Antin, M., 235, 238, 239, 240
Apple, M. W., 7, 113, 114
Arden, E., 177, 178
Arnold, K. 186
Aronowitz, S., 4, 8, 17, 18, 21
Asher, S., 218
Avent, J. E., 258, 264, 266, 271, 274, 275, 281
Averill, L. A., 264, 266, 267, 278
Ayers, W., 45

Baez, J., 170, 171
Bagley, W. C., 261, 262, 265, 269, 270
Ball, D., 57
Barber, M. A., 245, 253
Bargar, G. W., 219
Barth, J., 228–229
Beale, H. K., 274
Bellah, R. N., 257
Berenstain, J., 196
Berenstain, S., 196
Berrol, S., 232
Berry, C., 166, 167, 168
Bettelheim, B., 118
Biklen, S. K., *See* Bogdan, R. C.
Blume, J., 197
Bogdan, R. C., 76
Bowers, C. A., 57
Bowlby, J., 41, 47
Brooks, T., 188
Brooks, R., 148
Brown, M., 201, 202, 203, 206, 208, 209, 210
Browne, R. B., 233, 235, 238, 239

Bruner, J., 41, 51
Buber, M., 30–31, 40, 49
Butchart, R. E., 171

Callahan, R. E., 280
Campbell, J., 41
Carew, J. V., 4
Carney, M., 245, 255
Carnoy, M., 8
Carpenter, W. W., 275
Carruth, J., 196, 208, 209
Carter, K., 4
Cazet, D., 196, 198, 204, 208, 209
Chapman, D. W., 7
Charters, W. W., 258
Chase, M. E., 245, 248, 249, 252, 253, 254, 255, 256
Christensen, H.B., 245, 248, 250, 254
Clandinin, D. J., 6
Clark, J., 153, 154
Cohen, M.,196, 200–201, 203–204, 205–206, 208, 209, 210, 211
Cohn, M. M., *See* Provenzo, E. F.
Cole, J., 226
Cole, M., 65
Coles, R., 50
Colgrove, C. P., 268, 269, 272
Connor, R., 245, 247, 249, 251, 253
Conroy, P., 150, 151
Cooley, C. H., 55
Cooper, B. L., *See* Butchart, R. E.
Cosby, B., 180, 183, 187
Cottom, D., 20
Counts, G., 269
Covello, L., 232, 236, 238
Cox, W., 175
Creager, E., 217–218
Cronyn, H., 151

Crow, N. M., 61
Crume, M. T., 13–14
Cuban, L., 232, 257
Curti, M., 280

Danziger, P., 224, 225
Davis, M., *See* Pugh, S.
Davis, S. E., 263, 270, 273, 275, 277
Dearborn, N. H., 263
dePaola, T., 199–201
Dern, L., 152
De Tocqueville, A., 256
Dewey, J., 29, 40, 49
Donovan, F. R., 245, 272, 277, 278
DuBois, F. R., 45, 170, 172
Duke, C. W., 258, 263
Dunn, W. 171

Eco, U., 227
Eisner, E. W., 57
Elsbree, W. S., 274
Engelhard, N. L. *See* Strayer, G. D.
Epstein, J. L., 68–69
Escalante, J., 154, 155

Farber, P., *See* Holm, G.
Farrell, J. T., 233
Favat, F. A., 118
Feinman-Nemser, S., 6
Fine, M., 8, 16, 17
Fish, S., 216
Foght, H. W., 245
Folden, R. E. *See* Feinman-Nemser, S.
Ford, G. 148
Fowke, E., 164
    and J. Glazer, 165
Freedman, M., 153
Freeland, G. E., 270
Frith, S., 172

Gans, H. J., 13, 21, 216
Geertz, C., 8
Geller, L. G., 117
Giff, P. R., 201, 203
Gilson, J., 225
Giroux, H. A., 16
    and R. I. Simon, 7, 9, 17, 21
Gist, A. S., 258, 260, 263, 275
Glaser, B. G., 76
Glazer, J., 164; *See also* Fowke, E.
Gold, M., 232, 233, 235
Golden, H., 236, 237, 238
Goodlad, J., 51

Grant, E. B., 268, 269, 270, 272
Grant, J. R., 262, 271, 273
Green, N., *See* Joseph, P. B.
Griswold, J., 117
Gross, A., 208, 209
Grossberg, L., 8, 13
Grumet, M. R., 18

Haley, B., 148
Hamilton-Merrit, J., 196, 204, 205
Handlin, O., 240
Havel, V., 44
Henry, X., *See* Salzberger-Wittenberg, I.
Hicks, J., *See* Pugh, S.
Hines, H. C., 262, 263, 270
Hirsch, J., 152
Hoff, S., 197, 208, 209
Hofstadter, R., 15
Holley, C. E., 270, 271
Holm, G., 159, 171
Howe, J., 198, 206, 208
Hoy, W. K. and Rees, D. E., 5
Hunter, M., 219, 222

Jackson, K., 196
John, E., 168
Johnson, S. M., 93
Jordon, R. H., 262, 274, 275
Joseph, P. B., 18
Jung, C. G., 41

Kantor, K., 178
Kaplan, G., 181, 183
Keith, J. A., *See* Bagley, W. C.
Kellogg, S., 198
Kennedy, J., 245, 250
Kerr, M. E., 225
Kiesel, S., 215, 216, 225
Kirkpatrick, M. G., 245, 247
Knudsen, C. W., 274, 280
Kotarba, J., 171
Kottkamp, R. B., *See* Provenzo, E. F.

La Gumina, S., 236
Lang, A. R., *See* Almack, J. C.
Lasker, J., 210
Lee, E. A., 262, 265, 266, 271
L'Engle, M., 217, 226–227
Lewis, E. E., 263, 273
Lieberman, A., 55, 68, 71–72, 109, 110
Lightfoot, S. L., *See* Carew, J. V.
Lipsitz, G., 8, 13

Lortie, D. C., 18, 41, 56, 61–62, 64, 82, 109–113
Lowry, L., 220–221
Lowth, F. J., 245, 246, 247, 250
Lowther, M. S., *See* Chapman, D. W.
Lull, J., 171
Lulu, 165

M. C., Young, 167, 168
McAfee, L. O., *See* Knudsen, C. W.
Maccio, R., 153
McCloskey, G. N., *See* Provenzo, E. F.
McCully, E. A., 198, 203, 208, 209
McFee, I. N., 265, 266, 268, 271, 273
McLaughlin, M. W., 6
McNeil, L., 17
Madsen, R., *See* Bellah, R. N.
Mannes, M., 239
Marsh, J. F., 265, 267, 274, 275, 278
Marshall, J., 199, 203, 204
Marshe, E., 188
Marx, H., 233
Mead, M., 6, 16–17, 55
Measor, L., 65
Melby, E. O., 263, 270
Meyrowitz, J., 172
Miller, L., *See* Lieberman, A.
Milner, F., 262, 263, 264, 266, 267, 268, 279, 276
Mitz, R., 178, 183, 188
Morrow, V., 150
Munsch, R., 203, 204, 208, 209

Nias, J., 55, 68
Nielsen, J. M., 5
Noble, T. H., 198, 202
Noddings, N., 114; *See also* Witherall, C.

Olmos, E. J., 154
Oppenheim, J., 197–198, 203, 210
Osbourne, X., *See* Salzberger-Wittenberg, I.
Overn, A. V., 263, 272

Palmer, G. H., 258, 263, 265, 266, 267, 268
Parish, P., 198
Paterson, K., 219–220, 221, 227–228
Perry, A. C., 264, 271
Pfeiffer, R. S., *See* McLaughlin, M. W.
Phillips, L. D., 154
Poitier, S., 149, 164
Popkewitz, T. S., 4

Provenzo, E. F., 56, 57
Pugh, S., 57
Pulliam, R., 265, 274, 277

Quackenbush, R., 196

Ravage, M. E., 234, 237, 240
Rees, D. E., *See* Hoy, W. K.
Relf, P., 196, 197, 210
Richardson, E., 50
Ricoeur, P., 57
Ritt, M., 150
Roe, K., 172
Rosenholtz, S. J., 68–69
Roskolenko, H., 237
Rosten, L., 233, 239
Ruckman, I., 223
Rufi, J., *See* Carpenter, W. W.

Sachar, L., 215, 216
Sachs, M., 223
St. Marie, B., 170, 171
Salvo, P. W., 167
Salzberger-Wittenberg, I., 47, 48
Sandford, C. M., 258, 263, 271, 273, 277, 280
Saroyan, W., 234, 237
Schwartz, A., 196, 206, 208, 210
Sebastian, J., 165
Sellers, R., 169
Shanice, 165
Shreve, S., 223
Shumway, D. R., 8
Silver, E., 233
Simon, H. W., 266, 269, 272, 273, 275, 276, 277, 278
Simon, R. I., *See* Giroux, H. A.
Slacks, J. R., 245, 246
Smedman, M. S., 221–222
Smith, B., 232, 233, 234
Snyder, A., 263, 264, 265, 267, 269, 275
Spradley, J. P., 100
Spring, J., 5, 16, 218
Stevens, S., 164
Sting, 168, 169
Stratton-Porter, G., 245, 254
Strauss, A. L., *See* Glaser, B. G.
Strayer, G. D., 263, 269
Sullivan, W. M., *See* Bellah, R. N.
Sutherland, N., 21
Swanson-Owens, D., *See* McLaughlin, M. W.
Swidler, A., *See* Bellah, R. N.

Taba, H., *See* Zirbes, L.
Taxel, J., 8, 17
Taylor, M., 227
Tester, S. R., 196, 198, 206, 207, 211, 212
Thaler, M., 196, 198
Thomas, J., 55
Thompson, F. V., 232
Tipton, S. M., *See* Bellah, R. N.
Tracy, D., 43
Travis, M., 164
Travolta, J., 181
Tyack, D., 244, 256

Valentine, P. F., 269, 270, 271, 275
Van Halen, E., 168, 169
Van Manen, M., 80
Van Nice, C. R., 273, 275, 277
Venstra, T., *See* Pugh, S.
Viorst, J., 202
Voight, J., 150

Waller, W., 272, 278, 279
Walsh, M. J., 262, 273, 280
Waples, D., *See* Charters, W. W.
Watson, G., 269

Weber, S. E., 275
Weiler, K., 83
Wells, R., 196, 208, 209
Wiggin, K. D., 245, 247, 253
Wigginton, E., 12, 50
Wilder, L. I., 247, 248, 249, 251, 252, 254, 255
Winfield, P. 151
Winship, A. E., 262, 265, 267, 270, 276
Wister, O., 247
Witherall, C., 4
Wolfe, N., 152
Woods, P., 65
Woofter, T. J., 245, 247, 251
Wright, H. P., 265, 269, 272

Yee, S., *See* McLaughlin, M. W.
Yezierska, A., 236, 237, 239, 240
Yolen, J., 117

Zach, C., 227
Zindel, P., 224
Zipes, J., 117
Zirbes, L., 268, 269, 270

# Subject Index

Abuse, of students, 11, 15, 47, 118, 121, 139, 151–152, 195, 201, 202, 222, 232, 233, 234, 235, 248, 249, 250, 252

Administrators, 4, 7, 14, 20, 30, 42, 55, 56, 71–75, 77, 94, 98, 100, 107, 113–115, 124, 126–129, 131, 133, 138, 142, 147, 149, 150–154, 163, 167, 171, 176, 178, 180, 182, 188, 204, 226, 234–236, 238, 249, 272–274

Adolescents, 6, 8–9, 12–13, 17, 22, 63, 143, 148–149, 159, 161–162, 168, 171–173, 175, 178, 180, 190, 217–218, 222, 224, 227

Advocacy for students, 10, 12, 16, 31, 38, 42, 43, 46, 47, 49, 58, 61, 87, 94, 111, 133, 134, 141, 181, 183, 197, 202, 209, 223, 224

American culture, 3, 4, 8–9, 13, 15, 16, 18, 19–20, 23, 24, 51, 86, 106, 259, 262–264

Anger, 10, 13, 15, 20, 56, 104, 164, 170, 182, 201, 222, 249

Archetype, 116, 117, 209, 258, 265

Authority, 7, 12, 15, 41, 48, 57, 67–68, 69, 75, 82, 88–89, 119, 204, 217–218, 224–225, 249, 271–273

Autobiography, 20, 22, 30, 40, 170, 201, 241

Autonomy, 17, 37, 43, 55, 73, 93, 97, 104, 105, 109, 116, 118, 207, 223, 275

Career options of teachers, 6, 18, 29, 32, 41, 55, 56, 63, 77, 83–86, 89, 95, 96, 107, 111, 178, 277

Caricature, 10, 12, 14, 15, 16, 86, 187, 215, 222, 276–279

Caring, *See* Nurturing

Character of teachers, 18, 31, 44, 52, 201, 246–248, 255, 275

Childhood, 17, 21, 22, 23, 24, 46, 61, 71, 83, 90, 141, 162, 196, 220–221, 234, 243, 263, 265

Children, 4–6, 9–12, 15–17, 27, 29, 31–39, 41, 45–48, 52, 58, 63–64, 66, 69, 71, 73, 75, 79, 81, 83–114, 116–141, 147, 151, 156, 163, 170, 195–214, 215–230, 231–242, 243, 248, 250, 254, 256, 259, 263, 269–270, 272, 275–276, 278–279

Children's literature, 8, 10–11, 18, 23, 36–37, 41, 53, 113, 116–119, 195–214, 215–230, 245

Colleagues, teachers as, 11, 30, 32, 43, 44, 74, 78, 79, 80, 87, 95, 104, 106, 110, 147, 152, 169

Comedy, *See* Humor

Communities, 4–7, 9–11, 16, 18, 21, 41, 45, 52, 55, 62, 69–70, 72, 75–76, 88, 90, 94, 96–98, 101, 104–106, 108–110, 142, 148, 152, 156, 183, 218–219, 224, 226, 229, 234, 243, 244, 253, 256, 259, 272–276, 278–279

Complexities, 6, 9–10, 14–15, 30, 56–57, 66, 68, 71, 76, 104, 155, 195, 198, 216, 228

Conformity, 17, 60, 168, 200–201, 226, 228, 272, 276

Conservatism, 109, 178, 218–219, 275

Control, 10, 11, 15–17, 29, 34, 40, 44, 47, 49, 57, 62, 63, 66, 67, 72, 75, 111–113, 133, 151, 155. 157, 161, 169, 186, 198, 202–204, 217–219, 246, 248–251, 255, 271–274, 275–276, 280–281

Creativity, 14, 18–19, 45, 52, 58, 75, 104,
   105, 107, 150, 152, 171, 184, 219–
   222, 225, 227, 270–271, 275
Critical inquiry, 5, 7, 16, 21–23, 84, 95,
   185–186, 213, 256, 268–270
Culture, 5, 8–9, 15–17, 20–22, 32, 41, 45,
   51, 52, 97, 106, 109, 111, 113, 158–
   159, 170–171, 190, 209, 211, 217,
   219, 222, 253, 259, 285
Curriculum, 7–8, 17, 23, 41, 73–75, 77,
   78, 85, 88, 95, 97, 103, 155, 167,
   169, 178, 182, 184, 186, 189, 211,
   224, 246, 252–255, 258

Dedication in teaching, 7, 11, 75, 101–
   102, 107–114, 147, 151, 154–156,
   161, 238, 244, 247, 255, 262, 264,
   267
Discipline, 17, 18, 31, 59, 60, 68, 71, 86,
   89, 149, 155, 221, 223, 234, 244,
   246, 248, 250–252, 254–255, 271–
   272

Empowerment
   of students, 10, 48–49, 186, 239, 267–
   272
   of teachers, 7, 16, 18, 74, 107
Ethnicity, 22, 24, 25, 67–68, 76, 81, 97–
   100, 107, 120, 148–151, 154, 156,
   164, 170–171, 180–183, 187–188,
   209–212, 218, 228, 233, 235–238,
   244
Ethnographic research, 100, 115, 119–120
Expectations
   of administrators, 73, 272
   of children, 226–227
   of parents, 4, 41, 56, 69, 101, 104, 108,
   110, 142, 154
   of teachers, 4, 6–7, 17, 25, 40, 41, 46,
   47, 55, 62–66, 75, 86, 98, 101, 110,
   114, 128, 168, 236

Fairy tales. See Folklore
Families, 4, 6, 8, 11, 18, 32, 83–85, 89, 91,
   94, 96–98, 100, 102, 117, 147, 156,
   175, 180, 186–187, 195, 211, 227,
   234–240, 243
Fathering role of teachers, 16, 33, 48, 60,
   121, 186
Fears
   about teachers, 12, 14, 15, 17, 38, 70–
   71, 117, 157, 161, 163, 196, 218–
   219, 249, 270, 274

   of teachers, 6, 34, 156, 203, 251, 272,
   275, 276
Female teachers, 5, 11, 17–18, 23–24, 80,
   83–89, 96, 101, 107, 109, 111, 113–
   114, 152, 166, 176–178, 180, 188,
   196, 202, 204, 206–213, 218–219,
   222, 231–233, 236–237, 247–249,
   280, 283
Feminist research, 5, 23, 113–115
Film, 3–4, 6, 8–9, 10–14, 18, 20, 147–
   156, 161, 163–165, 167, 181, 183,
   190, 217
Folklore, 45, 116–118, 141, 163, 215

Gender, 18, 22, 24, 76, 83, 111–114, 118,
   142, 166, 168, 175, 187, 204, 206–
   207,209, 228, 257, 277, 280–281

Heroism of teachers, 3, 10, 19, 118, 147,
   149, 152–153, 156, 161, 190, 224,
   226–227, 247, 262
Human beings, teachers as, 10, 12, 14, 93,
   95, 121, 201, 226, 232, 237–239
Humor, 11, 13, 29, 117, 134–135, 139,
   163–164, 168, 175–177, 180–184,
   186–188, 196, 198, 202–204, 206,
   208, 233, 238–239, 246

Ideal teachers, 4–5, 9–11, 20, 24, 40–41,
   47, 59, 112–113, 143, 220, 238, 243,
   258, 259, 262, 264–268, 272, 276,
   279, 282
Images, influence of, 4, 5, 8, 17, 20, 21, 43,
   52, 55, 57, 61, 86, 272, 285
Image-makers, 5, 7, 11, 13, 20
   film-makers, 147–148, 171
   novelists, 8, 11, 12, 14, 20, 22, 213,
   217, 219, 221, 227–228, 241
   producers, film and television, 13, 188
   publishers, 13, 209, 218
   songwriters, 171
   textbook writers, 245, 280
Imagination, 3–8, 12, 14, 16, 19–21, 24,
   34, 44, 57, 63, 66–68, 71, 74, 77, 81,
   82, 90, 92–95, 110, 132, 135, 139,
   198, 200–201, 225–226, 241
Imaging, 30, 39, 40, 41, 50–52, 216
Immigrants, 211, 231–233, 236–242
Incompetent teachers, 46, 70, 120–126,
   130, 148, 152, 195, 215, 250, 255,
   272
Individuality and individualism, 21, 43,
   109, 209, 226, 257, 271, 275, 276

Inexperienced teachers, 6, 51, 63–64, 84,
    86, 118, 120–123, 149, 155, 187,
    225, 247–248, 254–255, 297
Influence of teachers, 18, 41, 59–63, 67–
    68, 70, 155, 160, 166, 180–181,
    184, 185–187, 201, 204, 217, 219,
    225–227, 231, 238–239, 240–241,
    252, 264, 268–269, 274
Instruction, See Pedagogy
Intellectual role of teachers, 8, 15, 16, 41,
    56, 98, 105–106, 110–111, 121–
    122, 155, 178, 185–186, 267–271
Isolation of teachers, 7, 69, 94, 110, 278

Leadership, 3, 12, 18, 41–43, 59, 61, 63,
    74, 76, 98, 114, 150, 238, 263, 267,
    270, 275
Literature, 3, 7–8, 10–12, 14, 18, 20–21,
    86, 186, 215–217, 227–228, 231–
    242, 244–245, 247–248, 254, 284
Love of children, 21, 52, 66, 84, 86, 90, 94,
    96, 98, 102, 103, 104, 106, 108, 132,
    150, 201, 239, 241, 248–249

Mainstream culture of teachers, 17–18,
    22, 67, 80, 178, 180, 187–188, 209–
    213, 218–219, 222, 225, 235, 283
Male teachers, 24, 112, 122, 147, 152, 164,
    180, 188, 206–208, 218–219, 262,
    280
Media, 3–4, 6–8, 10, 13–16, 19, 24, 40,
    91, 159, 165, 170, 172, 216
Memories, 3, 6–9, 11–14, 17–20, 22–25,
    35, 44, 50, 56, 62–63, 66, 71–72,
    76, 84, 120–121, 136, 143–144,
    158, 161, 163, 172, 175, 188, 190,
    215–217, 219–221, 228, 239, 243–
    244
Men as teachers, See Male teachers
Mentoring, See Nurturing
Metaphors, 14, 19, 54–62, 66, 69, 76–78,
    118, 143, 158, 168, 262–264, 267,
    280
Moral purposes of teachers, 6, 9–10, 15,
    32, 41–42, 48, 76, 155, 180, 186,
    231, 262, 266, 270
Mothering role of teachers, 11–13, 16, 33,
    36, 44, 47, 49, 61–62, 66, 84–90,
    92, 94, 98, 103, 109, 115, 118–119,
    122, 131, 186, 196, 198, 202, 222–
    224, 227, 265
Music, See Song
Myth, 13, 76, 118, 148, 162, 172

Narrative, 4, 10, 12, 14, 16, 18, 23, 40, 55,
    56, 95, 110, 118, 167
Negative images of teachers, 9, 13–15, 67,
    157, 176, 195, 198, 201–202, 206,
    213, 232, 237, 240, 277
Nonconformity, See Resistance
Nurturing role of teachers, 11, 16, 18, 22,
    33, 45, 48–49, 51–52, 60–61, 75,
    84, 86–87, 93, 101–103, 110–111,
    113–114, 141, 144, 180, 184, 195–
    196, 198, 202, 207, 209, 211, 219,
    221, 223, 231–232, 237, 239

Oral histories, 81, 96, 143
Order in classroom, 6, 16–18, 48, 60, 67,
    87, 98, 122, 134, 140–141, 151, 155,
    198, 202–203, 205, 231, 246, 248,
    250–252, 264, 271–273, 278

Paragons, 9–11, 14, 15, 187, 247, 255,
    259, 264, 267–271, 274, 276, 279
Parents
    expectations of, See under Expecta-
    tions
    teachers as, 11, 33, 34, 41, 42, 43, 45,
    48, 49, 58, 61, 62, 66, 68, 85, 87–89,
    122, 132, 143, 178, 186
    relationships with teachers, 6, 7, 9, 11,
    13–15, 20, 46, 55–56, 68–72, 76,
    78, 88–90, 93, 95, 101, 103, 105–
    106, 111, 118, 143, 153–154, 178,
    186, 219, 229, 233, 238, 256, 262,
    274, 283
Pedagogy, 9, 22–24, 29, 35, 41, 45, 59, 88,
    92, 104, 177, 187, 200, 232, 246,
    252, 254, 270
Personalities of teachers, 4, 31, 44, 67, 97,
    119, 122, 141, 179, 209, 246–247,
    258, 268–270, 272–275, 277–279,
    282–283.
Physical appearance of teachers, 10, 86–
    87, 122, 131, 133, 147, 149–154,
    161, 163–164, 167, 171, 176, 178–
    180, 182, 186, 188, 196, 202, 204,
    206–207, 226, 232–236, 238, 249,
    272–274, 276–278
Polarities, 9–10, 12, 14–15, 58, 60–61,
    227
Politics, 9, 16–17, 20, 22–23, 73, 93, 113,
    115, 172, 274
Popular culture, 3–4, 6, 8–10, 12–15, 17–
    23, 119, 173, 216, 229, 243, 285
Powerlessness of teachers, 7–8, 11, 18, 22,

70, 73, 118, 121, 136, 155, 164, 204, 207, 273, 275–276

Power of teachers, 7, 9, 11–12, 16, 18, 49, 55, 57, 59, 61–63, 66–67, 69, 74–76, 87, 108, 112, 119, 157, 162, 168, 202–205, 221–222, 241, 271–272, 278

Prejudice, of teachers, 21, 117, 149, 156, 180, 187, 220, 235–236, 269

Presence of teachers, 18–19, 31–32, 42–44, 52, 60, 65, 223, 264, 269–270

Principals, *See* Administrators

Professionals, professionalism, 4, 6–7, 11–12, 16, 18, 22, 30, 32, 42, 53, 55–57, 65–66, 71, 81, 83, 86, 94–95, 109, 112–115, 120, 151, 169, 265–268, 273–276, 279–280, 282

Public, the, 4, 6, 14, 15, 70, 72, 75, 101, 108–109, 142, 148, 155, 218, 226–263, 265, 273, 279

Reality versus imagery, 6, 8, 13, 36, 45, 57–58, 64–65, 84, 87, 93, 114, 117–119, 152, 176, 226, 243

Resistance
of students, 13, 46, 162–163, 172, 222, 234, 240, 248–249
of teachers, 3, 112–114, 183, 186, 218–219, 224–227, 266, 276

Respect, for teachers, 4, 13, 15–17, 24, 33, 46, 48, 56, 60, 62, 66–69, 70–75, 81, 84, 88, 92, 105–109, 111, 114, 119, 121, 176, 203, 226, 236, 238–239, 249, 267, 274

Retired teachers, 79–95, 97–115, 142–143, 284

Rewards of teaching
financial, 7, 11, 30, 55, 70, 101–102, 105, 107, 108–112, 115, 184, 265–266
intrinsic, 16–17, 25, 34, 57, 66, 69, 72, 76, 84, 102, 105–108, 111–112, 115, 264–266

Rural schooling, 11, 56, 63, 73, 82, 97–100, 107, 120, 143. 243–257, 284

Schooling
as battlefield, 11, 65, 88, 147–148, 152, 154, 165, 198, 256, 280
as factory, 17, 58–60, 108, 236, 262–263, 271, 280
as family, 18, 33, 49, 83–84, 85, 86, 90, 91, 94, 95, 106, 113

School reform, 29, 32, 44, 52 , 152, 216, 256

Self-definition of teachers, 4, 7, 14–15, 18, 55–58, 76, 86, 213, 226, 285

Sentimentalism, 88, 110, 150–151, 187, 243, 245–248, 250, 252, 256, 284

Sexuality in teacher images, 149, 152, 158–159, 168–169, 186, 188, 210, 218–219, 232, 275, 277

Social changes and schooling, 84, 88, 90–92, 95, 100, 115, 148, 170

Social class, 8, 17, 25, 69, 81, 97, 109, 143, 148–149, 178, 180, 187–188, 218–219, 222, 228, 235, 283

Social order, 7, 18, 78, 110, 263–264, 269, 280–282

Society
images defined by, 3–10, 13, 16, 17, 20–22, 40, 52, 71, 105, 113, 118, 143, 153, 176, 178, 216, 219, 229, 278
impact of and influence on teachers, 31, 33, 34, 64, 90, 94, 115, 226, 263–264, 267

Song, 83, 157–174, 178, 190

Status of teachers, 4, 7, 25, 52, 69, 104, 106–107, 152, 209, 266–267, 279, 282

Stereotypes, 3, 7, 8, 12–18, 20, 97, 110, 112, 148, 155, 175–177, 182–183, 186–188, 195, 206, 210, 222–223, 228, 232, 236, 276–279

Students' relationships with teachers, 4, 6–12, 14–19, 21, 24, 30, 32–37, 40–41, 43–51, 52–53, 55, 56, 58–63, 66–69, 76, 87, 93, 95–96, 107–111, 114–115, 122, 126–142, 143–144, 169, 177, 186, 203, 207, 218, 220, 228–229, 239–240, 283

Submission, *See* Powerlessness of teachers

Teacher education, 5–6, 10, 12, 15, 18–19, 22–23, 25, 64, 79, 86, 97–100, 108, 113, 216, 235, 245–247, 254–255, 258, 282

Teacher-researchers, 41, 78–80, 96

Teaching methods, *See* Pedagogy

Teaching profession, 4–7, 10, 14–15, 21, 24–25, 30, 37, 42, 45, 51–52, 56, 63–64, 66, 68, 72, 76, 81, 85–86, 95, 97–98, 101–102, 105, 108, 110–111, 113–117, 161, 191, 201, 213,

218, 234, 258–259, 262, 266–267,
271, 274, 277, 279, 281, 283
Television, 3, 6–8, 11, 12, 13, 15, 18, 23,
24, 35, 64, 87, 89, 91, 92, 137, 175–
188, 191, 217
Textbooks, 4, 10–11, 13, 15, 18, 19, 21–
22, 81, 113, 115, 141, 166, 182–
184, 231, 245, 250, 255, 258–282,
284

Uniqueness, of teachers, 4, 11, 31, 43,
274, 279
Urban schooling, 8, 22, 38, 56, 60–63, 65,
66–68, 71–74, 78, 91–92, 94, 97–
100, 120, 143, 148, 181, 231–242,
257

Women as teachers, *See* Female teachers